A Practical Introduction to Management Science

BUSINESS ADMINISTRATION SERIES

Consulting Editor: Gordon Anderson
University of Strathclyde

Published in association with the Strathclyde Business School

A Practical Introduction to Management Science

C. D. J. Waters
University of Calgary

 ADDISON-WESLEY PUBLISHING COMPANY

Wokingham, England · Reading, Massachusetts · Menlo Park, California
New York · Don Mills, Ontario · Amsterdam · Bonn
Sydney · Singapore · Tokyo · Madrid · San Juan

To Elizabeth

© 1989 Addison-Wesley Publishers Ltd.
© 1989 Addison-Wesley Publishing Company, Inc.

Many of the designations used by manufacturers and sellers to distinguish their products are claimed as trademarks. Addison-Wesley has made every attempt to supply trademark information about manufacturers and their products mentioned in this book. A list of the trademark designations and their owners appears on p. xvii.

Cover designed by Crayon Design of Henley-on-Thames and printed by The Riverside Printing Co. (Reading) Ltd.
Text design by Lesley Stewart.
Typeset by Columns of Reading.
Printed and bound in Great Britain by The Bath Press, Avon.

First printed 1989

British Library Cataloguing in Publication Data
Waters, C. D. J.
 A practical introduction to management science.
 1. Management. Decision making. Quantitative methods
 I. Title. II. Series
 658.4′03′028

 ISBN 0–201–41630–1

Library of Congress Cataloging in Publication Data
Waters, C. D. J. (C. Donald J.), 1949–
  A practical introduction to management science / C. D. J. Waters.
   p. cm. — (Business administration series)
  Includes bibliographical references.
   ISBN 0–201–41630–1
   1. Management science. I. Title. II. Series: Business administration series (Wokingham, England)
 T56.W38 1989
 650—dc20   89–15203
                                                                  CIP

Preface

Approach and style

This book gives an introduction to management science. This is a broad subject which considers the application of scientific ideas and methods to the problems met by managers. We will not start a long discussion about the precise meaning of 'the scientific method', but will say it provides a logical way of analysing problems and suggesting rational solutions.

There are many views of science and many ways in which scientific methods can be used in management. The potential applications are so numerous that we must limit ourselves to specific areas to allow a book of reasonable length. In this book a deliberate decision has been made to take a quantitative viewpoint. Even this is too wide an area, with many ways in which quantitative ideas can be presented. Again, a deliberate decision has been made to avoid rigorous mathematics and concentrate on applications rather than theory. Formal mathematical proofs are avoided and models are described by examples rather than theoretical argument. This practical orientation is reinforced by case studies which accompany most of the chapters.

Many textbooks on management science emphasize one particular topic, often at the expense of others. Typically, linear programming is discussed in detail, while other topics (which are at least as useful in practice) are covered more briefly. It has been suggested that linear programming has more mathematical neatness than many other techniques, but this is an argument which belongs in a book on mathematics and not management science. Similarly, a number of books emphasize statistical approaches, but by the time the background details have been covered with enough rigour there is not enough space to consider the application of these ideas.

This book gives a balanced view of several areas and does not concentrate on one area at the expense of others. It introduces a range of ideas which have proved useful to management. Some topics, such as integer, non-linear and quadratic programming, markov processes, dynamic programming and simplex-based procedures have been deliberately omitted. Although these are useful in some circumstances they are not as widely used as, say, network analysis or decision trees. They are also far more complicated. All textbooks must limit their material and in this case a line has been drawn which omits topics whose complexity seems excessive in relation to their practical use. References are given at the end of each chapter and anyone wanting a more detailed coverage is recommended to read some of these.

Market

There are several types of student who take introductory courses in management science. Perhaps the majority of these are doing a degree or equivalent course in some area of business studies. Typically, such students include core or optional courses in management science, operational research or quantitative methods in their second, third or fourth years. More specialized undergraduate courses may include a first year core course in management science. Related subjects, such as accountancy and economics, may include an optional course in the final year. This book has almost no mathematical prerequisites and can be widely used for this type of course.

As well as undergraduate courses there are many postgraduate courses available in areas of business studies. Most of these contain core courses in management science (often called quantitative methods for business or a related title). These include general MBA courses as well as more specialized postgraduate/post-experience ones.

A third route to management science is for students who do a degree in science or engineering and who are interested in seeing how their skills might be applied in business. Many science and engineering courses include a business or management option in the final year and there are obvious links between physical sciences and management science.

Contents

The contents of the book are laid out in a logical manner. Chapter 1 introduces the ideas of quantitative methods, discusses their applications and the role of models. A systematic approach for tackling problems, or methodology, is developed.

Students of management science come from a variety of backgrounds and some may be unsure of basic mathematical techniques. Before moving to the rest of the book, anyone who has doubts about their numerical skills is advised to read Appendix A. This contains a summary of the basic quantitative techniques used in later chapters. The Appendix might be used as general revision, a reference for specific points, or simply read by anyone who is not confident of their numerical skills.

Chapter 2 gives some illustrations of quantitative models and shows how these can be used in a variety of situations. Chapters 3 to 7 look in more detail at specific areas where models are used. In particular, Chapter 3 describes inventory control models, Chapter 4 looks at forecasting, Chapter 5 considers project network analysis, Chapter 6 describes linear programming and Chapter 7 looks at some problems of sequencing, scheduling and routing.

Many people find statistical ideas difficult to understand. Deterministic models can be quite straightforward, but probabilities and distributions of values are much more difficult to visualize. For this reason the first seven chapters are limited to deterministic models. Chapters 8 to 11 include statistical ideas, so the book can be considered in two parts:

Chapters 1 to 7 – deterministic
Chapters 8 to 11 – probabilistic

In particular, Chapter 8 outlines the statistics which are used in the following chapters. Chapter 9 describes a number of models based on these statistical ideas. Chapters 10 and 11 look in more detail at two areas where probabilistic ideas are used, decision analysis and simulation.

Chapter 12 reviews the material covered in the book and makes some comments on issues which may be met in practice.

The relationship between chapters is shown in Figure I.

Format

Each chapter uses a consistent format. This starts with a list of contents. A synopsis outlines the material to be covered and then a set of objectives lists the things which readers should be able to do by the end of the chapter. This is followed by the main material of the chapter, divided into coherent sections. Summaries and self-assessment questions ensure the material is being understood, while worked examples are used to illustrate the models. Each chapter has a conclusion to summarize the main points, followed by a set of numerical problems. Most of the chapters have a case study which illustrates the context in which decisions are made. Solutions to self-assessment questions and references for further reading are given at the ends of chapters.

Many people have access to computers and there is little point in doing intricate arithmetic by hand. This book certainly does not assume access to a computer, but there are several points where results from a computer package are described, or it is suggested that calculations could readily be done using a standard package. Spreadsheet packages (such as Lotus 1–2–3, Multiplan or VisiCalc) are common and are useful for many applications.

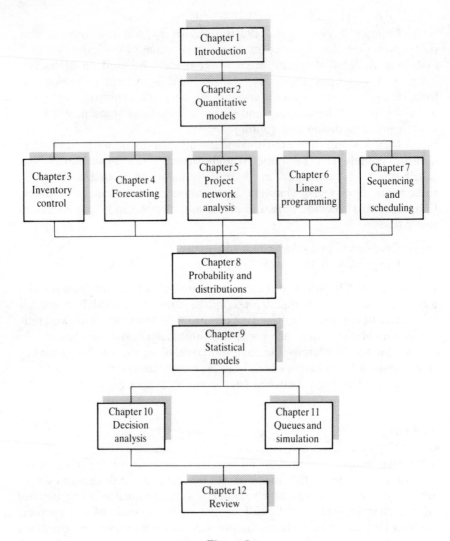

Figure I

It is worth mentioning the notation used for arithmetic throughout the book. Variables are given one or two character names and arithmetic operators ($+$, $-$, $*$ and $/$) are written explicitly. This follows the pattern needed by computers (both programs and packages) and is generally clearer than traditional mathematical notation. Equations are written in the form:

$$CT = 22 * DE + \frac{B * (AF + AT)}{D}$$

Apart from its use with computers this notation has the advantages of:

- being easy to understand;
- allowing useful variable names (for example, a fixed cost in period 2 would be written as $FC(2)$ rather than C_f^2 or $C_{f,2}$;
- removing ambiguities (does C_f^2 mean the second value of C_f or its square?);
- making meanings clear ($1.11 * 2.22$, for example, is clearer than 1.11×2.22, $1.11\ 2.22$ or $1.11.2.22$).

More details of this notation are given in Appendix A.

C. D. J. Waters
Calgary, February 1989

Contents

Contents

Chapter 1

Introduction to management science

SYNOPSIS

This chapter introduces the scope and methods of management science. It starts by defining management science as the application of scientific methods to the problems met by managers. No organization would deliberately act irrationally, so we can assume that managers try to tackle decisions sensibly and logically. Management science provides a framework for the necessary analyses.

Interest in management science has grown substantially in recent years. This growth has been caused by a number of factors, including an increased availability of computers, more intense competition, development of new methods and more widespread knowledge of available techniques.

Management science is a broad subject. Before looking at details we need some way of dividing its characteristic approach into coherent parts and this may be done by:

- the types of problems tackled
- the types of solution procedures used, or
- a general methodology.

This book describes a number of solution procedures. We could have adopted many approaches to this, but have decided to concentrate on the development of quantitative models. These allow alternatives to be compared, good policies to be identified, and overall decision making to be improved.

The development and implementation of a quantitative model can be viewed as a management science project. Such projects usually have a number of stages, typically consisting of observation, modelling, experimentation and implementation. A more detailed methodology is described by Ackoff (1962).

Note

This book is based on models which have a quantitative element. This does not mean it is a mathematics text book and it does not assume a high level of mathematical ability. Appendix A describes the basic mathematics which are needed in the rest of the book. If you are worried by the mathematics, need some revision or simply need a bit of confidence, reading this appendix would be useful. If you need a more formal text you could look at some of those listed at the end of Appendix A.

OBJECTIVES

After reading this chapter and doing the numerical exercises you should be able to:

- define 'management science';
- discuss reasons why scientific ideas are useful for tackling management problems;
- appreciate the scope for quantitative analyses in management problems;
- start to classify management science according to type of problem tackled or solution procedure used;
- appreciate the use of models;
- describe a general methodology for management science;
- list the stages which might be found in a management science project;
- make some useful comments about each of these stages.

1.1 MANAGEMENT SCIENCE

1.1.1 Definition and aims

Management science is the application of scientific methods to the problems met by managers. In this context, 'managers' are those who make decisions about the running of an organization, and the overall aim is to improve their decision making by the use of rational analyses. These analyses frequently involve some quantitative reasoning. This does not mean that *all* management problems can be tackled scientifically, or that *all* scientific approaches use quantitative arguments. In this book we are deliberately concentrating on problems which have proved amenable to scientific analysis, and particularly those for which practical quantitative models are available.

We expect managers to be rational and make sensible decisions on the basis of their skills and expertise rather than guesswork. It may, then, be obvious that putting decision making on a scientific footing has advantages. If this is not already clear we could try a formal justification along the following lines.

In recent years organizations have tended to become bigger, and they have certainly got more complicated. Decision making in these large, complex organizations is likely to be difficult. At the same time improved communications and more intense worldwide competition have meant that decisions must be made quickly. Delaying a decision might allow a competitor to gain an advantage which might not easily be overcome.

These two factors:

- more difficult decisions, and
- faster decisions

inevitably increase the chances of making errors. If a complex situation is examined with inadequate information and a decision is needed quickly, there is a good chance that a wrong decision will be made. Unfortunately, the costs of making errors can be high.

Consider an oil company which is offered the chance of exploring a new area in the Irish Sea. A decision about accepting this offer may be complex and based on financing, alternative uses of money, current operations, short and medium term forecasts for crude oil requirements, alternative sources, refining capacity, world oil prices, longer term company objectives, and so on. Unfortunately, a quick decision is needed as any delay might allow a competitor to take up all the exploration rights. If the company makes a wrong decision it may spend millions of pounds on fruitless exploration, or it may decide not to explore an area which could give high, long term profits.

Based on this need for better, faster decisions it is not surprising that organizations have actively looked for ways of putting their decision making on a more logical footing. They have looked for methods which will improve the quality of decision making and one such method is the scientific method (see Figure 1.1).

Management science is steadily growing in importance. It is being used by more organizations and is tackling an increasing range of problems. There are several reasons for this growth. We have already mentioned that increased competition and faster communications need improved decisions, but we should also mention the obvious impact of computers. Quantitative analyses have become much easier in the past few years and this has encouraged the development of new methods and moves into new areas. This success has brought attention to the subject and its growth has been encouraged by a broader awareness of its potential.

1.1.2 Quantitative analyses

The aim of management science is to improve decision making within an organization. This aim can be achieved by putting the decision making on a scientific footing. We do not want a long discussion about the precise

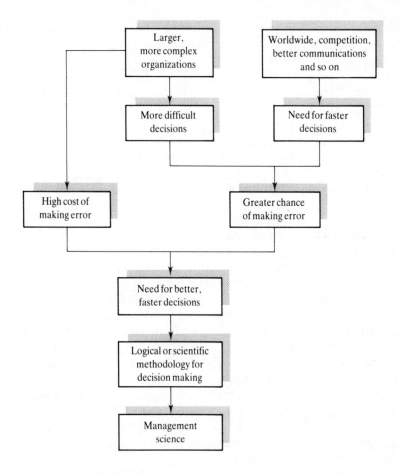

Figure 1.1 A rationale for the development of management science.

meaning of 'the scientific method', so we will simply say that it involves systematic and logical analyses of situations and the development of rational solutions. To be more specific, we will develop a quantitative view of management problems.

It is, perhaps, misleading to suggest that problems are tackled quantitatively. Almost inevitably a range of factors which cannot be quantified have to be taken into account. It would also be wrong to suggest that management science makes decisions. It can do relevant analyses and suggest actions, but ultimately it is managers who make the decisions. It is their job to assess all available information, both quantitative and qualitative, and on the basis of their skills, knowledge and experience make the final decision. This process is described in Figure 1.2.

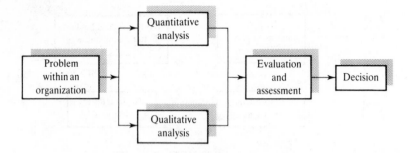

Figure 1.2 Quantitative and qualitative aspects of decision making.

It should not be surprising that we want to take a quantitative approach to management decisions. Quantitative analyses are accepted practice in many circumstances; civil engineers are expected to do calculations when they design bridges, doctors prescribe measured quantities of drugs, accountants give quantitative views of a company's performance. Unfortunately, there is often an assumption that managers do not need such formal analyses, but are somehow expected to 'know' the right decisions intuitively. Here we are trying to overcome this view, that decision making is an art which cannot be learnt, by illustrating the benefits of quantitative analysis in a number of areas.

This is not a new idea. There are examples of scientists helping managers dating back to Archimedes and before. More recently, some advances came at the end of the nineteenth century when economists began to think in quantitative terms, but the importance of quantitative analysis has increased significantly since the Second World War. In the early 1940s scientists from different backgrounds began working in multi-disciplinary teams to analyse wartime operations. This work became known by a number of names including Management Science, Operational Research, Operations Research, Quantitative Methods, Quantitative Analysis and Decision Analysis. Here we will use the single term 'management science', but recognize that the same approach is known by many different names.

Quantitative methods can be applied to many areas, but we have already said it would be wrong to suggest it is useful for *all* problems. Many decisions require experience, creative thinking or intuition. There are many areas, such as industrial relations, negotiations, recruitment, identification of objectives, personal relations and pattern recognition, which have hardly been touched by quantitative methods. There are, however, many areas where scientific ideas are essential and many others where they give substantial benefits.

Problems tackled by management science often share a number of characteristics, including:

Table 1.1 Problems that can be tackled by management science.

Problem	Some characteristics of problem area
Stock control	demand pattern, replenishment pattern, costs, service levels
Forecasting	historic demand patterns, changes, related variables
Project planning	ordered activities, duration times
Allocation	objectives, resources available, demands
Maintenance	operating efficiency, repair pattern, costs
Queueing	arrival pattern, service pattern, costs
Scheduling	objectives, arrival pattern, priorities
and so on	

- they should be complex, so that a solution is not obvious without some kind of formal analysis
- they should be relatively important, so the analysis is worthwhile
- they should be new, so there is limited experience with similar problems.

1.1.3 Classifications of management science

We can classify the management science approach in several ways:

- by considering the types of problem tackled;
- by considering the types of solution procedure used;
- by describing a general methodology.

Taking the first of these, we could say that management science has had a significant impact on the areas shown in Table 1.1. Almost all organizations do some forecasting and stock control, so this alone should indicate that management science is widely applied.

An alternative classification would look at the type of solution procedures developed to tackle these problems as shown in Table 1.2. The third option mentioned above is the description of a general approach to problems, or a standard 'methodology'. The identification of such a methodology avoids the temptation to concentrate on one solution procedure and adjust all problems until they fit neatly into the required form, or conversely to concentrate on one problem area and assume that management science cannot help in other areas. Many descriptions of management science put heavy emphasis on linear programming (described in Chapter 6). This can have the undesirable effect of making all problems appear to be linear programmes even if the problem has to be changed markedly to get it into the right form. Conversely, much work

Table 1.2 Management science as a solution.

Solution	Characteristics of solution procedures
Forecasting	projection of time series, identifying causal relationships
Linear programming	optimization with linear objective function and constraints
Network analysis	project representation by related activities and events
Inventory models	cost minimizing models for stock systems
Statistics	descriptive or probabilistic
Decision theory	alternatives, events, consequences
Simulation	any dynamic situation
and so on	

has been done on inventory control (see Chapter 3), but it would be wholly inadequate to suggest this is the area where most useful work is done. We should take a wider view and suggest that management science can be useful for any problem where a logical, rational analysis can bring benefits. In section 1.2 we will describe how such scientific analyses can be undertaken.

In summary
Management science is concerned with the application of scientific principles to the problems of management. Although this is not a new idea, a number of factors have recently encouraged its development.

We will concentrate on quantitative approaches to problems, but this does not mean that we shall be excluding qualitative ideas or that we shall be studying pure mathematics.

Management science can be classified according to the problems it tackles, or the solution procedures it uses, or the general methodology.

SELF ASSESSMENT QUESTIONS

1.1 What is 'Management Science'?

1.2 What are the benefits of using management science?

1.3 Is management science based on mathematics?

1.4 Does management science make decisions?

1.5 Why has the use of quantitative analyses of management problems increased markedly in the past twenty years?

1.6 How might the approach of management science be classified?

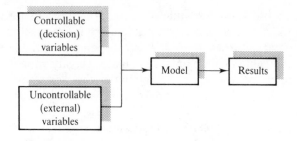

Figure 1.3 Construction of a model.

1.2 MANAGEMENT SCIENCE METHODOLOGY

1.2.1 Models

A distinct scientific methodology has been recognized for some time, but it is difficult to get agreement about the details of this. The basis of the method is certainly the development of a 'model'. Here model is used not in the sense of a toy, but as an abstraction of reality, or representation of a situation. There are three distinct types of model:

- iconic
- analogue
- symbolic.

Model cars are examples of iconic models. These have things in reality represented by the same things in the model, but on a different scale. A model car has small wheels to represent real wheels, a small engine to represent a real engine and so on.

Analogue models have properties in reality which are represented by other properties in the model. The time of day can be represented by the position of hands on a clock, temperature can be represented by the height of a column of mercury, speed can be represented by the position of a speedometer needle, and so on.

Most of science is concerned with symbolic models where real properties are represented by some kind of symbols. A scientific model may be in the form of a graph or chart, but more commonly will consist of a set of mathematical relationships (see Figure 1.3). If a company makes a product for £20 a unit and sells it for £30 a unit, a symbolic model of this would be:

Profit = number sold * (selling price − cost)

or $P = N * (30 - 20)$

or $P = N * (S - C)$

Here P and N are variables while S and C are constants (at least in the short term). N is an independent variable since it can take any value and does not depend on anything else. P is a dependent variable as its value depends on the value taken by N. We can also classify variables according to whether they are decision variables under the control of the decision maker (which might include S) or external variables which are outside their control (like N).

The main characteristics of models are:

- they represent the properties, states, events, objectives, etc. of reality
- they are simplified, with only relevant details included
- properties in reality are represented by other properties in the model.

The main purpose of using models is to allow experiments without changing the real system. In the example above, described by the model $P = N * (S - C)$, the profit for various production levels could have been found by direct experimentation on the real system. This has obvious disadvantages of being time consuming, difficult to implement, expensive and possibly causing permanent damage to the company (if, for example, a very low production level was tried which did not cover costs and caused the company to go into liquidation). It would be much easier to experiment with the model by substituting different values for N and calculating the consequent values for P.

Experimenting with real operations can be damaging, but it may also be impossible. The best location for a warehouse, for example, could not be found by experimentally trying different locations and keeping the best. As experiments with reality are, at best, expensive the only feasible alternative is to build a model of the situation and experiment with this.

Models are simplified representations of reality and include only the relevant details. This allows easier analysis by ignoring everything which is not directly relevant to the problem, but it also means that models are not exact duplicates of reality. They are approximations, and this implies there can be several equally good models for any situation. These could, perhaps, emphasize different features or make different assumptions. Many different models of national economic performance have been developed, and while these usually give similar results for, say, projected balance of trade figures, there are inevitably differences between the models. Similarly, meteorologists forecast the weather using very complex symbolic models of weather patterns: other people hang seaweed on a wall to build a much simpler analogue model. It is certainly good practice to start with a simple model and only add complications when the simple model fails. The essence of models is not that they

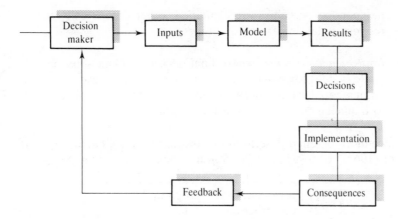

Figure 1.4   Feedback in decision making.

duplicate reality, but they concentrate on the main features and help decision making within an organization. Building a model is not an end in itself, and the quality should be judged by how useful it is rather than how closely it represents the real situation.

1.2.2 Stages in a management science project

The use of models in business can be described as a feedback loop, where experiments are done on the model, results are examined and decisions made. The consequences of implementing these are fed back to the decision makers who can use this additional information to modify the model (see Figure 1.4).

This gives a general picture, but we are particularly interested in the detailed stages leading to an appropriate model. The process of building, testing and experimenting with models can be described as a project with four distinct stages:

(1) *Observation stage*, where the problem is examined, data is collected, details of the problem are identified, objectives are set, context is considered, various ideas are discussed and so on.

(2) *Modelling stage*, where data is analysed, a model is built and tested, initial solutions are obtained.

(3) *Experimental stage*, where solutions are tested to see if they match predictions, optimal solutions are searched for, movements away from optimal solutions are considered, alternative values for

independent variables are examined, other data is collected, recommendations are made etc.

(4) *Implementation stage*, where final decisions about solutions are made, values for independent variables are set, these decisions are implemented, actual performance is monitored, feedback is given to management, models are kept updated.

A rather more detailed description of these stages has been proposed by Ackoff (1962), who suggests the following six phases for a project:

(1) formulating the problem
(2) constructing a model
(3) testing the model
(4) deriving a solution to the problem
(5) testing and controlling the solution
(6) implementing the solution

This is obviously a simplified view, and while it is not meant to be a recipe for an investigation it does suggest several stages which are common to most studies. The stages are not necessarily followed in strict order. A more realistic approach would involve some cycling, with perhaps, testing revealing faults in the model formulation which can then be adjusted.

The rest of this section makes some brief points about each of these six stages.

(1) Formulating the problem

Formulating the problem is the first important step of a project (and the one where many projects fail). This stage requires all aspects of a problem to be investigated, described and defined as fully as possible. A conceptual picture of the problem is built which might involve:

- determining the precise problem (which may not be the problem originally presented);
- finding the ultimate decision makers;
- finding their relevant objectives;
- determining the variables used in the problem;
- listing possible alternatives or courses of action;
- describing the context of the problem.

(2) Constructing a model

There are two main stages in model building:

- identification and measurement of relevant variables;
- establishing relationships between variables.

Some of the variables are under the control of the decision maker (production quantity, selling price, advertising expenditure, etc.) others are not (demand, raw material costs, competition, etc.). These decision and external variables can be combined into a number of constraints and objectives.

Guidance in the formulation of models of various types is given in the rest of this book. One useful approach is to start with simple models, test them and extend them only if they prove inadequate.

(3) Testing the model

Is the model an adequate representation of reality? The testing of the model finds an answer to this question. Such testing is not a separate stage at the end of modelling but occurs continuously as the model is being built. Initial tests can be made on various parts of the model as they are being built, with final testing of the model as a whole.

The usual way of testing a model is to use historic data. When this is substituted into the model its predictions can be compared with actual performance, and if the difference between the two is acceptably small the model is considered satisfactory. If the difference between the two is not small it might be caused by:

- the model containing variables which are not relevant;
- the model excluding variables which are relevant;
- errors in the functions relating variables;
- wrong numerical values assigned to variables.

(4) Deriving a solution to the problem

It is no use building a model unless a solution can be found. Several solution methods are available, varying from complete enumeration to efficient optimizing algorithms (or procedures). One classification of solution procedures has:

- analytical techniques
- numerical techniques
- simulation techniques.

We will meet these later in the book.

Some procedures give optimal solutions to problems, but heuristics are often used to give 'satisfycing' solutions. These are based on rules-of-thumb and experience to give satisfactory rather than optimal solutions, but with much less effort. It may, for example, be preferable to use heuristics which give results within 5% of optimal but only take a tenth of the effort needed to get optimal results.

(5) Testing and controlling the solution

Having tested the model and found it gives reasonable results with historic data, the next step is to implement the model and see how it works with current data. This is not as easy as it sounds because:

- only one decision is implemented and there is no comparison with alternatives;
- subjective criteria are used;
- the implementation might not have been done as planned;
- external factors might change;
- with decisions containing uncertainty there is always some variability in results.

The testing and controlling of the solution is the stage which takes these factors into account and adjusts the model and solution accordingly. This is particularly important in the longer term. Circumstances inevitably change with time and continuous monitoring is needed to ensure the model keeps performing adequately.

(6) Implementing the solution

Even if the previous stages have been done well, there is little benefit if the solution is not implemented. The aim of management science in general, and this methodology in particular, is to produce a solution which is an improvement on existing practice. If the revised solution is not implemented there seems little point in doing the work.

In practice, however, there are a number of reasons why the work may not be implemented:

- the new solution may not be much better than the existing solution and changes would not be worthwhile;
- the supply of money may be tight and there is not enough for the necessary investment;
- the problem may change or go away;
- decision makers may change their minds about objectives;
- the presentation of the solution may not be good enough to convince decision makers of its value.

In summary

A model is a simplified representation of reality. Most models used in management science are symbolic. The building, testing and implementing of a model can be considered as a project. There are several stages in such projects, typically based on observation, modelling, experimentation and implementation. More detailed descriptions can be given, including the six stages described by Ackoff.

SELF ASSESSMENT QUESTIONS

1.7 What is a model?

1.8 Why are models used?

1.9 What kind of model is most widely used in management science?

1.10 Is there a single correct model for any situation?

1.11 Generally speaking, what are the major phases in a management science project?

1.12 What are the six stages of a project described by Ackoff?

1.13 Should these stages be done:

(a) in exactly the order described
(b) in roughly the order described
(c) in the most appropriate order?

1.14 Is this description of a project the only one possible?

CONCLUSIONS

This chapter introduced the scope and methods of management science. It started by defining management science as the application of scientific methods to the problems met by managers and then developed a rationale for such studies.

Management science is a broad subject which can be classified according to:

- types of problems tackled
- types of solution procedures used
- a general methodology.

Emphasis in the rest of this book is on the solutions to a variety of management problems. These are largely based on the development of quantitative models which aim at improving the decision making within an organization. Not all problems can be tackled quantitatively.

The development and implementation of a quantitative model can be considered as a project with a number of stages. Typically such projects consist of observation, modelling, experimentation and implementation stages. A more detailed description was given of one methodology which divides a project into six stages.

SOLUTIONS TO SELF ASSESSMENT QUESTIONS

1.1 It is not easy to give a simple definition of management science, just as it is not easy to give a simple definition of physics. One definition suggests: 'Management science is the application of scientific methods to the problems met by managers'.

1.2 It allows rational analysis of problems so that decisions can be made on a logical footing rather than on the basis of intuition, subjectivity and guesswork.

1.3 No. Some of management science uses quantitative ideas but certainly not all of it. This book describes an essentially quantitative approach but there is a difference between this and pure mathematics.

1.4 No. Managers make decisions and they should base them on the best information they have available (both qualitative and quantitative) and on their own experience, judgement and so on.

1.5 There are several reasons for this, including:

- increased availability of computers
- fiercer competition requiring better, faster decisions
- development of new quantitative methods
- good experiences with earlier analyses encouraging managers to expand their use
- better education of managers making available techniques more widely known.

1.6 According to the problems tackled, the solution procedures used or the general methodology adopted.

1.7 A simplified representation of reality.

1.8 To develop solutions for real problems, allow experimentation without risk to actual operations, allow experiments which would not be possible in reality, assess the consequences of decisions, see how sensitive operations are to change, and so on.

1.9 Symbolic models (rather than iconic or analogue models).

1.10 No. Many models can be developed for a situation (particularly a complex one). The aim of these models is to help in decision making rather then be perfect representations of situations.

1.11 Observation, modelling, experimentation and implementation. There are several other views about these which are equally acceptable.

1.12 Formulating the problem, constructing a model, testing the model, deriving a solution to the problem, testing and controlling the solution, implementing the solution.

1.13 (c) in the most appropriate order

1.14 No. Projects take many forms and there are large numbers of factors and interactions to consider. The description given is not a menu to be followed blindly, but a suggestion for the major stages.

REFERENCES FOR FURTHER READING

Ackoff R. (1962). *Scientific Method: optimising applied research decisions* New York: John Wiley

Ackoff R. and Sasieni M. W. (1967). *Fundamentals of Operations Research* New York: John Wiley

Anderson D. R., Sweeney D. J. and Thomas A. W. (1988). *An Introduction to Management Science* 5th edn. St Paul: West Publishing

Blackett P. M. S. (1962). *Studies of War* London: Oliver and Boyd

Bross I. D. J. (1965). *Design for Decision* Free Press

Churchman C. W., Ackoff R. L. and Arnoff E. L. (1957). *Introduction to Operations Research* New York: John Wiley

Davis K. R., McKeown P. G. and Rakes T. R. (1986). *Management Science: an introduction* Boston: Kent Publishing

Lee S. M., Moore L. J. and Taylor B. W. (1985). *Management Science* 2nd edn. Dubuque: Wm. C. Brown Publishing

Medawar P. (1967). *The Art of the Soluble* London: Methuen

Popper K. R. (1968). *The Logic of Scientific Discovery* 2nd edn. London: Hutchinson

Rivett P. (1980). *Model Building for Decision Analysis* Chichester: John Wiley

Shogan A. W. (1988). *Management Science* New Jersey: Prentice Hall

Waddington C. H. (1973). *OR in World War 2* London: Paul Elek (Scientific Books)

White D. J. (1975). *Decision Methodology* London: John Wiley

Chapter 2

Quantitative models in business

SYNOPSIS

Chapter 1 introduced the use of quantitative models. The aim was to show that quantitative analysis could help decision making within an organization. In this chapter we are going to expand this theme and give some more detailed examples of commonly used quantitative models. These form a link between the general introduction given in Chapter 1 and the specific applications considered in later chapters. The models are illustrated by worked examples rather than rigorous mathematical derivation and analysis.

The first model looks at break-even analyses and cost calculations. This production theme is continued by looking at equipment utilization and capacity measurement. Section 2.3 considers some financial models based on the changing value of money over time. These emphasize discounting rates and net present values with extensions to decisions about equipment replacement. Finally, simple scoring models are mentioned.

You will probably have met some problems of this type when considering the best time to replace a car, the value of an educational course, how much output to expect from a machine, whether it is better to pay cash for something or take a loan, deciding a reasonable selling price for an item, and so on. You may have done some of the calculations without even considering them to be 'quantitative models'. One of the main aims of this chapter is to reinforce the idea that quantitative models can be easy and you should not be intimidated by the use of numbers. We would certainly not do quantitative analyses for the 'pleasure' of mathematics. They are used because some calculations are easy to apply in business and have been found to bring substantial benefits.

OBJECTIVES

After reading this chapter and doing the numerical exercises you should be able to:

- define fixed and variable costs and note their relationship to profit;
- calculate break-even points;
- do some analyses of capacities and utilization;
- appreciate the changing value of money over time;
- calculate net present values and use them to compare alternative projects;
- understand the basis of internal rate of return;
- analyse some equipment replacement decisions;
- use scoring models.

2.1 BREAK-EVEN ANALYSIS

2.1.1 Developing a model

The first model in this chapter describes the widely used idea of a break-even analysis. The basis of this model is the belief that most organizations are interested in making a profit of some kind, where 'profit' is defined as the difference between revenue and total cost:

profit = revenue − total cost

If a company makes and sells a number of different products, it will almost certainly want to know how much profit or loss is made on each one. Taking any particular item which sells at a fixed price per unit, we can define the revenue as:

revenue = price per unit * number of units sold

Looking at the costs is a little more awkward as some are fixed regardless of the number of units made, while others vary with the output. If a machine is leased to make a certain product, the cost of leasing may be fixed regardless of the number of units made, but the cost of raw materials will vary. A traditional view of costs gives:

total cost = fixed cost + variable cost

= fixed cost + cost per unit * number of units made

This gives a total cost which rises linearly with the output, as shown in Figure 2.1.

An everyday example of this separation is the cost of running a

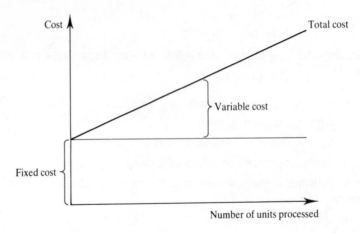

Figure 2.1 Variation of costs with number of units processed.

car, which can be divided into a fixed cost (repayment of purchase loan, road tax, insurance, etc.) and a variable cost for each mile travelled (petrol, oil, tyres, depreciation, etc.). This example also shows that the description of the model is phrased in manufacturing terms, but this is just for convenience and it could equally be phrased in terms of services provided or any other convenient units.

An important concept in many organizations is the break-even point. This is the number of units which must be processed before the company starts to make a profit. To illustrate this, we can consider a new product which has a total of £100,000 spent on research and development, tooling and other preparations needed before production can start. During normal production each unit costs £10 to make and is sold for £15. The company will only start to make a profit when the original £100,000 has been recovered, and the point when this occurs is the break-even point. In this example each unit sold contributes £15 − £10 = £5 to the company and therefore 100,000/5 = 20,000 units must be sold to cover the original investment. After this point the excess of revenue over expenditure will be profit.

This model (see Figure 2.2) defines a break-even point when:

$$revenue = total\ cost$$

$$price\ per\ unit * units\ made = fixed\ cost + cost\ per\ unit * units\ made$$

The description can be abbreviated by using symbols to represent the values, so we can let:

FC = fixed cost
UC = variable unit cost of manufacture
UP = unit price of selling
N = number of units made

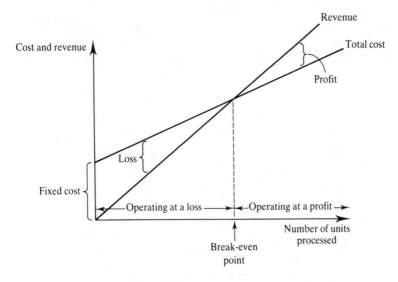

Figure 2.2 Illustrating a break-even point.

Replacing the variables in the above equation by their symbols (see Figure 2.3) gives a break-even point when:

$$N * UP = FC + N * UC$$

or $\qquad \boxed{N = FC/(UP - UC)}$

If the number of units processed is greater than the break-even point the profit is:

$$N * (UP - UC) - FC$$

If the number of units processed is less than the break-even point the net loss is:

$$FC - N * (UP - UC)$$

This analysis is useful for the obvious purpose of seeing how many units must be made and sold to operate at a profit, but also helps with decisions such as the choice between buying or leasing equipment, ensuring adequate capacity when buying new equipment, whether to buy an item or make it within the company, choice of competitive tenders for services and so on.

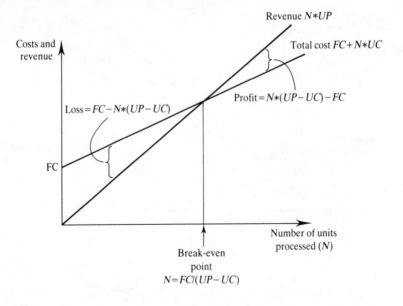

Figure 2.3 Break-even point and associated symbols.

WORKED EXAMPLE 2.1

A company makes and sells 100 units of a product every week; associated fixed costs for buildings, machines and employees amount to £6000 a week, while raw material and other variable costs amount to £50 a unit.

   (a)   What is the profit if the selling price is £130 a unit?

   (b)   What is the profit if the selling price is £80 a unit?

   (c)   What is the profit if the selling price is fixed at £80 but production is raised to 250 units a week?

   (d)   How many units must be sold at £80 a unit to break even?

SOLUTION

   (a)   Using the symbols defined above and substituting the weekly values given:

$$\text{fixed cost} = FC$$
$$= 6000$$

$$\text{variable cost} = \text{cost per unit} * \text{units made}$$
$$= UC * N$$
$$= 50 * 100$$
$$= 5000$$

$$\text{total cost} = \text{fixed cost} + \text{variable cost}$$
$$= 6000 + 5000$$
$$= £11,000 \text{ a week}$$

$$\text{revenue} = \text{price per unit} * \text{units sold}$$
$$= UP * N$$
$$= 130 * 100$$
$$= £13,000 \text{ a week}$$

$$\text{profit} = \text{revenue} - \text{total cost}$$
$$= 13,000 - 11,000$$
$$= £2000 \text{ a week}$$

The profit is an apparently healthy £2000 a week.

(b)   Repeating the above analysis but with a selling price of £80 gives:

$$\text{total cost} = £11,000 \text{ a week (the same as before)}$$

$$\text{revenue} = 80 * 100$$
$$= £8000 \text{ a week}$$

$$\text{profit} = \text{revenue} - \text{total cost}$$
$$= 8000 - 11,000$$
$$= -£3000 \text{ a week}$$

With the new figures the revenue does not cover costs and the item is being made and sold at a loss of £3000 a week. In these circumstances some thought should be given to reducing the costs of production, increasing the selling price or stopping production of the item.

(c)   Repeating the analysis with weekly production of 250 units gives:

$$\text{total cost} = \text{fixed cost} + \text{variable cost}$$
$$= 6000 + 50 * 250$$
$$= £18,500 \text{ a week}$$

$$\text{revenue} = 80 * 250$$
$$= £20,000 \text{ a week}$$

$$\text{profit} = \text{revenue} - \text{total cost}$$
$$= 20,000 - 18,500$$
$$= £1500 \text{ a week}$$

This shows that a profit can still be made with a low selling price provided production is high enough. The point where production is large enough to just cover total cost is the break-even point (see Figure 2.4).

(d)   This asks the question, 'When does revenue equal total cost?' The answer can be found from the equation:

$$N = FC/(UP - UC)$$

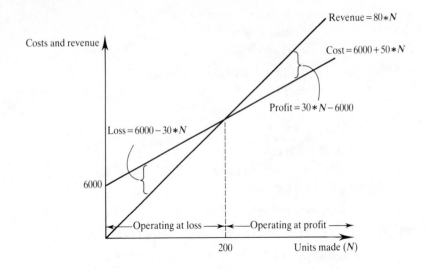

Figure 2.4 Break-even analysis for Worked example 2.1.

Substituting the known values gives:

$N = 6000/(80 - 50)$
$\quad = 200$ units

If 200 units are made a week revenue exactly covers total cost.
If less than 200 are made the company does not cover costs and the item is produced at a loss of $6000 - (80 - 50) * N$. If more than 200 units are made the company covers all costs and operates at a profit of $(80 - 50) * N - 6000$.

WORKED EXAMPLE 2.2

An airline is considering a new service between Aberdeen and Calgary. Its existing airplanes, each of which has a capacity of 240 passengers, could be used for one flight a week with fixed costs of £30,000 and variable costs amounting to 50% of ticket price. If it is planned to sell tickets at £200 each, how many passengers will be needed for the airline to break even on the proposed route? Does this seem a reasonable number?

SOLUTION

To break even revenue must equal total costs, or:

$$revenue = passengers * ticket\ price$$
$$= passengers * 200$$

$$costs = fixed\ cost + variable\ cost$$
$$= 30,000 + passengers * 0.5 * 200$$

Equating these two gives

$$passengers * 200 = 30,000 + passengers * 0.5 * 200$$
$$passengers * 100 = 30,000$$
$$passengers = 300$$

We could have saved time in this calculation by directly using the result:

$$N = FC/(UP - UC)$$
$$= 30,000/(200 - 100)$$
$$= 300$$

This number exceeds the airplane capacity of 240 passengers and shows the route could not run at a profit. If the airline could easily attract 240 passengers a week it might increase prices to cover all costs.

To break even with 240 passengers

$$240 * ticket\ price = 30,000 + 240 * 0.5 * ticket\ price$$
or $$120 * ticket\ price = 30,000$$
$$ticket\ price = 250$$

Alternatively it could try to reduce costs. One option which would not work is to put on a second flight for the extra 60 passengers. Costs for the second flight would be the same as for the first flight and the airline would then need 600 passengers to break even.

WORKED EXAMPLE 2.3

A local electricity board offers two alternative prices for domestic consumers. The normal rate has standing charges of £18.20 a quarter, with each unit of electricity consumed costing £0.142. A special economy rate has standing charges of £22.70 a quarter, with each unit of electricity during the day costing £0.162, but each unit consumed during the night costing only £0.082. What consumption pattern would make it cheaper to use the economy rate?

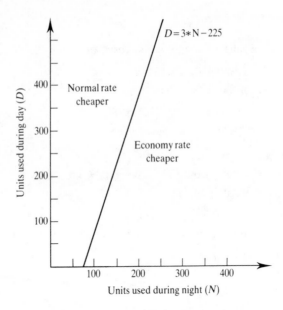

Figure 2.5 Cheapest option for buying electricity in Worked example 2.3.

SOLUTION

If a consumer uses an average of D units per quarter during the day and N units a quarter during the night, their costs would be:

normal rate: $18.20 + 0.142 * (D + N)$

economy rate: $22.70 + 0.162 * D + 0.082 * N$

It would be cheaper to use the economy rate when

$$22.7 + 0.162 * D + 0.082 * N < 18.2 + 0.142 * (D + N)$$
$$4.5 < 0.06 * N - 0.02 * D$$
$$D < 3 * N - 225$$

If consumption during the day is less than three times the night consumption minus 225 units it would be cheaper to use the economy rate, otherwise it would be cheaper to use the standard rate. This is illustrated in Figure 2.5.

2.1.2 Economies of scale

Returning for a moment to the equation for total cost:

total cost = fixed cost + variable cost

$$TC = FC + N * UC$$

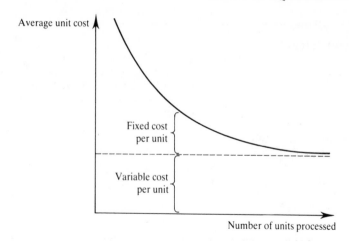

Figure 2.6 Variation of average unit cost with number of units processed.

The average total cost per unit can be found by dividing this by N, the number of units processed (see Figure 2.6):

$$TC/N = FC/N + UC$$

As N increases the average cost per unit will decline, because the proportion of fixed cost to be covered by each unit produced is reduced. This is the basis of 'economies of scale'. The implication is that large facilities are cheaper to operate than small ones, and operating costs can be reduced by making factories, warehouses or other facilities as large as possible. This simple view does not represent the whole picture and there are many instances where 'diseconomies of scale' apply. Here the advantage of reduced fixed cost per unit is more than offset by increased costs of supervision and management, difficulties of communication, more complex management hierarchies, perceived reduction of the importance of individuals, and so on.

In summary
Costs can be classified as either fixed or variable and revenue must cover both of these before a profit is made. The production quantity at which revenue equals total cost is called the break-even point. Economies of scale may be achieved by spreading fixed costs over a larger number of units processed.

SELF ASSESSMENT QUESTIONS

2.1 What does the 'variable cost' vary with?

2.2 What is the 'break-even point'?

2.3 The break-even point for a product is calculated at 1500 units a week. If actual production is 1200 units a week does this mean:
(a) the product is making a profit,
(b) the product is making a loss,
(c) the product could be making either a profit or a loss?

2.4 Because of economies of scale it is always better to have a single large factory than a number of smaller ones. Is this statement true or false?

2.2 CALCULATION OF CAPACITY AND UTILIZATION

In worked example 2.2 above the calculated break-even point of 300 passengers could not be achieved because of the capacity of the airplanes. When planning any process (whether it is production from a factory, sales from a shop, patients in a hospital, policemen on a beat, or anything else) a check must be kept on available capacity to ensure the designed throughput is realistic.

The capacity of a process is the maximum amount which can be processed within a specified time. All processes have some limitation on their capacity: a factory will have a maximum output a week, a machine will have a maximum throughput per hour, an airplane will have a maximum number of passengers on a flight, and so on. Sometimes the capacity is obvious (the number of seats in a theatre, for example) but at other times it is less clear and may need some calculation.

A factory which has N machines, each working H hours on each of S shifts a day, has a total available machine time of $N * H * S$ hours a day. An appropriate measure of capacity may be the number of units the machines can produce in a year. If the machines work for D days a year and each unit of product takes M minutes to process, the total annual capacity of the machines is:

$$\text{capacity} = \frac{\text{time available in year}}{\text{time to make one unit}}$$

$$= N * H * S * D/(M/60) \text{ units a year}$$

$$= N * H * S * 60 * D/M \text{ units a year}$$

This equation could be turned around to see how many machines would

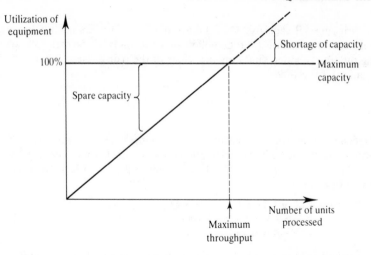

Figure 2.7 Variation of equipment utilization with throughput.

be needed to produce a certain number of parts, or at what utilization the plant is working if a specified number of units are actually produced.

If there is an annual production target of PT units, the total machine time available must be greater than, or at least equal to, the total time required. With calculations in minutes, this gives

$$\text{time available} \geq \text{time required}$$
$$N * H * S * 60 * D \geq PT * M$$

or

$$N \geq \frac{PT * M}{H * S * 60 * D}$$

If original plans were to use less than N machines, either production plans must be changed or more machines must be found. If there are more than N machines available they will be working at a utilization of

$$\text{utilization} = \frac{\text{time used for production}}{\text{time available for production}}$$
$$= \frac{PT * M}{N * H * S * 60 * D}$$

WORKED EXAMPLE 2.4

A ski lift consists of pairs of chairs pulled on a continuous wire from the bottom of a ski run to the top. Ordinarily one pair of chairs arrives at the bottom of the slope every six seconds. If the lift works for 8 hours a day for 100 days a year, what is its normal capacity? On a typical day 10% of users need help getting on the lift, and they cause average delays of 10 seconds. A further 15% of people using the lift are alone, and only one chair of the pair is used. What is the actual utilization of the lift?

SOLUTION

Two chairs arrive at the bottom of the slope every six seconds, so this is equivalent to two machines working in parallel taking 0.1 minutes to process each chair. Then $N = 2$, $H = 8$, $S = 1$, $D = 100$ and $M = 0.1$, to give an annual capacity of

$$\text{capacity} = N * H * S * 60 * D/M \text{ people a year}$$
$$= 2 * 8 * 1 * 60 * 100/0.1$$
$$= 960{,}000 \text{ people a year}$$

The number of people a year which the lift can carry might be a useful measure, but it would probably be more interesting to talk in terms of people per hour. Changing the units gives:

$$\text{capacity} = 2 * 60/0.1 = 1200 \text{ people an hour}$$

10% of people cause an average delay of ten seconds. The average time between each pair of chairs arriving at the bottom of the slope can be found by adding the times of 90% which take 6 seconds and 10% which take 16 seconds. This gives an average time of:

$$0.9 * 6 + 0.1 * 16 = 7 \text{ seconds}$$

The number of chairs per hour is then:

$$2 * 60 * 60/7 = 1028.6$$

If this calculation is unclear, it can be checked by saying, 1028.6 chairs per hour is equivalent to 514.3 pairs of chairs per hour. 90% of these take 6 seconds and 10% take 16 seconds, so the total time taken for 514.3 pairs of chairs is:

$$514.3 * 0.9 * 6 + 514.3 * 0.1 * 16 = 3600 \text{ seconds} = 1 \text{ hour.}$$

We can allow for the 15% of single people by saying 85% of the 514.3 pairs of chairs carry two people while 15% carry one person. The number carried per hour is then:

$$514.3 * 0.85 * 2 + 514.3 * 0.15 * 1 = 951.5$$

$$\text{Actual utilization} = \text{number carried/capacity}$$
$$= 951.5/1200$$
$$= 0.79 \text{ or } 79\%$$

WORKED EXAMPLE 2.5

A bottling hall has three distinct parts:
- three bottling machines each with a maximum throughput of 8 gallons a minute;
- two labelling machines each with a maximum capacity of 3000 bottles an hour;
- a packing area with a maximum throughput of 10,000 cases a day.

The hall is set to fill pint bottles and put them in cases of twelve bottles during a twelve-hour working day.

(a) What is the capacity of the hall?

(b) What is the utilization of each part of the hall?

(c) What extra equipment would be needed to increase capacity by 40%?

SOLUTION

The bottling hall can be viewed as the simple production line shown in Figure 2.8.

(a) All measurements must be in consistent units, and here pint bottles per day would seem most useful (this is only for convenience as any other consistent units would give the same results). The capacities of each stage are:

bottling
8 gallons/min on 3 machines   = 24 gallons a minute

$$= 24 * 60 * 12 * 8 \text{ bottles a day}$$

$$= 138,240 \text{ bottles a day}$$

labelling
3000 bottles/hr on 2 machines = 3000 * 2 * 12 bottles a day

$$= 72,000 \text{ bottles a day}$$

packing
10,000 cases/day = 10,000 * 12 bottles a day

$$= 120,000 \text{ bottles a day}$$

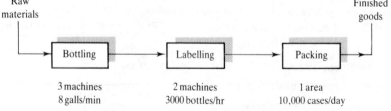

Figure 2.8 Process within the bottling hall.

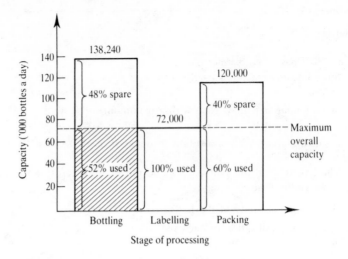

Figure 2.9 Capacity and utilization of the bottling hall for Worked example 2.5.

The limiting constraint is clearly labelling which has a much smaller capacity than the other two stages. As the capacity of the whole line is determined by the smallest capacity at any point along the line, the maximum throughput of the bottling hall is 72,000 bottles a day (see Figure 2.9).

(b) If a throughput of 72,000 bottles a day were achieved, the utilizations of each part of the line would be:

$$\text{utilization} = \frac{\text{time used for process}}{\text{time available for process}}$$

$$= \frac{\text{actual throughput of bottles}}{\text{maximum throughput of bottles}}$$

bottling: 72,000/138,240 = 0.52 or 52% of capacity

labelling: 72,000/72,000 = 1.00 or 100% of capacity

packing: 72,000/120,000 = 0.60 or 60% of capacity

(c) If planned throughput were increased by 40%, to 100,800 bottles a day, there would still be spare capacity in bottling and packing, but capacity in labelling would need to be increased by 40%. There are two labelling machines at present, so assuming identical machines would be bought to increase capacity, one additional machine would raise capacity to 3000 * 3 * 12 = 108,000 bottles a day. Utilizations would then be:

bottling: 100,800/138,240 = 0.73 or 73% of capacity

labelling: 100,800/108,000 = 0.93 or 93% of capacity

packing: 100,800/120,000 = 0.84 or 84% of capacity

Part (c) of this example illustrates a recurring problem when planning the

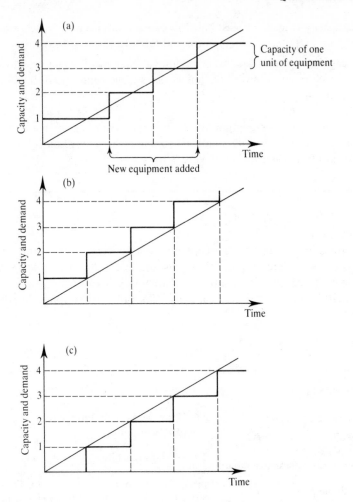

Figure 2.10 Alternative strategies to meet increasing demand when extra capacity must be added in discrete amounts: (a) capacity more or less matching demand; (b) capacity always greater than demand; (c) capacity always lagging behind demand.

resources needed to meet target throughput. Demand can take any value, but capacity may only be supplied in discrete amounts. Typically, an additional machine can add a fixed amount of capacity or employing an extra person gives a discrete increase in throughput. If demand increases steadily there are three ways of adjusting capacity:

(1) capacity is more or less matched to demand so that sometimes there is excess capacity and sometime a shortage;

(2) capacity is made at least equal to demand at all times (which requires more investment in equipment and leads to lower utilizations);

(3) capacity is only added when additional equipment would be fully used (which requires lower investment, gives higher utilizations, but constrains output).

Each of these would be appropriate in different circumstances, but it should be recognised that there is seldom an ideal solution where all resources are used at 100% of available capacity (see Figure 2.10).

In summary

There are always limits to the capacity of a process. These limits may be obvious or need calculating. With reasonable estimates for capacity, it is possible to find actual utilizations. Difficulties may occur when demand rises steadily but additional capacity can only be supplied in discrete amounts.

SELF ASSESSMENT QUESTIONS

2.5 What is the capacity of a process:

(a) amount of processing actually used during some time period;

(b) maximum amount of processing available in some period;

(c) proportion of available processing used during some period;

(d) minimum amount of processing which covers costs?

2.6 How would you find the maximum output of a production line?

2.7 If eight machines work for eight hours a day, 345 days a year, each making one unit of an item every eight minutes, what is the annual capacity of the machines? If actual output is 150,000 units a year what is the utilization of the machines?

2.3 VALUE OF MONEY OVER TIME

2.3.1 Interest rates

The responsibility for break-even analyses may be assigned to the operations area of a company, or it may be considered a financial function. Viewing it as the latter, we can continue this theme by looking at other models concerned with finance. One particularly useful study considers the changing value of money over time. This can be

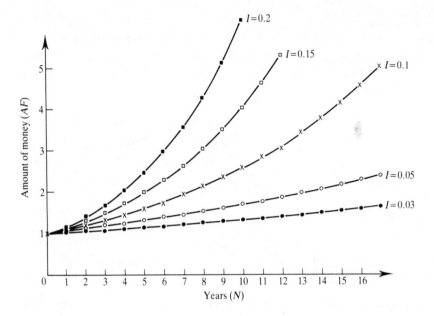

Figure 2.11 Increase of amount after earning interest with varying interest rates (initial investment = 1.0).

demonstrated by reference to interest rates, rates of return and net present values.

If money is put into a bank account it will accumulate interest and the amount in the account will increase. Suppose an amount AP is put into a bank account at the present time and is left untouched for a year earning interest at a rate I. At the end of the year there will be an amount

$$AP * (1 + I)$$

For this calculation the interest rate, I, is a decimal fraction, or proportion rather than a percentage, so an interest rate of 10% would be represented by $I = 0.1$, an interest rate of 15% by $I = 0.15$ and so on (see Figure 2.11).

If the money, AP, is left untouched for a second year it will earn interest not only on the initial amount deposited but also on the interest earned in the first year. This amounts to

$$\{AP * (1 + I)\} * (1 + I)$$

or

$$AP * (1 + I)^2$$

The amount of money will increase in this compound way, and at any time N years in the future the amount of money in the bank account, AF, will be:

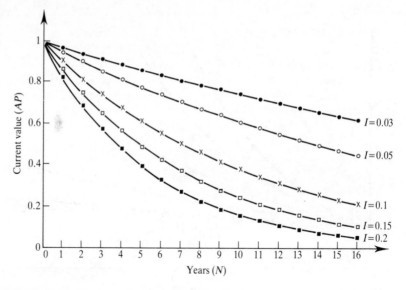

Figure 2.12 Decrease of present value of money N years in the future (future value = 1.0).

$$AF = AP * (1 + I)^N$$

Provided consistent units are used the time period need not be years, so an amount of money AP at present will have a value of $AP * (1 + I)^N$ at some time N periods in the future. Turning this the other way around, we could say that an amount, AF, N periods in the future has a present value of

$$AP = AF/(1 + I)^N = AF * (1 + I)^{-N}$$

For most purposes it would be an over-simplification to use an interest rate for I, as this would ignore the effects of inflation, opportunity costs and other factors. Sometimes these can be taken into account by defining I as a more general discounting factor (or percentage discounting rate). One step towards this would set I as a real interest rate, with

real interest rate = actual interest rate − inflation

If the rate of inflation is low the real interest rate will be positive and the value of money invested will grow. If the rate of inflation is high the real interest rate will be negative and any money invested will decrease in value (see Figure 2.12).

WORKED EXAMPLE 2.6

Several years ago a couple invested in an endowment insurance policy which has recently matured. They have the option of receiving £10,000 now or £20,000 in ten years' time. Because they are now retired and pay no income tax, they could invest the money with a real interest rate expected to remain at 10% a year for the foreseeable future. Which option should they take?

SOLUTION

This problem needs a comparison of amounts of money at two different points in time. The way to make such comparisons is to find the values of both amounts at the same point. Any convenient time may be used, but there are two obvious alternatives:

(a) calculate the values of both amounts when they are available ten years in the future;

or

(b) calculate the present value of both amounts.

As these are different ways of viewing the same problem they must come to the same conclusion, so either could be adopted.

Calculating the values for ten years in the future:

(i) take the option of £10,000 now. This can be increased by 10% a year for ten years and will then have the value $10,000 * (1 + 0.1)^{10}$, or £25,937.

(ii) take the option of £20,000 in ten years' time.

Clearly £10,000 now can be invested to give a higher value in ten years' time (29.7% higher), and this is the option which should be adopted.

The same problem can be tackled using the present value of each amount:

(i) take the option of £10,000 now;

(ii) take the option of £20,000 in ten years' time. This can be discounted by 10% a year for ten years and will have an equivalent present value of $20,000/(1 + 0.1)^{10}$, or £7711.

Again £10,000 now has a higher value (29.7% higher), and this is the option which should be adopted.

2.3.2 Net present value

This worked example illustrates a useful approach for comparing projects which have payments and incomes spread over varying time periods. The general strategy is to calculate, for all amounts of money paid or received, the equivalent value at some convenient point in time. This would allow direct comparison. The usual convention is to find the equivalent *present* values of all sums. Then subtracting the present value of all costs from the present value of all revenues gives a 'net present value'.

Net Present Value = Sum of Discounted Revenues − Sum of Discounted Costs

---

WORKED EXAMPLE 2.7

Three alternative projects have been proposed with initial costs and projected revenues (each in thousands of pounds) for the next five years as shown below.

	Initial cost	\multicolumn{5}{}{Net revenue generated in each year}

	Initial cost	1	2	3	4	5
A	1000	500	400	300	200	100
Project B	1000	200	200	300	400	400
C	500	50	200	200	100	50

If the company has enough resources to start only one project which should it consider?

SOLUTION

Conventional accounting often takes an 'average rate of return' as a useful measure. This is found by taking the average annual revenue as a percentage of initial investment. In this example the average rates of return are:

Project	A	B	C
Initial cost	1000	1000	500
Total revenue	1500	1500	600
Average annual revenue	300	300	120
Average rate of return	30%	30%	24%

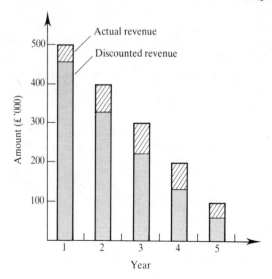

Figure 2.13 Actual and discounted revenues for Project A. (Similar graphs could be drawn for the other two projects).

Projects A and B have the same average rate of return, but project C offers a lower rate and would only be considered if the company could not afford the initial investment of £1 million, if 24% were considered an acceptable rate of return, or if some other factor made projects A and B less acceptable.

Looking in more detail at the money flows for projects A and B, we see that the revenues vary over time and in particular A offers more in early years while B offers more in later years. To give a valid comparison between these we can transform all amounts to present values and compare the net present value of each project. No discounting factor is specified, so we can select the most appropriate. We will assume this to be 10% a year.

For project A:

500 in year 1 has a present value of $500/1.1 = 454.545$
400 in year 2 has a present value of $400/1.1^2 = 330.579$
300 in year 3 has a present value of $300/1.1^3 = 225.394$
and so on (see Figure 2.13).

It is relatively straightforward to make a table (see Table 2.1) of these results, incorporating the discounting factors 1.1, 1.1^2, 1.1^3 etc. Although such tables might appear unwieldy, they can easily be developed using a spreadsheet package such as Multiplan, Supercalc, Lotus 1–2–3, Symphony or one of the many equivalent packages.

Table 2.1

Year	Discounting factor	Project A		Project B		Project C	
		Revenue	Present value	Revenue	Present value	Revenue	Present value
1	1.1	500	454.545	200	181.818	50	45.455
2	1.21	400	330.579	200	165.289	200	165.289
3	1.331	300	225.394	300	225.394	200	150.263
4	1.4641	200	136.603	400	273.205	100	68.301
5	1.61051	100	62.092	400	248.369	50	31.046
Totals		1500	1209.213	1500	1094.075	600	460.354

Subtracting the present values of costs (in this case the single initial project costs) from the present values of revenues gives net present values of:

	Project A	Project B	Project C
Present value of revenue	1209.213	1094.075	460.354
Present value of costs	1000.000	1000.000	500.000
Net present value	209.213	94.075	−39.646

Project A has the highest net present value and should, all other things being equal, be the one adopted. Project C has a negative net present value, indicating a loss, and this alternative should clearly be avoided. One other consideration which might be important is that the revenues from A are declining, implying the project has a limited life span of around five years, while revenues from project B are rising, implying a longer potential life span. Considerations of this kind must be taken into account before any final decisions are made.

Many people have an aversion to debts, and although these are usually expensive they can have benefits. Given a choice between £100 now or in a year's time we should take the money now because it has a higher value. This reasoning can be used as a justification for some debts; they allow us to receive money now and then make repayments in the future using money which has a lower value. Whether debts are beneficial or not obviously depends on the purpose to which the money is being put, real interest rates, inflation rate and so on.

2.3.3 Internal rate of return

To compare the three projects in worked example 2.7 we assumed the discounting factor was fixed and calculated the three net present values. It is frequently difficult to find a suitable discounting rate which takes into account interest rates, inflation, taxes, opportunity costs, exchange rates and everything else. An alternative would be to find the discounting rate which would lead to a specified net present value. In other words keep the same net present value for each project and calculate three different discounting rates. The usual approach is to calculate the discounting rate which will lead to a net present value of zero and this is called the 'internal rate of return' for the project. Projects can then be compared by calculating the internal rate of return for each and adopting the one with the highest value.

Unfortunately, there is no straightforward formula for calculating the internal rate of return and an iterative approach must be used. In project B above, for example, a discounting factor of 0.1 gave a net present value of £94,075. If a discounting factor of 0.14 is used the net present value is −£23,597. A discounting rate of 10% gives a positive net present value while a discounting rate of 14% gives a negative value, so the internal rate of return (which gives a net present value of zero) must lie between these two. By doing more calculations the internal rate of return can be found more accurately.

One convenient way of doing such calculations is to use a spreadsheet and Figure 2.14 shows the result from one spreadsheet model. Here the net present value is calculated for a number of discounting factors, and the internal rate of return is confirmed as lying between 10% and 14% (between 10% and 12% in fact). Such models are easy to develop and many are widely available (see, for example, Zimmerman and Zimmerman, 1988).

(If you are unfamiliar with spreadsheet packages you might skip the following description.) In detail the elements in this spreadsheet model are:

$$D6 \quad \text{initial discounting rate}$$

C3   increment in discounting rate

B8–B13   revenues in each year

C8–C13   costs in each year

D8–D13   discounted values with initial discounting rate

E8–H13   discounted values with other discounting rates

D15–H15   net present values with different discounting rates

The discounted values are calculated as described above, with, for example, $D8 = (B8 - C8)/(1 + D6/100)$.

A practical introduction to management science

	A	B	C	D	E	F	G	H
1			CALCULATION	FOR INTERNAL	RATE OF	RETURN		
2								
3	Discount Rate Step		2%					
4								
5				--------Discount Rates ---------------------				
6	Year	Revenue	Costs	8.00	10.00	12.00	14.00	16.00
7	---	---	---	---	---	---	---	---
8	0	0	1000	-1000.00	-1000.00	-1000.00	-1000.00	-1000.00
9	1	200	0	185.19	181.82	178.57	175.44	172.41
10	2	200	0	171.47	165.29	159.44	153.89	148.63
11	3	300	0	238.15	225.39	213.53	202.49	192.20
12	4	400	0	294.01	273.21	254.21	236.83	220.92
13	5	400	0	272.23	248.37	226.97	207.75	190.45
14	---	---	---	---	---	---	---	---
15		1500.00	1000.00	161.05	94.08	32.72	-23.60	-75.39
16	===	===	===	===	===	===	===	===
17								
18								
19								
20								

19-Jan-80   01:24 AM

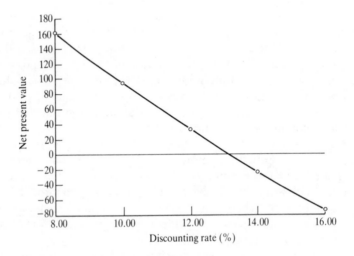

Figure 2.14 Calculation of internal rate of return for Project B above.

Changing the values in *D*6 and *C*3 allows an accurate value for the internal rate of return to be found quickly. For this example the value is between 13.14 and 13.15% as illustrated in Figure 2.15.

2.3.4 Continuous discounting

If interest is paid more frequently than every year, say every month or even every day, the calculation of present value can be done differently.

```
H20:                                                                    READY

       A        B        C        D        E        F        G        H
 1                     CALCULATION FOR INTERNAL    RATE OF  RETURN
 2
 3  Discount Rate Step      0.01%
 4
 5                              --------Discount Rates --------------------
 6      Year  Revenue    Costs     13.13    13.14    13.15    13.16    13.17
 7     --------------------------------------------------------------------
 8        0        0    1000 -1000.00 -1000.00 -1000.00 -1000.00 -1000.00
 9        1      200       0   176.79   176.77   176.76   176.74   176.73
10        2      200       0   156.27   156.24   156.21   156.19   156.16
11        3      300       0   207.20   207.14   207.09   207.03   206.98
12        4      400       0   244.20   244.12   244.03   243.94   243.86
13        5      400       0   215.86   215.76   215.67   215.57   215.48
14     --------------------------------------------------------------------
15           1500.00  1000.00     0.32     0.03    -0.24    -0.53    -0.79
16     ====================================================================
17
18
19
20
19-Jan-80   01:18 AM
```

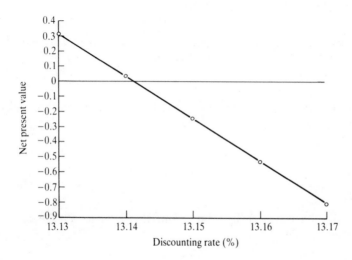

Figure 2.15 More accurate value for internal rate of return.

With compounding M times in a period the future value of the amount AP is:

$$AF = AP * (1 + I/M)^{N*M}$$

This can become messy when M gets large (when compounding is done every day, for example) and it is easier to approximate this equation by:

$$AF = AP * e^{I*N}$$

where e is the exponential constant with value 2.71828. . . . This is the basis of a widely used scheme of continuous discounting. The calculations

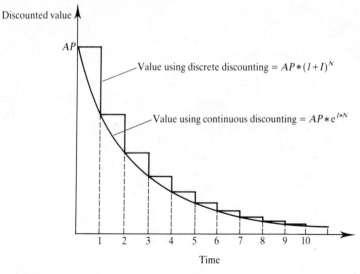

Figure 2.16 Discounted value of money using continuous and discrete discounting.

for continuous discounting are exactly the same as for discrete discounting except:

$$(1 + I)^N$$

is replaced by

$$e^{I*N}$$

Figure 2.16 illustrates this. Apart from this change all aspects of the calculations remain the same.

WORKED EXAMPLE 2.8

How much will an initial investment of £1000 earning interest of 8% a year be worth at the end of 20 years?

SOLUTION

Using discrete compounding

$$AF = AP * (1 + I)^N$$
$$= 1000 * (1.08)^{20}$$
$$= £4661$$

Using continuous compounding

$$AF = AP * e^{I*N}$$
$$= 1000 * e^{0.08*20}$$
$$= £4953$$

These answers are slightly different and the 'correct' one will depend on whether interest is paid annually or is compounded more frequently. Generally the latter is true and continuous compounding will be more reliable.

WORKED EXAMPLE 2.9

Part of a major project is to be done by sub-contractors. Two firms submit tenders for the work with projected cash flows as follows (with negative figures representing payments and positive figures revenues).

	Year 1	Year 2	Year 3
Firm A	−50,000	20,000	60,000
Firm B	−80,000	10,000	100,000

If inflation and opportunity costs suggest a discounting rate of 8% a year, which of the firms should get the contract?

SOLUTION

These two tenders can be compared by calculating the net present value of each. We will start by using discrete discounting and follow this by continuous discounting to see if there is much difference.

Table 2.2 shows discrete discounting using $(1 + I)^N$.

Table 2.2

Year	Discounting factor	Firm A Revenue	Firm A Discounted revenue	Firm B Revenue	Firm B Discounted revenue
1	1.080	−50,000	−46,296	−80,000	−74,074
2	1.166	20,000	17,153	10,000	8,576
3	1.260	60,000	47,619	100,000	79,365
Totals		30,000	18,476	30,000	13,867

The figures in Table 2.2 suggest using Firm A which gives a net present value of £18,476.

Table 2.3 shows continuous discounting using e^{I^*N}.

Table 2.3

Year	Discounting factor	Firm A Revenue	Firm A Discounted revenue	Firm B Revenue	Firm B Discounted revenue
1	1.083	−50,000	−46,168	−80,000	−73,869
2	1.174	20,000	17,036	10,000	8,518
3	1.271	60,000	47,207	100,000	78,678
Totals		30,000	18,075	30,000	13,327

The figures in Table 2.3 are very similar to the first set and again show that Firm A should be used. The net present value of this tender is around £18,000, but the exact value will depend on accounting conventions used and in particular whether continuous discounting is preferred to discrete.

In summary

The value of money varies over time. A given amount available at present will have a value equivalent to a larger amount in the future. Calculating present values allows revenues and payments made at different times to be compared. The difference between these is the net present value which can be used to compare projects which extend over different time periods. Discounting may be either continuous or at discrete intervals.

SELF ASSESSMENT QUESTIONS

2.8 Is £1000 now worth

(a) more than £1000 in five years' time
(b) less than £1000 in five years' time
(c) the same as £1000 in five years' time
(d) cannot say without more information?

2.9 How could you compare the net benefits of two projects, one of which lasts for five years and the other for seven years?

2.10 What is a discounting factor?

2.11 What is meant by continuous discounting?

2.4 REPLACEMENT OF EQUIPMENT

The performance of almost everything declines with age. Schedules of routine maintenance can reduce the effects of aging and keep equipment working fairly efficiently, but a point will come when maintenance and repairs become too expensive and it will be cheaper to buy new equipment. We will now illustrate a method for determining this point.

Replacement decisions are obviously important for expensive plant (when, for example, a power station is removed from service or a ship is laid up). Although the costs are not so dramatic, less expensive equipment should also have planned replacement to maintain acceptable levels of reliability, costs, quality and quantity of output. Decisions of this type also occur when we consider buying a new car (for economic reasons rather than status), a new television set or, in a more extreme example, having worn hip joints replaced by artificial ones.

Figure 2.17 illustrates two possible approaches to the problem. Firstly, equipment may be replaced when its performance declines to the point where it is no longer acceptable; the output may be too low, quality too poor, breakdowns too frequent, etc. A drawback of this approach is that its response is too late as the equipment is already unsatisfactory. A better alternative would be to analyse costs and keep the equipment operating for the specific time which minimizes total costs.

One useful approach adds the cost of operating a machine over a number of years and then divides this total cost by the machine's lifetime to give an average annual cost. Repeating this calculation for several values of lifetime will identify the optimal age of replacement.

WORKED EXAMPLE 2.10

On the first of February each year a company reviews the performance of its production machines so that any replacements can be delivered before the end of the financial year. The cost of replacing each machine is £100,000 and expected resale values at the end of each year are given in the following table. Records of machine operations have been used to find average annual operating and maintenance costs, which are also shown in the table below. What is the best age to replace the machines?

Age of machine	1	2	3	4	5
Resale value	50,000	30,000	15,000	10,000	5,000
Running cost in previous year	5,000	9,000	15,000	41,000	60,000

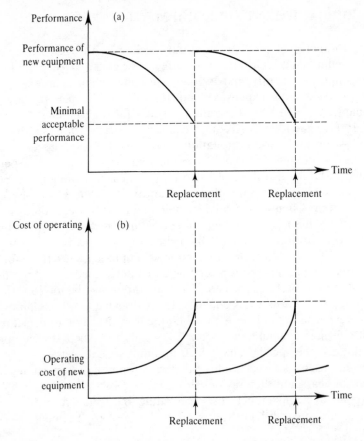

Figure 2.17 Performance varying with age: (a) Performance deteriorating over time until replacement when a minimal acceptable performance is reached; (b) Increasing operating cost over time minimized by replacement policy.

SOLUTION

The approach is to find the total cost of operating a machine over a number of years, then dividing this by the lifetime gives an average annual cost. Repeating this calculation for different lifetimes will identify the optimal age of replacement.

When a machine is sold the total cost of use during its lifetime is in two parts:

(a) a capital cost equal to the difference between the price of a new machine and the resale value of the old one;

(b) a running cost which is the cumulative cost of maintenance and operation over the machine's life.

Here, if a machine is sold after one year of use:

> capital cost will be 100,000 − 50,000 = £50,000
> running cost is £5000.

The total cost of using the machine for one year is £55,000.
> If the machine is sold after 2 years:

> capital cost will be 100,000 − 30,000 = £70,000
> running cost will be 5000 in the first year plus 9000 in the second year.

The total cost of using the machine for two years is £84,000, which is an average of £42,000 a year.

> Repeating these calculations for other ages of replacement gives the values in Table 2.4.

Table 2.4

Age of replacement	1	2	3	4	5
Capital cost	50,000	70,000	85,000	90,000	95,000
Running cost	5,000	14,000	29,000	70,000	130,000
Total cost	55,000	84,000	114,000	160,000	225,000
Av. annual cost	55,000	42,000	38,000	40,000	45,000

Replacement after three years gives the lowest average annual cost, as shown in Figure 2.18.

> So far we have assumed that a new machine will be bought: an alternative would be to buy a secondhand one. When resale value declines quickly, as it does in this example, secondhand equipment can be bought which is both cheap and relatively new. This may be better than buying new machines, but there are obvious problems with reliability, availability of spare parts, status, use of outdated technology, etc. Many organizations function quite happily with secondhand equipment and the analysis of costs is a simple extension to the model above.

> If a machine is bought when it is two years old and used until it is four years old:

> capital cost will be 30,000 − 10,000 = £20,000
> running cost will be £15,000 in the first year plus £41,000 in the second year.

The total cost over two years is £76,000, or an average of £38,000 a year.
> If a machine is bought when it is two years old and used until it is five years old:

> capital cost will be 30,000 − 5000 = £25,000
> running cost will be £15,000 in the first year, £41,000 in the second year and £60,000 in the third year.

The total cost over three years is £141,000, or an average of £47,000 a year.

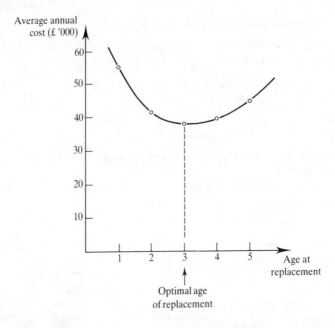

Figure 2.18 Graph of average annual cost against age of replacement for Worked example 2.10.

Repeating this calculation for combinations of ages bought and ages sold gives the following table of average annual costs (entries are in thousands of pounds).

		Age sold			
	1	2	3	4	5
0	55	42	38	40	43
1	–	29	29.5	35	42.5
Age bought 2	–	–	30	38	47
3	–	–	–	46	55.5
4	–	–	–	–	65

The cheapest alternative is to buy one-year-old machines and sell them a year later.

This calculation can give useful results, but an obvious flaw is the assumption that the value of money is constant. Earlier in the chapter we saw how discounting factors could be used to reduce amounts of money in the future to their discounted present value. It would be fairly simple to introduce this idea into this analysis and check the results.

For simplicity we will use a discounting rate of 1% a month, or slightly over 12% a year. In addition we will use discrete discounting and only consider buying new machines.

If the machines are replaced after one year of operation:

(a) capital cost consists of the purchase price minus the resale value, but the resale value has to be discounted by 1.01^{12}.

(b) running costs have to be discounted similarly. As these occur more or less uniformly over the year (i.e. months 1 to 12) we can use an average discounting factor based on the middle of the year (i.e. month 6) equal to 1.01^6.

Total cost then becomes:

$$\text{capital cost} = 100,000 - 50,000/1.01^{12}$$
$$= 100,000 - 44,372$$
$$= 55,628$$

$$\text{running cost} = 5000/1.01^6$$
$$= 4710$$

$$\text{total cost} = 55,628 + 4710$$
$$= £60,338$$

Similarly, selling the machines after two years of operation has:

$$\text{capital cost} = 100,000 - 30,000/1.01^{24}$$
$$= 100,000 - 23,627$$
$$= 76,373$$

$$\text{running cost} = 5000/1.01^6 + 9000/1.01^{18}$$
$$= 4710 + 7524$$
$$= 12,234$$

$$\text{total cost} = £88,607 \text{ or } £44,304 \text{ a year}$$

Repeating these calculations for other operating periods gives the results shown in Table 2.5.

Table 2.5

Age at replacement	1	2	3	4	5
Capital cost	55,624	76,373	89,516	93,797	97,248
Running cost	4,710	12,234	23,363	50,358	85,417
Net present cost	60,334	88,607	112,879	144,155	182,665
Average cost/year	60,334	44,303	37,626	36,039	36,533

With discounted values the best solution is to replace the machines every four years. This can be compared with the previous solution, without discounts, which recommended replacement every two years. The difference arises because future operating and maintenance costs have been discounted to give lower present values. If this is unrealistic and there is an expectation that costs will rise and maintain their real values, the calculation could be repeated on this basis.

WORKED EXAMPLE 2.11

New cars cost a company £12,000 each, with resale values and maintenance costs shown below. What is the optimal age of replacement if a continuous discounting rate of 1% a month is used?

Age of car (years)	1	2	3	4	5	6
Resale value	8000	5000	3000	2000	1200	600
Annual maintenance	1000	1200	1500	2000	3000	8750

SOLUTION

Continuous discounting, with I equal to 0.01, uses a factor of $e^{0.01*N}$. Resale values are discounted for full years, but we will assume that maintenance is notionally paid in the middle of the year. Then the discounting factor for the first year is $e^{0.06}$, for the second year is $e^{0.18}$ and so on. The calculations for this decision are shown in Table 2.6.

Table 2.6

Age of car when sold	1	2	3	4	5	6
Resale value	8,000	5,000	3,000	2,000	1,200	600
Discounting factor	1.127	1.271	1.433	1.616	1.822	2.054
Discounted resale value	7,095	3,933	2,093	1,238	659	292
Capital cost	4,905	8,067	9,907	10,762	11,341	11,708
Maintenance cost	1,000	1,200	1,500	2,000	3,000	8,750
Discounting factor	1.062	1.197	1.350	1.522	1.716	1.935
Discounted maintenance	942	1,002	1,112	1,314	1,748	4,522
Total discounted cost	5,847	9,069	11,018	12,076	13,089	16,230
Average annual cost	5,847	4,535	3,673	3,019	2,618	2,705

The average annual cost of cars reaches a minimum when they are replaced every five years (see Figure 2.19) and this should be considered as the optimal replacement age (all other things being equal).

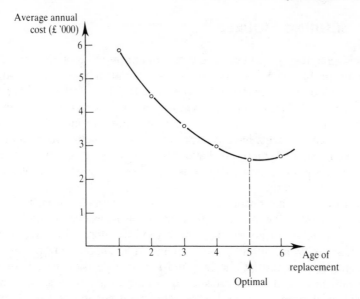

Figure 2.19 Average annual operating cost against age of replacement for
Worked example 2.11.

In summary

The performance of almost everything declines with age. Maintenance
will reduce the effects of aging, but eventually equipment should be
replaced. The optimal time for this can be found by calculating average
annual costs over various lifetimes and selecting the lowest. Discounting
to present values can be used for longer life expectancies.

SELF ASSESSMENT QUESTIONS

2.12 Is it likely that maintenance costs for a
machine will decline over time?

2.13 When should a machine be replaced:

(a) when it breaks down and can no longer
be repaired;
(b) when the operating costs rise above the
cost of a new machine;
(c) when the average annual cost is a
minimum;
(d) when the operating cost rises above the
resale value?

2.14 The optimal age of replacement for a
machine has been calculated, with no
discounting, to be six years. If future
maintenance costs are now raised in line with
expected inflation and the calculation is
repeated will this:

(a) lower the optimal age of replacement;
(b) raise the optimal age of replacement;
(c) either lower or raise the optimal age of
replacement;
(d) have no effect on the optimal age of
replacement?

2.5 SCORING MODELS

In this chapter we have developed quantitative models for several common problems. Such models are useful, but many situations are too complex to be represented by simple models. Then decisions have to be made when all factors are not known, when interactions are unclear, information is unavailable and under pressure of time. Often (if not usually) such decisions have a large subjective element which can not be quantified. Several methods have been developed to try and add a rational viewpoint to such decisions and scoring models are one of the most useful of these.

Consider the problem of finding the best location for a new factory. Quantitative models for location decisions are often complex, time consuming and not readily understood by those who have to make the decisions. More often than not, quantitative analyses are not used and someone assesses the alternatives and makes a decision based solely on their judgement. One aid for such decisions would be a simple scoring model, which would not reduce the judgement needed by managers, but would allow them to base comparison of alternatives on a more logical footing.

For scoring models the important factors in a decision are identified and given a maximum possible score based on their relative importance. Financial considerations might be given a maximum score of 20, marketing considerations are half as important and are given a maximum score of 10 and so on. Then each alternative is examined and is given a number of points for each factor (usually on a subjective basis and often agreed after wide discussion). The points are added and the alternative with the highest total is, all other things being equal, the most attractive.

The procedure for scoring models is:

---

(1) decide the relevant factors in a decision;

(2) give each factor a weighting (or maximum score);

(3) consider each alternative in turn and assign points for each factor;

(4) add the total points for each alternative to identify the best.

This may be viewed as a way of introducing some numerical foundation to qualitative decisions (harsher critics suggest it is a way of building a defence for decisions which may turn out to be wrong).

WORKED EXAMPLE 2.12

A new electronics factory is planned in an area which is encouraging industrial growth, and there are three alternative sites. A management team is considering these alternatives and has suggested the important factors are government grants, attitude of the local community, availability of trained electronics engineers, availability of experienced workforce, nearby suppliers of components, education centres for collaborative research, and housing for employees. Each of these factors has been assigned a maximum score, as shown below. For each alternative site the management team discussed the actual achievement of each factor and assigned it an agreed number of points. Thus government grants were assigned a maximum score of 10: locations A and B qualified for reasonably high government grants and were given eight points each while location C qualified for a lower grant and was given five points. Repeating this process for other factors gave the results in Table 2.7.

Table 2.7

Factor	Max Score	Points given at location		
		A	B	C
Government grants	10	8	8	5
Community attitude	10	8	7	5
Electronic engineers	15	10	8	8
Experienced workforce	20	20	15	15
Nearby suppliers	5	2	3	3
Education centres	10	8	6	5
Housing	5	2	3	5
Totals	85	58	50	46

The total number of points show that A has advantages over the other locations, while B would be the second choice. This rating can be incorporated with other tangible factors (such as construction costs, transport, rent and local taxes) to allow a final decision.

WORKED EXAMPLE 2.13

A company wants to expand its product range by manufacturing a new item. There are three alternatives available and the company must select the best of these. A project team has been formed and has reported that the most important factors, with relevant weights, are shown in Table 2.8. After considerable discussion the team also agreed a number of points for each product. Which product should be introduced?

Table 2.8

Factor	Maximum	Points A	B	C
Product:				
Time to develop product	10	8	4	7
Research and development requirements	20	15	8	10
Experience with similar products	10	9	4	7
Similarity with existing products	10	9	2	5
Expected life	20	10	6	12
Ease of manufacture	25	20	12	18
Requirements of raw materials	5	4	4	3
Finance:				
Research and development expenditure	20	18	14	17
Capital outlay	15	10	10	10
Return on investment	25	12	15	20
Net present value	20	10	17	18
Market:				
Existing demand	25	23	12	16
Marketing effort	10	10	4	7
Advertising requirements	5	4	2	6
Competition	15	5	15	10
Stability of market	5	3	2	4
Market trends	10	4	9	7
Totals	250	174	140	177

SOLUTION

The total points show products A and C to be about equally attractive, while product B is some way behind. Details of A and C would now be looked at in detail and other factors considered before a final decision is made.

In summary

Many decisions are made in complex situations and involve an amount of subjective judgement. Scoring models are one way of allowing some rational comparison of these opinions.

SELF ASSESSMENT QUESTIONS

2.15 Can scoring models be used:

(a) when quantitative models are available;
(b) when qualitative views are to be considered;
(c) only for complex situations;
(d) in any circumstances?

2.16 If a scoring model indicates a particular location is the best site for a new warehouse would any further analysis be necessary?

CONCLUSIONS

In this chapter we have examined a number of quantitative models. We started by looking at break-even analyses which defined the throughput necessary to make a profit. This was followed by the related calculation of capacity to see if planned throughput can be achieved. If there is spare capacity some measure of utilization can be defined. Financing production decisions leads to ideas about the changing value of money over time. This is relevant for comparing projects and may be used in replacement decisions. Finally we looked at scoring models which allowed comparisons of subjective views.

The overall approach we have adopted is to illustrate principles by worked examples rather than getting bogged down in mathematical formulae. This is consistent with an overall aim of illustrating the usefulness of quantitative ideas, and suggesting that quantitative models need not be complex or difficult to understand.

This chapter may be considered a link between the general ideas expressed in the introduction of Chapter 1, and the more specific applications in following chapters.

PROBLEMS

2.1 A taxi driver has fixed costs of £4500 a year. Each mile he drives costs 30 pence and he charges an average of 45 pence.

    (a)   How many miles a year does he need to travel before he starts making a profit?

    (b)   Last year he drove 90,000 miles. What were his total and net incomes?

2.2 A company makes knives, forks and spoons. The variable costs, selling prices and proportions of each are given in the following table.

	Knives	Forks	Spoons
Variable cost	£2	£2.50	£1.50
Selling price	£4	£5.25	£4.50
Proportion of total production	45%	20%	35%

Fixed costs are £60,000 a year and the company has a target of making £30,000 a year profit. How many units of each should be made?

2.3 Four machines work two shifts of eight hours each for six days a week. When adjusted properly each machine can produce one unit of an item every 10 minutes. Last year total production was 84,372 units. What was the utilization of the machines?

2.4 An assembly line consists of five stages as shown.

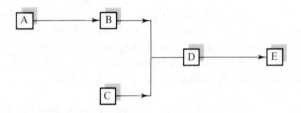

Two sub-assemblies are made, one on stages A and B and the other on stage C. These are assembled at stage D and finished at stage E. The number of machines at each stage and the capacity of each machine are given below.

Stage	A	B	C	D	E
Number of machines	2	2	4	3	2
Capacity of each machine (units per hour)	600	450	220	250	800

(a) What is the utilization of each stage if the line is working at full capacity?

(b) If one more machine is bought (of an identical type to those already operating), what would be the new utilization?

2.5 Given the cash flows in Table 2.9 for a project, calculate the net present value using a discounting rate of 12% a year. What is the internal rate of return for the project?

2.6 Use continuous discounting on the data for problem 2.5 to see if there is much difference. Which of the two answers is more reliable?

Table 2.9

Year	Income	Expenditure
0	0	18,000
1	2,500	0
2	13,500	6,000
3	18,000	0
4	6,000	2,000
5	1,000	0

2.7   A machine costs £75,000 with resale values and maintenance costs shown below.

Age of machine (years)	1	2	3	4	5	6	7
Resale value	60,000	50,000	40,000	25,000	12,000	1,000	0
Maintenance in year	5,000	7,000	9,000	15,000	20,000	60,000	140,000

What is the optimal age for replacing the machine if a continuous discounting rate of 1.5% a month is used?

CASE STUDY – THE LEWIS EDUCATION CENTRE

In the mid 1980s George Lewis had been a school teacher for over 25 years. He was dedicated to teaching, but was depressed by the poor performance of some of his pupils, particularly able ones who suddenly began to fall behind the rest of the class. He analysed school records for the past five years, interviewed many pupils whose performance had declined and found a common pattern. This would start with a pupil being ill or missing an important lesson. When they returned to school they would not understand what was happening in class and would lose interest. Then they would fall further behind, lose self-confidence and often become disruptive. Sometimes a pupil would not miss any school but would simply be slow to understand an important point and the pattern would again be followed.

It seemed clear to Mr Lewis that if pupils with problems were caught early, a small effort could help them back to their previous performance levels. Unfortunately this kind of help was not possible within the existing school system. Teachers had only a limited amount of time and if special attention were given to one pupil the rest of the class would be affected. Private tutors were available but these tended to be expensive and covered an entire course rather than concentrate on the specific needs of a pupil.

After much thought, Mr Lewis decided to leave teaching and start his own business, the 'Lewis Education Centre'. This would supplement the existing education service and:

- allow parents whose children were having problems at school to discuss their problems;
- do a detailed test of student's knowledge;
- identify those specific areas which the student did not understand;
- design a programme to remedy the specific areas of weakness;
- organize and administer the programme;
- retest the pupil at the end of the programme and ensure progress had been made.

It took Mr Lewis three years to test his ideas on a number of pupils and prepare necessary material. His test pupils almost always showed considerable progress.

The general format of courses which evolved during trials was to have 26 hours of teaching with at most three pupils per teacher. Students would come to the centre (initially in Mr Lewis's home) after school for two hours a week. They would study the material which was specifically designed for them and had virtually individual teaching. Based on his own experience, and that of part-time teachers hired to prepare other material, Mr Lewis could offer courses on a range of subjects to pupils between the ages of 5 and 14, with a number of specialized courses for older students (life skills, preparing for university entrance, effective communication and so on). The courses needed to be relatively expensive to cover costs, and Mr Lewis guaranteed results so that a pupil not achieving an agreed objective had all money refunded.

The next stage in the development of the Lewis Education Centre was to open an office near the town centre and attract customers. Because it was a new venture the initial cost of advertising was high, but in time referrals from schools, advice from related organizations and word of mouth should ensure the centre's long term future.

Arrangements for the opening of the new centre were carefully made, including recruitment of a number of staff who were trained as teachers but who were currently not working in schools. A list of suitable teachers, who would be sympathetic to the aims and approaches of the centre, was kept and they were employed by the hour as needed. The centre was administered by a full time manager, and an educational co-ordinator and secretary working part time.

The layout of the centre caused some discussion, but the final plan consisted of four tables in an open plan area; a teacher would sit at each table and would teach at most three pupils at any time.

Advertising started in April 1987 and the formal opening of the centre was in May with pupils enrolled from June. The process of enrolling a new student was usually in several stages:

- a parent would phone or write to the centre for more information;
- a talk with parents and tour of the centre;
- an assessment test to identify the specific needs of the student;
- actual enrollment in the centre.

The centre would then design an individual programme based on weaknesses, give 26 hours of tuition followed by a final test to assess progress. Sometimes pupils would enroll for a second 26 hour-course.

Mr Lewis kept records of enquiries each week and the numbers who eventually enrolled, as shown in Table 2.10. It was felt that roughly 40% of enquiries lead to visits to the centre, about 90% of these lead to tests and about 95% of students taking tests enrolled in a programme. This table also shows the advertising expenditure and number of student hours taught. Because of holidays, illness or other factors all students enrolled did not attend every week. George Lewis was fortunate in his choice of staff and the centre manager ensured that everything ran smoothly. He was pleased with the performance of the centre and the results obtained from students. He felt that his business was going to be a success, but began to worry about a few things.

Students had to attend the centre outside normal school hours and there were times when it seemed a bit crowded. Conversely, most of the time there was plenty of space. Mr Lewis had no clear idea of the capacity of the centre, the utilization he was achieving or the time when he would have to think of expanding. He felt that he could fit one more desk into the existing centre but would then have to find larger premises.

There was also some doubts about the profitability of the Centre. There was not enough time to prepare detailed costs, but Mr Lewis did some tentative calculations. He charged a flat rate of £12 an hour, with a reduction of 10% if the student re-enrolled for a second 26 hours or if a brother or sister was already enrolled. From this income he paid teachers £11 an hour, salaries of £370 a week (for himself and the centre manager), advertising and other overheads of about £350 a week. Any expansion in the current premises would not add significantly to the fixed costs, but teachers would be paid for more hours. He also guessed that no more than 3% of students would have money refunded for not attaining their targets.

The town he had chosen to open his centre had a population of 115,000, but another town with a population of 185,000 was only 45 miles away. He felt that opening a second centre would be an obvious move, but he needed some ideas for fixing its capacity. The demand might depend on the amount of advertising, but he had little feel for the effectiveness of this.

Table 2.10 Weekly results for Lewis Education Centre.

	Week	Enquiries	Test	Enrolled	Hours	Advertising
May	2	10	–	–	–	£2,750
	3	14	1	1	–	£2,950
June	1	10	4	3	8	£1,750
	2	12	4	2	12	£1,100
	3	9	5	5	24	£ 660
	4	11	4	4	30	£ 425
July	1	8	4	4	36	£ 415
	2	11	3	2	40	£ 395
	3	12	6	5	51	£ 385
	4	16	6	4	58	£ 350
August	1	9	5	5	68	£ 350
	2	10	5	3	75	£ 340
	3	12	7	6	81	£ 335
	4	12	5	4	86	£ 345
September	1	10	4	4	90	£ 340
	2	11	7	3	102	£ 350
	3	13	8	6	104	£ 335
	4	14	7	2	110	£ 325
October	1	8	5	4	106	£ 295
	2	10	5	2	113	£ 305
	3	10	5	4	121	£ 290
	4	12	8	4	127	£ 285
November	1	10	7	6	119	£ 275
	2	9	5	4	122	£ 270
	3	11	4	3	123	£ 285
	4	9	4	2	125	£ 275
December	1	9	4	3	135	£ 250
	2	6	2	2	123	£ 250
	3	3	1	1	117	£ 235
	4	4	2	1	96	£ 195
January	1	6	2	2	101	£ 215
	2	10	3	3	129	£ 235
	3	11	5	3	137	£ 255
	4	12	8	5	133	£ 240

Overall it was clear that this was a time when Mr Lewis should sit back and put some careful thought into the next stage of his plans.

Suggested questions

- What are the objectives of the centre?
- Describe in detail the operation of the centre.
- How accurate is the data collected?

- What are the capacity, utilization and break-even point of the centre?
- Will the centre run at a profit?
- What is the effect of advertising?
- How might enrolment of the centre be increased?
- What changes could be suggested for running the centre?
- Should Mr Lewis open another centre, and if so how big should it be?

SOLUTIONS TO SELF ASSESSMENT QUESTIONS

2.1 Variable cost varies with the number of units processed (numbers produced, throughput etc.). It is distinct from the fixed cost which stays the same regardless of the throughput.

2.2 The break-even point is the number of units which must be processed before a profit is made. It is the point at which total revenue equals total (fixed + variable) cost.

2.3 (b) The product is making a loss as revenue from 1200 units will not cover all fixed costs.

2.4 False. Economies of scale suggest that it is *usually* better to have a single large factory than a number of smaller ones, but there are also diseconomies of scale, such as communication costs, increased management hierarchies, increased bureaucracy and increased supervision needs.

2.5 (b) the maximum amount of processing available during some period.

2.6 The maximum output is determined by the smallest capacity at any point along the line. Observation of a line can show the bottlenecks fairly quickly, and the throughput at these points can either be calculated or found by observation.

2.7 The total availability of machine time in minutes a year is $8 * 60 * 8 * 345$. Each unit of the item takes eight minutes to make, so the maximum capacity for the item is this number divided by eight, which equals $1,324,800/8 = 165,600$ units a year. If actual output is 150,000 units the utilization of machines is $150,000/165,600 = 0.906$ or 90.6%.

2.8 (a) more than £1000 in five years' time, as:

- the money could be invested and earn interest for five years;
- inflation may reduce the value of money in the future.

It may be argued that (d) is a possible answer because of uncertainties, but this would be a very cautious viewpoint.

2.9 By reducing all costs and revenues to present values, then subtracting, for each project, the present value of costs from the present value of revenues. Direct comparisons can then be made between these net present values.

2.10 An estimate of the proportional increase or decrease in the value of money in each time period. This may take into account interest rates, inflation, opportunity costs and a number of other factors.

2.11 Discounting where values are assumed to decline continuously over time rather than in discrete steps. In practice this means replacing the discounting factor $(1 + I)^N$ by e^{I*N}.

2.12 No. As machines get older their reliability deteriorates and they need more maintenance with consequent higher costs. There may be some reduction when machines are new (with teething troubles) but this is usually short term.

2.13 In general the answer to this question is (**c**), when the average annual cost is a minimum. (**a**) is also possible as a machine which breaks down may cost more to repair than to replace.

2.14 (**a**) lower the optimal age of replacement. Maintenance costs are raised in the second calculation to allow for inflation and the costs of keeping the machine will rise. In consequence the minimum average annual cost will occur earlier than before.

2.15 (**d**) in any circumstances. They are widely applicable and can be used to support other models, formalize qualitative judgements and in complex situations.

2.16 Yes. Managers should make decisions based on all available information and not just the results from one analysis.

REFERENCES FOR FURTHER READING

There are many books describing quantitative models of the kind illustrated in this chapter. The following references give some idea of the range of books available and can be used to find other examples of quantitative models.

Bierman H., Bonini C. P., and Hausman W. H. (1986). *Quantitative Analysis for Business Decisions* Homewood: Irwin

Davis K. R., McKeown P. G. and Rakes T. R. (1986). *Management Science: an introduction* Boston: Kent Publishing

De Lisle C. (1979). *The Martin Book of Management Calculations* Cambridge: Martin Books

Evans J. R., Anderson D. R., Sweeney D. J. and Williams T. A. (1987). *Applied Production and Operations Management* 2nd edn. St Paul: West Publishing

Forgionne G. A. (1986). *Quantitative Decision Making* Belmont: Wadsworth

Johnson D. (1986). *Quantitative Business Analysis* London: Butterworths

Krajewski L. J. and Ritzman L. P. (1987). *Operations Management* Reading: Addison Wesley

Lee S. M. (1987). *Introduction to Management Science* 2nd edn. Chicago: Dryden Press

Levin R. I., Kirkpatrick C. A. and Rubin D. S. (1982). *Quantitative Approaches to Management* McGraw-Hill International

Shogan A. W. (1988). *Management Science* New Jersey: Prentice Hall

Taylor B. W. (1986). *Introduction to Management Science* 2nd edn. Dubuque: Wm Brown Publishers

Computers may be used for some calculations and there are a number of books covering this area including:

Chang Y.-L. and Sullivan R. S. (1986). *Quantitative Systems for Business* New Jersey: Prentice-Hall

Dennis T. L. and Dennis L. B. (1988). *Microcomputer Models for Management Decision-Making* St Paul: West Publishing

Erikson (1980). *Computer Models for Management Science* 3rd edn. Wokingham: Addison-Wesley

Nathan J. and Cicilioni R. Y. (1987). *A Spreadsheet Approach to Production and Operations Management* St Paul: West Publishing

Whitaker D. (1984). *OR on the Micro* Chichester: John Wiley & Sons

Zimmerman S. M. and Zimmerman S. M. (1988). *Operations Management Problems* St Paul: West Publishing

Chapter 3

Inventory control

SYNOPSIS

In Chapter 1 we introduced the idea of quantitative models and illustrated their use with some general examples. This theme was extended in Chapter 2 where specific models were described in more detail. Here we are going to look at the use of models to solve problems in one specific area, inventory or stock control.

In the chapter we introduce some ideas of 'scientific inventory control'. In particular, we are going to discuss the reasons why stocks are needed, how much they cost and how these costs can be controlled. We will examine two distinct approaches to inventory control: quantitative modelling and materials requirement planning. Quantitative models are covered first, starting with the classic 'economic order quantity'. Extensions to this are described, including finite lead times and production rates. The approach of materials requirement planning is then discussed and illustrated by examples. A batching rule is developed for MRP, or any other situation which has discrete variable demand.

Although there is some numerical work, we will not get bogged down in arithmetic manipulation. Instead, we will cover general principles and by the end of the chapter you should appreciate the ways in which quantitative analyses can tackle a range of stock control problems.

OBJECTIVES

After reading this chapter and doing the numerical exercises you should be able to:

- appreciate the need for stocks of varying types;
- define the costs associated with stock holding;
- calculate economic order quantities using the 'classic analysis';
- calculate the effect of moving away from the economic order quantity;
- calculate reorder levels;
- calculate the effects of finite production rates;
- use materials requirement planning to schedule orders;
- use a batching rule for discrete, variable demand;
- appreciate the scope of real inventory control systems.

3.1 STOCK HOLDINGS AND THEIR CONTROL

3.1.1 Stock holdings within organizations

Problems of inventory control have been around for a very long time. The need to collect food when it is readily available and then store it for times of shortage is perhaps the fundamental stock holding problem, which was tackled long ago by man (and almost every other living creature). Nowadays we usually think of stocks being held by industry to allow efficient and continuous operations.

Almost all organizations hold stocks of various kinds and there are always costs associated with these (to cover warehouse operations, tied-up capital, deterioration and so on). An obvious question is, therefore, 'Why do organizations hold stock?'. The simple answer is, 'To allow for short term fluctuations in supply and demand'. This can be illustrated by a common situation where components are assembled to give finished products. It might be possible to arrange for components to be delivered just as they are needed and deliveries of finished goods to be sent out just as they are requested. In this idealized system there would be no need to hold stocks. Unfortunately, such exact matching of supply and demand is almost always impossible. Some variation in supply is inevitable (caused by delays to delivery vehicles, disruptions to the supplier's production,

Figure 3.1 Stock as a buffer between supply and demand.

rejections of poor quality materials, and so on). Demand for finished goods will also contain random variations. The only reasonable way to allow for such variations and continue efficient operations is to hold stocks. On a national scale the value of stocks held amount to around 25% of GNP[1].

In most circumstances stocks are needed as a buffer between supply and demand (see Figure 3.1). They allow organizations to meet demands larger than expected, or at unexpected times, and allow them to maintain operations when deliveries are delayed or too small. Sometimes there are other reasons for holding stocks, including:

- to take advantage of price discounts on large orders;
- to buy items when the price is low and expected to rise;
- to buy items which are going out of production or are difficult to find;
- to make full loads and reduce transport costs;
- to decouple stages in a production process;
- to provide cover for emergencies.

Whatever the reason for holding stocks, there are associated costs and these are often surprisingly high. Typically, the annual cost of holding stock varies (depending on the items held, how they are stored, financial arrangements, and so on) from about 15% of value to over 50%, with an average figure around 25%.

As the costs associated with inventories are high, there are obvious incentives to look for policies to reduce these. Work started in the area at the end of the last century, with quantitative models developed shortly after. Harris[2] is often credited with early work in 1915, while Raymond[3] was able to write the first reasonable book on inventory control in 1931. There has been continuous progress up to the present day when computerized systems and Japanese ideas of manufacturing are leading to further improvements in efficiency. This can, perhaps, be illustrated by the steady decline in national inventories from 35% of GNP in the mid 1960s to 25% in the mid 1980s.

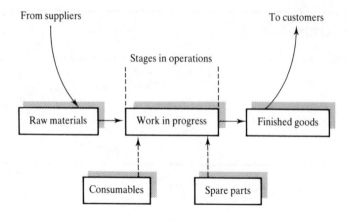

Figure 3.2 Classification of stock holdings.

3.1.2 Types of inventories held

Just about everything is held as stock somewhere, whether it is raw materials in a factory, finished goods in a shop or tins of baked beans in a pantry. These stocks are often classified, as shown in Figure 3.2, according to:

- raw materials
- work in progress
- finished goods.

This is a fairly arbitrary classification, as one company's finished goods will be another company's raw materials. Some organizations (notably retailers and wholesalers) have stocks of finished goods only, while others (manufacturers, say) have all three types in different proportions. Figures[4] suggest that on a national scale around 30% of stocks are raw materials, 40% work in progress and 30% finished goods. Some stock items do not fall easily into these categories, and two additional types are:

- spare parts (for machinery, equipment, etc.);
- consumables (oil, paper, etc.).

In summary
If an adequate service is to be maintained through variations in supply and demand, the need to carry stock of various types is an inevitable consequence. This incurs costs which are often high.

3.1.3 Approaches to inventory control

We are looking for policies which reduce the costs of stock holding, and one option would be to supply all goods using back-orders. For these a company does not carry stocks itself but guarantees to deliver within a specified time. This policy works if someone else holds stocks (perhaps a manufacturer, wholesaler, importer or main distributor) which can be accessed with an acceptably short delay. The centralized stock implied by this arrangement may reduce costs, but the service, measured by delivery time, is inevitably reduced. An extreme form of back-orders has demand met directly from production. Stocks of finished goods are then eliminated, but any variation in demand must be met by varying the guaranteed delivery time or rescheduling production.

In normal circumstances stock holdings of some kind are inevitable and there are two distinct approaches to their control:

- quantitative models
- materials requirement planning.

Materials requirement planning is designed for manufacturers and has become more popular in recent years. The approach is to take a detailed production plan and 'explode' it using a partslist or bill of materials. This gives a detailed timetable for requirements of all components and raw materials. These are then ordered to arrive in time to meet demands.

The alternative approach, using quantitative models, is more generally applicable and is the one we will consider first. A model of an inventory system is built relating costs, demand patterns, order sizes, and other variables. The model is then used to find the order patterns which minimize costs.

Both approaches look for solutions to three basic questions of stock control.

What items should be stocked?

No item, however cheap, should be stocked without considering the related benefits and costs. This means that checks are needed to stop new items being introduced unnecessarily, and regular searches should be made to remove obsolete or dead stock.

When should an order be placed?

This depends on the inventory control system used, type of demand (high or low, steady or erratic, known exactly or estimated), value of the item, lead time between placing an order and receiving it into stock, supplier reliability, and a number of other factors. Two different ordering policies are common:

- 'fixed order quantity' system, where an order of fixed size is placed whenever stock falls to a certain level. A central heating plant, for example, may order 5000 gallons of oil whenever the amount in the tank falls to 500 gallons. Such systems need continuous monitoring of stock levels and are better suited to low irregular demand for relatively expensive items.
- 'periodic review' system, where orders of varying size are placed at regular intervals to raise the stock level to a specified value. Goods on supermarket shelves, for example, may be refilled every evening to replace whatever was sold during the day. The operating cost of this system is generally lower and it may be used for high regular demand of low value items.

Variations in the stock levels over time for these two approaches are illustrated in Figure 3.3.

How much should be ordered?

If large, infrequent orders are placed average stock levels will be high but the costs of placing and administering orders will be low; if frequent small orders are placed average stock levels will be low but the costs of placing and administering orders will be high (see Figure 3.4). In an attempt to compromise between these competing costs it is possible to calculate an optimal order size (commonly called the 'economic order quantity', EOQ). This is described in section 3.2.

In summary

There are two basic approaches to inventory control, materials requirement planning and quantitative modelling. These try to minimize the total costs of carrying stock by determining what items should be stocked, when orders should be placed and how large orders should be.

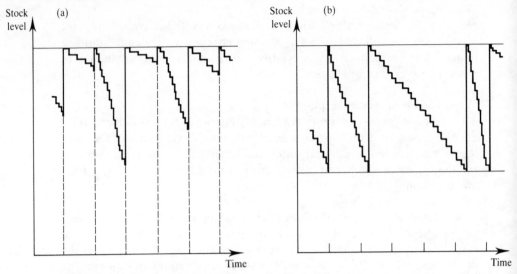

Figure 3.3 Comparison of inventory control systems: (a) periodic review system (variable order size placed at fixed intervals); (b) fixed order quantity system (fixed order size placed at variable intervals).

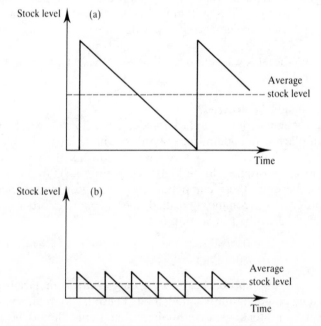

Figure 3.4 Comparing large infrequent orders with small frequent ones to meet the same demand.

SELF ASSESSMENT QUESTIONS

3.3 List three differences between materials requirement planning and quantitative modelling for inventory control.

3.4 What does inventory control try to do:

(a) minimize costs
(b) maximize customer service
(c) maximize profit
(d) minimize stock levels?

3.5 Which inventory control system would you use for controlling the stock of nuts and bolts in a company store:

(a) fixed order quantity
(b) periodic review
(c) either
(d) cannot say without more information?

3.2 COSTS OF CARRYING STOCK

We want to develop policies for stock control which emphasize the minimization of costs. An obvious starting point is to consider the costs in more detail, and define a number of distinct types.

Unit Cost (*UC*)
This is the price of the item charged by the supplier, or the cost to the company of acquiring one unit of the item. It may be fairly easy to find values by looking at quotations or recent invoices from suppliers, but it may be more difficult if there are several suppliers offering alternative products or giving different purchase conditions. If the company makes the item itself it may be difficult to set a production cost or to calculate a valid transfer price.

Reorder Cost (*RC*)
This is the cost of placing a repeat order for an item and might include allowances for drawing-up an order (with checking, signing, clearance, distribution and filing), computer time, correspondence and telephone costs, receiving (with unloading, checking and testing), supervision, use of equipment and follow-up. Sometimes costs such as quality control, transport charges, sorting and movement of received goods are included in the reorder cost.

This cost should ideally be for repeat orders and not a first order (which might have additional allowances for searching for suitable suppliers, checking reliability and quality, negotiations with alternative suppliers and so on). In practice, the best estimate for a reorder cost might be found by dividing the total annual cost of the purchasing department (plus any other relevant costs) by the number of orders sent out.

Table 3.1

	% of unit cost
Cost of money	10–20
Storage space	2–5
Loss	4–6
Handling	1–2
Administration	1–2
Insurance	1–5
Total	19–40

A special case of the reorder cost occurs when the company makes the item itself and is concerned with stocks of finished goods. Here the reorder cost is a batch set-up cost and might include production documentation costs, allowance for production lost while resetting machines, idle time of operators, material spoilt in test runs, time of specialist tool setters and so on.

Holding Cost (*HC*)

This is the cost of holding one unit of an item in stock for a unit period of time. The obvious cost is for tied-up money which is either borrowed (with interest payable) or could be put to other use (in which case there are opportunity costs). Other holding costs are due to storage space (supplying a warehouse, rent, rates, heat, light, etc.), loss (due to damage, deterioration, obsolescence and pilferage), handling (including special packaging, refrigeration, putting on pallets, etc.), administration (stock checks, computer updates, etc.) and insurance. Typical annual values for these, as percentages of unit cost, are shown in Table 3.1.

Shortage Cost (*SC*)

If an item is needed but cannot be supplied from stock, there is usually a cost associated with this shortage. In the simplest case a retailer may lose direct profit from a sale, but the effects of shortages are usually much more widespread. Goodwill and loss of potential future sales might be added as well as an element for loss of reputation. Shortages of raw materials for a production process could cause disruption and force rescheduling of production, re-timing of maintenance periods, laying-off employees, and so on. Also included in shortage costs might be allowances for positive action to counteract the shortage, perhaps sending out emergency orders, paying for special deliveries, storing partly finished goods or using alternative, more expensive suppliers.

Shortage costs are almost invariably difficult to find. There is general agreement, however, that they can be very high, particularly if production is stopped by a shortage of raw materials. This allows us to look at the purpose of stocks again and rephrase our earlier statement by saying, 'the cost of shortages can be very high and to avoid these organizations are willing to incur the relatively lower costs of carrying stock'.

Now we have described the separate costs we can combine them with other variables to develop a model of an inventory system. In the first instance we will take a simple view and make a lot of assumptions, but as the analysis progresses these assumptions can be relaxed and more realistic models developed.

SELF ASSESSMENT QUESTIONS

3.6 List four types of cost associated with stock holdings.

3.7 Is holding cost defined as

(a) a cost per unit
(b) a cost per order
(c) a cost per unit time
(d) a cost per unit per unit time?

3.8 Costs are difficult to determine for inventory systems. Is this statement

(a) true
(b) false
(c) partly true?

3.3 THE CLASSIC ANALYSIS OF INVENTORY CONTROL

This analysis was first described in the 1920s and is often attributed to Wilson[5], although it has been developed independently several times. The results are widely used and form the basis of most 'scientific inventory control'.

3.3.1 Assumptions of the analysis

We will consider a single item where the demand is known to be continuous and constant at exactly D per unit time. Then a graph of the demand over time has the pattern shown in Figure 3.5.

We assume that replenishment of the stock is instantaneous and that lead time (between placing an order and it arriving) is zero: when we decide to replenish stock a delivery is made immediately. Finally, it is assumed that unit cost (UC), reorder cost (RC) and holding cost (HC) are all known exactly, while the shortage cost (SC) is so large that all demands must be met and no shortages are allowed. These assumptions

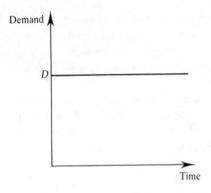

Figure 3.5 Constant demand over time.

may appear unrealistic, but the model developed can give surprisingly useful results which are, at worst, good guidelines.

The assumptions of zero lead time and instantaneous replenishment mean there is no point in placing orders until existing stock is completely exhausted. Moreover, if an optimal order quantity exists, orders will always be placed for the same quantity. Then, as units are removed from stock to meet a continuous, steady demand, D, the stock level will follow the saw-tooth pattern shown in Figure 3.6.

The overall approach of this analysis is to find costs for a single stock cycle, then dividing this by the cycle length gives a cost per unit time. Minimizing this cost per unit time allows us to find an optimal order quantity.

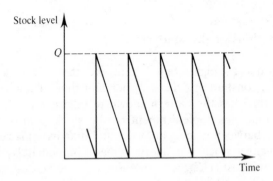

Figure 3.6 Saw-tooth stock level over time.

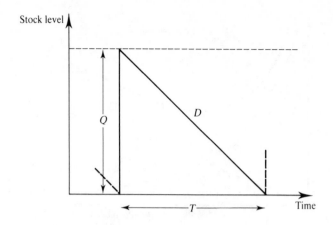

Figure 3.7 A single stock cycle.

3.3.2 Cost of a single stock cycle

Consider one cycle of the saw-tooth pattern shown in Figure 3.6 (see Figure 3.7).

At some point an order is placed for a quantity, Q, which arrives instantly. This is used at a constant rate, D, until no stock remains, at which point another order is placed. The resulting stock cycle has length T and we know:

amount entering stock = amount leaving stock
        in the cycle   in the cycle

$$Q = D * T$$

The total cost for the cycle is found by adding the three components of cost (unit, reorder and holding), remembering there are no shortage costs.

Total cost for cycle

total unit cost: = number of units ordered(Q) * unit cost(UC)
        $= UC * Q$

total reorder cost: = number of orders(1) * reorder cost(RC)
        $= RC$

total holding cost: = average stock level($Q/2$) * time held(T) *
                                                holding cost(HC)

$$= \frac{HC * Q * T}{2}$$

79

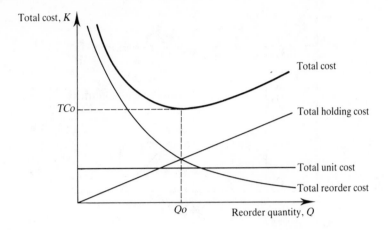

Figure 3.8   Total cost versus reorder quantity (Qo = optimal reorder quantity, TCo = minimum cost).

Adding these three gives the total cost per cycle as:

$$UC * Q + RC + \frac{HC * Q * T}{2}$$

If this is divided by the cycle length, T, we can find the total cost per unit time, TC.

$$TC = \frac{UC * Q}{T} + \frac{RC}{T} + \frac{HC * Q}{2}$$

Then substituting $Q = D * T$ gives

$$TC = UC * D + \frac{RC * D}{Q} + \frac{HC * Q}{2}$$

This finishes the first part of the analysis as we have an expression for the cost per unit time. The three cost elements on the right of this equation can be plotted separately against Q, as shown in Figure 3.8.

The total unit cost ($UC * D$) is independent of Q and can be considered 'fixed'; the total holding cost rises linearly with Q and the total reorder cost falls as Q increases. Clearly, large infrequent orders give high total holding costs and low total reorder costs; small frequent orders give low total holding costs and high total reorder costs. Adding the three contributing costs gives a total cost curve which is an asymmetric 'U' shape with a distinct minimum. This minimum corresponds to the optimal order size which we will call Qo. To find the value Qo (which is often called the economic order quantity, EOQ) we differentiate the total cost function with respect to Q, and set this equal to zero.

$$0 = -\frac{RC * D}{Qo^2} + \frac{HC}{2}$$

or

$$Qo = \sqrt{\frac{2 * RC * D}{HC}} \qquad \text{Economic Order Quantity}$$

This result can be substituted back into the equations for stock cycle length ($T = Q/D$) and total cost to give the corresponding optimal values:

Optimal Cycle Length $\qquad To = \sqrt{\dfrac{2 * RC}{HC * D}}$

Minimum Total Cost $\qquad TCo = UC * D + \sqrt{2 * RC * HC * D}$

The equation for minimum total cost contains a 'fixed' element, $UC * D$, which does not vary with order quantity and a 'variable' element, VCo, which does:

$$TCo = UC * D + VCo$$
$$VCo = \sqrt{2 * RC * HC * D}$$

WORKED EXAMPLE 3.1

In a small warehouse the demand for an item is constant at 100 units a year. Unit cost is £50, cost of processing an order is £20 and holding cost is estimated at £10 per unit per annum. What is the economic order quantity, corresponding cycle length and costs?

SOLUTION

Listing the values we know:

$D = 100$ units a year
$UC = £50$ a unit
$RC = £20$ an order
$HC = £10$ a unit a year.

Then substitution gives:

$$Qo = \sqrt{\frac{2 * RC * D}{HC}} = \sqrt{\frac{2 * 20 * 100}{10}} = 20 \text{ units}$$

$$To = \sqrt{\frac{2 * RC}{HC * D}} = \sqrt{\frac{2 * 20}{10 * 100}} = 0.2 \text{ years} = 10.4 \text{ weeks}$$

$$VCo = \sqrt{2 * RC * HC * D} = \sqrt{2 * 20 * 10 * 100} = £200 \text{ a year}$$

$$TCo = UC * D + VCo = 40 * 100 + 200 = £5200 \text{ a year}$$

The optimal policy (with total costs of £5200 a year) is to order 20 units every 10.4 (say 10 or 11) weeks.

WORKED EXAMPLE 3.2

A company works 50 weeks a year and has demand for an item which is constant at 100 units a week. The cost of each unit is £20 and the company aims for a return of 20% on capital invested. Annual warehouse costs are estimated to be 5% of the value of goods stored. The purchasing department of the company costs £45,000 a year and sends out an average of 2000 orders. Determine the optimal order quantity for the item, the optimal time between orders and the minimum annual cost of carrying the item.

SOLUTION

Listing the values we know and making sure the units are consistent:

$$D = 100 * 50 = 5000 \text{ units a year}$$

$UC = £20$ a unit

$$RC = \frac{\text{annual cost of purchasing department}}{\text{number of orders raised a year}} = \frac{45,000}{2000}$$

$$= £22.50 \text{ an order}$$

$$HC = (20\% + 5\%) \text{ of unit cost a year} = (0.2 + 0.5) * UC$$

$$= £5 \text{ a unit a year}$$

Then substitution gives:

$$Qo = \sqrt{\frac{2 * RC * D}{HC}} = \sqrt{\frac{2 * 22.5 * 100}{5}} = 212.1 \text{ units}$$

$$To = \sqrt{\frac{2 * RC}{HC * D}} = \sqrt{\frac{2 * 22.5}{5 * 5000}} = 0.042 \text{ years} = 2.1 \text{ weeks}$$

$$VCo = \sqrt{2 * RC * HC * D} = \sqrt{2 * 22.5 * 5 * 5000}$$

$$VCo = £1060.66 \text{ a year}$$

$$TCo = UC * D + VCo = 20 * 5000 + 1060.66 = £101,060.66 \text{ a year}$$

The optimal policy (with variable costs around £1060 a year) is to order 212 units every 2 weeks or so.

In summary
Using the variables:

D = demand per unit time

Q = order quantity

T = stock cycle length

UC = unit cost

RC = reorder cost

HC = holding cost

TC = total cost per unit time

a model of an inventory system was built to give optimal values of:

$$Qo = \sqrt{\frac{2 * RC * D}{HC}}$$

$$To = \sqrt{\frac{2 * RC}{HC * D}}$$

$$VCo = \sqrt{2 * RC * HC * D}$$

$$TCo = UC * D + VCo$$

SELF ASSESSMENT QUESTIONS

3.9 List seven assumptions made in the 'classic analysis'.

3.10 What is the economic order quantity:

(a) only possible order size;
(b) minimum order quantity;
(c) order size which minimizes average stock level;
(d) order size which minimizes inventory costs?

3.11 If small orders are placed frequently (rather than placing large orders infrequently) does this

(a) reduce total costs;
(b) increase total costs;
(c) either increase or decrease total costs;
(d) have no effect on total costs?

3.3.3 Moving away from the economic order quantity

In worked example 3.2 above, the economic order quantity was calculated as 212.1 units. This is clearly an awkward order size and it would be interesting to see what happens to costs if orders are placed for, say, 200 or 250 units. For this we can use the total cost curve shown in Figure 3.8, where for any value of Q the total cost is given by:

$$TC = UC * D + \frac{RC * D}{Q} + \frac{HC * Q}{2}$$

The optimal value of this has been found for Qo, when:

$$TCo = UC * D + \sqrt{2 * RC * HC * D}$$

If we ignore the constant terms, the ratio of actual to optimal variable cost can be found as:

$$\frac{VC}{VCo} = \frac{\dfrac{RC * D}{Q} + \dfrac{HC * Q}{2}}{\sqrt{2 * RC * HC * D}}$$

This can be simplified to:

$$\boxed{\frac{VC}{VCo} = \frac{1}{2} \left\{ \frac{Q}{Qo} + \frac{Qo}{Q} \right\}}$$

As VC must be greater than VCo, this ratio is always greater than one and shows the proportional rise in variable cost as we move away from Qo.

Using an order quantity of 200 instead of 212.1 in worked example 3.2 gives:

$$\frac{VC}{VCo} = \frac{VC}{1060.66} = \frac{1}{2} \left\{ \frac{212.1}{200} + \frac{200}{212.1} \right\}$$

or

$$VC = 1.0017 * 1060.66 = £1062.46$$

A reduction of almost 6% in order size increases the variable cost by only 0.17%. Similarly, an order size of 250 (an increase of almost 18%) increases variable cost by 1.4% to £1075.03 (see Figure 3.9). This illustrates one of the reasons why the classic analysis is so widely used; it is recognized that the calculation is based on a series of assumptions and approximations but the total cost rises slowly with small changes around the optimal. The EOQ gives a good guideline for order size in many circumstances.

Substituting specific values into the equation above shows the movement away from the optimal order quantity which raises the variable cost by a specific amount, say, 10%.

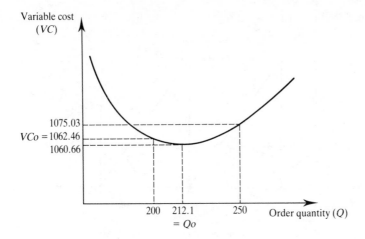

Figure 3.9 Alteration in variable cost moving away from Qo.

$$\frac{VC}{VCo} = \frac{1.1}{1} = \frac{1}{2}\left\{\frac{Q}{Qo} + \frac{Qo}{Q}\right\}$$

Setting Q as a proportion of Qo, so that $Q = f * Qo$ gives:

$$2.2 = \frac{f}{1} + \frac{1}{f}$$

or

$$f^2 - 2.2 * f + 1 = 0$$

Solving this quadratic equation gives either $f = 0.64$ or $f = 1.56$. In other words, Qo can be increased to 156% of the optimal value or reduced to 64% and only raise variable costs by 10%.

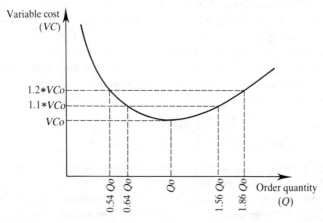

Figure 3.10 Alteration in variable cost moving away from Qo.

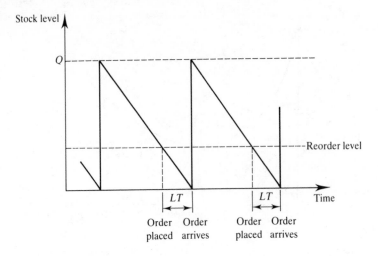

Figure 3.11 Inventory level with fixed lead time (*LT*).

In the example where the economic order quantity was calculated to be 212.1 units, any order quantity between 135.7 and 330.9 would have a variable cost within 10% of optimal. Extending the analysis shows that any order quantity between 114.5 (= 0.54 * *Qo*) and 394.5 (= 1.86 * *Qo*) would have variable costs within 20% of optimal (see Figure 3.10).

3.3.4 Adding a finite lead time

A useful extension to the basic model would add a finite lead time, *LT*, between placing an order and having it arrive in stock. To start with we will assume that *LT* is constant. Then the stock level will follow the same saw-tooth pattern shown in Figure 3.6, with stock rising when a delivery is made and falling slowly back to zero. To ensure a delivery arrives just as stock is running out, the order must be placed a time *LT* earlier. The easiest way of finding this point is to look at the current stock and place an order when there is just enough left to last the lead time. With constant demand of *D*, an order is placed when the stock level is $LT * D$ and this point is called the reorder level (see Figure 3.11).

Reorder Level = Lead Time * Demand

$$ROL = LT * D$$

One way of using such a system in practice is called the 'two-bin system'. In this, stock is kept in two bins, one of which holds an amount equal to the reorder level and the second of which has all remaining stock. Demand is met from the second bin. When this is empty the total stock has declined to the reorder level and it is time to place an order.

WORKED EXAMPLE 3.3

Demand for an item is steady at 100 units a week and the economic order quantity has been calculated at 212.1 units. If the lead time is one week calculate the reorder level.

SOLUTION

The stock level varies as shown in Figure 3.12 (using a previous example again).
Calculating the reorder level as lead time demand gives:

$$ROL = LT * D = 1 * 100 = 100 \text{ units}$$

and we should place an order for 212.1 units every time actual stock declines to 100 units.
If the lead time in this example were two weeks the calculation could be repeated with

$$ROL = LT * D = 2 * 100 = 200 \text{ units.}$$

An order would then be placed every time stock declined to 200 units. Suppose, though, that the lead time is three weeks. As before we would have

$$ROL = LT * D = 3 * 100 = 300 \text{ units.}$$

The problem is that stock fluctuates between 212.1 units and zero and never rises to 300 units. Because the lead time is longer than stock cycle there will always be at least one order outstanding, as shown in Figure 3.13.
The way around this problem is to realize that the calculated reorder level relates to both stock on hand and stock on order (and arriving shortly). Then a new order should be placed when stock on hand plus stock on order equals the lead time demand:

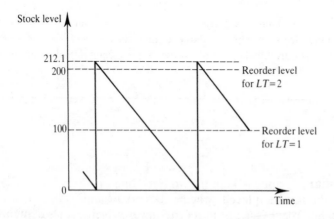

Figure 3.12   Variation of stock level over time.

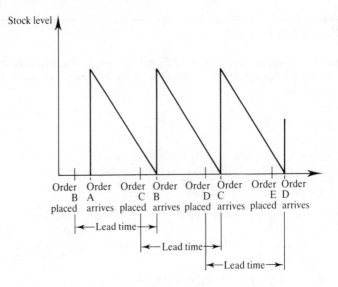

Figure 3.13 Stock levels with lead time greater than cycle length.

$$ROL = \text{stock on hand} + \text{stock on order}$$

In the example, when an order is placed there is still one order for 212.1 units outstanding, so:

ROL = stock on hand + stock on order

300 = stock on hand + 212.1

or

stock on hand = 87.9.

An order for 212.1 units is placed whenever stock on hand falls to 87.9 units.

In practice both demand and lead time can vary and some spare stock, the safety stock, is normally kept as a reserve. Some calculations for safety stocks are discussed in Chapter 9.

In summary

Orders should be placed when stock on hand (plus stock in any outstanding order) falls to the reorder level, which equals demand during lead time.

3.12 If a finite lead time is added to the classic analysis what is the reorder level:

(a) the lead time demand
(b) the optimal order size
(c) the lead time
(d) zero?

3.13 If the lead time is greater than the length of the stock cycle does the reorder level consider:

(a) stock on hand only
(b) stock on hand plus stock on order
(c) stock on order only?

3.4   INVENTORY CONTROL FOR PRODUCTION SYSTEMS

If an item is manufactured at some finite rate, it may be moved into stock at this rate rather than arrive in batches. If, for example, components are made at a rate of 100 a day, the stock of these should rise steadily by 100 a day (assuming none are used). We will now extend the classical analysis by removing the assumption of instantaneous replenishment and allowing units to be moved into stock at a finite rate, P. We will again assume that the stocks have to meet a constant demand of D as shown in Figure 3.14.

If the rate of production is less than the rate of demand (i.e., P is less than D) there is no problem with stock holding. Supply is not keeping up with demand and as soon as a unit is made it is transferred straight out to customers. Inventory problems only arise when the rate of production is higher than the demand (P is greater than D). Then stock builds up at a rate ($P - D$) for as long as production continues. Production must be stopped when a reasonably sized batch of the item has been made. We will say that production stops after some time TP, when facilities are transferred to make other items.

When production is stopped, demand from customers continues at a rate D and is met from the accumulated stock. After some further time, TD, all the stock will be used and production must restart. If we again assume the lead time is zero, production need only restart when stock is exhausted. Alternatively, if there is a fixed lead time, LT, production

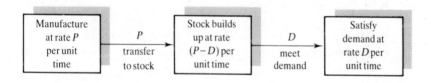

Figure 3.14   A manufacturer producing for stock.

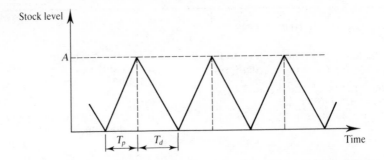

Figure 3.15 Variation in stock level with finite production rate.

must be started when stock falls to the lead time demand $LT * D$. The resulting stock level is shown in Figure 3.15.

We want to find an optimal batch size and consequent optimal values for TP, the production cycle length, and A, the maximum actual stock level. We can use the same approach as for the classic analysis, which involves finding the total cost for a single stock cycle, dividing this by the cycle length to give a cost per unit time and then minimizing this cost.

Consider one cycle of the stock pattern shown in Figure 3.16.

Batches of size Q are made and if replenishment were instantaneous this would be the maximum stock level. As units are actually fed into stock at a finite rate and are continuously being removed to meet demand, the maximum stock level will be lower than Q and will occur at the point where production is stopped. The value for A, the highest actual stock level, can be found in terms of other variables as follows.

Looking at the productive part of the cycle, TP, we have:

$$A = (P - D) * TP$$

We also know that total production during the period is:

$$Q = P * TP \text{ or } TP = Q/P$$

Substituting this value for TP into the equation for A gives:

$$A = Q * \frac{(P - D)}{P}$$

We can now continue the analysis, remembering that in this case RC, the reorder cost, is really a production set-up cost.

Total cost for cycle:

total unit cost: = number of units made(Q) * unit cost(UC)

$$= UC * Q$$

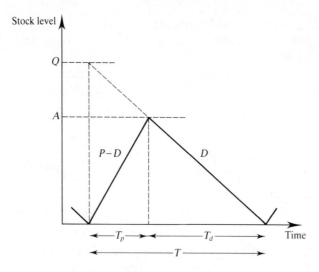

Figure 3.16 One stock cycle with finite production rate.

total set-up cost: = number of production set-ups (1)
$*$ set-up cost(RC)

$= RC$

total holding cost: = average stock level ($A/2$) $*$ time held(T)
$*$ holding cost(HC)

$$= \frac{HC * A * T}{2} = \frac{HC * Q * T}{2} * \frac{(P - D)}{P}$$

Adding these three gives the total cost per cycle as:

$$UC * Q + RC + \frac{HC * Q * T}{2} * \frac{(P - D)}{P}$$

Dividing this by the cycle length, T, gives a total cost per unit time, TC:

$$TC = \frac{UC * Q}{T} + \frac{RC}{T} + \frac{HC * Q}{2} * \frac{(P - D)}{P}$$

Then substitution of $Q = D * T$ gives:

$$TC = UC * D + \frac{RC * D}{Q} + \frac{HC * Q}{2} * \frac{(P - D)}{P}$$

Comparing this with the result for the classic analysis shows the only difference is the factor $(P - D)/P$. The analysis could be continued by plotting this total cost curve against batch size, Q, and finding an asymmetric 'U' shaped curve with a distinct minimum. Differentiating the total cost equation with respect to Q and setting the derivative to equal

91

zero would give the optimal batch quantity, Qo. We will not repeat the arithmetic, but note the results only differ from the classic analysis by the factor $(P - D)/P$.

Finite Production Rate	Classic Analysis
$Qo = \sqrt{\dfrac{2 * RC * D}{HC}} * \sqrt{\dfrac{P}{P - D}}$	$Qo = \sqrt{\dfrac{2 * RC * D}{HC}}$
$To = \sqrt{\dfrac{2 * RC}{HC * D}} * \sqrt{\dfrac{P}{P - D}}$	$To = \sqrt{\dfrac{2 * RC}{HC * D}}$
$VCo = \sqrt{2 * RC * HC * D} * \sqrt{\dfrac{P - D}{P}}$	$VCo = \sqrt{2 * RC * HC * D}$
$TCo = UC * D + VCo$	$TCo = UC * D + VCo$

Again there is a compromise between large, infrequent batches (with consequent high holding costs but low set-up costs) and small frequent batches (with low holding costs but high set-up costs). With a finite production rate the stock level is somewhat lower that it would be with instantaneous replenishment, so we would expect, all other things being equal, to make larger batches. This is confirmed by the results above where batch size increases by $\sqrt{P/(P - D)}$.

WORKED EXAMPLE 3.4

Worked example 3.1 described a small warehouse which has a constant demand for an item of 100 units a year. Unit cost is £50, the cost of processing an order is £20 and holding cost is estimated to be £10 per unit per annum. The economic order quantity for this item was calculated at 20 units with variable costs of £200 a year. Suppose the warehouse could only be supplied at a finite rate of 10 units a week; how would this alter the calculations?

SOLUTION

Listing the values we know:

$$D = 100 \text{ units a year}$$
$$P = 10 * 52 = 520 \text{ units a year}$$
$$UC = £50 \text{ a unit}$$
$$RC = £20 \text{ an order}$$
$$HC = £10 \text{ a unit a year.}$$

Then substitution gives:

$$Qo = \sqrt{\frac{2 * RC * D}{HC}} * \sqrt{\frac{P}{P - D}}$$

$$Qo = \sqrt{\frac{2 * 20 * 100}{10}} * \sqrt{\frac{520}{520 - 100}}$$

$$= 20 * 1.11 = \text{(about)} \ 22 \ \text{units}$$

Some time may be saved by calculating $\sqrt{P/(P - D)}$ separately as this is used in the remaining calculations.

$$\sqrt{P/(P - D)} = \sqrt{520/(520 - 100)} = 1.1.$$

$$To = \sqrt{\frac{2 * RC}{HC * D}} * \sqrt{\frac{P}{P - D}} = \sqrt{\frac{2 * 20}{10 * 100}} * 1.11$$

$$= 0.22 \ \text{years} = 11.44 \ \text{weeks}$$

$$VCo = \sqrt{2 * RC * HC * D} * \sqrt{\frac{P - D}{P}}$$

$$= \sqrt{2 * 20 * 10 * 100} * \left(\frac{1}{1.11}\right)$$

$$= \text{£}180.18 \ \text{a year}$$

$$TCo = UC * D + VCo = 50 * 100 + 180.18$$

$$= \text{£}5180.18 \ \text{a year}$$

The optimal policy, with total costs of £5180 a year, is to make batches of 22 units every 11.44 (say 11 or 12) weeks.

WORKED EXAMPLE 3.5

Demand for an item is 1200 units a month and relevant costs have been estimated as

- production set-up cost of £3.20 an order
- shop order preparation of £2.50 an order
- scheduling of shop order at £5.90 an order
- insurance of 0.5% of unit cost a year
- obsolescence, deterioration and depreciation allowance of 2% of unit cost a year
- capital costs of 20% of unit cost a year
- storage space at £3.50 per unit per annum
- handling costs of £0.60 per unit per annum.

Each unit costs the company £10 and the rate of production is 2500 units a month. Determine the optimal batch quantity and the minimum variable cost a year.

By rescheduling work the company could reduce its effective rate of production to 200 units a month at an additional cost of £12 a month. Would this be worthwhile?

SOLUTION

In this example we must remember the definitions of costs. Every cost must be classified as unit, reorder or holding (with no shortage costs). Then:

$$D = 1200 * 12 = 14,400 \text{ units a year}$$
$$P = 2500 * 12 = 30,000 \text{ units a year}$$
$$UC = £10 \text{ a unit}$$

Collecting together all costs which arise per order gives:

$$RC = 3.2 + 2.5 + 5.9 = £11.60 \text{ per order}$$

Holding costs are of two types, a percentage (0.5%, 2% and 20%) of unit costs and a fixed amount (£3.50 + £0.60) a unit a year.

$$HC = (3.5 + 0.6) + (0.005 + 0.02 + 0.2) * 10$$
$$= £6.35 \text{ a unit a year}$$

Substituting these values gives

$$\sqrt{\frac{P}{P - D}} = \sqrt{\frac{30,000}{30,000 - 14,400}} = 1.387$$

$$Qo = \sqrt{\frac{2 * RC * D}{HC}} * \sqrt{\frac{P}{P - D}}$$

$$= \sqrt{\frac{2 * 11.6 * 14,400}{6.35}} * 1.387$$

$$= 318 \text{ units}$$

$$VCo = \sqrt{2 * RC * HC * D} * \sqrt{\frac{P - D}{P}}$$

$$= \sqrt{2 * 11.6 * 6.35 * 14,400} / 1.387$$

$$= 1456.5/1.387 = £1050 \text{ a year}$$

At first it may seem strange to pay more to reduce the production rate, but the reason is obvious after a moment's thought. If production could be matched exactly to demand, there would be no need to hold stock (assuming both are continuous at constant rates). Stock is only held because of the mismatch in production and demand rates, and the smaller this mismatch can be made the smaller will be stock holding costs. By paying to reduce the production rate we might save money by more closely matching supply and demand. Reducing P to $2000 * 12$ units a year gives:

$$VCo = \sqrt{2 * RC * HC * D} * \sqrt{\frac{P - D}{P}}$$

$$= 1456.51 * \sqrt{\frac{24{,}000 - 14{,}400}{24{,}000}}$$

$$= \text{£}921 \text{ a year}$$

If we add the additional rescheduling cost of £12 a month the total cost becomes $921 + 144 = \text{£}1065$ a year and the rescheduling is obviously not worthwhile.

SELF ASSESSMENT QUESTIONS

3.14   Finite production rates are only important for stock control when:

(a)   production rate is greater than demand
(b)   production rate is less than demand
(c)   production rate equals demand
(d)   never?

3.15   If a batch of size Q is produced at a finite production rate of P units per unit time the highest actual stock level, A, is

(a)   equal to Q
(b)   greater than Q
(c)   less than Q?

3.16   When compared with instantaneous replenishment, does a finite production rate lead to:

(a)   larger batches
(b)   smaller batches
(c)   same size batches
(d)   could be either larger or smaller batches?

3.17   What effect does a finite production rate have on the values Qo, TCo and To calculated using the classic analysis?

3.5   MATERIALS REQUIREMENT PLANNING

3.5.1 The MRP process

We have looked at some quantitative models for stock control and could continue extending these, making them more realistic and removing assumptions, until we have models which are accurate representations of real situations. The detail involved in such analyses can be quite extensive and are described in the specialist texts listed at the end of the chapter. Here we are going to consider the alternative approach of materials requirement planning (MRP).

MRP is designed for manufacturing industries and is based on an accurate assessment of demand for inventory items. It does not rely on a formal model of the inventory system, but works on the principle that demand for parts is determined by planned production. If ten tables are to be made in a month's time, there will be a consequent demand for ten table tops and 40 legs. A way of minimizing inventories would be to have these parts delivered just before they are needed. This is the basis of MRP.

It is essential to have a detailed production plan, known some time in advance, before MRP can be considered. This plan is exploded using a parts list or bill of materials to give detailed requirements for components and raw materials; these are ordered to arrive just before they are needed. The process can best be described using an example.

WORKED EXAMPLE 3.6

A company assembles tables using bought-in parts of a top and four legs. These have lead times of one week and three weeks respectively, and assembly takes a week. The company receives orders for 20 tables to be delivered in week 5 of a production period and 40 tables in week 7, but has current stocks of only two complete tables, 22 tops and 40 legs. When should it order parts?

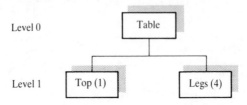

Figure 3.17 Relationship of parts.

SOLUTION

We can represent the simple production process by Figure 3.17, where 'level 0' refers to final products and 'level 1' to the parts.

Starting at the lowest level, we can draw a production plan for tables as shown in Table 3.2. Here 'Gross requirements' shows what the company needs

Table 3.2

Week	1	2	3	4	5	6	7
Tables							
Gross requirements					20		40
Stock on hand	2	2	2	2	0	0	0
Net requirements					18		40
Start assembly				18		40	

Table 3.3

Week	1	2	3	4	5	6	7
Tops							
Gross requirements				18		40	
Stock on hand	22	22	22	4	4	0	0
Net requirements						36	
Place order					36		
Legs							
Gross requirements				72		160	
Stock on hand	40	40	40	0	0	0	0
Net requirements				32		160	
Place order	32		160				

while 'Stock on hand' shows what it currently has; the difference between the two forms 'Net requirements'. Thus, the opening stock of two tables is carried through to week 5 where it is used to meet the first order and still leaves a net requirement of 18. There is an assembly time of one week so production for these 18 must start in week 4. Similarly assembly of 40 units must start in week 6.

Now we can repeat this type of analysis for level 1 items, whose gross requirements are determined by the planned assembly times for level 0 items (see Table 3.3). 18 table tops are required in week 4, 40 in week 6; 72 legs are required in week 4 and 160 in week 6. There may be enough stock on hand to meet gross requirements, but if there is not, subtracting stock on hand gives net requirements. To ensure the parts arrive on time they must be ordered the lead time in advance (that is, one week for tops and three weeks for legs).

This result can be summarized as a weekly schedule with:

> week 1 order 32 legs
>
> week 3 order 160 legs
>
> week 4 assemble 18 tables
>
> week 5 order 36 tops
>
> week 6 assemble 40 tables

The main advantages of MRP are that a clear timetable of activities is produced and stock is matched directly to production needs; parts can be scheduled to arrive just in time for their use and stock levels can be minimized.

WORKED EXAMPLE 3.7

A company which makes a final product, A, receives orders for 50 units for delivery in week 12 of a production cycle, 60 units for week 13 and 40 units for week 16. To make a unit of A needs one unit of component B and two units of components C, with assembly taking two weeks. Components B and C are bought from suppliers with lead times of three and two weeks respectively. Current free stocks are 5, 10 and 20 units respectively for A, B and C and an order for 40 units of C is expected to arrive in week 7. Devise a production and order plan for the company.

SOLUTION

This analysis proceeds exactly as before, starting by defining the relationship of parts.

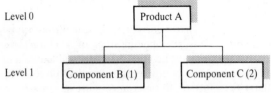

Taking the lowest level first, a production plan for product A can be developed as shown in Table 3.4.

Table 3.4

Week	7	8	9	10	11	12	13	14	15	16
Product A										
Gross requirements						50	60			40
Stock on hand	5	5	5	5	5					
Net requirements						45	60			40
Start production				45	60			40		

Now we can take the next level and expand the production plan for A into demands for components B and C (see Table 3.5). Here an extra line is added for component C to register 'Scheduled receipts', which are added to the stock on hand.

The overall plan would then be:

week 7 order 35 units of B

week 8 order 60 units of B and 30 units of C

week 9 order 120 units of B

week 10 start production of 45 units of A

week 11 start production of 60 units of A

week 12 order 80 units of C

week 14 start production of 40 units of A.

Table 3.5

Week	7	8	9	10	11	12	13	14	15	16
Component B										
Gross requirements				45	60			40		
Stock on hand	10	10	10							
Net requirements				35	60			40		
Place order	35				40					
Component C										
Gross requirements				90	120			80		
Scheduled receipts	40									
Stock on hand	20	60	60							
Net requirements				30	120			80		
Place order	35	120				80				

WORKED EXAMPLE 3.8

A company makes three sizes of filing cabinet with 2, 3 and 4 drawers. Each cabinet consists of a case, drawers and a lock. Each case is made from drawer slides and a formed case (which is itself made from a sheet of steel). Each drawer is made from roller supports, a handle and a formed drawer (which is made from a sheet of steel). Assembly of the four drawer cabinet can be represented as follows, with the figures below the boxes giving lead times in weeks.

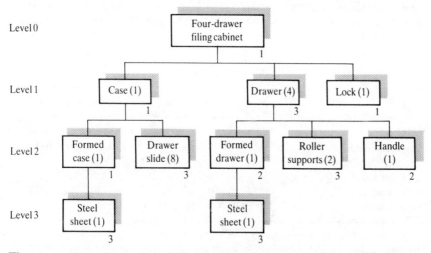

There are currently stocks of 50 complete drawers and 100 roller supports, and a delivery of 300 roller supports is expected in period 1. The master production schedule for the next 12 periods is as follows:

Week	1	2	3	4	5	6	7	8	9	10	11	12
Two-drawer cabinet						100			100		100	50
Three-drawer cabinet						60	120		60			
Four-drawer cabinet					150			150		90		

Devise a plan for ordering and production.

SOLUTION

We are not going to tackle all of this problem, as it is easy to get bogged down in arithmetic and this kind of analysis can really only be done with computers. The full analysis for this example is left as an exercise and we will illustrate only the first part (see Table 3.6).

Table 3.6

Level 0 Week	1	2	3	4	5	6	7	8	9	10	11	12
Two-drawer cabinets												
Gross requirements						100			100		100	50
Scheduled receipts												
Stock on hand												
Net requirements						100			100		100	50
Start assembly					100			100		100	50	

Similar tables can be drawn for three- and four-drawer cabinets before we move on to level 1 items. From the production plan the gross requirement for drawers can be found (150 * 4 in week 4, 100 * 2 + 60 * 3 in week 5 and so on) and Table 3.7 is produced.

Table 3.7

Week	1	2	3	4	5	6	7	8	9	10	11	12
Drawers												
Gross requirements				600	380	360	600	380	360	200	100	
Scheduled receipts												
Stock on hand	50	50	50									
Net requirement				550	380	360	600	380	360	200	100	
Place orders	550	380	360	600	380	360	200	100				

The rest of this analysis would continue in the same way, moving progressively up the levels of items.

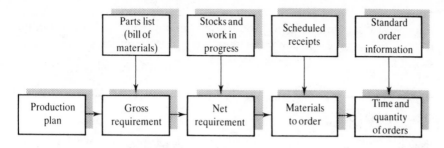

Figure 3.18 The MRP process.

3.5.2 Extensions to MRP

MRP has become increasingly popular in recent years and has been extended in several ways. Allowance can easily be made for variable supply (or other measures of supplier reliability), wastage, defective quality, etc. and the overall MRP process is summarized in Figure 3.18. Another extension to MRP is to cover more aspects of planning than materials delivery. The production plan could, for example, allow a similar analysis to determine machinery and equipment use in each period. This could be extended again by looking at manning implications and so on. Eventually the production plan could be used to plan most of the resources of a factory. This process has become known as Manufacturing Resource Planning, or MRP II.

A variation of MRP, which originated in Toyota factories in Japan, is to aim for 'stockless production'. In this, materials arrive just in time for their use. Most operations work on the basis that stock is expensive, but is needed to allow for short term variations in supply and demand. The basis of Just-in-Time (JIT) systems is that rather than hold stock, the reasons for short term variations should be investigated and eliminated. Then deliveries can be scheduled just in time for their use. Such systems are based on very short lead times, complete reliability of suppliers, total quality control and the belief that problems in production should be recognized and solved rather than simply avoided. These principles are described in detail in some of the suggested reading at the end of the chapter.

In summary
MRP has proved very useful in practice and has the advantages of keeping inventories low, ensuring a valid production schedule is devised and maintained, giving early warning of shortages or problems and assigning priorities to certain areas. There are, however, difficulties such as the need for computers to run the system, the large amount of

processing needed to link production schedules with bills of material and the need for a valid, detailed production plan covering some period in the future. Several extensions to the basic MRP process have been developed.

SELF ASSESSMENT QUESTIONS

3.18 What is meant by MRP?

3.19 What are the advantages of MRP over quantitative models for stock control?

3.20 When developing delivery plans using MRP do you start by considering:

(a) low level items
(b) high level items
(c) any items?

3.5.3 Batching rules for MRP – discrete variable demand

The ordering pattern in worked example 3.8 has orders planned every week, yet in the first part of this chapter we suggested that frequent small orders lead to high costs. It would be useful to look at this kind of demand pattern (which is variable and occurs at discrete times) and develop a model to see if it would be cheaper to batch several of the separate demands together into a single order.

With batching of several orders, stock levels vary over time as shown in Figures 3.19 and 3.20.

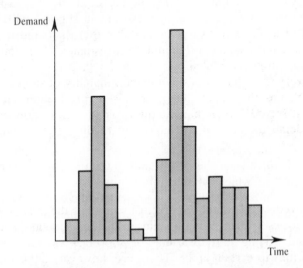

Figure 3.19 Discrete variation of demand over time.

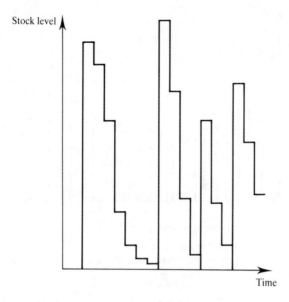

Stock level

Time

Figure 3.20 Discrete variation of stock level over time.

We can approach this problem in the same way as before, and find the total cost for a stock cycle, divide this by the cycle length to give a cost per unit time and then minimize this value. Unfortunately, because the information is discrete, we cannot find a minimum cost by differentiation.

If enough stock is bought to last the next cycle of n periods, we can calculate a cost for the cycle. A small value for n (i.e., small order quantity) would give low holding costs, but high reorder costs; a high value for n would give low reorder costs but high holding costs. By direct analogy with the classic analysis for continuous data, we would sketch the variation of total cost with n as shown in Figure 3.21.

Small values of n give high reorder costs and hence high total costs, while large values of n give high holding costs and hence high total costs. Between these two a compromise optimal value for n can be found which minimizes the total costs.

One way of finding this optimal value is to start with short stock cycles at the lefthand side of the graph and follow the graph down until costs begin to rise, at which point the minimum has been found. This process can be formalized as follows. First calculate the cost of buying for a single period and compare this with the cost of buying for two periods. If it is cheaper to buy for two periods than for one we are obviously going down the lefthand side of the graph in Figure 3.21 and the cost is reducing as the cycle length is increasing. Next compare the cost of buying for two periods with the cost of buying for three periods. If it is

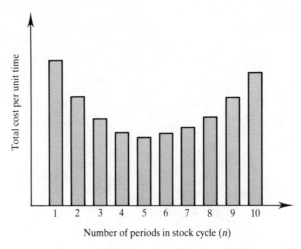

Figure 3.21 Variation in total cost with stock cycle for discrete values.

cheaper to buy for three periods we are still on the declining part of the graph and have not yet reached the point of minimum cost, in which case we would continue and compare the cost of buying for three periods with the cost of buying for four periods. In general, we will always compare the cost of buying for the next n periods with the cost of buying for the next $n + 1$ periods. This process is continued until at some point it becomes cheaper to buy for n periods than for $n + 1$ periods and then we have reached the bottom of the graph and found the point of minimal cost. Any further increases in the cycle length would have increasing total costs as we climb up the righthand side of the graph.

This procedure finds a good (though not necessarily optimal) length for the next stock cycle. Unfortunately, because demand varies over time we cannot calculate a single, fixed value for the optimal cycle length and always use this. The procedure must be repeated for every new cycle. Fortunately, there is a short cut to the arithmetic which removes most of the work and this is described in the following section.

Consider one stock cycle where enough is bought at the beginning to last for n periods. The demand is variable so we can no longer refer to it as D, but must represent the demand in period i by the value $D(i)$. Hence $D(1)$ is the demand in the first period, $D(2)$ the demand in the second period and so on (see Figure 3.22).

For a cycle of n periods the total amount ordered and hence the highest actual stock level, A equals

$$\sum_{i=1}^{n} D(i)$$

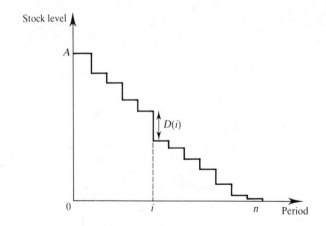

Figure 3.22 Stock level declining over time with discrete demand.

and the average stock level can be approximated by $A/2$. Then total costs for the cycle are:

$$\text{total unit cost} = \text{number ordered}(A) * \text{unit cost}(UC)$$
$$= A * UC$$
$$= UC * \sum_{i=1}^{n} D(i)$$

$$\text{total reorder cost} = \text{number of orders}(1) * \text{reorder cost}(RC)$$
$$= RC$$

$$\text{total holding cost} = \text{average stock level}(A/2) * \text{time held}(n)$$
$$* \text{holding cost}(HC)$$
$$= \frac{HC * n * \sum_{i=1}^{n} D(i)}{2}$$

Adding these three elements gives the total cost for n periods

$$UC * \sum_{i=1}^{n} D(i) + RC + \frac{HC * n * \sum_{i=1}^{n} D(i)}{2}.$$

Dividing this by n gives the average cost per unit time when an order is placed for n periods, $TC(n)$:

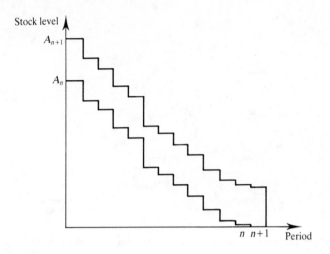

Stock level

A_{n+1}

A_n

n $n+1$ Period

Figure 3.23 Stock level against time period for discrete demand.

$$TC(n) = \frac{UC * D(i)}{n} + \frac{RC}{n} + \frac{HC * \sum\limits_{i=1}^{n} D(i)}{2}$$

The first term represents the fixed cost and the other two the variable cost, so concentrating on the latter gives:

$$VC(n) = \frac{RC}{n} + \frac{HC * \sum\limits_{i=1}^{n} D(i)}{2}$$

Suppose that instead of buying for n periods we buy for $n + 1$ periods, as shown in Figure 3.23.

The cost for this cycle can be found by simply replacing n by $n + 1$ in the above equation:

$$VC(n + 1) = \frac{RC}{n + 1} + \frac{HC * \sum\limits_{i=1}^{n+1} D(i)}{2}$$

We are interested in finding the point at which $VC(n + 1)$ becomes larger than $VC(n)$, so:

$$VC(n + 1) > VC(n)$$

$$\frac{RC}{n + 1} + \frac{HC * \sum\limits_{i=1}^{n+1} D(i)}{2} > \frac{RC}{n} + \frac{HC * \sum\limits_{i=1}^{n} D(i)}{2}$$

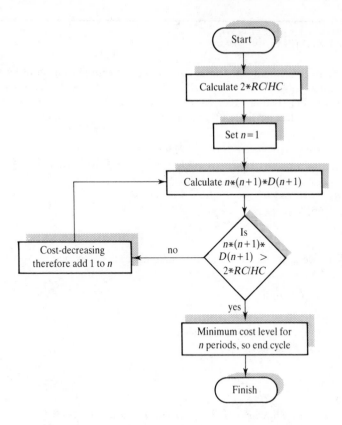

Figure 3.24 Flow diagram for the solution procedure.

With some manipulation this can be simplified to:

$$n * (n + 1) * D(n + 1) > \frac{2 * RC}{HC}$$

This is now the solution procedure: set n equal to 1 and compare the costs of ordering for one or two periods. If it is cheaper to order for two periods than for one (that is, the inequality is invalid) then set n equal to 2 and compare the costs of ordering for two and three periods. n is incremented while the inequality is invalid, but as soon as it becomes valid we have reached the optimal value for n and stop the process. This procedure is illustrated in the flow diagram of Figure 3.24.

WORKED EXAMPLE 3.9

A supplies manager estimates the total cost associated with placing an order to be £45 while annual holding costs are 24% of unit cost. If the forecast monthly demand for an item costing £100 is given below, find an approximately optimal order policy and calculate the cost for this policy.

month	1	2	3	4	5	6	7	8	9	10	11	12
forecast demand	1	3	5	8	8	5	2	1	1	5	7	9

SOLUTION

For simplicity we will take the monthly holding cost to be one-twelfth of the annual cost, then:

UC = £100 a unit

RC = £45 an order

HC = 0.02 * 100 = £2 a unit a month

and the ratio:

$$\frac{2 * RC}{HC} = \frac{2 * 45}{2} = 45$$

Starting with $n = 1$ we have $n + 1 = 2$, $D(n + 1) = 3$ and $n * (n + 1) * D(n + 1)$ = 1 * 2 * 3 = 6. As this is less than 45 the inequality is invalid and we have not reached the minimum.

Next take $n = 2$. Then $n + 1 = 3$, $D(n + 1) = 5$ and $n * (n + 1) *$ $D(n + 1) = 2 * 3 * 5 = 30$. As this is less than 45 the inequality is invalid and we have not reached the minimum.

Next take $n = 3$. Then $n + 1 = 4$, $D(n + 1) = 8$ and $n * (n + 1) *$ $D(n + 1) = 3 * 4 * 8 = 96$. This is greater than 45 so the inequality is valid and we have reached a minimum cost with n equal to three periods. This means that we must buy enough to last for periods 1, 2 and 3 (i.e., 1 + 3 + 5) to arrive by the beginning of period 1.

It is easier to do these calculations in a table, so we can repeat this calculation and continue the analysis in Table 3.8. The only thing to remember is that every time a new cycle is started n returns to 1 and the demand figures are updated accordingly.

Consider the costs for the first cycle:

total unit cost: = number of units(9) * unit cost(100)

= £900

total reorder cost: = number of orders(1) * reorder cost(45)

= £45

Table 3.8

month (i)	1	2	3	4	5	6	7	8	9	10	11	12
demand (D(i))	1	3	5	8	8	5	2	1	1	5	7	9

n	1	2	3	1	2	3	4	5	6	1	2
n * (n + 1) * D(n + 1)	6	30	96	16	30	24	20	30	210	14	54
delivery	9			25						12	

first	second	third
←———→←—	————→←—	————→
cycle	cycle	cycle

total holding cost: = average stock(9/2) * time held(3) * holding cost(2)

= £27

Similarly for the second cycle:

total unit cost: = 25 * 100 = £2500

total reorder cost: = 1 * 45 = £45

total holding cost: = 25/2 * 6 * 2 = £150

Again for the third cycle:

total unit cost: = 12 * 100 = £1200

total reorder cost: = 1 * 45 = £45

total holding cost: = 12/2 * 2 * 2 = £24

Adding these separate costs for the three cycles gives a total of £4936 over 11 months or about £450 a month.

WORKED EXAMPLE 3.10

An item of stock costs £5 a unit and the future demand is known to be:

month	1	2	3	4	5	6	7	8	9	10	11	12	13
demand	100	50	60	60	100	100	80	60	40	70	80	100	140

If the cost of placing an order (including delivery) is £100 and effective interest rates are 2.5% a month, determine a good ordering policy and the corresponding cost.

SOLUTION

We have:

$$UC = \text{£5 a unit}$$
$$RC = \text{£100 an order}$$
$$HC = 0.025 * 5 = \text{£0.125 a unit a month}$$

Then,

$$\frac{2 * RC}{HC} = \frac{2 * 100}{0.125} = 1600$$

Building a table of the calculations:

month (i)	1	2	3	4	5	6	7	8	9	10	11	12
demand ($D(i)$)	100	50	60	60	100	100	80	60	40	70	80	100

n	1	2	3	4	1	2	3	4	5	1	2	3
$n * (n + 1) * D(n + 1)$	100	360	720	2000	200	480	720	800	2100	160	600	1680
delivery		270				380					250	

The costs can be calculated as shown in Table 3.9.

Table 3.9

	Total unit cost	*Total reorder cost*	*Total holding cost*	*Total cost*
Cycle 1	270 * 5	100	270/2 * 4 * 0.125	1517.5
Cycle 2	380 * 5	100	380/2 * 5 * 0.125	2118.75
Cycle 3	250 * 5	100	250/2 * 3 * 0.125	1396.88

Adding the costs gives a total of £5033.13 over 12 periods or about £420 a month.

In summary

A model for discrete, variable demand such as met in MRP systems, leads to the batching rule 'order for n periods when $n * (n + 1) * D(n + 1) > 2 * RC/HC$'.

SELF ASSESSMENT QUESTIONS

3.21 What is a batching rule?

3.22 At a certain point in an MRP system it is found that $n * (n + 1) * D(n + 1) > 2 * RC/HC$. Does this mean

(a) nothing
(b) an optimal solution has been found
(c) an approximately optimal solution has been found
(d) an approximately optimal solution has not yet been found?

3.23 Why does the batching rule developed only give an 'approximately optimal' policy?

3.6 COMMENTS ON REAL STOCK CONTROL PROBLEMS

In this chapter we have looked at several approaches to stock control. These only cover a small set of problems and we have emphasized that assumptions have been made in each model. Real problems can differ from those described in a number of ways.

- Some of the assumptions will not hold in a particular situation: demand may not be constant or known in advance, costs may be estimates reached by agreement rather than by calculation and so on.

- The demand will probably be a forecast which contains errors.

- More items should be considered. We have only considered a single item, but several items coming from the same supplier (and other interactions) will affect decisions.

- When limited resources are available for stock control, most emphasis should be put on expensive items and less attention given to cheaper ones. A useful ABC analysis is described in Chapter 9.

- Lead time may vary and need an additional allowance for safety stock.

- The implementation of inventory control systems is important. Information should be updated properly and results used sensibly.

- It is difficult to measure the performance of an inventory system. Is a high service level a good measure, or should a number of shortages be allowed to balance competing costs? Is it cheaper not to hold some items in stock or are the intangible costs associated with lost customers too high? Such questions are a matter for company policy rather than calculation.

EOQ results for stock

EOQ input data:

Demand per year (D) = 2500

Order or setup cost per order (Co) = 45

Holding cost per unit per year (Ch) = 20

Shortage cost per unit per year (Cs) = 250

Shortage cost per unit, independent of time (π) = 150

Replenishment or production rate per year (P) = 5000

Lead time for a new order in year (LT) = 0.1

Unit cost (C) = 50

EOQ output:

EOQ	= 150.000
Maximum inventory =	75.000
Maximum backorder =	0.000
Order interval =	0.060 year
Reorder point	= 100.000
Ordering cost	= 750.000
Holding cost	= 750.000
Shortage cost =	0.000
Subtotal of inventory cost per year =	1500.000
Material cost per year	= 125000.000
Total cost per year	= 126500.000

Figure 3.25 Sample output from an inventory control package.

Perhaps the main difference with real systems is the use of computers, as almost all stock holdings of any size are computerized. The quality of software is highly variable, but a good system will allow close control of information and goods. Inventory control systems can be large and complex, but are based around models like those described in this chapter. A flavour for the calculations in such systems is given in Figure 3.25, which shows the output from a package when forecasts of demand and other data are input.

MRP systems have a large number of simple calculations which make computer use essential. Specialized packages are generally used for these, but spreadsheets can demonstrate the basic calculations.

CONCLUSIONS

This chapter has described some quantitative approaches to inventory control. The reasons for holding stocks and associated costs were discussed. This showed the need to minimize costs by using scientific inventory control. Two distinct approaches were suggested, quantitative models and materials requirement planning.

A model was developed for the classic economic order quantity and this was extended to cover finite lead time and production rate. Although such models are simplifications, their application can produce considerable benefits. More complex and accurate models could be used, but the results from simple models can give guidelines which are certainly useful. Where the existing inventory control system gives the appearance of working well, quantitative analyses may pinpoint weaknesses, or they might simply confirm that everything is being handled efficiently.

MRP systems are fairly new developments which link stock holdings of parts to a production plan. Although there may be difficulties in implementing such systems, they have potential for minimizing inventory costs. There are several extensions of the MRP idea, including Just-in-Time systems.

PROBLEMS

3.1   The unit cost of an item is £24; reorder cost is £80 and holding cost is £8 a unit a year. Demand for the item is 1800 a year and lead time is three weeks. What would be an optimal inventory policy for the item?

3.2   A wholesaler buys microwave cookers for £250 each and sells about 80 a week at £300 each. Each order sent to the manufacturers costs an average of £45 for administration, £445 for transport, £30 for testing and £20 for miscellaneous costs. Annual holding costs are £40 a cooker for warehouse space plus 15% for use of capital.

The wholesaler currently buys 1000 cookers at a time. What is the total cost of holding a stock of microwaves? How much does this add to the price of each cooker?

What is the optimal policy for the inventory of cookers? What savings would this policy give?

What size of order would give variable costs within 15% of optimal?

3.3   Annual demand for an item is 2000 units, each order costs £10 to place and the annual holding cost is 40% of the unit cost. The unit cost depends on the quantity ordered as follows:

- for quantities less than 500 unit cost is £1;
- for quantities between 500 and 1000 unit cost is £0.80;
- for quantities of 1000 or more unit cost is £0.60;

What is the optimal ordering policy for the item?

3.4   In a small warehouse the demand for an item is constant at 100 units a year. The unit cost is £50, the cost of processing an order is £20 and the annual holding cost is estimated to be £10 a unit. If the warehouse could be supplied at a finite rate of 10 units a week what would be the best inventory policy for the item?

3.5   A manufacturer estimates that it will need 1800 computer chips of a particular type over a 200-day working year. If there are any shortages production will be disrupted with very high costs. The holding cost for the chips is £2 a unit a year and the cost of placing an order is estimated to be £40 an order. Determine:

- the economic order quantity;
- the optimal number of orders a year;
- the total annual cost of operating the system (including the cost of purchases) if the real interest rate is 20% a year.

What would be the effect on this inventory system if the supplier of chips could only supply them at a finite rate of 40 a day?

3.6   A company assembles trolleys, each consisting of a body and four wheels. They must have six of these finished in the sixth week of a production cycle, and a further ten finished in the eighth week. Assembly takes one week.

The bodies are bought from an outside supplier with an average lead time of two weeks. At the beginning of the production cycle there are four bodies already in stock.

Wheels are made in another part of the company with a lead time of two weeks. At the beginning of the production cycle there are ten wheels in stock, but company policy is to keep at least 8 wheels in stock.

Each wheel consists of two rims and a tyre which are bought from suppliers with lead times of one and two weeks respectively. There are opening stocks of six tyres but no rims, and the rim supplier will only deliver in batches of 100 units.

Use MRP to devise a timetable for placing orders and starting production.

3.7   A factory assembles desks, each consisting of a top, two drawers and four legs. Each drawer is made from two 'wood kits' and one 'metal kit'. At the start of a 13-week production cycle it is decided to have 20 desks ready for weeks 5 and 13, and 40 desks ready for weeks 7 and 10. Opening stocks and lead times for purchased items are:

	Opening stock	Lead time
Tops	40	3 weeks
Legs	0	2 weeks
Metal Kit	70	4 weeks

Opening stock and assembly time for items made in the factory are:

	Opening stock	Assembly time
Desks	25	1 week
Drawers	10	1 week
Wood kits	80	2 weeks

The supplier of metal kits only delivers batches of 200 units and it is company policy to keep 20 finished desks and 20 tops in stock at all times.

Use MRP to find a schedule of events for this production cycle.

3.8 The reorder cost for an item (costing £20 a unit) is £20, while the holding cost is £1 a unit a week. If the demand for the item is as follows, when should orders be placed?

Week	1	2	3	4	5	6	7	8	9	10	11	12
Demand	2	4	2	3	3	5	6	6	5	3	2	3

What is the average weekly cost of this policy?

CASE STUDY – THE MIDLAND PILL SUPPLY COMPANY

In the United Kingdom, pharmaceuticals are supplied to around 12,000 retail pharmacies, hospitals, dispensing doctors and a few other outlets. Historically, deliveries were made directly by manufacturers, but during the 1960s the range of pharmaceuticals and related goods grew rapidly and a wholesale industry developed to allow fluctuating demands to be met speedily from efficient centralized stock holdings.

There was a period of stability in this wholesale sector up to the mid 1970s when several hundred depots operated around the country. Then in 1978 retail price maintenance was removed from pharmaceuticals and this strengthened the competition which was developing as a result of:

- smaller retail pharmacies closing and being replaced by fewer, larger ones;
- the growth of national wholesalers;

- wholesalers offering price discounts;
- the government tightening its control on prices (as the National Health Service was by far the largest customer);
- a limited list of acceptable drugs for National Health Service prescription was introduced in 1985;
- some parallel imports of cheaper (usually lower quality) drugs;
- computerized systems to assist operations.

Overall the market was becoming increasingly competitive and a small number of national wholesalers began to dominate the wholesale pharmaceutical market.

The Midland Pill Supply Company (MPS) is a medium sized private company which is run efficiently and, by offering a good service to customers in a relatively small area, is competing successfully with the national wholesalers. The three main activities of MPS can be described as:

- order taking and processing
- stock holding and control
- delivery to customers.

To ensure its survival the company has to make continuous improvements to efficiency and keep a firm control on all costs.

A short while ago the management of MPS were concerned that the costs of deliveries to customers were beginning to account for an increasing proportion of their turnover. The distribution system had been reviewed occasionally as the company grew, but it was essentially designed for a much smaller operation. As there was little expertise in transport planning within the company, MPS hired a management consultant to advise them on transport operations, vehicle schedules, and general materials management. This consultant did some work which was well received by the company and saved them a substantial amount in transport running costs. In his final report the consultant also suggested that the company might look at its stock holding policies as this seemed an area where additional savings could be made.

The company started to look at its inventory control system. This had been introduced five years earlier, when MPS bought a new computer, and it appeared to be functioning quite effectively. When the system was examined in detail it was soon noticed that stock levels had been drifting upwards for the past three years. The purchasing department explained that the company was successful because it had a reputation for reliability and service. In particular, an order could be phoned in at any time during the working day and delivery would normally be guaranteed within three hours. Unfortunately there had been occasions when they had run out of stock and had let down customers (their own lead time from manufacturers averaged about a week). To make sure this happened as infrequently as possible the purchasing department had adopted a policy of keeping three weeks demand in reserve to cover for late deliveries from manufacturers or sudden, unexpectedly high demands from customers.

The stock in MPS was computer controlled, with the purchasing department setting parameters. They had decided the most important factor was the average demand for an item over the past three weeks. This value, F, was used as a forecast of future demand and a stock of three weeks' demand was held in reserve. Lead time averaged a week so the reorder level was set at $4 * F * FACTOR1$, where $FACTOR1$ was a variable between 1 and 2 which was a subjective view of the reliability of the supplier.

Order quantities were calculated on the basis of the workload which could be handled within the purchasing department. The equivalent of four full-time people worked in the department and they could each process a maximum of forty orders a day. In 200 working days the purchasing department could process 32,000 orders and as there were 3500 items kept in stock this meant that on average an item could have 9.1 orders a year. An element of safety was added to this and each order was made large enough to last for seven weeks, including a subjective allowance for the 'importance' of the item. The same inventory policy was used for all items.

The computer recorded all stock transactions for the past 13 weeks and although it was not set-up to produce summarized reports, raw data was readily available. Management looked at a small sample of this, but they did not have time to make much progress. Table 3.10 shows some data collected for seven items.

When the company accountant was asked for information on the inventory he was reluctant to give advice and explained that there was little hard information available. The unit cost varied from a few pence to several hundred pounds, and no attempt had been made to cost the stock holding or purchasing functions. Wages were paid at slightly over union agreed rates for the industry. Turnover of MPS was £750,000 a week and the company expects to make a net profit of 2.5% (slightly above the average of similar companies).

The management of MPS are keen to make progress in this area as their initial examination has, they feel, confirmed the consultant's belief that savings can be made.

Suggested questions on the case study

- Why might the introduction of a wholesale sector in the 1960s be more effective than having manufacturers supply directly to 'retailers'?

Table 3.10

Week	Item number 132/75	741/33	884/65	884/92	331/21	175/88	303/18
1	252	27	145	1235	567	121	987
2	260	32	208	1098	664	87	777
3	189	23	177	987	548	223	743
4	221	22	195	1154	602	304	680
5	232	27	211	1559	530	76	634
6	195	30	179	1209	650	377	655
7	217	31	205	993	612	156	598
8	225	23	187	1313	608	198	603
9	186	28	156	1405	596	94	621
10	265	23	182	1009	637	355	564
11	245	25	171	985	555	187	559
12	212	28	169	1237	589	209	519
13	224	31	210	1119	601	304	485
ROL	1057	162	1121	6101	2517	893	4415
Q	1509	245	1443	7926	4517	1945	6432
UC	10.02	8.73	13.67	1.25	2.49	6.55	14.20

- What are the main difficulties faced by MPS when competing with large national companies?
- Why might a consultant looking at transport operations become interested in stock control?
- Why did MPS not know that its stock control system was not functioning effectively?
- Describe in detail the existing stock control system at MPS.
- What were the main faults with the existing system?
- What information can be found from the sample of product data?
- Describe an improved stock control system that MPS could use.
- What information would be needed before this new system could be implemented?

SOLUTIONS TO SELF ASSESSMENT QUESTIONS

3.1 (c) to allow for fluctuations in supply and demand. Although some stocks may increase in value more than inflation, this is not the main reason for holding them. Similarly profits may (or may not) be maximized by holding stock.

3.2 There are many possible classifications, but a useful one is:

- raw materials
- work in progress
- finished goods
- spare parts
- consumables.

3.3 Materials requirement planning is best suited to manufacturing companies, demand is calculated by exploding a production schedule and order size is determined by some batching rule rather than calculation of an optimal order quantity. (Do not worry if you stumble over this question, as the differences will become more apparent when we look at each approach in more detail.)

3.4 Inventory control might try to do any of the objectives stated as they are all beneficial. In the analyses described cost minimization is emphasized.

3.5 **(d)** cannot say without further information. We could be tempted by the periodic review system as this is preferable for high regular demand of low value items, but there is really not enough information to form a valid opinion. Nuts and bolts can often be controlled very well using a two-bin system.

3.6 Unit cost (*UC*), reorder cost (*RC*), holding cost (*HC*) and shortage cost (*SC*).

3.7 **(d)** a cost per unit per unit time (for example £5 per unit per year).

3.8 **(c)** partly true. Certainly some costs might be very difficult to find, particularly shortage costs, but others might be quite easy; the unit cost might simply be the price paid for an item last time it was bought. Reorder costs and holding costs can usually be estimated with reasonable accuracy.

3.9 A single item is considered, demand is known exactly, demand is continuous and constant, costs are known exactly, replenishment is instantaneous, no shortages are allowed, lead time is zero.

3.10 **(d)** order size which minimizes inventory costs.

3.11 **(c)** either increases or decreases costs. Costs are minimized by placing orders of the size determined by the economic order quantity. This might lead to small frequent orders (when holding costs are high) or large infrequent orders (when reorder costs are high).

3.12 **(a)** the lead time demand. An order should be placed when there is just enough stock to last the lead time. If the lead time is less than the stock cycle the reorder level (of stock on hand) equals the lead time demand.

3.13 **(b)** orders are placed when the lead time demand equals the stock on hand plus any stock on order.

3.14 **(a)** production rate is greater than demand. If production rate is less than demand there is no stock at all and demand is not being met.

3.15 **(c)** less than Q. Customer demand removes stock during production cycles so that the maximum stock level, A, is always less than Q.

3.16 **(a)** larger batches (all other things being equal).

3.17 Values are multiplied (Qo and To) or divided (TCo) by the factor $\sqrt{P/(P - D)}$.

3.18 MRP is a process where production plans are exploded to show detailed parts requirements. These are scheduled to arrive just before they are needed.

3.19 Supplies are closely matched to demands, stocks are kept low, a valid production plan must be devised and maintained, early warning is given of shortages or other problems, priority areas are identified.

3.20 **(a)** low level items. The planning is started with level 0 items and moves progressively up through other levels of items.

3.21 A batching rule gives guidance for the optimal size of batches, or the number of periods of demand which should be joined together to give orders of reasonable size.

3.22 (c) an approximately optimal solution has been found (corresponding to an order to cover n periods' demand).

3.23 The policy described is approximately optimal because of the assumptions made during the formulation and analysis, notably:

- costs are approximations;
- forecast demands involve some error;
- demand figures are discrete (i.e. they are considered to occur at one point in a time period);
- average stock levels in a cycle are approximated;
- an n period cycle may be cheaper than an $n + 1$ period cycle but more expensive than an $n + 2$ period one.

REFERENCES FOR FURTHER READING

1. Central Statistics Office (1988). *National Income and Expenditure* London: HMSO
2. Harris F. (1915). *Operations and Cost* Chicago: A. Shaw
3. Raymond F. E. (1931). *Quantity and Economy in Manufacture* Chicago: McGraw-Hill
4. Central Statistics Office (1986). *United Kingdom National Accounts* London: HMSO
5. Wilson R. H. (1934). A scientific routine for stock control *Harvard Business Review* XIII

Further Reading

There are many books on stock control and the following list gives a flavour for some of these.

Buffa E. S. and Miller J. G. (1979). *Production-Inventory Systems: planning and control* 3rd edn. Homewood: Irwin

Hadley G. and Whitin T. M. (1963). *Analysis of Inventory Systems* New Jersey: Prentice-Hall

Hall R. W. (1983). *Zero Inventories* Harewood: Dow Jones Irwin

Lewis C. D. (1970). *Scientific Inventory Control* London: Butterworths

Lewis C. D. (1975). *Demand Analysis and Inventory Control* Saxon-House

Orlicky J. (1975). *Materials Requirement Planning* New York: McGraw-Hill

Tersine R. J. (1982). *Principles of Inventory Management* 2nd edn. New York: North-Holland

Silver E. A. and Peterson R. (1985). *Decision Systems for Inventory Management and Production Planning* 2nd edn New York: John Wiley

Wight O. W. (1983). *MRP II* Williston: Oliver Wight

Chapter 4

Forecasting

SYNOPSIS

There is a widespread need, or at least desire, to predict what will happen in the future. We constantly make predictions about a whole range of things; whether it will rain, how much money we will spend over a bank holiday, which horse will win a race, whether we should invest in certain shares, when a bout of flu will clear up, and so on. All decisions become effective at some point in the future, so they should be based on forecasts of circumstances prevailing at the time. Managers should make decisions which are not based on present circumstances, but on circumstances as they will be when the decisions become effective. In this sense, forecasting is of fundamental importance.

Despite its importance, progress in many aspects of forecasting has been limited. It is still difficult to get a reliable weather forecast; the winner of a horse race still eludes us; the price of gold still appears to fluctuate randomly; excess bread goes stale in the bread bin. There are, however, many situations in which good forecasts can be found. If forecasts are unreliable it could be because the problems faced are complicated and not well understood, or because insufficient analysis has been done. If we guess the future price of gold we should not be surprised if the guess is wrong; if a company guesses the future sales of a product it should not be surprised at making a mistake. Fortunately the consequences of most wrong guesses are small. Only when these consequences get more serious do we begin to worry about the reliability of forecasts and look for some procedure to take the guesswork out of predictions. This chapter describes some of these methods.

The chapter starts by looking at the role of forecasting within an organization and classifying forecasting methods according to judgemental, projective and causal. Some judgemental methods are then outlined.

Projective forecasting is covered next, with simple averages, moving averages, exponential smoothing and models for seasonality and trend. The quality of these forecasts is measured by mean error, mean absolute deviation and mean squared error.

Finally, causal forecasts are considered, based on regression models. Linear regression is described with its performance measured by the coefficients of determination and correlation.

OBJECTIVES

After reading this chapter and doing the numerical exercises you should be able to:

- appreciate the need for forecasting;
- discuss how forecasts are used within an organization;
- describe the characteristics of judgemental forecasting;
- discuss a variety of judgemental forecasting methods;
- define 'time series' and appreciate their importance;
- calculate forecast errors using mean error, mean absolute deviation and mean squared error;
- describe the characteristics of projective forecasting;
- forecast using actual averages, moving averages and exponential smoothing;
- vary the sensitivity of projective forecasts by using appropriate parameters;
- make forecasts for time series with seasonality and trend;
- describe the characteristics of causal forecasts;
- find lines of best fit using linear regression;
- calculate coefficients of determination and correlation and appreciate their importance.

4.1   FORECASTING WITHIN AN ORGANIZATION

The need to forecast arises in many different circumstances. Information is needed to make reasoned decisions, but these decisions become effective at some point in the future. They must, then, be based on circumstances not as they are at present, but as they will be when the decision becomes effective. Information required for a decision must, almost inevitably, be forecast.

The list of things which could be forecast is endless: demand for products, interest rates, productivity, output, resources, manpower, time to complete a building, production rates, and so on. It follows that forecasting is found throughout an organization and should not be done by an isolated group of specialists. The integration of forecasting within an organization is illustrated in Figure 4.1.

It would be convenient to say that 'Much work has been done on forecasting and the best method is . . .'. Unfortunately this is not possible. Because of the diversity of things to be forecast and the different situations in which forecasts are needed, there is no single best

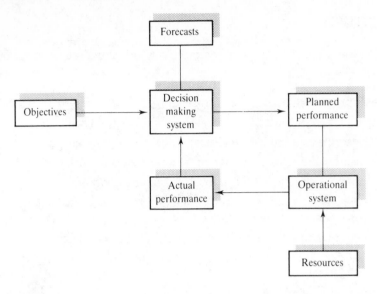

Figure 4.1   Forecasting within the context of decision making.

method. Some guidelines can be given and the intention here is to describe a variety of methods and indicate the circumstances in which each might be used.

One classification of forecasting methods concerns the time in the future which is forecast. In particular:

- short term forecasts might cover the next four months (the continuing demand for a product, for example);
- medium term forecasts might look ahead between four months and two years (say, the time needed to replace an old product by a new one);
- long term forecasts might look ahead several years (the time needed to build a new factory).

The time horizon affects the choice of forecasting method because of the availability and relevance of historic data, the time available to do the forecasting, the cost involved and the effort considered worthwhile.

Another classification of forecasting methods is shown in Figure 4.2.

The first distinction is between qualitative and quantitative approaches. Qualitative methods are used in a variety of circumstances and these are generally referred to as Judgemental methods. They rely on subjective assessments and opinions.

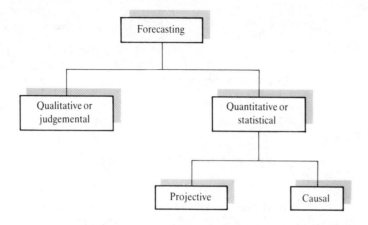

Figure 4.2 Classification of forecasting methods.

If things to be forecast can be quantified there are two separate approaches:

- projective methods examine past patterns and extend these into the future. If sales of an item for the past four weeks have been 250, 300, 350 and 400, it would be reasonable to suggest that sales for the following week would be around 450.
- causal methods analyse the effects of outside influences and use these to produce forecasts. Productivity of a factory might depend on the bonus rates paid to employees and it would be more reliable to set an appropriate bonus rate than to project the last few months' productivity.

This classification of methods does not mean that each must be used in isolation. Managers must look at all available information and then make the decision they feel most appropriate. This implies that forecasts will inevitably have some subjective review before they are adopted.

The rest of this chapter describes different types of forecasting (see Figure 4.3).

4.2 JUDGEMENTAL FORECASTING

Judgemental forecasting methods are subjective assessments, often based on the opinions of experts. These are sometimes called qualitative or subjective methods.

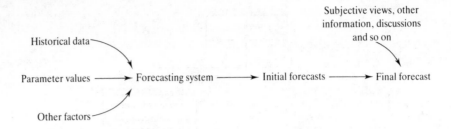

Figure 4.3 Stages in forecasting.

If there is no historic data on which to base a forecast, we may look to experts in the field to supply the best information. When a company is about to market an entirely new product, or a medical team is considering a new organ transplant or a board of directors is considering plans for 15 years in the future, there is no appropriate historic data and judgements have to be made. One common problem of this type is to assess the effects of new technologies. Such 'technological forecasting' might, for example, assess the demand for oil in 25 years' time, bearing in mind the possible developments of electric cars, nuclear power and river barrages to generate electricity.

Here we will outline five specific methods of judgemental forecasting:

- personal insight
- panel consensus
- market surveys
- historic analogy
- Delphi method.

4.2.1 Personal insight

A single person who is familiar with the situation produces a forecast based on their own judgement. This is the most widely used forecasting method, and is the one which managers should try to avoid. It relies entirely on one person's judgement (opinions, prejudices and ignorance). It can give good forecasts, but often gives very bad ones and there are countless examples of experts being totally wrong. Perhaps the major weakness of the method is its unreliability. This may not matter for minor decisions, but when the consequences of errors are large some more reliable method should be used.

One clear finding from comparisons of forecasting methods is that someone familiar with a forecasting situation, using experience and subjective evaluation to find a forecast, will consistently produce worse forecasts than someone who knows nothing about the situation but uses a more formal method.

4.2.2 Panel consensus

A single expert can easily make a mistake, but collecting together several experts and allowing them to talk freely to each other should lead to a consensus which is more reliable. If there is no secrecy and the panel are encouraged to talk openly, a genuine consensus may be found. Conversely, there may be difficulties in combining the views of different experts when a consensus can not be found.

Although it is more reliable than one person's insight, panel consensus still has the major weakness that all experts can make mistakes. There are also problems of group working, where 'He who shouts loudest gets his way', everyone tries to please the boss, some people do not speak well in groups, and so on. Overall, panel consensus is an improvement on personal insight, but results from either method should be viewed with caution.

4.2.3 Market surveys

Large amounts of information may be needed for a decision and if this is not already available a market survey might be a convenient method of collecting it. A typical application is to assess demand for a new product before full production starts. There would be no data on which to base projective or causal forecasts, so judgemental methods must be used. In essence, this replaces the small panel of experts by a large number of randomly selected people.

This approach can give useful information but relies on:

- a survey sample which is representative
- useful, unbiased questions
- reliable analysis of the replies
- valid conclusions drawn from the analysis.

Many surveys have proved useless because of failures in one or more of these. Another problem with surveys is the cost and time needed to organize them.

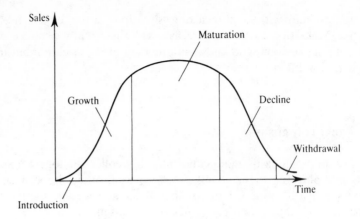

Figure 4.4 Stages in the life cycle of a product.

4.2.4 Historic analogy

Demands for many products follow a similar pattern through their lifetime. In particular, sales can be expected to go through periods of

- introduction
- growth
- maturation
- decline
- withdrawal

as illustrated in Figure 4.4.

Suppose a product was launched some time ago and sales are now going through a period of growth. It would be nonsensical to project this growth into the long term future, as demand is likely to settle down to some more stable level. This effect was noticed in sales of home computers, which started steadily in the late 1970s and then had a tremendous growth in the early 1980s. Some companies assumed this growth would continue and increased production accordingly. When demand began to stabilize in the mid 1980s these manufacturers were unable to sell their products.

Historical analogy requires demand to be monitored and compared with similar products which were introduced earlier. This can give a good idea of the demand at various points in the life-cycle, but there are often difficulties in finding similar products or fitting the characteristic life-cycle curve.

4.2.5 Delphi method

This is the most formal of the judgemental methods and has a well defined procedure. A number of experts are contacted by post and each is given a questionnaire to complete. The replies from these questionnaires are analysed and summaries are passed back to the experts. Each is then asked to reconsider their original reply in the light of the summarized replies from others. Each reply is anonymous so that undue influences of status and the pressures of face-to-face discussions are avoided. This process of modifying responses in the light of replies made by the rest of the group is repeated several times (often between three and six). By this time, the range of opinions should have narrowed enough to help with decisions.

The following example illustrates the Delphi approach. One of the most rapidly changing areas of technology is associated with extracting oil from off-shore fields. A company may be interested in knowing when under water inspections on platforms will be done by robots rather than divers. A number of experts would be contacted to start the Delphi forecast. These people would come from various backgrounds, including divers, technical staff from oil companies, ships captains, maintenance engineers and robot designers. The overall problem would then be explained and each of the experts would be asked when they thought robots would replace divers. The initial returns would probably give a wide range of dates from, say, 1993 to 2050 and these would be summarized and passed back. Each person would then be asked if they would like to reassess their answer in the light of other replies. After repeating this several times, views might converge so that 80% of replies suggested a date between 2005 and 2015, and this would be enough to help planning.

4.2.6 Comparison of judgemental forecasts

A comparison of these approaches is given in Table 4.1.

Table 4.1

| Method | Accuracy in term | | | Cost |
	Short	Medium	Long	
Personal insight	poor	poor	poor	low
Panel consensus	poor to fair	poor to fair	poor	low
Market survey	very good	good	fair	high
Historical analogy	poor	fair to good	fair to good	medium
Delphi method	fair to very good	fair to very good	fair to very good	medium to high

In summary

Forecasting is an important part of a manager's function and should be integrated into the decision making within an organization. Forecasts may be classified according to judgemental, projective or causal. Judgemental forecasts rely on subjective views, as demonstrated by personal insight, panel consensus, market surveys, historic analogy and the Delphi method. Each of these is useful in different circumstances.

SELF ASSESSMENT QUESTIONS

4.1 Why is forecasting important to an organization?

4.2 'Forecasting is best done by a group of experts working in isolation.' Is this statement:

(a) true
(b) false
(c) partly true?

4.3 List three fundamentally different approaches to forecasting.

4.4 What factors should be considered in choosing a forecasting method?

4.5 What are 'Judgemental Forecasts'?

4.6 List five types of judgemental forecast.

4.3   TIME SERIES AND MEASURES OF FORECAST ERROR

We will now move on to quantitative forecasts, but need to cover some related material first. Probably the most common use of quantitative forecasting is for 'time series', which are series of observations taken at regular intervals of time. Thus, monthly unemployment figures, daily rainfall, weekly demand, and annual population statistics are examples of time series.

One good way of showing the behaviour of a time series is to draw a graph. This allows underlying patterns to be seen more clearly. Three common patterns in time series are:

- constant series (where values take roughly the same value over time, such as annual rainfall);
- series with a trend (which either rise or fall steadily, such as the GNP per capita);
- seasonal series (which have a cyclical component such as the weekly sales of soft drinks).

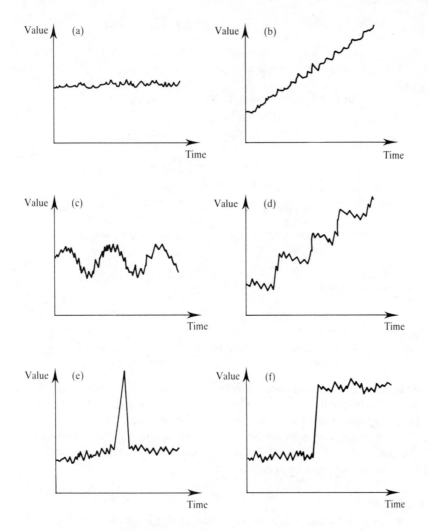

Figure 4.5 Common patterns in time series: (a) constant series; (b) series with trend; (c) series with seasonality; (d) series with seasonality and trend; (e) constant series with impulse; (f) series with step.

A number of other underlying patterns are seen, some of which are illustrated in Figure 4.5.

There are almost always differences between the actual observations and the underlying pattern. A random 'noise' is superimposed on the underlying pattern so that a constant series, for example, does not always take exactly the same value, but is somewhere close. Thus

100   105   94   95   108   103   100   93   101   98

would be a constant series with superimposed noise.

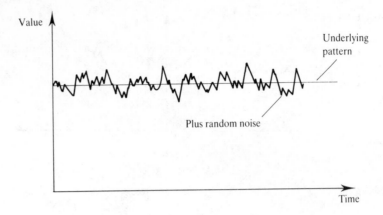

Figure 4.6 Addition of random noise to a time series.

> Actual value = underlying pattern + random noise

This random noise makes accurate forecasting very difficult. If the noise is relatively small it can be easy to get good forecasts, but if the noise is large this becomes more difficult. See Figure 4.6.

The random noise in time series means that forecasts almost always contain errors, but we really need some way of measuring these. This measure could then be used to:

- minimize the errors;
- give a measure for the accuracy of the forecast;
- show how confident we should be in the forecast;
- monitor forecasts to see if they are going seriously wrong;
- compare different forecasting methods.

A number of different measures have been developed and three of these are described below.

For the rest of this chapter the thing being forecast is called 'demand'. This is simply a convenient name and is not meant to imply that forecasts are only used for sales. We will also use the convention:

t = time
$D(t)$ = demand at time t
$F(t)$ = forecast *for* time t (*not* the forecast made *at* time t)

4.3.1 Mean error

Suppose a forecast, $F(t)$, is made for the demand at some time t, and the actual demand turns out to be $D(t)$. There is an error of:

$$E(t) = D(t) - F(t)$$

If this is repeated for a number of periods, n, an obvious measure of forecast error would be the mean error per period.

$$\text{Mean error} = 1/n * \sum_{t=1}^{n} E(t) = 1/n * \sum_{t=1}^{n} [D(t) - F(t)]$$

The drawback with this measure is that positive and negative errors cancel each other, and very poor forecasts can have zero error. If the mean error has a positive value it implies that the forecast is consistently too low, and if the mean error has a negative value the forecast is consistently too high. The mean error is a measure of bias rather than accuracy.

WORKED EXAMPLE 4.1

Forecasts have been calculated for the following two time series. What are the mean errors of each?

Series 1	t	1	2	3	4	5
	$D(t)$	18	23	28	23	25
	$F(t)$	20	22	26	24	27

Series 2	t	1	2	3	4	5	6	7
	$D(t)$	20	20	20	20	20	20	20
	$F(t)$	1	4	9	16	25	36	49

SOLUTION

Calculating the errors for each period from $E(t) = D(t) - F(t)$ gives:

Series 1	t	1	2	3	4	5
	$D(t)$	18	23	28	23	25
	$F(t)$	20	22	26	24	27
	$E(t)$	-2	1	2	-1	-2

The mean error is $(-2 + 1 + 2 - 1 - 2)/5 = -0.4$ and on average each forecast is 0.4 too high.

Series 2	t	1	2	3	4	5	6	7
	$D(t)$	20	20	20	20	20	20	20
	$F(t)$	1	4	9	16	25	36	49
	$E(t)$	19	16	11	4	-5	-16	-29

Here the forecasts are obviously poor, but the mean error is zero.

Mean error = $(19 + 16 + 11 + 4 - 5 - 16 - 29)/7 = 0$

This reinforces the observation that mean error is primarily a measure of bias and not forecast accuracy.

4.3.2 Mean absolute deviation and mean squared error

The mean error allows positive and negative errors to cancel each other, but there are two ways around this:

(a) take absolute values of the errors and calculate the mean absolute deviation:

$$\text{Mean absolute deviation} = 1/n * \sum_{t=1}^{n} \text{ABS}[D(t) - F(t)]$$

$$= 1/n * \sum_{t=1}^{n} \text{ABS}[E(t)]$$

(b) square the errors and calculate the mean squared error:

$$\text{Mean squared error} = 1/n * \sum_{t=1}^{n} [D(t) - F(t)]^2$$

$$= 1/n * \sum_{t=1}^{n} [E(t)]^2$$

The mean absolute deviation has an obvious meaning; when it takes a value of, say, 2.5 the forecast is on average 2.5 away from actual demand. The mean squared error has a less clear meaning, but is useful for some statistical analyses. The larger the value of either measure, the worse is the forecast.

WORKED EXAMPLE 4.2

Calculate the mean absolute deviation and mean squared error for the time series used in worked example 4.1.

SOLUTION

Series 1	t	1	2	3	4	5
	$D(t)$	18	23	28	23	25
	$F(t)$	20	22	26	24	27
	$E(t)$	−2	1	2	−1	−2
	ABS[$E(t)$]	2	1	2	1	2
	$[E(t)]^2$	4	1	4	1	4

Mean absolute deviation = $(2 + 1 + 2 + 1 + 2)/5 = 1.6$

Each forecast is, on average, 1.6 away from actual demand.

Mean squared error = $(4 + 1 + 4 + 1 + 4)/5 = 2.8$

Series 2	t	1	2	3	4	5	6	7
	$D(t)$	20	20	20	20	20	20	20
	$F(t)$	1	4	9	16	25	36	49
	$E(t)$	−19	−16	−11	−4	5	16	29
	ABS[$E(t)$]	19	16	11	4	5	16	29
	$[E(t)]^2$	361	256	121	16	25	256	841

Mean absolute deviation = $100/7 = 14.3$

Mean squared error = $1876/7 = 268$

The mean error for this series is zero. These two other measures are high and suggest that the forecasts are inaccurate.

In summary

Many forecasts are concerned with time series, which are observations taken at regular intervals. There are several common patterns in time series, with actual observations having a random noise element super-imposed on the underlying pattern. The noise means that forecasts will contain errors. There are several ways of measuring these errors, including mean error, mean absolute deviation and mean squared error.

4.7   Why do forecasts always contain errors?

4.9   Define two other measures of error.

4.8   What is the mean error of a forecast and why is it of limited value?

4.4   PROJECTIVE FORECASTING

Projective forecasting examines historic data and projects the patterns found into the future. This is sometimes called intrinsic forecasting as it ignores any external influences and only looks at past values of demand to suggest future values. There are several ways of projecting time series, the most important of which are described below.

4.4.1 Simple averages

Suppose we are going away on holiday and want to know the daily hours of sunshine to expect. The easiest way of finding this would be to look up records for previous years and take an average. With a holiday due to start on 1 July we could find the average hours of sunshine on 1 July over, say, the past ten years.

This forecasting uses simple averages with:

$$F(t+1) = 1/n * \sum_{t=1}^{n} D(t)$$

where:

n = number of periods of historic data

t = time period

$D(t)$ = demand at time t

$F(t)$ = forecast for time t

The forecast hours of sunshine on 1 July might be 7.6, but random noise will give an actual value which is somewhere around this. We could have used more data to give a forecast (say the past 50 years) but the value is likely to be fairly stable and this should make little difference.

WORKED EXAMPLE 4.3

Forecast demand for period six of the following time series and comment on the accuracy of each forecast.

Period	t	1	2	3	4	5
Series 1	$D(t)$	98	100	98	104	100
Series 2	$D(t)$	140	66	152	58	84

SOLUTION

Series 1 $F(6) = 1/n * \sum_{t=1}^{n} D(t) = 1/5 * \sum_{t=1}^{5} D(t) = 100$

Series 2 $F(6) = 1/5 * \sum_{t=1}^{5} D(t) = 100$

Although the forecasts are the same, there is clearly more noise in the second series than the first. Consequently we would be more confident in the first forecast and expect the error to be less.

Using actual averages to forecast demand is easy and can work well for constant demands. Unfortunately, if there is a change in the demand pattern, older data tends to swamp the latest figures and the forecast is very unresponsive to the change. Suppose weekly demand for an item has been constant at 100 units for the past two years. Using actual averages would give a forecast demand for week 105 of 100 units. If the actual demand suddenly rises to 200 in week 105, using actual averages would give a forecast of:

$$F(106) = (104 * 100 + 200)/105 = 100.95$$

A rise in demand of 100 leads to an increase of 0.95 in the forecast. If demand continued at 200 units a week subsequent forecasts are:

$$F(107) = 101.89 \qquad F(108) = 102.80 \qquad F(109) = 103.70$$

and so on. The forecasts are rising but the response is very slow.

In summary

Using actual averages can give reasonable results if the demand is constant. For any other pattern some alternative method should be used.

4.4.2 Moving averages

Hardly any time series is stable over long periods and the restriction that actual averages can only be used for constant series makes this approach of limited value. It can only be used in the short term for stable series. The problem is that old data, which may be out of date, tends to swamp newer, more relevant data. One way around this is to ignore old data and only use a number of the most recent values. Demand might be forecast using, say, the average weekly demand over the past twelve weeks. Any data older than this is ignored.

This is the basis of moving averages, where instead of taking the average of all historic data, only the latest N periods of data are used, and as new data becomes available the oldest data is ignored. Moving average forecasts are found from:

$$F(t + 1) = \text{average of } N \text{ most recent pieces of data}$$
$$= [\text{latest data} + \text{next latest} + \ldots N\text{th latest}]/N$$
$$= [D(t) + D(t - 1) + \ldots D(t - N + 1)]/N$$

WORKED EXAMPLE 4.4

The demand for an item over the past six months is as follows:

t	1	2	3	4	5	6
$D(t)$	425	500	475	525	525	450

The market for this item is unstable, and any data over three months old is no longer valid. Use a moving average to forecast demand for the item.

SOLUTION

Only data more recent than three months is valid, so we can use a three month moving average for the forecast. If we consider the situation at the end of period 3, the forecast for period 4 is:

$$F(4) = [D(1) + D(2) + D(3)]/3 = (425 + 500 + 475)/3 = 466.7$$

At the end of period 4, when actual demand is known to be 525, this forecast can be updated to give:

$$F(5) = [D(2) + D(3) + D(4)]/3 = (500 + 475 + 525)/3 = 500.0$$

Then

$$F(6) = [D(3) + D(4) + D(5)]/3 = (475 + 525 + 525)/3 = 508.3$$

and

$$F(7) = [D(4) + D(5) + D(6)]/3 = (525 + 525 + 450)/3 = 500.0$$

The error at each stage could be calculated to see how the forecast is performing. It is clearly responding to changes, with a high demand moving the forecast upwards and vice versa. At the same time the forecast is smoothing out fluctuations. The responsiveness of the forecast can be adjusted by using an appropriate value of N. Using a large N takes the average of a large number of observations and will be unresponsive: the forecast will smooth out random variations, but may not follow genuine changes. Conversely, a small N will give a responsive forecast which will follow genuine changes in demand, but it may be too sensitive to random fluctuations. A compromise value of N is needed to give reasonable results and a moving average of about six periods is often useful.

WORKED EXAMPLE 4.5

The following table shows monthly demand for a product over a two year period. Use moving averages with $N = 3$, $N = 6$ and $N = 9$ to produce one period ahead forecasts.

Month	1	2	3	4	5	6	7	8	9	10	11	12
Demand	26	25	27	24	26	25	28	24	25	26	37	38

Month	13	14	15	16	17	18	19	20	21	22	23	24
Demand	37	36	25	22	23	24	25	26	25	27	26	24

SOLUTION

The earliest forecast which can be made using a three-period moving average (i.e. $N = 3$) is $F(4) = [D(1) + D(2) + D(3)]/3$. Similarly the earliest forecast for a six and nine period moving average are $F(7)$ and $F(10)$ respectively. The forecasts are shown in Table 4.2.

Plotting these forecasts shows the differences, with the three-month moving average being the most responsive to change and the nine month moving average being least responsive (see Figure 4.7).

One particularly useful property of moving averages is seen when they are used to forecast demands which have strong seasonal variations. If N is chosen to equal the number of periods in a season, a moving average will effectively deseasonalize the data. This is illustrated in the following example.

Table 4.2

| Month | Demand | Forecasts | | |
		$N = 3$	$N = 6$	$N = 9$
1	26	–	–	–
2	25	–	–	–
3	27	–	–	–
4	24	26	–	–
5	26	25.3	–	–
6	25	25.7	–	–
7	28	25	25.5	–
8	24	26.3	25.8	–
9	25	25.7	25.7	–
10	26	25.7	25.3	25.6
11	37	25	25.7	25.6
12	38	29.3	27.5	26.9
13	37	33.7	29.7	28.1
14	36	37.3	31.2	29.6
15	25	37	33.2	30.7
16	22	32.7	33.2	30.7
17	23	27.7	32.5	30
18	24	23.3	30.2	29.9
19	25	23	27.8	29.8
20	26	24	25.8	29.7
21	25	25	24.2	28.4
22	27	25.3	24.2	27
23	26	26	25	25.9
24	24	26	25.5	24.8
25		25.7	25.5	24.7

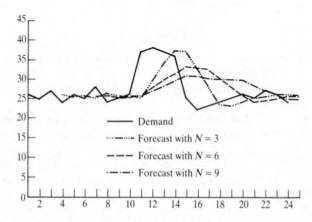

Figure 4.7 Comparison of moving average forecasts with varying N.

WORKED EXAMPLE 4.6

Use a moving average with two, four and six periods to calculate the one period ahead forecasts for the following data.

t	1	2	3	4	5	6	7	8
$D(t)$	200	100	40	300	220	110	50	280

t	9	10	11	12	13	14	15	16
$D(t)$	190	90	60	290	200	110	60	300

SOLUTION

Calculating the moving averages gives the results shown in Table 4.3.

Table 4.3

Period	Demand	Forecast		
		$N = 2$	$N = 4$	$N = 6$
1	200	–	–	–
2	100	–	–	–
3	40	150	–	–
4	300	70	–	–
5	220	170	160	–
6	110	260	165	–
7	50	165	168	162
8	280	80	170	137
9	190	165	165	167
10	90	235	158	192
11	60	140	153	157
12	290	75	155	130
13	200	175	158	160
14	110	245	160	185
15	60	155	165	157
16	300	85	165	135
17	–	180	168	170

These results can be seen most clearly in a graph (see Figure 4.8).

The moving average with both $N = 2$ and $N = 6$ has responded to the peaks and troughs of the demand, but neither has got the timing right: both forecasts lag behind demand. The two-period moving average is much more responsive than the six-period one, but the interesting result is the four-period moving average which has almost completely deseasonalized the data.

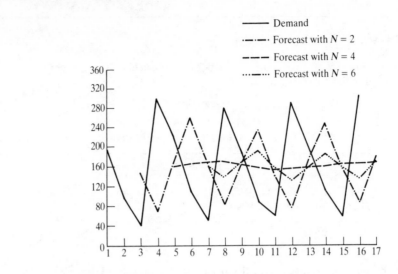

Figure 4.8 Selecting the value of *N* to deseasonalize data.

In summary

Moving averages give forecasts based on the latest data and ignoring any older values. Their sensitivity can be changed by altering the value of *N*. Time series can be deseasonalized by setting *N* to the number of periods in the season.

4.4.3 Exponential smoothing

Exponential smoothing is currently the most widely used forecasting method. It is based on the idea that as data gets older it becomes less relevant and should be given less weight. This is also the basis of moving averages, where each value is given a weight of $1/N$ until it is $N + 1$ periods old, when the weight switches to zero. A more sensible approach, achieved by exponential smoothing, is to give a steadily declining weight, as shown in Figure 4.9.

This can be achieved using only the latest demand figure and the previous forecast. Suppose we calculate a new forecast by taking a proportion, α, of the latest demand and adding a proportion, $1 - \alpha$, of the previous forecast.

New Forecast = α * latest demand + $(1 - \alpha)$ * last forecast

or

$$F(t + 1) = \alpha * D(t) + (1 - \alpha) * F(t)$$

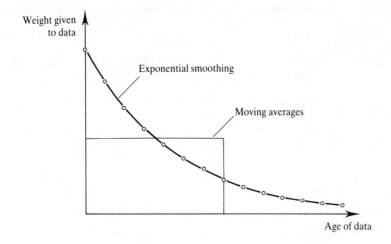

Figure 4.9 Decreasing weight given to older data with exponential smoothing.

This is the equation for exponential smoothing, where α is the smoothing constant and generally takes a value between 0.1 and 0.2.

To illustrate the way exponential smoothing adapts to changes in demand, we can look at a forecast which was optimistic and suggested a value of 1100 for a demand which actually turns out to be 1000. Taking a value of $\alpha = 0.2$, the forecast for the next period is:

$$F(t + 1) = \alpha * D(t) + (1 - \alpha) * F(t)$$
$$= 0.2 * 1000 + (1 - 0.2) * 1100$$
$$= 1080$$

The optimistic forecast is noted and the value for the next period is adjusted downwards. The reason for this adjustment is clear if we rearrange the exponential smoothing formula.

$$F(t + 1) = \alpha * D(t) + (1 - \alpha) * F(t)$$
$$= F(t) + \alpha * [D(t) - F(t)]$$

but

$$E(t) = D(t) - F(t)$$

Therefore

$$F(t + 1) = F(t) + \alpha * E(t)$$

The error in each forecast is noted and a proportion is added to adjust the next forecast. The larger the error in the last forecast the greater is the adjustment to the next forecast.

WORKED EXAMPLE 4.7

Use exponential smoothing with $\alpha = 0.3$ and an initial value of $F(1) = 84$ to produce one period ahead forecasts for the following time series.

Month	1	2	3	4	5	6	7	8	9	10	11	12
Demand	89	90	78	75	81	79	77	66	72	69	63	73

SOLUTION

We know the $F(1) = 84$ and $\alpha = 0.3$. Therefore substitution gives:

$$F(2) = \alpha * D(1) + (1 - \alpha) * F(1) = 0.3 * 89 + 0.7 * 84 \quad = 85.5$$
$$F(3) = \alpha * D(2) + (1 - \alpha) * F(2) = 0.3 * 90 + 0.7 * 85.5 = 86.9$$
$$F(4) = \alpha * D(3) + (1 - \alpha) * F(3) = 0.3 * 78 + 0.7 * 86.9 = 84.2$$

and so on, as shown in the following table.

t	1	2	3	4	5	6	7	8	9	10	11	12
$D(t)$	89	90	78	75	81	79	77	66	72	69	63	73
$F(t)$	84	85.5	86.9	84.2	81.4	81.3	80.6	79.6	75.5	74.4	72.8	69.9

Although we have described its operations, it may not be obvious that exponential smoothing actually does give less weight to data as it gets older. We can demonstrate this by taking an arbitrary value for α, say 0.2. Then:

$$F(t + 1) = 0.2 * D(t) + 0.8 * F(t)$$

But substitution of $t - 1$ for t gives:

$$F(t) \quad = 0.2 * D(t - 1) + 0.8 * F(t - 1)$$

and using this in the equation above gives:

$$F(t + 1) = 0.2 * D(t) + 0.8 * [0.2 * D(t - 1) + 0.8 * F(t - 1)]$$
$$= 0.2 * D(t) + 0.16 * D(t - 1) + 0.64 * F(t - 1)$$

But $F(t - 1) = 0.2 * D(t - 2) + 0.8 * F(t - 2)$

so $F(t + 1) = 0.2 * D(t) + 0.16 * D(t - 1) + 0.64 * [0.2 * D(t - 2)$
$$+ 0.8 * F(t - 2)]$$

$$= 0.2 * D(t) + 0.16 * D(t - 1) + 0.128 * D(t - 2)$$
$$+ 0.512 * F(t - 2)$$

The weight put on older data is getting progressively less, and the above calculation could be continued to give the figures shown in Table 4.4.

Table 4.4

Age of data	Weight
0	0.2
1	0.16
2	0.128
3	0.1024
4	0.08192
5	0.065536
6	0.0524288
and so on	and so on

In this calculation we took an arbitrary value of $\alpha = 0.2$. Repeating the calculations with other values of α would lead to similar results, but the value given to α is important in setting the sensitivity of the forecasts. Changing the value gives a different balance between the last forecast and the latest demand. To give responsive forecasts a high value of α is used (say 0.3 to 0.35): to give less responsive forecasts a lower value is used (say 0.1 to 0.15).

WORKED EXAMPLE 4.8

The following time series has a clear step upwards in demand in month 3. Using an initial forecast of 500 compare exponential smoothing forecasts with varying values of α.

Period	1	2	3	4	5	6	7	8	9	10	11
Value	480	500	1500	1450	1550	1500	1480	1520	1500	1490	1500

SOLUTION

Taking values of $\alpha = 0.1, 0.2, 0.3$ and 0.4 gives the results shown in Table 4.5.

All these forecasts would eventually follow the sharp step and raise forecasts to around 1500. Higher values of α make this adjustment more quickly and give a more responsive forecast (see Figure 4.10).

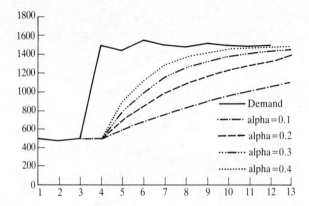

Figure 4.10 Forecast sensitivity with changing value of alpha.

Table 4.5

Period	Value	Forecast			
		$\alpha = 0.1$	$\alpha = 0.2$	$\alpha = 0.3$	$\alpha = 0.4$
1	480	500.00	500.00	500.00	500.00
2	500	498.00	496.00	494.00	492.00
3	1,500	498.20	496.80	495.80	495.20
4	1,450	598.38	697.44	797.06	897.12
5	1,550	683.54	847.95	992.94	1,118.27
6	1,500	770.19	988.36	1,160.06	1,290.96
7	1,480	843.17	1,090.69	1,262.04	1,374.58
8	1,520	906.85	1,168.55	1,327.43	1,416.75
9	1,500	968.17	1,238.84	1,385.20	1,458.05
10	1,490	1,021.35	1,291.07	1,419.64	1,474.83
11	1,500	1,068.22	1,330.86	1,440.75	1,480.90

WORKED EXAMPLE 4.9

Use a smoothing constant of 0.2 and an initial forecast of 15 to calculate the one period ahead forecast for the following time series. Find the error in the forecast for each period. What conclusions can you draw from these results?

Period	1	2	3	4	5	6	7	8	9	10	11	12	13	14	15	16
Value	16	13	18	14	20	16	14	18	22	30	41	48	59	67	75	80

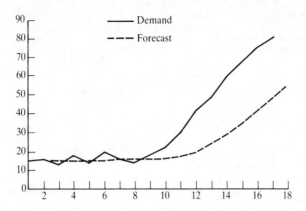

Figure 4.11 Response of exponential smoothing to a trend.

Table 4.6

Period	Demand	Forecast	Forecast error
1	16	15.00	1.00
2	13	15.20	−2.20
3	18	14.76	3.24
4	14	15.41	−1.41
5	20	15.13	4.87
6	16	16.10	−0.10
7	14	16.08	−2.08
8	18	15.66	2.34
9	22	16.13	5.87
10	30	17.31	12.69
11	41	19.84	21.16
12	48	24.08	23.92
13	59	28.86	30.14
14	67	34.89	32.11
15	75	41.31	33.69
16	80	48.05	31.95
17	–	54.44	–

SOLUTION

Substitution gives the results in Table 4.6.

The forecast appears to work well for the first half of the data, but the errors increase in the second half. A graph of the results shows a clear trend in the second half and the conclusion is that exponential smoothing performs well for relatively stable time series, but does not perform well if there is a steady trend (see Figure 4.11).

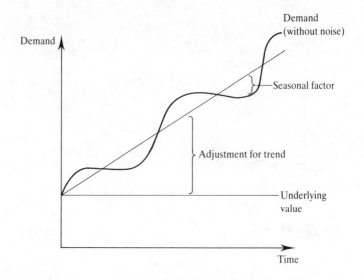

Figure 4.12 Components making-up a demand pattern with seasonality and trend.

In summary

Exponential smoothing steadily reduces the weight given to data as its age increases. The latest demand is balanced against the previous forecast, with the sensitivity of the forecast adjusted by the value given to the smoothing constant, α. Changes are needed to cope with trends and other underlying patterns.

4.4.4 Models for seasonality and trend

The methods described so far are reasonably good for constant time series, but need some adjustment if there are other patterns. In this section we will develop a model which can be used for data with both seasonality and trend. Here the actual demand figures are made up of a number of components:

- an underlying value, which is the basic value of the series;
- adjustment for trend, which is an addition (or subtraction) to allow for steady increases (or decreases);
- seasonal index, which allows for regular cyclical variation;
- noise, which is the random factor which cannot be forecast.

These are illustrated in Figure 4.12.

Table 4.7

(1)	deseasonalize values and then use exponential smoothing to give the smoothed underlying value
(2)	use exponential smoothing on the trend to give a smoothed adjustment for trend
(3)	use exponential smoothing on the seasonal index to give the smoothed index for the period
(4)	add the basic value to the trend adjustment and multiply by the seasonal index to give the forecast.

$$F(t + 1) = \begin{bmatrix} \text{smoothed} & \text{smoothed} \\ \text{underlying} + \text{adjustment} \\ \text{value} & \text{for trend} \end{bmatrix} * \begin{matrix} \text{smoothed} \\ \text{seasonal} \\ \text{index} \end{matrix}$$

Then: $D(t) = (\text{underlying} + \text{adjustment}) * \text{seasonal} + \text{noise}$
value   for trend   index

The approach to this problem is shown in Table 4.7.

Thus $F(t + 1) = [U(t) + T(t)] * I(n)$

where $U(t)$ = smoothed underlying value for period t

$T(t)$ = smoothed trend for period t

$I(n)$ = smoothed seasonal index for period t, which is the nth period of a cycle

This may seem a little complex, but is quite straightforward as illustrated by the following example. Suppose we have eight periods of data which show a season of two periods. The first half of the data has been used to get initial values of

- seasonal index for first period in cycle = 1.2
- seasonal index for second period in cycle = 0.8
- initial underlying value = 100
- initial trend = 10.

The rest of the data is:

Period	5	6	7
Period in cycle	1	2	1
Values	130	96	160

Experience has suggested a value of $\alpha = 0.15$ be used.

To start the forecast, we know that:

$$F(t + 1) = [\text{underlying} + \text{adjustment}] * \text{seasonal}$$
$$\text{value} \qquad \text{for trend} \qquad \text{index}$$

so substituting the initial values of $U(4) = 100$, $T(4) = 10$ and $I(1) = 1.2$, gives:

$$F(5) = [U(4) + T(4)] * I(1)$$
$$= (100 + 10) * 1.2$$
$$= 132$$

The forecast for period 6 can now be found by updating values using the procedure described above.

Step 1

Deseasonalize the latest demand and use exponential smoothing to find the smoothed underlying value. The deseasonalized element of the last demand is $U(4) = 100$. The latest demand is $D(5) = 130$ and the seasonal index for the first period of the cycle is $I(1) = 1.2$, so the latest deseasonalized demand is $130/1.2 = 108.3$. Exponential smoothing is used to give the smoothed underlying value.

$$U(5) = \alpha * [D(5)/I(1)] + (1 - \alpha) * [U(4) + T(4)]$$
$$= 0.15 * 108.3 + 0.85 * 110$$
$$= 109.75$$

In general this calculation is:

$$U(t) = \alpha * [D(t)/I(n)] + (1 - \alpha) * [U(t - 1) + T(t - 1)]$$

Step 2

Use exponential smoothing on the trend to give a smoothed adjustment for trend. The latest value for trend is the difference between the last two values for the deseasonalized, underlying value. These are $U(5) = 109.75$ and $U(4) = 100$, so the latest trend figure is $109.75 - 100 = 9.75$. The last value for trend was 10, so a smoothed value is found using exponential smoothing:

$$T(5) = \alpha * [U(5) - U(4)] + (1 - \alpha) * T(4)$$
$$= 0.15 * 9.75 + 0.85 * 10$$
$$= 9.96$$

In general this calculation is:

$$T(t) = \alpha * [U(t) - U(t - 1)] + (1 - \alpha) * T(t - 1)$$

Step 3

Use exponential smoothing on the seasonal index to find the smoothed index for the period. The latest figure for the deseasonalized, underlying value is $U(5) = 109.75$. The latest actual demand for period 5 is 130. Hence the latest seasonal index for the first period in the cycle is $130/109.75 = 1.18$. The last value was 1.2, so a smoothed seasonal index is calculated using exponential smoothing:

$$I(1) = \alpha * [D(5)/U(5)] + (1 - \alpha) * \text{last value for } I(1)$$
$$= 0.15 * [130/109.75] + 0.85 * 1.2$$
$$= 1.20$$

In general this calculation gives:

$$I(n) = \alpha * [D(t)/U(t)] + (1 - \alpha) * I'(n)$$

where $I'(n)$ is the previous value of the seasonal index.

Step 4

Add the basic value to the trend adjustment and multiply by the seasonal index to give the forecast. All the elements for the next forecast have now been found, so we can do the substitution. We have just updated a value for $I(1)$, but the next forecast is for period six which is the second period in the cycle so the latest value for $I(2)$ is used.

$$F(t + 1) = [\text{underlying} + \text{adjustment}] * \text{seasonal}$$
$$\qquad\qquad \text{value} \qquad \text{for trend} \qquad \text{index}$$
$$= [U(t) + T(t)] * I(n)$$
$$F(6) = [U(5) + T(5)] * I(2)$$
$$= [109.75 + 9.96] * 0.8$$
$$= 95.77$$

This procedure can be repeated to give the next forecast.

Step 1

Latest figure for deseasonalized, underlying value:

$$U(t) = \alpha * [D(t)/I(n)] + (1 - \alpha) * [U(t - 1) + T(t - 1)]$$
$$U(6) = \alpha * [D(6)/I(2)] + (1 - \alpha) * [U(5) + T(5)]$$
$$= 0.15 * [96/0.8] + 0.85 * [109.75 + 9.96]$$
$$= 119.75$$

Step 2

Latest figure for trend:

$$T(t) = \alpha * [U(t) - U(t - 1)] + (1 - \alpha) * T(t - 1)$$
$$T(6) = \alpha * [U(6) - U(5)] + (1 - \alpha) * T(5)$$

$$= 0.15[119.75 - 109.75] + 0.85 * 9.96$$
$$= 9.97$$

Step 3
Latest figure for seasonal index for the second period of the cycle:

$$I(n) = \alpha * [D(t)/U(t)] + (1 - \alpha) * I'(n)$$
$$I(2) = \alpha * [D(6)/U(6)] + (1 - \alpha) * I'(2)$$
$$= 0.15 * [96/119.75] + 0.85 * 0.8$$
$$= 0.80$$

Step 4
Next forecast:

$$F(t + 1) = [U(t) + T(t)] * I(n)$$
$$F(7) = [U(6) + T(6)] * I(1)$$
$$= [119.75 + 9.97] * 1.20$$
$$= 155.66$$

This could be continuously updated for as long as latest demand figures are available.

Two problems with this approach are the need to initialize variables and the selection of smoothing constants. As the exponential smoothing process reacts to errors, the initial values are not so important, provided the process is allowed to run itself in. If there are a number of periods of historic data the first half of these might be used to get rough estimates for initial values while the remaining half is used to run in the system and get reliable, current, starting values. The values for α could

```
H20:                                                                 READY

          A        B        C        D        E        F        G        H
 1                 PROJECTIVE FORECASTING WITH SEASONALITY AND TREND
 2
 3     ALPHA  =        0.15
 4     SEASON =        2.00 PERIODS
 5
 6     ================================================================
 7     Period   t          4.00     5.00     6.00     7.00     8.00     9.00
 8     Demand   D(t)               130.00    96.00   160.00   110.00
 9     ----------------------------------------------------------------
10     Basic    U(t)      100.00   109.75   119.75   130.30   139.93   127.43
11     Trend    T(t)       10.00     9.96     9.97    10.06     9.99     6.62
12     Season   I(t)                1.20     0.80     1.20     0.80     1.20
13     ----------------------------------------------------------------
14     Forecast F(t)                         95.77   155.37   112.32   180.23
15     ================================================================
16
17
18
19
20
19-Jan-80   01:34 AM
```

Figure 4.13 Sample output from a spreadsheet package.

be set arbitrarily at around 0.15, but there is no need to use the same value for all updates. A forecast could be used which is more responsive to changes in underlying values than to trend. As such forecasts tend to be sensitive to values of smoothing constant it is worthwhile putting some effort into the selection of these. Perhaps the most useful way of doing this is to see how different values perform on historic data, doing trial runs with several values of α and comparing the resulting errors.

The calculations may seem daunting, but they can be done quickly either using a worksheet, or a spreadsheet package. Figure 4.13 illustrates the output from a spreadsheet for the problem above.

WORKED EXAMPLE 4.10

Quarterly demand for a product has been recorded over the past three years as follows.

Quarter	1	2	3	4	5	6	7	8	9	10	11	12
Demand	182	105	77	168	210	126	119	161	217	140	133	189

Use a constant value of $\alpha = 0.15$ to produce forecasts for the next year.

SOLUTION

This problem differs from the illustration above as initial values have not been set. We will use the first two-thirds of the data to find initial values. These can then be tuned using the last third of the data, and finally the forecasting can be done.

The mean demand in the first four quarters is 133 and in the second four quarters is 154. This suggests a trend of 21/4 = 5.25 a quarter. Drawing a graph of the data (Figure 4.14) and fitting a straight line by eye suggests a deseasonalized demand during the first period of about 125, then $D(2) = 125 + 5.25 = 130.25$, $D(3) = 125 + 2 * 5.25 = 135.5$, $D(4) = 125 + 3 * 5.25 = 140.75$ and so on. The graph also shows that the data has a cycle length of four periods.

We now have actual demands and estimates of deseasonalized demand, so dividing actual by deseasonalized demand will give a seasonal index for each period (see Table 4.8).

The average seasonal index for the first period in the cycle is $(1.46 + 1.44)/2 = 1.45$. Similarly the average seasonal indices for the other periods are 0.82, 0.67 and 1.10 respectively.

We now have all the initial values needed and the next step is to tune these over the last third of the data using the updating procedure described above. This gives the results in Table 4.9.

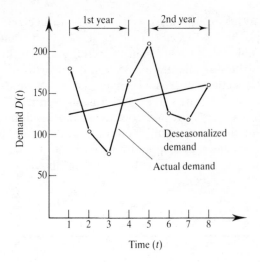

Figure 4.14 Deseasonalizing original demand data.

Table 4.8

t	$D(t)$	Seasonality removed	Seasonal index
1	182	125.00	1.46
2	105	130.25	0.81
3	77	135.50	0.57
4	168	140.75	1.19
5	210	146.00	1.44
6	126	151.25	0.83
7	119	156.50	0.76
8	161	161.75	1.00

Table 4.9

Period	t	8	9	10	11	12
Demand	$D(t)$	161	217	140	133	189
Basic Series	$U(t)$	161.75	164.40	169.48	177.99	181.69
Trend	$T(t)$	5.25	4.86	4.89	5.44	5.17
Seasonal Index	$I(n)$	1.45	0.82	0.67	1.10	1.43
Forecast	$F(t)$			138.79	116.83	201.77

The updated seasonal indices are 1.43, 0.82, 0.68 and 1.09 respectively. At the end of this tuning, reasonable values have been found and we can do the actual forecasting for the next year.

period 13 forecast = (181.69 + 5.17) * 1.43 = 267.21

period 14 forecast = (181.69 + 10.34) * 0.82 = 157.46

period 15 forecast = (181.69 + 15.51) * 0.68 = 134.10

period 16 forecast = (181.69 + 20.68) * 1.09 = 220.58

In summary

Forecasts can be made for data with seasonality and trend. The calculations for this appear messy, but they are straightforward applications of exponential smoothing on the underlying value, trend and seasonal indices. Computer use has obvious benefits.

SELF ASSESSMENT QUESTIONS

4.10 Why are actual averages of limited use for forecasting?

4.11 A moving average forecast can be made more responsive to change by:

(a) using a higher value of α
(b) using a higher value of N
(c) using a lower value of N
(d) changing initial values?

4.12 How can data be deseasonalized using moving averages?

4.13 Why is the forecasting method called 'exponential smoothing'?

4.14 An exponential smoothing forecast can be made more responsive by:

(a) using a higher value of α
(b) using a higher value of N
(c) using a lower value of N
(d) changing initial values?

4.15 How can exponential smoothing be used to forecast demand which has a trend?

4.16 Define all the terms in the equation

$$F(t + 1) = [U(t) + T(t)] * I(n)$$

4.5 CAUSAL FORECASTING

So far in this chapter we have looked at two approaches to forecasting (judgemental and projective) and can now move on to the third (causal). This looks for a cause or relationship which can be used to prepare forecasts. The sales of an item, for example, might depend on the price being charged, so setting the price at a particular value would allow sales

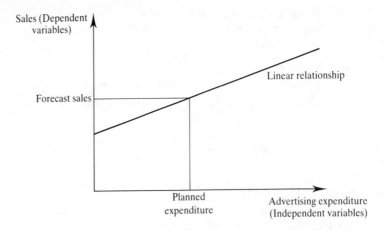

Figure 4.15 Illustrating a linear relationship between independent and dependent variables.

to be forecast. Similarly, advertising expenditure determines demand, bonus payments determine productivity, interest rates determine borrowing, amount of fertilizer sets crop size, and so on. These are examples of true relationships where changes in the first (independent) variable will cause changes in the second (dependent) variable (see Figure 4.15).

4.5.1 Linear regression

The rest of this chapter concentrates on simple linear regression, where the relationship between two variables is a straight line. The approach is best illustrated by an example.

WORKED EXAMPLE 4.11

A local amateur dramatic society is staging a play and wants to know how much to spend on advertising. Its objective is to attract as many people as possible up to the limit of the hall capacity. For the past eleven productions the spending on advertising (in hundreds of pounds) and subsequent audience is shown in the following table. If the hall capacity is now 300 people how much should be spent on advertising?

Spending	3	5	1	7	2	4	4	2	6	6	4
Audience	200	250	75	425	125	300	225	200	300	400	275

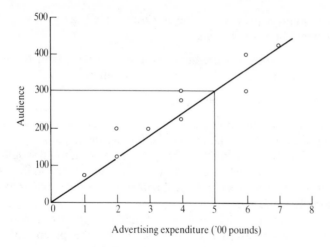

Figure 4.16 Scatter diagram for Worked example 4.11.

SOLUTION

A scatter diagram (Figure 4.16) of spending on advertising (the independent variable, X) and attendance (the dependent variable, Y) shows a clear linear relationship.

A reasonable straight line can be drawn by eye through the data and the hall capacity of 300 people corresponds to an advertising expenditure of around £500. If £500 is spent we would forecast an attendance of 300. Forecasts always contain errors, but in this case the error seems relatively small and we would expect the audience to be fairly close to 300. As it would be a bad policy to turn people away at the door, an advertising expenditure of somewhat less than £500 may finally be used.

In worked example 4.11 above we drew a scatter diagram, noticed a linear relationship and then fitted a line of best fit by eye. Although this informal approach can work quite well, we really need some more reliable way of identifying the relationship. One guideline is 'make sure the same number of points are above and below the line', but we could guarantee better results using some calculation. In particular we are going to derive the equation of the line of best fit. This involves finding values for the constants a and b in the equation:

$$Y = a + b * X$$

where X = independent variable
Y = dependent variable

a = point at which the line intersects the Y axis

b = gradient of the line.

As the line through the data will not be a perfect fit there will be an error in each point, $E(i)$. Taking the ith values

$$Y(i) = a + b * X(i) + E(i)$$

the line of best fit will minimize some measure of these errors. We saw earlier that simply adding the errors and finding the mean is not useful, as positive and negative errors cancel. Better alternatives would be to minimize the mean absolute deviation or the mean squared error. Because it is used for other statistical analyses, the mean squared error is conventionally preferred.

The derivation of the equation for the line of best fit is not difficult, but we are more interested in the results. (References given at the end of the chapter give the derivation.) Using the abbreviations:

$$\Sigma X = \overset{n}{\underset{i=1}{\Sigma}} X(i) \text{ and so on}$$

$MEAN(X)$ = mean value of X and so on

N = number of observations

the line of best fit is found from:

$$Y = a + b * X$$

$$b = \frac{N * \Sigma(X * Y) - \Sigma X * \Sigma Y}{N * \Sigma X^2 - (\Sigma X)^2}$$

$$a = MEAN(Y) - b * MEAN(Y)$$

WORKED EXAMPLE 4.12

Calculate the line of best fit through the following data for advertising budget (in hundreds of pounds) and units sold. Hence forecast the number of units sold if the advertising budget is £2500.

Month	i	1	2	3
Advertising budget	$X(i)$	10	20	30
Units sold	$Y(i)$	80	230	280

SOLUTION

Putting the data and calculated values for $X * Y$ and X^2 into Table 4.10:

Table 4.10

i	X	Y	$X * Y$	X^2
1	10	80	800	100
2	20	230	4,600	400
3	30	280	8,400	900
Totals	60	590	13,800	1,400

The number of observations, N, is equal to 3, and substitution gives:

$$\text{MEAN}(X) = 60/3 = 20$$
$$\text{MEAN}(Y) = 590/3 = 196.7$$

$$b = \frac{N * \Sigma(X * Y) - \Sigma X * \Sigma Y}{N * \Sigma X^2 - (\Sigma X)^2}$$

$$= \frac{3 * 13,800 - 60 * 590}{3 * 1400 - 60 * 60}$$

$$= 10$$

$$a = \text{MEAN}(Y) - b * \text{MEAN}(X)$$
$$= 196.7 - 10 * 20$$
$$= -3.3$$

The line of best fit is $Y = -3.3 + 10 * X$. With an advertising budget of £2500 $X = 25$, so

$$\text{Units sold} = Y = -3.3 + 10 * 25$$
$$= 246.7$$

WORKED EXAMPLE 4.13

Ten experiments were done to assess the effects of bonus rates paid to salesmen on sales, with the following results.

% Bonus	0	1	2	3	4	5	6	7	8	9
Sales ('00s)	3	4	8	10	15	18	20	22	27	28

What is the line of best fit through this data?

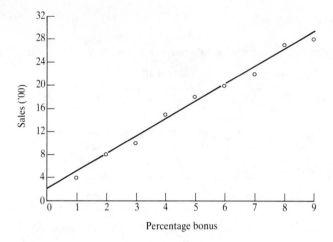

Figure 4.17 Scatter diagram for Worked example 4.13.

SOLUTION

The independent variable, X, is the bonus rate and the dependent variable, Y, is the consequent sales. Then, a table of the data has:

											Totals
X	0	1	2	3	4	5	6	7	8	9	45
Y	3	4	8	10	15	18	20	22	27	28	155
XY	0	4	16	30	60	90	120	154	216	252	942
X^2	0	1	4	9	16	25	36	49	64	81	285

With $N = 10$, substitution leads to:

$$b = (10 * 942 - 45 * 155)/(10 * 285 - 45 * 45) = 2.96$$
$$a = 155/10 - 2.96 * 45/10 = 2.18$$

The line of best fit is:

$$Y = 2.18 + 2.96 * X$$

or   Sales ('00s) = 2.18 + 2.96 * Bonus percentage

This is illustrated in Figure 4.17.

4.5.2 Coefficient of determination

We can now calculate a line of best fit, but we need some way of telling how good this line is. For this we will use a measure called the coefficient of determination.

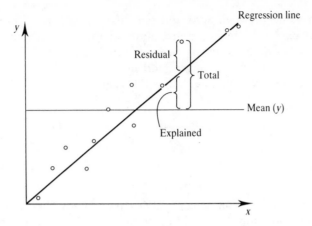

Figure 4.18 The relation between total, explained and residual deviations from mean.

In estimating a and b we minimized the sum of squared errors. This sum of squared errors (SSE) can be separated into components as follows. Observations of $Y(i)$ will have some variability about the mean value. This is the total sum of squared errors:

$$\text{Total } SSE = \Sigma[Y(i) - \text{MEAN}(Y)]^2$$

When we build a regression model, the estimates, $Y'(i)$, show what the observations would be if all noise is eliminated. Thus the regression model explains some of the variation from the mean.

$$\text{Explained } SSE = \Sigma[Y'(i) - \text{MEAN}(Y)]^2$$

Because of noise, the regression model does not explain all the variation, and there is some residual left unexplained.

$$\text{Unexplained } SSE = \Sigma[Y(i) - Y'(i)]^2$$

With a little algebra it can be shown that:

$$\text{Total } SSE = \text{Explained } SSE + \text{Unexplained } SSE$$

This is illustrated in Figure 4.18.

The greater the amount of the total variation explained by the regression, the more accurate is the linear relationship. The coefficient of determination is defined as the proportion of total SSE explained by the regression model.

$$\text{Coefficient of Determination} = \frac{\text{Explained } SSE}{\text{Total } SSE}$$

This has a value between zero and one: if it is near to 1, most of the variation is explained by the regression and the straight line is a good fit. Conversely, if the value is near to zero, most of the variation is unexplained and the line is not a good fit.

The easiest way of calculating the coefficient of determination is the rather messy looking equation:

$$\text{Coefficient of Determination} = \left[\frac{N * \Sigma(X * Y) - \Sigma X * \Sigma Y}{\sqrt{[\{N * \Sigma X^2 - (\Sigma X)^2\} * \{N * \Sigma Y^2 - (\Sigma Y)^2\}]}} \right]^2$$

All values in this equation, except ΣY^2, have already been calculated to find the regression line (but again it should be said that such calculations are well suited to computer spread sheets or specialized programs).

WORKED EXAMPLE 4.14

Calculate the coefficient of determination for the data in worked example 4.12.

SOLUTION

Drawing the table of results as before, and adding the values for ΣY^2 gives:

i	X	Y	$X * Y$	X^2	Y^2
1	10	80	800	100	6,400
2	20	230	4,600	400	52,900
3	30	280	8,400	900	78,400
Totals	60	590	13,800	1,400	137,700

We already know the line of best fit is $Y = -3.3 + 10 * X$, but are now checking to see how good this line is. The coefficient of determination is calculated as:

$$\text{Coefficient of Determination} = \left[\frac{N * \Sigma(X * Y) - \Sigma X * \Sigma Y}{\sqrt{[\{N * \Sigma X^2 - (\Sigma X)^2\} * \{N * \Sigma Y^2 - (\Sigma Y)^2\}]}} \right]^2$$

$$= \left[\frac{3 * 13,800 - 60 * 590}{\sqrt{[\{3 * 1400 - 60 * 60\} * \{3 * 137,700 - 590 * 590\}]}} \right]^2$$

$$= 0.96^2$$

$$= 0.92$$

92% of the variation can be explained by the regression model and only 8% is unexplained. This is evidence for a very good fit, but we would have expected this with only three data points.

4.5.3 Coefficient of correlation

A second useful measure is the coefficient of correlation which asks the question 'are X and Y linearly related?'. The coefficients of correlation and determination answer very similar questions, and a standard calculation (which we will not describe) shows:

> coefficient of correlation = $\sqrt{\text{coefficient of determination}}$

The coefficient of determination is usually referred to as r^2 and the coefficient of correlation as r.

The correlation coefficient has a value between +1 and −1.

- a value of $r = 0$ shows there is no correlation at all between the two variables and no linear relationship;
- a value of $r = 1$ shows the two variables have a perfect linear relationship with no noise at all, and as one increases so does the other;
- a value of $r = -1$ shows the two variables have a perfect linear relationship and as one variable increases the other decreases.

With correlation coefficients near to +1 or −1 there is a stronger linear relationship between the two variables. When r is less than about 0.7 the coefficient of determination is less than 0.49 and less than half the sum of squared errors is explained by the regression model. Thus values of r between 0.7 and −0.7 suggest a linear regression line is not very reliable (see Figure 4.19).

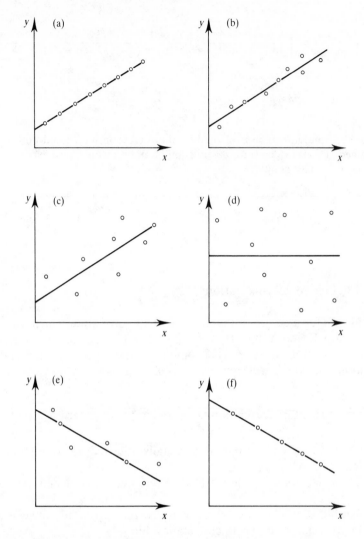

Figure 4.19 Showing the variation of r, coefficient of correlation: (a) $r = +1$ (perfect positive correlation); (b) r is close to $+1$ (line is good fit); (c) r is getting smaller; (d) $r = 0$ (random points); (e) r close to -1 (line is good fit); (f) $r = -1$ (perfect negative correlation).

WORKED EXAMPLE 4.15

Calculate the coefficients of correlation and determination for the data used in worked example 4.13. What conclusions can be drawn from these?

SOLUTION

Using a table for the data:

											Totals
X	0	1	2	3	4	5	6	7	8	9	45
Y	3	4	8	10	15	18	20	22	27	28	155
XY	0	4	16	30	60	90	120	154	216	252	942
X^2	0	1	4	9	16	29	36	49	64	81	285
Y^2	9	16	64	100	225	324	400	484	729	784	3135

Substitution then gives

$$r^2 = \left[\frac{N * \Sigma(X * Y) - \Sigma X * \Sigma Y}{\sqrt{[\{N * \Sigma X^2 - (\Sigma X)^2\} * \{N * \Sigma Y^2 - (\Sigma Y)^2\}]}} \right]^2$$

$$= \left[\frac{10 * 942 - 45 * 155}{\sqrt{[\{10 * 285 - 45 * 45\} * \{10 * 3135 - 155 * 155\}]}} \right]^2$$

$$= 0.995^2$$
$$= 0.99$$

The coefficient of determination shows that 99% of variation is explained by the linear model, so the model should be very useful. The coefficient of correlation = 0.995 which shows a strong linear relationship.

WORKED EXAMPLE 4.16

One section of a steel works consumes a lot of electricity. The actual quantity depends on the amount of steel produced, with figures for the past 10 months given below.

Output ('00 tons)	15	13	14	10	6	8	11	13	14	12
Electricity used ('00s KWh)	105	99	102	83	52	67	79	97	100	93

(a) Draw a scatter diagram to illustrate the relationship between electricity consumption and output.

(b) Calculate the correlation coefficient and see if there is a linear relationship between output and electricity consumption.

(c) Assuming that planned output is known before the month starts, calculate a regression equation to forecast the electricity consumption.

(d) What assumptions are implicit in these calculations? What do the two figures obtained represent in words?

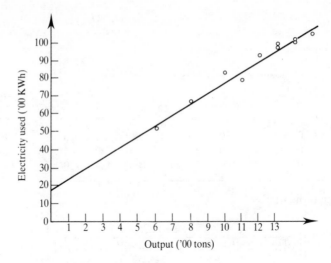

Figure 4.20 Scatter diagram for data in Worked example 4.16.

(e) Management is planning to increase production to roughly 2000 tons a month. Forecast the expected electricity consumption.

(f) Does the linear model seem a good representation?

SOLUTION

The independent variable, X, is the steel output and the dependent variable, Y, is the electricity consumption. Then:

$$\Sigma X = 116 \quad \Sigma X^2 = 1420 \quad \Sigma X * Y = 10,614 \quad \text{MEAN}(X) = 11.6$$
$$\Sigma Y = 877 \quad \Sigma Y^2 = 79,611 \quad N = 10 \quad \text{MEAN}(Y) = 87.7$$

(a) A scatter diagram for the problem is shown in Figure 4.20.

(b) Coefficient of correlation $= \dfrac{10 * 10,614 - 116 * 877}{\sqrt{[\{10 * 1420 - 116 * 116\} * \{10 * 79,611 - 877 * 877\}]}}$

$= 0.93$

This suggests a very strong linear relationship.

(c) For the regression:

$$b = \frac{10 * 10,614 - 116 * 877}{10 * 1420 - 116 * 116} = 5.925$$

$$a = 87.7 - 5.925 * 11.6 = 18.973$$

and

$$Y = 18.973 + 5.925 * X$$

(d) The main assumption is that a linear relationship is valid over the range of available data and that this relationship extends as far as we wish to forecast.

a is the quantity of electricity (1897.3 KWh) required to keep the plant going without producing any steel: *b* (592.5 KWh) is the amount of electricity needed to make each additional ton of steel.

(e) The forecast amount of electricity needed to make 2000 tons (i.e. $X = 20$) is:

$$Y = 18.973 + 5.925 * 20 = 137.473$$

or

13,747 KWh a month.

(f) In part (b) we calculated the correlation coefficient, *r*, as 0.98, so the coefficient of determination, r^2, = 0.96. This shows 96% of the variation is explained by the regression line and 4% is residual noise, so the model developed is a very good representation.

In summary

Causal forecasts look for relationships which allow forecasts to be made for some variables by considering the values taken by other variables. Linear regression finds the equation of the line of best fit (measured by the sum of squared errors). The proportion of the total variation explained by the regression line is given by the coefficient of determination, r^2, while the coefficient of correlation, *r*, shows how strong the linear relationship is.

SELF ASSESSMENT QUESTIONS

4.17 What is meant by 'linear regression'?

4.18 Define each of the terms in the linear regression equation $Y = a + b * X + E$.

4.19 What is measured by the coefficient of determination?

4.20 What values can be taken by the coefficient of correlation and how is this related to the coefficient of determination?

CONCLUSIONS

This chapter has discussed various aspects of forecasting. It started by considering the need to forecast and where such forecasting might fit into an organization. Then it looked at ways in which forecasts can be made.

There are essentially three approaches to forecasting, judgemental, projective and causal. In many situations judgemental forecasts, which are based on opinions and qualitative considerations, are the most appropriate. There are several ways in which such forecasts can be obtained, ranging from personal insight to the more formal Delphi method.

If the thing being forecast can be quantified, either projective or causal methods might be appropriate. Projective methods are widely used for time series, where moving averages or exponential smoothing can work well with constant time series. Exponential smoothing is generally the better method, but it needs some adjustment to deal with patterns, such as seasonality and trend. These adjustments are straightforward but can involve some tedious arithmetic.

Causal forecasts were illustrated by linear regressions. This checks to see if a linear regression model is appropriate (using the coefficients of determination and correlation) and then calculates the line of best fit.

Whatever forecasting method is used, there will be some error, because of the noise which is almost always present. The larger the contribution of noise, the less reliable is the forecast. Three measures of forecast error were considered, mean error, mean absolute deviation and mean squared error.

PROBLEMS

4.1   The productivity of a factory has been recorded over a ten month period, together with forecasts made the previous month by the production manager, the foreman and the management services department. Compare the three sets of forecasts in terms of bias and accuracy.

Month	1	2	3	4	5	6	7	8	9	10
Productivity	22	24	28	27	23	24	20	18	20	23

	1	2	3	4	5	6	7	8	9	10
Prodn Manager	23	26	32	28	20	26	24	16	21	23
Foreman	22	28	29	29	24	26	21	21	24	25
Mgmt Services	21	25	26	27	24	23	20	20	19	24

4.2   Find the two, three and four period moving average for the following time series, and by calculating the errors say which gives the best results.

t	1	2	3	4	5	6	7	8	9
$D(t)$	140	120	180	170	150	110	100	180	210

4.3   Find deseasonalized forecasts for the following time series and hence identify the underlying trend.

t	1	2	3	4	5	6	7	8	9	10	11	12
$D(t)$	750	300	520	880	320	530	900	300	560	960	340	600

4.4   Use exponential smoothing with smoothing constant equal to 0.1, 0.2, 0.3 and 0.4 to produce one period ahead forecasts for the following time series. Use an initial value of $F(1) = 10.4$ and say which value of α is best.

t	1	2	3	4	5	6	7	8	9
$D(t)$	10.6	10.8	21.2	24.3	10.6	10.4	10.4	10.2	10.8

4.5   Forecast values for periods 10 to 15 of the following time series using a smoothing constant of 0.15 where appropriate.

t	1	2	3	4	5	6	7	8	9
$D(t)$	112	151	142	174	207	212	247	283	268

4.6   The following data has a trend but no seasonality. Use values of $\alpha = 0.2$, $F(1) = 100$ and initial trend $= 15$ to give forecasts for period 10 to 13.

t	1	2	3	4	5	6
$D(t)$	100	120	135	140	155	170

4.7   The number of shifts worked per month and the consequent output are shown in the following table. If 400 units are needed next month, how many shifts should be planned? How reliable is this result?

Month	1	2	3	4	5	6	7	8
Shifts worked	50	70	25	55	20	60	40	25
Units made	352	555	207	508	48	498	310	153

4.8   Sales over the past 10 months have been as shown below. Use linear regression to forecast sales for the next 6 months. How reliable are these figures?

Month	1	2	3	4	5	6	7	8	9	10
Sales	6	21	41	75	98	132	153	189	211	243

4.9 Figures for the demand and cost of an item have been collected from five suppliers as follows.

Supplier	1	2	3	4	5
Cost	14	25	18	28	20
Demand	24	18	20	16	20

It is thought that demand can be calculated from:

$$\text{demand} = a + b/\text{cost}$$

Use linear regression to find the expected demand for a cost of 16.

CASE STUDY – LOCH ERICHSAE KNITWEAR COMPANY

Hamish Macdonald started manufacturing knitwear in the Scottish borders in 1883. The company has continued to operate in the same location and is still run by the Macdonald family. The range of articles knitted has evolved to meet current demands, and nowadays the most important product is high quality, lambswool sweaters. These are made in a number of styles aimed primarily at the golf and other sports markets.

Sales of sweaters have risen steadily in recent years as more people have taken up leisure activities and sweaters have become increasingly popular. The highest sales are for a plain sweater, which is available in two styles (roll collar and V-neck), 12 colours and seven sizes. This accounts for 70% of sales while other styles (sports shirts, intarsias, sleeveless pullovers, speciality sweaters and special orders) make up the remaining 30%.

The premises occupied by the company for the past 100 years are now in need of major renovation. This would be a considerable expense and the company is reluctant to spend so much to repair an old building. An alternative has been suggested by a local construction company. The factory is near the town centre and is now surrounded by modern houses. The construction company has approached Macdonalds to see if they would sell the site, allowing the factory to be demolished and more houses to be built. In return the developer would pay for the move to new custom built premises on a nearby industrial estate. The question asked by the management of Macdonalds is how big the new factory should be.

If a move is made, the new factory should be big enough to cover expected demand for some time in the future. At the same time the company does not want to run a factory which is too large for their needs, and the construction company would be reluctant to finance a very large expansion. Although the demand for sweaters is rising, there have been periods in the past when demand has declined for long periods and the company has concentrated on other products.

Another problem with sweaters is the variation in demand, with peaks in the summer (when more outdoor sports are played) and near Christmas (where high quality sweaters are a popular present). This gives a fluctuating demand with consequent difficulties in production planning. One way around this would be to keep large stocks of finished sweaters, but this has proved expensive and should be avoided. An alternative, which is now giving substantial benefits, is to develop an export market. By selling goods around the world the effects of seasons can be reduced. Export sales are less reliable than domestic ones since they depend on the value of international currencies and the competition from cheaper, lower quality products from the Far East. At one time the company tried importing finished sweaters to meet fluctuating demand but the quality could not be assured and the experiment was quickly stopped. Another way of stabilizing demand is to sell sweaters in bulk to clubs, associations etc. Golf club professionals are given discounts if they buy a reasonable number of sweaters which can be sold to club members.

There are several views within the company about the size of premises which should be bought. James Macdonald, the present company chairman, says the current premises are 50,000 square feet: this has been big enough for the last 100 years and the company should, therefore, move into new premises of the same size. An alternative view from the factory manager says that two years ago the company was producing 2000 sweaters a month, last year it was 3000 a month, now it is 4000 a month. In three years they could be making 7000 sweaters a month and should, therefore, move into a factory of at least 50,000/4000 * 7000 = 87,500 square feet.

To help planning, the actual sales of sweaters over the past two years have been collected for the domestic, export and bulk markets. Table 4.11 shows monthly sales for domestic and export and average monthly sales for bulk, calculated every quarter.

A space analysis by the company auditor shows that the factory is made up of 6000 square feet of offices, reception areas, cafeteria etc.; 22,000 square feet is occupied by the various stages in production on the factory floor; 16,000 square feet is for stocks and a factory shop and 6000 square feet which is unused or unusable. Based on this, and some estimates from past years, he suggests that 20,000 square feet is needed to keep the factory running and a variable amount of space is dependent on production. He feels that a year ago the factory effectively used 70% of its available space, while this year effective utilization was up to 80%. More than this was actually used as the space would otherwise remain empty.

Table 4.11

Month	Domestic	Export	Bulk
1	804	1108	174
2	680	974	
3	711	1072	
4	775	944	215
5	1014	996	
6	1480	1073	
7	1407	1044	293
8	1283	927	
9	1206	1020	
10	1333	1003	348
11	1622	838	
12	1947	902	
13	1830	805	406
14	1644	884	
15	1504	1055	
16	1613	967	485
17	1821	1036	
18	1941	1077	
19	1802	906	566
20	1664	732	
21	1598	763	
22	1712	719	617
23	2028	751	
24	2573	918	
25	2349	870	682

The sales manager added to the discussion by saying that he was not only interested in the overall number of sweaters made, but also the distribution of sizes, colours and quantities ordered. If the product range were reduced then stock levels, production set-up times and space needed could all be reduced. He put forward the figures in Tables 4.12 and 4.13 for sales and order quantities which had been collected over a random period. Although he was not sure how these figures could be used he felt they should be considered somewhere.

Suggested questions

- What advantages would a move to a new factory bring to Macdonalds?
- What are the effects of variable demand and how can the company deal with these?

Table 4.12

	Size	XXS	XS	S	M	L	XL	XXL
Colour								
White		0	1	6	15	17	9	1
Grey		0	1	6	18	19	9	1
Black		0	2	7	23	23	10	2
Dark blue		1	4	20	59	68	41	4
Mid blue		0	1	4	12	12	7	2
Light blue		1	4	12	25	28	15	2
Bright red		0	3	9	21	20	13	3
Dark red		0	2	7	20	22	11	1
Cream		0	2	10	24	25	11	1
Fawn		0	0	3	8	7	4	1
Brown		0	0	4	5	7	5	1
Green		0	1	6	17	21	10	1

Table 4.13

Units per order	% of orders	% of units
0–10	52.5	11.4
11–20	21.5	15.1
21–30	9.1	10.7
31–40	5.7	9.5
41–50	4.3	9.5
51–60	2.3	6.1
61–70	0.9	2.9
71–100	1.5	5.9
101–200	1.5	9.6
201+	0.6	19.2

- How valid are the views of the company chairman and factory manager?
- Based on historic data covering two years, what are forecast sales for the foreseeable future?
- What size of factory would be needed based on the company auditor's analysis?
- How should the figures collected by the sales manager be used?
- What other information would be useful to help with a decision?
- Based on the data available, what decisions should the company make?

SOLUTIONS TO SELF ASSESSMENT QUESTIONS

4.1 Planning is important for the survival and success of most organizations. Decisions are implemented at some point in the future, which means that the prevailing circumstances must be forecast.

4.2 **(b)** false. Forecasting may be done by experts but they should certainly not be working in isolation.

4.3 Judgemental, projective and causal forecasting.

4.4 Relevant factors include:

- what is to be forecast and why;
- can the thing being forecast be quantified;
- how does the forecast affect other parts of the organization;
- how far into the future are forecasts needed;
- is reliable data available and how frequently is it updated;
- what external factors are relevant;
- how much will the forecast cost and how much will errors cost;
- how much detail is required;
- how much time is available?

Many other points may also be listed.

4.5 Judgemental forecasts are subjective views based on opinions and intuition rather than quantitative analysis.

4.6 Personal insight, panel consensus, market surveys, historical analogy and Delphi method.

4.7 Forecasts are based on projecting the underlying pattern, but they cannot deal with short term, random noise. Hence errors are introduced by noise, incorrectly identifying the underlying pattern and changes in the system being forecast.

4.8 The mean error is defined as:

$$\text{Mean error} = 1/n * \sum_{t=1}^{n} E(t)$$

$$= 1/n * \sum_{t=1}^{n} [D(t) - F(t)]$$

Positive and negative errors cancel each other. The mean error should have a value around zero unless the forecasts are biased.

4.9 Mean absolute deviation

$$= 1/n * \sum_{t=1}^{n} \text{ABS}[D(t) - F(t)]$$

$$= 1/n * \sum_{t=1}^{n} \text{ABS}[E(t)]$$

Mean squared error

$$= 1/n * \sum_{t=1}^{n} [D(t) - F(t)]^2$$

$$= 1/n * \sum_{t=1}^{n} [E(t)]^2$$

4.10 Because older data tends to swamp more recent (and more relevant) data. Actual averages should only be used if the demand is known to be constant.

4.11 **(c)** using a lower value of N.

4.12 By using a moving average where N (the number of periods used) is the same as the seasonal length.

4.13 Because the weight given to data declines exponentially with the age of the data, and the method smooths the effects of noise.

4.14 **(a)** using a higher value of α.

4.15 Ordinary exponential smoothing is not good for data which has a trend, as the forecast always lags behind actual demand. An allowance for trend should be added to the forecasts (which is equivalent to using the model described for seasonality and trend with seasonal indices fixed at 1.0).

4.16

t = time period

$F(t)$ = forecast for time t

$U(t)$ = smoothed, deseasonalized underlying value for t

$T(t)$ = smoothed trend for t

$I(n)$ = smoothed seasonal index for period t, which is the nth period of a cycle.

4.17 If a relationship is observed between variables, regression identifies the nature of the relationship. If a linear relationship is observed between two variables, linear regression finds the equation of the line of best fit.

4.18 X and Y are the independent and dependent variables respectively; a is the point where the line crosses the Y axis, b is the gradient of the line; E is the noise.

4.19 The proportion of the total sum of squared error which is explained by the regression.

4.20 -1 to $+1$. This shows if there is a linear relationship between two variables. The coefficient of determination is the square of the coefficient of correlation.

REFERENCES FOR FURTHER READING

Benton W. K. (1972). *Forecasting for Managers* Reading, Mass: Addison Wesley

Bowerman B. L. and O'Connell R. T. (1979). *Forecasting and Time Series* Mass: Duxbury Press

Box G. E. P. and Jenkins G. M. (1976). *Time Series Analysis: forecasting and control* rev. edn. San Francisco: Holden Day

Hanke J. E. and Reitsch A. G. (1986). *Business Forecasting* 2nd edn. Boston: Allyn and Bacon

Linstone H. A. and Turoff M. (1975). *The Delphi Method: techniques and applications* Reading, Mass: Addison Wesley

Makridakis S., Wheelwright S. C. and McGee V. E. (1983). *Forecasting: methods and applications* 2nd edn. New York: John Wiley

Thomopoulos N. T. (1980). *Applied Forecasting Methods* New Jersey: Prentice Hall

Wheelwright S. C. and Makridakis S. (1985). *Forecasting Models for Management* 4th edn. New York: John Wiley

Willis R. E. (1987). *A Guide to Forecasting for Planners and Managers* New Jersey: Prentice-Hall

Younger M. S. (1979). *A Handbook for Linear Regression* Mass: Duxbury Press

Chapter 5

Project network analysis

SYNOPSIS

Project network analysis is an important aid for planning, scheduling and controlling projects. The aim of this chapter is to introduce the overall approach and give some feel for its scope and application. As usual we shall be looking at the ideas by reference to examples and illustrations.

This chapter describes how a project consists of related activities and how these may be represented by an 'activity on arrow' diagram (rather than the less common 'activity on node' diagram). In particular we will be looking at a standard approach for projects where estimates of activity durations can be found with relative certainty ('critical path method'). This is extended, in Chapter 9, to include probabilistic durations for the activities (PERT).

The first part of the chapter covers the need for project planning and the information required. This is followed by a description of the critical path method (CPM) of drawing project networks to describe relationships between activities. Having drawn a network the next stage is to analyse the timing of individual activities and the overall project. Adjustment of times may be needed to achieve objectives and an approach to resource levelling is outlined.

OBJECTIVES

After reading this chapter and doing the numerical exercises you should be able to:

- appreciate the need for planning complex projects;
- list the requirements of project planners;
- represent small projects by networks of connected activities and events;
- extend the use of networks to describe larger projects;
- calculate early and late times for events and hence their slacks;
- calculate earliest and latest start and finish times for activities and hence their floats;
- identify critical paths and hence overall project durations;
- change the times of activities to achieve stated objectives;
- draw Gantt charts for projects;
- find the resources needed during a project and reschedule activities to smooth the requirements.

5.1 BACKGROUND TO PROJECT NETWORK ANALYSIS

This chapter examines an important aid for planning projects, so we should start by defining a 'project'. A fairly loose definition describes a project as a self-contained piece of work which can be viewed as a distinct entity. Each of us does a number of small projects every day, such as preparing a meal, writing a report, building a fence or organizing a social function. Such projects need planning, and in particular the identification of:

- the activities which make up the project
- the order in which these activities must be done
- timing of each activity
- resources needed at each stage.

Fortunately, small projects need hardly any formal planning and a little thought generally ensures things run smoothly. With larger, complex projects (such as installing a new computer system, building a nuclear power station, organizing the Olympic Games, or building a multi-storey office block) it would be impossible to remember all the activities, let alone ensure that each is done by the time it is needed, or that resources are available at the right time. Without formal planning mistakes would be inevitable. Project network analysis is the most widely used technique for helping organize complex projects.

Project network analysis was developed independently in the late 1950s by two groups facing similar problems. The first group was concerned with the Polaris missile project for the United States Department of Defense. At the time the US government felt that progress in its development of missiles was too slow and it gave high priority to the huge Polaris project. To help control this project, which involved over 3000 contractors, a technique called PERT (programme evaluation and review technique) was developed. This was considered a major success and reduced the overall length of the project by two years.

The second group worked for Du Pont and developed CPM (critical path method) for planning maintenance programmes in chemical plants. PERT and CPM were always very similar, but any differences in the original ideas have disappeared over time. The one difference which still exists is that PERT stresses probabilistic durations of activities while CPM assumes fixed durations. In this chapter we will consider CPM while the small additions needed for probabilistic durations are covered in Chapter 9.

5.2   PROJECT MANAGEMENT

Project managers generally have a number of goals, including:

- allocation of resources so that objectives are achieved;
- effective monitoring and control of activities;
- anticipation and avoidance of problems;
- speedy reaction to deviations from plans;
- alteration of plans and schedules as required.

To help managers in the achievement of these goals, we would expect a reasonable planning tool to:

- present relevant information in an easily understandable form (preferably graphical);
- identify the order in which activities should be done and their interdependence;
- estimate how long the project will take;
- identify the time by which each activity must be finished if the project is not to be delayed;
- show the maximum delay in each activity which will not delay the

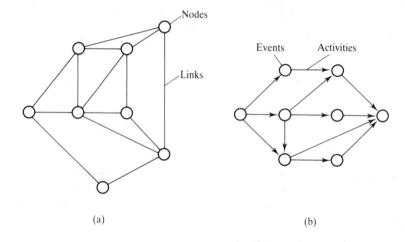

Figure 5.1 Representation of networks: (a) road network; (b) project network.

project and hence indicate which activities are most critical to the completion of the project;

- allow scheduling of resources to provide steady utilization during the project;
- enable effective monitoring and control of activities during the project;
- allow rapid adjustment for changes in activity duration or order.

Project network analysis provides this information. Although CPM can be used for almost any type of project, it has proved most useful for those which are fairly large (having a reasonable amount of money involved and making it worthwhile to do the data collection and analysis) and complex (so there are enough opportunities for things to go wrong). Such projects will probably be one-off so there is little previous experience which could be used directly. Typical projects include construction (roads, bridges or buildings), organization of large events, launch of new products, plans for equipment maintenance and manufacture of one-off items.

5.3 NETWORK REPRESENTATION

The term 'network' is familiar in the context of maps of road or rail networks. In these 'nodes' are used to represent towns, and lines are drawn to show direct links between nodes, as illustrated in Figure 5.1. Project networks are similar to these, as they represent projects by a

Figure 5.2   Activity and event representation.

series of nodes connected by lines. In a project network each 'activity' is represented by an arrow to indicate the sequence of activities (there is no importance to their orientation). Nodes represent points in time at which activities begin and end: the nodes are called 'events' and a network will consist of alternating activities and events.

In Figure 5.2 the arrow represents an activity, the event on the left represents the start of the activity and the event on the right the finish of the activity. Project networks are built up of connected chains of activities and events.

We can demonstrate the critical path method by taking a small example where a greenhouse is to be built from a kit. The instructions make it clear that the project can be considered in three parts:

- preparing the base (which will take three days)
- building the frame (which will take two days)
- fixing the glass (which will take one day).

These activities make up the project and there is a fixed order in which they must be done; building the frame must be done after preparing the base and before fixing the glass. The chain of activities for the project is shown in Figure 5.3.

The direction of the arrows in Figure 5.3 indicates precedence and each preceding activity must be finished before the following one is started. Preparing the base must be done first, and as soon as this is finished the frame can be built, then as soon as this is finished the glass can be fixed. This project could also be described by a precedence or dependence table such as Table 5.1 where each activity is listed along with those activities which immediately precede it.

Figure 5.3   Network for building greenhouse.

Table 5.1

Activity	Duration (days)	Description	Immediate predecessor
A	3	prepare base	–
B	2	build frame	A
C	1	fix glass	B

Labelling the activities A, B and C is a convenient shorthand and allows us to refer quickly to activity B having activity A as immediate predecessor, which is normally stated as 'B depends on A'. In this table only *immediate* predecessors are entered, so the fact that activity C (fixing the glass) depends on activity A as well as B need not be separately entered but can be inferred from other dependencies. Activity A has no immediate predecessors and can be started whenever convenient.

After drawing the basic network for the project we can now consider its timing. It is convenient to assume a notional starting time of zero. Then preparing the base can be finished by the end of day 3, building the frame takes another two days and can be finished by the end of day 5 and fixing the glass takes one day and can be finished by the end of day 6. This is added to the network as shown in Figure 5.4.

If the concrete of the base takes more than three days to set, or the glass is not delivered by day 5 the project will be delayed, but if building the frame takes less than two days the project may be finished early. This plan also allows us to schedule resources, as we know that a concrete mixer must be available for the first three days of the project, a frame builder must be there for days 4 and 5, and a glazier should be available on day 6.

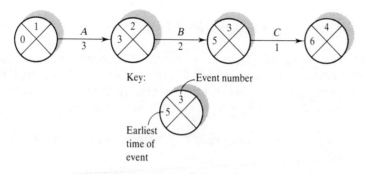

Figure 5.4 Times for the project.

We have now done most of the planning for this project and can summarize the steps taken as

- define the separate activities
- determine the dependence and duration of each activity
- draw the network
- analyse the timing of the project
- schedule resources

If, for some reason, the timings or resource requirements suggested by the initial plan are not acceptable, the project can be adjusted until a satisfactory solution is found. Finally, when the plan is implemented and the project is running, progress must be monitored and controlled to find any deviations from the plan, with adjustments made as necessary to compensate for these.

This initial example is very simple but with even slightly more complex projects it quickly becomes difficult to do the planning intuitively.

In summary

Planning is needed for most projects of reasonable size. CPM is a useful way of doing this planning. Projects are divided into a number of self contained activities which are represented by a network of alternating activities and events. After the network is drawn calculations can be done for timing and resource allocation.

5.4   DRAWING LARGER NETWORKS

In this section we will expand the scope of networks to cover larger projects, particularly those which include parallel activities. We have already developed some implicit rules for networks and before continuing should state these more formally. The two main rules are:

- before an activity can begin all preceding activities must be finished;
- the arrows representing activities imply precedence only and neither the length nor orientation is significant.

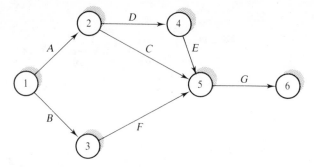

Figure 5.5 Network for opening office.

There are also, by convention, some other rules:

- a network has only one starting and finishing event;
- each event has a unique identifying number;
- any two events can only be connected by one activity.

These rules can now be applied to develop a network for a slightly more complex project. A company is planning to open a new office and identifies the main activities and dependencies as shown in Table 5.2.

Table 5.2

Activity	Description	Depends on
A	find office location	–
B	recruit new staff	–
C	make office alterations	A
D	order equipment needed	A
E	install new equipment	D
F	train staff	B
G	start operations	C, E, F

In this project activities A and B have no predecessors and can be started as soon as convenient. As soon as activity A is finished both C and D can start: E can start as soon as D is finished and F can start as soon as B is finished. G can only start when C, E and F have all finished. This network is shown in Figure 5.5.

The network conforms to the rules above, and in particular has a single starting and finishing event, unique event numbers and only one activity between any pair of events.

The network shows that the project can start with activities A and

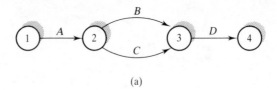

(a)

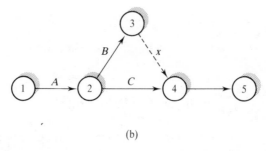

(b)

Figure 5.6 Networks illustrating the use of a 'uniqueness dummy': (a) incorrect network; (b) correct network using dummy activity x.

B, but this does not imply that these *must* start at the same time, only that both can start as soon as convenient and must be finished before any following activity can start. Similarly event 2 marks the point at which both C and D can start but this does not mean they must start at the same time. Conversely event 5 is the point where C, E and F are finished but this does not mean that they must finish at the same time, only that they must all be finished before G can start.

Using these principles we could now draw networks of almost any size, but there are still two situations which would cause difficulties. The first of these is illustrated by the dependence table:

Activity	Depends on
A	–
B	A
C	A
D	B, C

We may be tempted to draw this as shown in Figure 5.6(a), but this would break one of the rules above which says, 'Any two events can only be connected by one activity'. The conventional way around this is to define a 'dummy activity' which is not a part of the project, has zero duration and requires no resources, but is simply there to allow a sensible

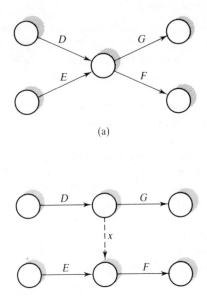

Figure 5.7 Networks illustrating the use of a 'logical dummy' x: (a) incorrect part of network; (b) correct network using dummy activity x.

network to be drawn. In this case the dummy ensures that only one activity goes between two events and is called a 'uniqueness dummy'. In Figure 5.6(b) the dummy activity is represented by the broken line, x.

A second situation which needs a dummy activity is illustrated by part of a dependence table shown below.

Activity	Depends on
D	not given
E	not given
F	D, E
G	D

We may be tempted to draw this part of the network as shown in Figure 5.7(a), but the dependence would clearly be wrong. Activity F is shown as depending on D and E, which is correct, but G is shown as having the same dependence. The dependence table shows that G can start as soon as D is finished but the network shows it as having to wait for E to finish as well. The way to avoid this relies on separating the dependencies by introducing a dummy activity, as shown in Figure 5.7(b). The dependence of F on D is shown through the dummy activity x. In effect the dummy can not start until D has finished and then F can not start until the dummy and E are finished: as the dummy activity has zero duration this does not add any time to the project. This type of dummy is called a 'logical dummy'.

These are the only two circumstances (ensuring only one activity goes between any two nodes and ensuring the logic is correct) in which dummies are used, so we are now able to draw networks to represent almost any project. Drawing networks from dependency tables is a matter of practice, but a useful starting point is to draw on the left hand side all those activities which have no preceding activities. Then activities which only depend on the first activities can be added and so on, systematically expanding the network from the initial activities and working through the project (left to right across the diagram). Mistakes are inevitable while drawing the network and these can be corrected most easily by using a blackboard, or a pencil, rubber and stack of cheap paper.

WORKED EXAMPLE 5.1

A project consists of the activities described by the dependence table shown in Table 5.3. Draw the network for this project.

Table 5.3

Activity	Depends on
A	–
B	–
C	A
D	A
E	C
F	D
G	B
H	G
I	E, F
J	H, I

SOLUTION

We can start by noting that activities A and B have no immediate predecessors and can both be started straight away. Then activities C, D and G, which only depend on A and B, can be added, followed by E, F and H. Activity I can not start until both activities E and F are finished, while the start of J must wait until both H and I are finished. The final network is shown in Figure 5.8.

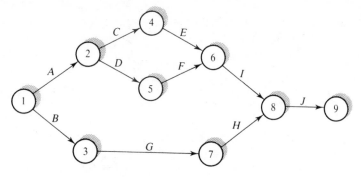

Figure 5.8 Network for Worked example 5.1.

This network conforms to the general rules and, in particular, has a single starting and finishing event, unique event numbers and only one activity between any pair of events.

The network shows that the project can start with A and B, but this does not imply that they *must* start at the same time. Similarly event 6 marks the point at which both E and F are finished, but this does not mean that they must finish at the same time, only that they must both be finished before I can start.

WORKED EXAMPLE 5.2

(a) An amateur dramatic society is planning its annual production and is interested in using a network to coordinate the various activities. What activities do you think should be included in the network?

(b) If discussions lead to the following activities, what would the network look like?

- assess resources and select play
- prepare scripts
- select actors and cast parts
- rehearse
- design and organize advertisements
- prepare stage, lights and sound
- build scenery
- sell tickets
- final arrangements for opening

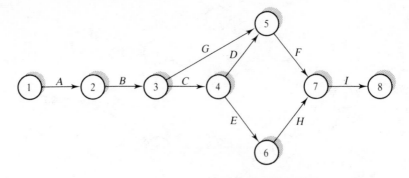

Figure 5.9 Network for Worked example 5.2.

SOLUTION

(a) One answer to the first part of this question is given in part (b). There are many alternatives and the most appropriate list of activities should be adopted.

(b) A dependence table must be drawn for activities and this might well arouse different views which must be reconciled. One version is shown in Table 5.4.

Table 5.4

Activity	Description	Depends on
A	assess resources and select play	–
B	prepare scripts	A
C	select actors and cast parts	B
D	rehearse	C
E	design and organize advertisements	C
F	prepare stage, lights and sound	D, G
G	build scenery	B
H	sell tickets	E
I	final arrangements for opening	F, H

The network for this dependence table is shown in Figure 5.9.

WORKED EXAMPLE 5.3

A project is described by the dependency table in Table 5.5. Draw a network of the project.

Table 5.5

Activity	Depends on		Activity	Depends on
A	J		I	J
B	C, G		J	–
C	A		K	B
D	F, K, N		L	I
E	J		M	I
F	B, H, L, M		N	M
G	A, E, I		O	M
H	G			

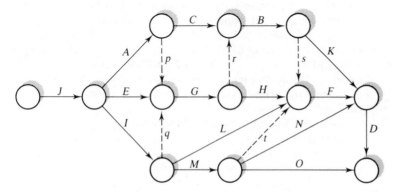

Figure 5.10 Network for Worked example 5.3.

SOLUTION

Although this seems a difficult network to draw the steps are fairly straight-forward. Activity J is the only one which does not depend on anything else, then A, E and I, which depend only on J can be added. Continuing this line of reasoning leads to the network shown in Figure 5.10, which includes five dummy activities.

WORKED EXAMPLE 5.4

The Management Science Group in a whisky distillery has examined the inventory control system to see how stock levels can be set to meet forecast demand. They have concluded that an expanded computer system is needed which will extrapolate past demand patterns and, based on these, set appropriate stock levels. These stock levels will then be passed to a production control module which varies the quantities bottled to meet inventory requirements.

The first part of this proposed system is called DFS (Demand Forecasting System) while the second part is ICS (Inventory Control System). The introduction of these is expected to take about 18 months, including linking to the production control module which is already operating. The introduction of DFS and ICS is a self-contained project for which the following activities have been identified. Draw a network for the project.

Activity	Description
A	examine existing system and environment of ICS
B	collect costs and other data relevant to ICS
C	construct and test models for ICS
D	write and test computer programs for ICS models
E	design and print data input forms for ICS data
F	document ICS programs and monitoring procedures
G	examine sources of demand data and its collection
H	construct and test models for DFS
I	organize past demand data
J	write and test computer programs for DFS models
K	design and print data input forms for DFS data
L	document DFS programs and monitoring procedures
M	train staff in the use of DFS and ICS
N	initialize data for ICS programs (ICS staff)
P	initialize data for DFS programs (DFS staff)
Q	create base files for DFS
R	run system for trial period

SOLUTION

In fairly complex projects there are usually several views on the dependence of activities. The information given above allows several opinions and these should be sorted out by discussion, preferably in the light of experiences with similar projects. One dependence table for the project is shown in Table 5.6 with the associated network shown in Figure 5.11.

Table 5.6

Activity	Depends on	Activity	Depends on
A	–	J	H, K
B	A	K	A, G
C	A	L	J
D	C	M	F, L
E	C	N	B, M
F	D, E	P	I, M
G	–	Q	P
H	A, G	R	N, Q
I	G		

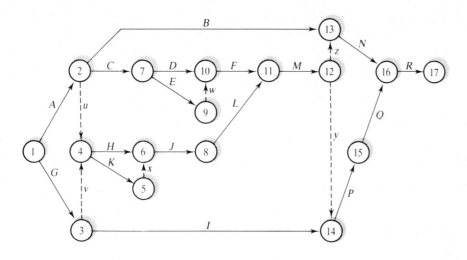

Figure 5.11 Network for Worked example 5.4.

In the initial example of building a greenhouse, the project was conveniently divided into three activities. It could have been divided into a lot more (such as determine location, clear vegetation, level and prepare ground, dig foundations, lay hard-core, mix concrete, lay concrete base, and so on) but the complexity of the network would increase with the number of activities and the importance of each activity would decline. In general a balance must be reached between using too few activities (and reducing the usefulness as a planning aid) and using too many (and needlessly increasing complexity).

If the number of activities gets above about 30 it is probably best to start using a computer package (many of which are available) but if the number of activities is very large the network will cover many pages, be complicated and difficult to follow. For large projects a useful approach would be to draw a general, master network of the major parts of the project, and then for each of these parts draw a separate, more detailed network. For very large projects it may be useful to go further and break down the more detailed networks into yet smaller parts. This approach would be particularly useful when there are a large number of contractors and subcontractors working on a single project. The owner of the project may construct a master network, each contractor could be given a network covering their own work, and any major subcontractors could be given separate networks of their parts of the work. At each stage the networks would cover less of the overall project but would show more detail.

SELF ASSESSMENT QUESTIONS

5.1 What is meant by 'project management' and why is the planning of projects necessary?

5.2 What are the aims of systematic project planning?

5.3 What information is needed to draw a project network?

5.4 What are the main rules of drawing a project network?

5.5 When are dummy activities used?

5.5 TIMING OF PROJECTS – EVENTS

The timing of events and activities is a major part of project planning. In particular, it is important to find the earliest time an activity can start and the latest time by which it must be finished. It would be difficult to find these intuitively for a project of any reasonable size and a more systematic approach must be used. The CPM approach is illustrated by the dependence table in Table 5.7. It does not matter what the activities are, so we will simply use reference letters and note that the durations are given in weeks.

Table 5.7

Activity	Duration	Depends on
A	3	–
B	2	–
C	2	A
D	4	A
E	1	C
F	3	D
G	1	B
H	4	G
I	5	E, F
J	2	H, I

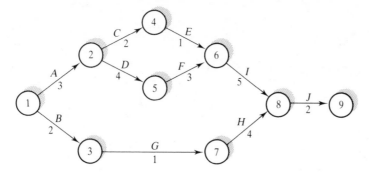

Figure 5.12 Basic network for text example.

This project is represented by the network shown in Figure 5.12, with durations noted under the activities.

We can start the analysis of times by finding the earliest possible time for each event, assuming a notional start time of zero for the project as a whole. The earliest time for event 1 is clearly 0. The earliest time for event 2 is when A finishes, which is three weeks after its earliest start at 0: the earliest time for event 4 is the time when C finishes, which is two weeks after its earliest start at 3 (i.e. week 5). Similarly, the earliest time for event 5 is 4 + 3 = 7 and for event 7 is 1 + 2 = 3.

When several activities have to finish before an event, the earliest time for the event is the earliest time by which all preceding activities can be finished. The earliest time for event 6 is when both E and F are finished. E can finish one week after its earliest start at 5 (i.e. week 6), F can finish 3 weeks after its earliest start at 7 (i.e. week 10) and the earliest time when both of these can be finished is, therefore, week 10. Similarly, event 8 must wait until both activities H and I are finished. Activity H can be finished by week 3 + 4 = 7 while activity I can be finished by week 10 + 5 = 15: the earliest time for event 8 is the later of these which is week 15.

Finally the earliest time for event 9, which marks the end of the project is week 15 + 2 = 17, and the overall duration of the project is 17 weeks. Figure 5.13 shows the earliest times for each event added to the network.

The formal statement of the calculations for earliest event time is:

$$ET(1) = 0$$

and

$$ET(j) = \text{MAX}_{i}[\ ET(i) + D(i,j)\ ]$$

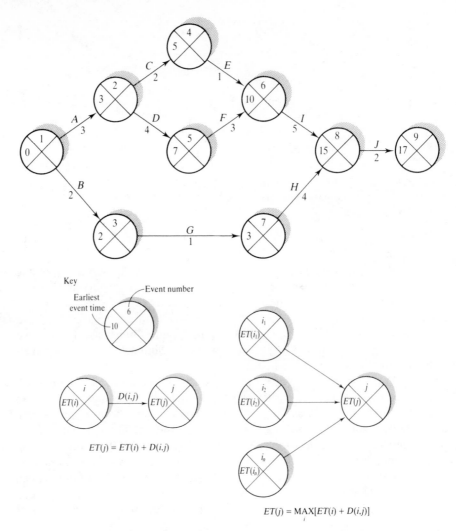

Figure 5.13 Network with earliest event times added.

where: $ET(i)$ = the earliest time of event i

$D(i,j)$ = duration of activity linking events i and j

> The earliest time of event j is the earliest time by which *all* preceding activities can be finished.

Having gone through the network and found the earliest time for each event we can do a similar analysis to find the latest time for each. This would then give an idea of those events which need strict control and those for which there is some slack. The procedure for this is almost the reverse of that used to find the earliest time. We start at the end of the project with event 9 and say that this has a latest time for completion of week 17. To allow activity J to be finished by week 17 it must be started two weeks before this, so the latest time for event 8 is week $17 - 2 = 15$. Now, the latest H can finish is week 15, so the latest time it can start is four weeks before this and the latest time for event 7 is week $15 - 4 = 11$. Similarly the latest time for event 3 is $11 - 1 = 10$, for event 6 is $15 - 5 = 10$, for event 5 is $10 - 3 = 7$ and for event 4 is $10 - 1 = 9$.

For events which have more than one following activity the latest time must allow all following activities to be completed on time. Event 2 is followed by activities C and D; C must be finished by week 9 so it must be started two weeks before this (i.e. week 7), while D must be finished by week 7 so it must be started four weeks before this (i.e. week 3). The latest time for event 2 which allows both C and D to start on time is the earliest of these, which is week 3.

Similarly the latest time for event 1 must allow both A and B to finish on time. The latest start time for B is $10 - 2 = 8$ and the latest start time for A is $3 - 3 = 0$. The latest time for event 1 must allow both of these to start on time and this means a latest time of 0. Figure 5.14 shows the network with latest times added for each event.

The formal statement of the calculation of latest event time is:

$$LT(n) = ET(n)$$

and

$$LT(i) = \underset{i}{\text{MIN}} \, [LT(j) - D(i,j)]$$

where: $LT(i)$ = latest time of event i

$\quad n \quad$ = number of events (with the terminal event numbered n)

> The latest time for an event is the latest time which allows *all* following activities to be started on time.

Some of the events have a certain amount of flexibility in timing (event 3, for example, can occur any time between week 2 and week 10, while event 7 can occur any time between weeks 3 and 11). Other events are fixed without any leeway (events 1, 2 and 5, for example). The amount an event can move is called the 'slack', which is defined as the difference between the latest and earliest times.

A practical introduction to management science

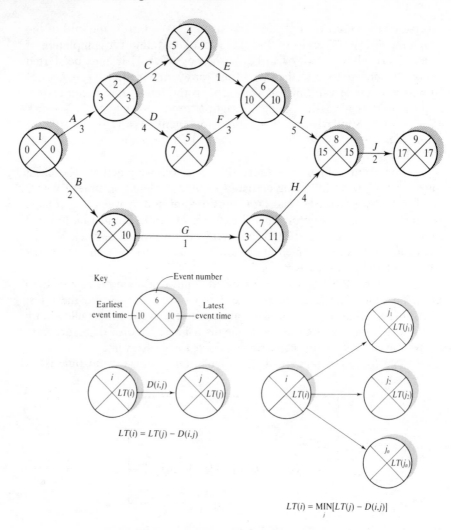

Figure 5.14 Network with latest event times added.

> Slack for = latest time − earliest time
> event i for i for i
>
> $S(i) = LT(i) - ET(i)$

The more slack an event has the more scope there is for adjustment and less chance of problems. If there is no slack an event must occur at the specified time and any delay will cause the whole project to be delayed. Slack values for the example above are shown in Figure 5.15.

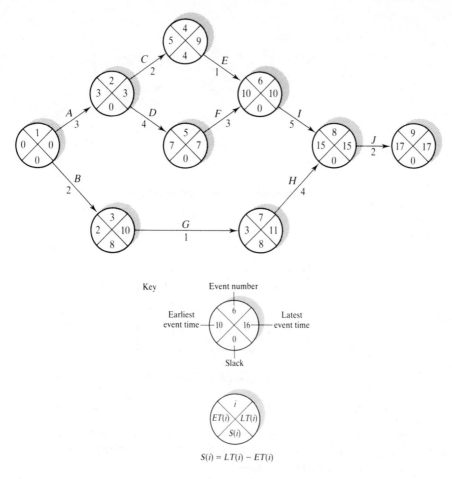

Figure 5.15 Network with event slacks added.

5.6 TIMING OF PROJECTS – ACTIVITIES

The analysis of project times can be extended to activities, where earliest and latest start times (and corresponding earliest and latest finish times) can be found.

The earliest start time for an activity is the earliest time of the preceding event. The earliest finish time is the earliest start time plus the duration (see Figure 5.16).

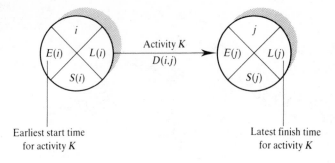

Figure 5.16   Illustrating earliest and latest activity times.

Then:

$$ES(k) = ET(i)$$
and
$$EF(k) = ES(k) + D(i,j)$$

where: $ES(k)$ = earliest start time of activity k which is between events i and j

$EF(k)$ = earliest finish time of activity k

Returning to the example shown in Figure 5.15 and taking one of the activities, say G, the earliest start time is week 2 and the earliest finish time is, therefore, week $2 + 1 = 3$.

The latest start and finish time for an activity can be found using similar reasoning, but working backwards. The latest finish time for an activity is the latest time of the following event: the latest start time is the latest finish time minus the duration.

Then:

$$LF(k) = LT(j)$$
and
$$LS(k) = LF(k) - D(i,j)$$

where: $LF(k)$ = latest finish of activity k which is between events i and j

$LS(k)$ = latest start time of activity k

Thus, for activity G the latest finish would be week 11 and the latest start would be week $11 - 1 = 10$.

Repeating these calculations for all activities in the project gives the figures in Table 5.8.

Table 5.8

Activity	Duration	Earliest start	Earliest finish	Latest start	Latest finish
A	3	0	3	0	3
B	2	0	2	8	10
C	2	3	5	7	9
D	4	3	7	3	7
E	1	5	6	9	10
F	3	7	10	7	10
G	1	2	3	10	11
H	4	3	7	11	15
I	5	10	15	10	15
J	2	15	17	15	17

In this table there are some activities which have flexibility in time: activity G, as we have seen, can start as early as day 2 or as late as day 10, while activity C can start as early as day 3 or as late as day 7. Conversely, there are other activities which have no flexibility at all: activities A, D, F, I and J have no freedom and their latest start time is the same as their earliest start time. These activities have to be done at a fixed time and if they are late the whole project is delayed. Such activities are 'critical' and they form a continuous path through the network which is called the 'critical path'. The length of this path determines the overall project duration. If one of the critical activities is extended by a certain amount the overall project duration is extended by this amount, or if one of the critical activities is delayed by some time the overall project duration is again extended by the time of the delay. Conversely, if one of the critical activities is reduced in duration the overall project duration may be reduced by this amount. Sometimes there is more than one critical path in a network, but we will return to the effects of this later.

Those activities which have some flexibility in timing are the 'non-critical' activities and these may be delayed or extended without necessarily affecting the overall project duration.

In the same way that slack defined the amount of movement available for an event, 'float' defines the amount of movement available in activities. We will consider three different kinds of float for an activity, each of which has a specific purpose. The first is 'total float' which is the difference between the maximum amount of time available for an activity and the time actually used.

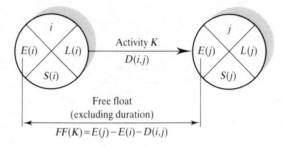

Figure 5.17 Calculation of total float for an activity.

$$\boxed{\begin{array}{c} \text{Total float} = \text{latest finish} - \text{earliest start} - \text{duration} \\ TF(k) = LT(j) - ET(i) - D(i,j) \end{array}}$$

This is zero for critical activities and will take some positive value for non-critical activities. The total float is the maximum expansion which is possible for an activity without affecting the completion date of the project (see Figure 5.17).

If all activities start at their earliest times, a 'free float' can be defined as the maximum expansion possible without affecting any following activity. This is illustrated in Figure 5.18.

$$\boxed{\begin{array}{c} \text{Free float} = \text{earliest time} - \text{earliest time} - \text{duration} \\ \text{of following} \quad \text{of preceding} \\ \text{event} \qquad \text{event} \\ FF(k) = ET(j) - ET(i) - D(i,j) \end{array}}$$

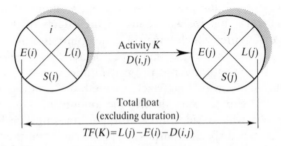

Figure 5.18 Calculation of free float for an activity.

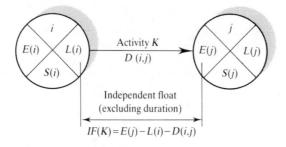

Figure 5.19 Calculation of independent float for an activity.

Finally, if every activity preceding an activity finishes as late as possible and every activity following starts as early as possible, there may still be some 'independent float' which is defined as:

> Independent float = earliest time − latest time − duration
> of following   of preceding
> event   event
>
> $$IF(k) = ET(j) - LT(i) - D(i,j)$$

This is illustrated in Figure 5.19.

This is the maximum expansion possible without affecting either preceding or following activities.

Calculating the floats for activity G in the example has

$$ET(i) = 2,\ LT(i) = 10,\ ET(j) = 3,\ LT(j) = 11\ \text{and}\ D(i,j) = 1.$$

Then:

$$TF(k) = LT(j) - ET(i) - D(i,j) = 11 - 2 - 1 = 8$$
$$FF(k) = ET(j) - ET(i) - D(i,j) = 3 - 2 - 1 = 0$$
$$IF(k) = ET(j) - LT(i) - D(i,j) = 3 - 10 - 1 = -8\ (= 0)$$

Activities only have independent float if there is still spare time when preceding activities finish as late as possible and following activities start as early as possible. Many activities which are squeezed for time will have zero independent float and in some cases it will go negative (when it is conventionally recorded as zero).

Repeating the calculations for other activities in the example gives the results in Table 5.9.

A practical introduction to management science

Table 5.9

Activity	Duration	ES	EF	LS	LF	Total	Free	Indep.	
A	3	0	3	0	3	0	0	0	*
B	2	0	2	8	10	8	0	0	
C	2	3	5	7	9	4	0	0	
D	4	3	7	3	7	0	0	0	*
E	1	5	6	9	10	4	4	0	
F	3	7	10	7	10	0	0	0	
G	1	2	3	10	11	8	0	0 (−8)	
H	4	3	7	11	15	8	8	0	
I	5	10	15	10	15	0	0	0	*
J	2	15	17	15	17	0	0	0	*

The *Float* columns are headed *Total*, *Free*, *Indep.*

Critical activities have zero floats, while non-critical activities all have some total float at least. Activity E, for example, could be expanded by up to 4 days without affecting either the overall duration of the project or any following activity. Activity C could also be expanded by up to four days, but following activities would then start at their latest time.

WORKED EXAMPLE 5.5

A small telephone exchange is to be built and the project is divided into ten major activities with estimated durations (in days) and dependencies shown in Table 5.10. Draw the network for this project, find its duration and calculate the floats of each activity.

Table 5.10

Activity	Description	Duration	Depends on
A	design internal equipment	10	–
B	design exchange building	5	A
C	order parts for equipment	3	A
D	order material for building	2	B
E	wait for equipment parts	15	C
F	wait for building material	10	D
G	employ equipment assemblers	5	A
H	employ building workers	4	B
I	install equipment	20	E, G, J
J	complete building	30	F, H

204

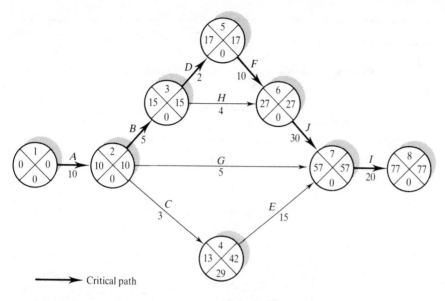

➤ Critical path

Figure 5.20 Network for Worked example 5.5.

Table 5.11

Activity	Duration	ES	EF	LS	LF	Total	Free	Indep.	
							Float		
A	10	0	10	0	10	0	0	0	*
B	5	10	15	10	15	0	0	0	*
C	3	10	13	39	42	29	0	0	
D	2	15	17	15	17	0	0	0	*
E	15	13	28	42	57	29	29	0	
F	10	17	27	17	27	0	0	0	*
G	5	10	15	52	57	42	42	42	
H	4	15	19	23	27	8	8	8	
I	20	57	77	57	77	0	0	0	*
J	30	27	57	27	57	0	0	0	*

SOLUTION

The network for this is shown in Figure 5.20 and repeating the calculations described above gives the results in Table 5.11.

The duration of the project is 77 days, defined by the critical path A, B, D, F, I and J.

WORKED EXAMPLE 5.6

Draw the network represented by the dependence table in Table 5.12 and calculate the floats for each activity.

Table 5.12

Activity	Duration (weeks)	Depends on
A	3	–
B	1	–
C	1	B
D	5	A
E	8	B
F	12	A, C
G	5	D, E
H	2	E
I	3	D

SOLUTION

The network for this project is shown in Figure 5.21 and the float calculations in Table 5.13. There are three dummy activities in the network and the analysis for these is exactly the same as for real activities.

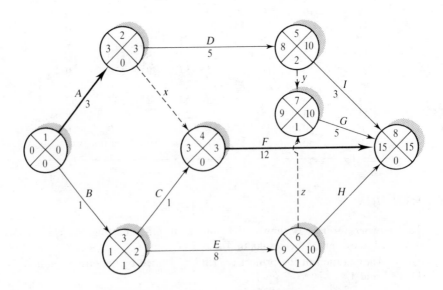

Figure 5.21 Network for Worked example 5.6.

Table 5.13

Activity	Duration	ES	EF	LS	LF	Total	Float Free	Indep.	
A	3	0	3	0	3	0	0	0	*
B	1	0	1	1	2	1	0	0	
C	1	1	2	2	3	1	1	0	
D	5	3	8	5	10	2	0	0	
E	8	1	9	2	10	1	0	0 (−1)	
F	12	3	15	3	15	0	0	0	*
G	5	9	14	10	15	1	1	0	
H	2	9	11	13	15	4	4	3	
I	3	8	11	12	15	4	4	2	
x	0	3	3	3	3	0	0	0	*
y	0	8	8	10	10	2	1	0 (−1)	
z	0	9	9	10	10	1	0	0 (−1)	

The critical path is A, x and F, which gives the project an overall duration of 15 days.

In summary

The determination of times for events and activities is an important part of project planning. An earliest and latest time can be found for each event, with 'slack' defined as the difference between these. An earliest and latest start and finish time can be found for each activity. The amount of leeway can be measured by the floats (total, free and independent). Critical activities have no leeway at all and form the critical path(s).

SELF ASSESSMENT QUESTIONS

5.6 How are the earliest and latest times for an event calculated?

5.7 What is meant by the 'slack' of an event?

5.8 What is meant by the 'float' of an activity and how is this defined?

5.9 What is a 'critical path'?

5.7 CHANGING PROJECT DURATIONS

Project durations may need changing for two main reasons:

(1) when a network is analysed the timing is unacceptable (it may, for example, take longer than the organization has available).

(2) during the execution of a project an activity might take longer than originally planned.

5.7.1 Delays in projects

Taking the second of these, we want to know how an increase in the duration of one activity effects the duration of the project as a whole. We already know that increasing the duration of a critical activity will extend the project by the same amount, so this analysis is primarily concerned with extending non-critical activities. The effects can be found from the floats, as illustrated in the following example.

WORKED EXAMPLE 5.7

Draw the network for the dependence table in Table 5.14 and calculate the total, free and independent float of each activity.

Table 5.14

Activity	Duration	Depends on
A	4	–
B	14	–
C	10	A
D	6	A
E	4	C
F	6	D, E
G	12	B

SOLUTION

The network for this is shown in Figure 5.22, with calculated times and floats given in Table 5.15.

The critical path is B and G and the project duration is 26.

A close look at activity D shows how delays in a non-critical activity affect the project duration. D has an independent float of 6 so any extension up to this would have no effect on any other activity in the project. If the duration increases above 6 other activities would be affected. If the duration of D is increased by 7 to 13, this makes no difference to the event times on the network, but other

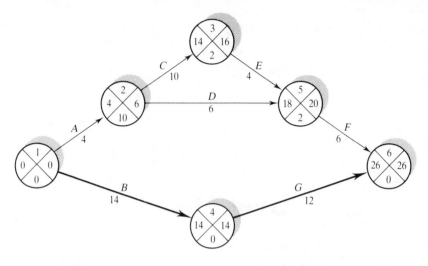

Figure 5.22   Network for Worked example 5.7.

Table 5.15

Activity	Duration	ES	EF	LS	LF	Float			
						Total	Free	Indep.	
A	4	0	4	2	6	2	0	0	
B	14	0	14	0	14	0	0	0	*
C	10	4	14	6	16	2	0	0 (−2)	
D	6	4	10	14	20	10	8	6	
E	4	14	18	16	20	2	0	0 (−2)	
F	6	18	24	20	26	2	2	0	
G	12	14	26	14	26	0	0	0	*

activities are now affected. Originally A could finish as late as 6 and F could start as early as 18. This is still true provided only one of them occurs; it is no longer possible for *both* A to finish at 6 and F to start at 18 as D does not fit in the gap.

If the duration of D is raised by 9 to 15 (see Figure 5.23) all its free float is used and following activities are affected. In particular the early start time for F is delayed from 18 to 19.

Finally, if D is expanded by 11 to 17, all the total float is used and the project will be delayed. Originally there was a total float of 10 and, as the activity has been expanded by 11, the project will be delayed by 1. This can be shown in Figure 5.24 where the critical path has switched from B and G to A, D and F.

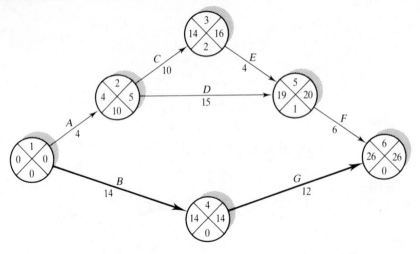

Figure 5.23 Showing the effect of increasing the duration of D to 15.

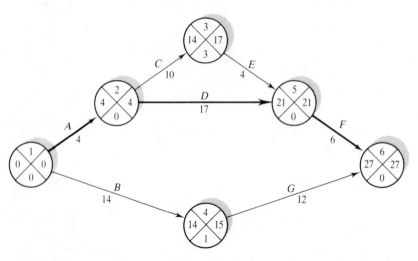

Figure 5.24 Showing the effect of increasing the duration of D to 17.

In summary

Whenever the duration of an activity expands beyond the independent float it begins to interfere with other activities. When it expands beyond the free float it affects following activities and when it expands by more than the total float the critical path changes and the project is delayed by an amount:

expansion of activity − total float of activity

WORKED EXAMPLE 5.8

A project consists of ten activities with estimated durations (in weeks) and dependencies shown in Table 5.16. What are the estimated duration of the project and the earliest and latest times for activities?

Table 5.16

Activity	Depends	Duration	Activity	Depends	Duration
A	–	8	F	C, D	10
B	A	6	G	B, E, F	5
C	–	10	H	F	8
D	–	6	I	G, H, J	6
E	C	2	J	A	4

If activity B requires special equipment to be hired when should this be scheduled?

Suppose a check on the project at week 12 showed that activity F is running two weeks late, that activity J would now take six weeks, and that the equipment for B would not arrive until week 18 what effect will this have on the overall project duration?

SOLUTION

The network for this project is shown in Figure 5.25 with the times and floats shown in Table 5.17.

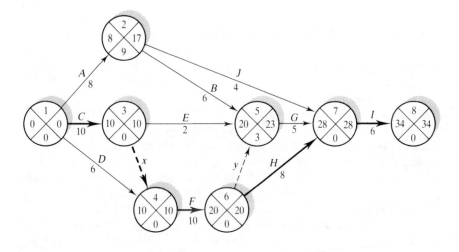

Figure 5.25 Network for Worked example 5.8.

211

Table 5.17

Activity	*Duration*	*ES*	*EF*	*LS*	*LF*	*Float* *Total*	*Free*	*Indep.*	
A	8	0	8	9	17	9	0	0	
B	6	8	14	17	23	9	6	0	
C	10	0	10	0	10	0	0	0	*
D	6	0	6	4	10	4	4	4	
E	2	10	12	21	23	11	8	8	
F	10	10	20	10	20	0	0	0	*
G	5	20	25	23	28	3	3	0	
H	8	20	28	20	28	0	0	0	*
I	6	28	34	28	34	0	0	0	*
J	4	8	12	24	28	16	16	7	
x	0	10	10	10	10	0	0	0	*
y	0	20	20	23	23	3	0	0	

Activity B can start as early as week 8 or as late as week 17 so the equipment could be hired for 6 weeks starting anywhere within this period.

Activity F is critical and if it is running two weeks late the whole project will be delayed by two weeks and will not finish until week 36. Activity D has four weeks of independent float, so an extension of two weeks will make no difference to the project. If the equipment for B is available between weeks 18 and 24 this would normally delay the project by a week (with the path B,G,I becoming critical), but as activity F is already delaying the project by two weeks this will have no additional effect.

5.7.2 Reducing the length of a project

The other problem of timing, where the initial length is excessive and must be reduced, can be tackled in a similar way. Firstly, we know that if the duration of a project is to be reduced this must be done by reducing the durations of critical activities; reducing the duration of non-critical activities will have no effect on the overall project duration. There must come a point, however, when the duration of the critical path is reduced so much that another path through the network becomes critical. This point can be found from the total float on paths parallel to the critical path. When the critical path is reduced by more than the total float of a parallel path, the parallel path becomes critical.

It should also be remembered that reductions in the duration of an activity will probably need more resources, and have a higher cost. A decision must be made about the optimal duration which combines reasonable timing and acceptable cost. The costs of 'crashing' activities will vary and reductions in project length should be found by crashing the cheapest critical activities.

WORKED EXAMPLE 5.9

The network shown in Figure 5.26 has a project duration of 14 with A, B and C as the critical path.

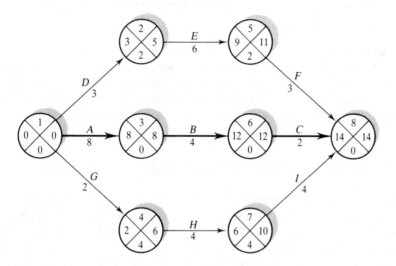

Figure 5.26 Network for Worked example 5.9 (with original times).

If each activity can be reduced by up to 50% of the original duration, how would you reduce the overall duration to:

(a) 13 weeks
(b) 11 weeks
(c) 9 weeks?

If reductions cost an average of £1000 per week what would be the cost of finishing the project by week 9?

SOLUTION

(a) A reduction of one week is needed in the critical path, so reducing the longest activity (as it is usually easier to find savings in longer activities) would give A a duration of 7 weeks and the project could be finished by week 13.

(b)   To finish in 11 weeks requires a further reduction of two weeks in the critical path, and this can again be removed from A. Unfortunately the path D, E, F now becomes critical with a duration of 12 weeks and a week must be removed from E (again chosen as the longest activity in the critical path).

(c)   To finish in nine weeks would need 5 weeks removed from the path A, B, C (say 4 from A and 1 from B), three weeks removed from the path D, E, F (say from E) and one week removed from the path G, H, I (say from H).

To achieve a five-week reduction in project duration has meant a total reduction of 5 + 3 + 1 = 9 weeks from individual activities, at a total cost of £9000.

In summary

A critical path can only be reduced up to a certain limit before another path becomes critical. This limit is the total float of the parallel path. When reducing project durations a check must be kept on the total floats of parallel paths to see if any are about to become critical.

5.8   GANTT CHARTS AND RESOURCE LEVELLING

After the initial planning of a project, there should be constant monitoring of progress to ensure activities are being done at the required times. This is rather difficult if working directly from a network, but a Gantt chart allows planned progress to be monitored much more easily. In essence, a Gantt chart (see Figure 5.27) has a time scale across the bottom, activities are listed down the lefthand side and times when activities should be done are drawn in the body of the chart.

The principles of a Gantt chart can be illustrated (Figure 5.28) for worked example 5.9 (using the initial duration values). If each activity starts as early as possible, the time taken is represented by a continuous line. The total float of an activity is added afterwards as a broken line. As the total float is the maximum expansion which still allows the project to finish on time, there should be no problem keeping to the planned duration while activities are completed before the end of the broken lines.

The main benefit of Gantt charts is that they show clearly the activities which should be in hand (as well as those which should be finished and those which are about to start) at any point in the project. Any necessary expediting, rescheduling and preparation can be easily identified.

Another benefit of Gantt charts comes with resource levelling, which is the final topic we will look at in this chapter.

Consider the Gantt chart shown in Figure 5.28 and assume, for simplicity, that each activity uses one unit of a particular resource (one

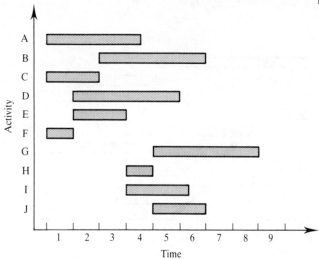

Figure 5.27 Example of a Gantt chart.

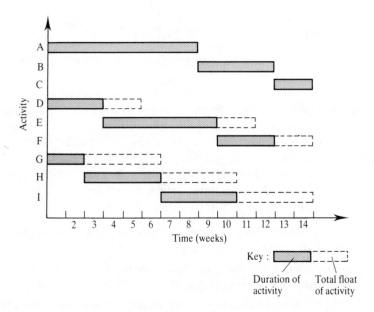

Figure 5.28 Gantt chart for Worked example 5.9.

team of men, say). If all activities start as soon as possible, we could draw a
bar chart to show the resources in use at any time. The project starts with
activities A, D and G so three teams will be used. At the end of week 2
one team can move from G to H, but three teams will still be needed.

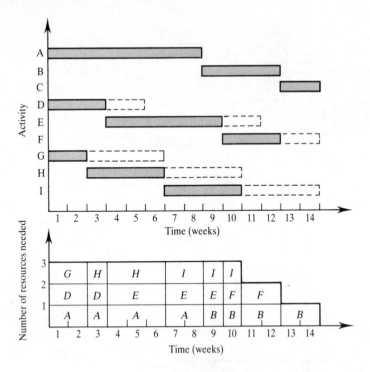

Figure 5.29 Resource use during project of Worked example 5.9.

In this example (see Figure 5.29), the use of resources is steady for most of the project and only begins to fall near the end. This pattern of level resource use is generally the most desirable. It is certainly not typical and there are usually a series of peaks and troughs which should be smoothed by rescheduling activities. As critical activities are at fixed times this smoothing must be done by rescheduling non-critical activities and in particular by delaying those activities with relatively large total floats. One useful approach to resource levelling is:

(1) schedule all activities at their earliest times and find the resources needed throughout the project

(2) for times when too many resources are used delay (or reschedule) non-critical activities to times when less resources are used

(3) if there are conflicts, always give priority to activities with least float, and it is usually easier to start rescheduling activities near the end of a project.

There are formal methods for scheduling workloads but these tend to need a lot of manipulation and are best done using standard computer software. This heuristic approach can be demonstrated in the following example.

WORKED EXAMPLE 5.10

The network shown in Figure 5.30 shows a project consisting of 11 activities over a period of 19 months. If each activity uses one work team, how many teams will be needed at each stage of the project?

Would it be possible to schedule the activities so that a maximum of three work teams are used at any time?

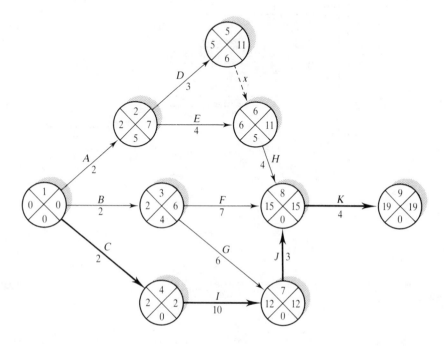

Figure 5.30 Network for Worked example 5.10.

SOLUTION

A Gantt chart for this project is shown in Figure 5.31 with the assumption that all activities start as early as possible. This uses a maximum of five work teams during months 3 to 5. If the number of work teams is to be smoothed, activities with large floats should be delayed. One schedule would delay the start of D until month 7, the start of F until 9 and the start of H until 10. This rescheduling reduces the maximum number of work teams required to 3 and gives a smoother workload (see Figure 5.32).

Rescheduling a project can be done easily if a computer is used for the calculations. Unfortunately the quality of software for network analysis is variable. Some programs need details of the network to be specified as input data and simply do the timing calculations. Others do not do the resource levelling. Most programs give results as printed tables, with very few actually drawing the network. The output from one simple package is shown in Figure 5.33.

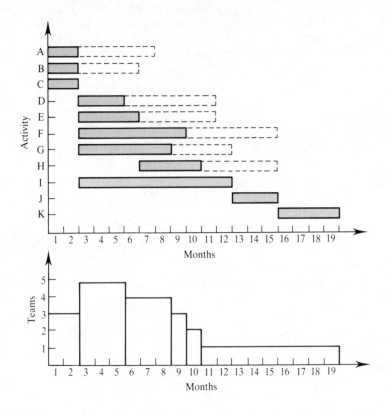

Figure 5.31 Gantt chart and work team requirements assuming all activities start as early as possible.

(a)

Input Data of The Problem Project Page 1

Activity number	Activity name		Start node		End node		Normal duration	Crash duration	Normal cost		Crash cost	
1	<Aone	>	<1	>	<2	>	<4.0000>	<3.5000>	<100.00	>	<150.00	>
2	<Btwo	>	<1	>	<3	>	<5.0000>	<4.5000>	<200.00	>	<250.00	>
3	<Cthree	>	<2	>	<4	>	<2.0000>	<2.0000>	<150.00	>	<150.00	>
4	<Dfour	>	<3	>	<5	>	<6.0000>	<5.5000>	<800.00	>	<1200.0	>
5	<Efive	>	<4	>	<6	>	<4.0000>	<3.5000>	<450.00	>	<800.00	>
6	<Fsix	>	<5	>	<6	>	<7.0000>	<6.5000>	<1200.0	>	<1500.0	>

Figure 5.33 Illustrating a typical network analysis package: (a) input data; (b) output analysis.

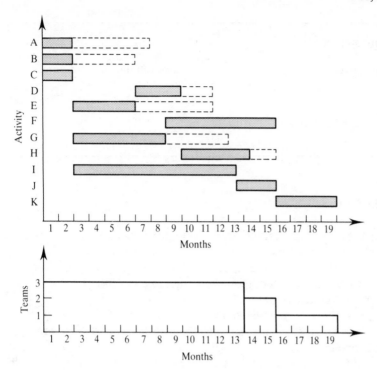

Figure 5.32 Gantt chart and work team requirements with activities rescheduled to smooth load.

(b)

```
                    CPM Analysis for Project    Page  1

   Activity  Activity  Earliest  Latest    Earliest  Latest    Slack
   Number    Name      Start     Start     Finish    Finish    LS-ES

      1       Aone      0         8.0000    4.0000    12.000    8.0000
      2       Btwo      0         0         5.0000    5.0000    Critical
      3       Cthree    4.0000    12.000    6.0000    14.000    8.0000
      4       Dfour     5.0000    5.0000    11.000    11.000    Critical
      5       Efive     6.0000    14.000    10.000    18.000    8.0000
      6       Fsix      11.000    11.000    18.000    18.000    Critical

            Completion time = 18    Total cost = 2900
```

Critical paths for Project with completion time = 18   Total cost = 2900

CP £ 1   :
    Btwo   Dfour   Fsix
  1========>   3========>   5========>   6

Figure 5.33   (cont.)

SELF ASSESSMENT QUESTIONS

5.10 By how much can the duration of a critical path usefully be reduced when trying to shorten a project?

5.11 What are the main benefits of Gantt charts?

5.12 How can the use of resources be smoothed during a project?

CONCLUSIONS

This chapter has described the way in which projects can be represented by networks and the ways in which these networks can be used in planning. The overall approach has been to divide projects into self-contained activities and then show the relationships between these on an 'activity on arrow' network.

The earliest and latest times for events can be found from the network, together with slacks. Earliest and latest start and finish times can be found for activities, together with total, free and independent floats. Critical paths can be found to identify those activities which set the duration of the project and need particular attention.

Gantt charts allow the progress of a project to be monitored and can be used to reschedule activities so that resource requirements can be smoothed over time.

PROBLEMS

5.1 Draw a network for the dependence table in Table 5.18.

Table 5.18

Activity	Depends on	Activity	Depends on
A	F	H	K
B	–	I	K
C	–	J	G, I, M
D	A, H, J	K	C
E	–	L	C
F	E	M	F
G	B, L		

5.2 Draw a network for the dependence table in Table 5.19.

Table 5.19

Activity	Depends on		Activity	Depends on
A	H		I	F
B	H		J	I
C	K		K	L
D	I, M		L	F
E	F		M	L, O
F	–		N	H
G	E, L		O	A, B
H	E			

5.3 If each activity in problem 5.2 has a duration of one week, find the earliest and latest times for each event and the slacks. Calculate the earliest and latest start and finish times for each activity and the corresponding total, free and independent floats.

5.4 Do a complete analysis of times for the project described by the dependence table in Table 5.20.

Table 5.20

Activity	Depends	Duration		Activity	Depends	Duration
A	B, E	3		J	K, L, Q	7
B	M	5		K	C, N	1
C	P	4		L	O	4
D	G, H, J	8		M	–	6
E	I	4		N	O	2
F	–	6		O	F	5
G	A	5		P	–	8
H	B, C, E, L	7		Q	O	2
I	–	2				

If each activity can be reduced by up to two, what is the shortest duration of the project and which activities are reduced?

5.5 Draw a Gantt chart for the project described in problem 5.4. If each activity uses one team of men, draw a graph of manpower requirements assuming each activity starts as soon as possible. How might these requirements be smoothed?

5.6 Analyse the times and resource requirements of the project described by the data in Table 5.21.

Table 5.21

Activity	Depends on	Duration	Resources
A	–	4	1
B	A	4	2
C	A	3	4
D	B	5	4
E	C	2	2
F	D, E	6	3
G	–	3	3
H	G	7	1
I	G	6	5
J	H	2	3
K	I	4	4
L	J, K	8	2

5.7 In the project described in problem 5.6 it costs £1000 to reduce the duration of an activity by 1. If there is £12,000 available to reduce the overall duration of the project how should this be allocated and what is the shortest time in which the project can be completed? What are the minimum resources needed by the revised schedule?

CASE STUDY – ACME PRODUCTS LTD

Background

Acme Products Ltd is a small manufacturing company based in the North of Italy. It designs and makes cheap gadgets for the home, usually for use in kitchens or cars. The general characteristics of these gadgets are that they are simple, contain few parts, are cheap, include a new gimmick of some kind and have a short life cycle. Acme makes the initial designs for its gadgets, manufactures them, markets them vigorously for a short time and, when sales decline, they withdraw old products and introduce new ones. Recent products have included a slicer for vegetables, a pocket coin holder, a windscreen de-icer which plugs into car cigarette lighters, a window cleaning brush which is attached to a hosepipe, a door chime that plays tunes and a sensor that stops saucepans from boiling over. The company is marketing about 20 products at any time.

Because the gadgets use simple technology and are aimed at rapidly changing demands, Acme's survival depends on a frequent change of products, with an average product manufactured for only six months. The stages between initial design and final marketing can usually be done within a few weeks. There is strong competition from other companies, mainly based in the Far East, and if a product is priced too highly or is not withdrawn quickly from the market, competitors introduce items which are very similar in design, usually lower quality and considerably cheaper. Sometimes a product catches the public imagination and sales are very heavy: in these cases it is not withdrawn and a few such items have been manufactured continuously for several years.

Most of the company's plans are based on experience of the market and do not involve any strategic planning or long term forecasts. Market surveys are only done to assess demand for a new product. Acme work on the assumption that if they make an item which has some gimmick, they can advertise it and create sufficient demand for the item to be produced for several months. If something goes wrong the company can respond very quickly and either increase or stop production. A recently introduced product did not sell as well as expected and Acme have decided to stop production and bring in a replacement item as soon as possible.

Although Acme has considerable practice in changing products it has recently been looking at ways of reducing the time needed to introduce new ones. In particular they want to know if project network analysis could be used effectively and they have decided to examine this for the introduction of their next product.

A meeting was held between various operational areas of the company to discuss the new product (a shelf system which would allow several dishes of varying size and depth to be put into a microwave oven at the same time). At this meeting each area put forward their views on the times necessary for various activities and an agreed summary of the meeting follows.

Design

The new product is slightly more complicated than usual, but quite a lot of work has already been done and initial designs could be ready in 14 days. These are submitted to Production who make a set of prototypes which are passed to Sales and Marketing for trials.

When the results from a market survey are returned the design team would make any changes necessary (taking 6 days) and again pass details to Production.

The design team also works on packaging for the product which takes five days and uses some of the artwork supplied by Advertising. The ideas on packaging are then sent to specialist manufacturers, who tender for the work (18 days). When the best tender is accepted, discussions may alter the design somewhat to reduce costs (three days) and the packaging is then available 14 days later.

Production

Preparations for manufacturing the product are in several stages. Initially a single machine is set-up (five days) to make prototypes (which takes eight days). This machine is then available for training production staff (for two days) so they are familiar with the new product.

With their experience of setting-up the single machine the final production is planned (taking four days) and when designs for the product are finalized the remaining production machines are set-up (10 days) and production starts on samples. With usual teething problems it is estimated that the first production samples will be ready five days after the start of production. The machines then have any necessary fine tuning (two days) and are ready to start final production in earnest.

Sales and Marketing

The Sales and Marketing department makes initial plans for the campaign to launch the product (five days), but their effort really starts with a market survey using the prototypes (10 days). The results of this survey are passed back to Design with suggested modifications.

Later, when the sample of final products is ready, Sales and Marketing arrange a series of demonstrations of the product in various department stores and shows. This campaign needs some planning (three days), followed by the recruitment of sufficient demonstrators (eight days) and their training (one day).

When the sample of products is available, company salesman take them around shops and obtain orders, usually taking five days for first orders to arrive at the company.

Sales and Marketing arrange delivery of the finished product to shops. Tenders are requested from transport companies (18 days) and the cheapest bid is accepted, with deliveries then made within two days of manufacture.

Advertising

Associated with the marketing effort is an advertising campaign which must be planned (six days) and run (10 days) starting at least two days after products are available in shops. The artwork for this campaign takes 10 days to prepare and is based on pictures of the initial sample of products. This artwork is also used in brochures (which take eight days to write and seven days to print) and for the packaging (which is worked on by Design).

Timing

A network is needed for the project. As the item is to be introduced as soon as possible, any possible savings in time should be identified.

Generally, each department is so small that it can only work on one activity at a time, but if pressure is exerted they might work over the weekends to meet deadlines. If this seems inadequate, extra staff might be employed, but both of these alternatives have associated costs.

Suggested questions on the case study

- Should Acme consider project network analysis? What would the advantages be?
- What are the activities involved in launching a new product?
- What are the dependencies of these activities?
- What does a network for the project look like?
- How long will the project take and what are the critical activities?
- How might the project duration be reduced and what are the associated costs? Would such a reduction be worthwhile?
- What assumptions have been made in these analyses?

SOLUTIONS TO SELF ASSESSMENT QUESTIONS

5.1 Project management is concerned with the planning, scheduling and controlling of activities in a project and hence the management of resources. Planning is necessary to ensure that projects run on time and that resources are used efficiently. For small projects this may be done informally, but for larger projects some formal method of planning is needed.

5.2 The aims are to:

- present relevant information in an easily understandable form (preferably graphical);
- identify the order in which activities should be done;
- estimate how long the project will take;
- find the maximum delay in each activity which will not delay the project and hence indicate which activities are most critical to the completion of the project;
- identify the time by which each activity must be finished if the project is not to be delayed;
- allow scheduling of resources to provide steady utilization during the project;
- allow rapid adjustment for changes in activity duration or order;

- enable effective monitoring and control of activities during the project.

5.3 A list of all activities in the project and the immediate predecessors of each activity. Durations, resources needed and other factors can be added but these are not essential for drawing the network.

5.4 The two main rules are:

- before an activity can begin all preceding activities must be finished;
- the arrows representing activities imply precedence only and neither the length nor orientation is significant.

There are also some secondary rules:

- a network has only one starting and finishing event;
- each event has a unique identifying number;
- any two events can only be connected by one activity.

5.5 The two uses of dummy activities are:

- to ensure only one activity is directly between any two nodes;
- to ensure the logic of the dependence table is maintained in the network.

5.6 The earliest time of event j is the earliest time by which *all* preceding activities can be finished.

$$ET(1) = 0$$
$$ET(j) = \text{MAX}_i[ET(i) + D(i,j)]$$

The latest time for an event is the latest time which allows *all* following activities to be started on time.

$$LT(n) = ET(n)$$
$$LT(i) = \text{MIN}_j[LT(j) - D(i,j)]$$

5.7 The slack of an event is the amount it can move without affecting the project duration. It is defined as the difference between the latest and earliest times.

$$S(i) = LT(i) - ET(i)$$

5.8 Float measures the amount of flexibility there is in an activities timing. Total float is the difference between the maximum amount of time available for an activity and the time actually used.

$$TF(k) = LT(j) - ET(i) - D(i,j)$$

Free float is the maximum expansion possible without affecting any following activity.

$$FF(k) = ET(j) - ET(i) - D(i,j)$$

Independent float is the maximum expansion possible without affecting any other activity.

$$IF(k) = ET(j) - LT(i) - D(i,j)$$

5.9 The critical path (or paths) is the chain of activities which have no float and therefore determine the project duration. It follows that if any critical activity is extended or delayed the whole project will be delayed.

5.10 A critical path can only usefully be shortened until another parallel path becomes critical. This point is found from the total float of activities on parallel paths: when a critical path is reduced by more than the total float of activities on a parallel path, the parallel path itself becomes critical.

5.11 Gantt charts show the activities which should be in hand, as well as those which should have finished and those which are about to start at any point in a project. Any necessary expediting, rescheduling and preparation can be identified quickly. They can also be used for resource levelling.

5.12 Resources used can be levelled by delaying non-critical activities to times when less resources are needed. Priority should be given to activities with least float and it is often easiest to reschedule activities starting near the end of the project and working backwards.

REFERENCES FOR FURTHER READING

Original descriptions

Kelley J. E. and Walker M. R. (1959). Critical Path Planning and Scheduling. *Proceedings of the Eastern Joint Computer Conference*, Boston, pp. 160–173

Special Projects Office, Department of the Navy (1958). *PERT, Program Evaluation Research Task*. Phase 1 Summary Report, pp. 646–669

Battersby A. (1970). *Network Analysis for Planning and Scheduling* London: Macmillan

Cleland D. I. and King W. R. (1983). *Project Management Handbook* New York: Van Nostrand Reinhold

Elmaghraby S. B. (1977). *Activity Networks: project planning and control by network models* New York: McGraw-Hill

Kerzner H. (1984). *Project Management for Executives* New York: Van Nostrand Reinhold

Martino R. L. (1970). *Critical Path Networks* New York: McGraw-Hill

Moder J. J., Phillips C. R. and Davis E. W. (1983). *Project Management with CPM, PERT and Precedence Diagramming* 3rd edn. New York: Van Nostrand Reinhold

Weist J. D. and Levy F. K. (1977). *A management guide to PERT/CPM* 2nd edn. New Jersey: Prentice Hall

Chapter 6

Linear programming

SYNOPSIS

A common problem in business is the allocation of resources to achieve some stated objective. There will inevitably be constraints on the options available and such problems are often referred to as problems of 'constrained optimization'. This chapter describes linear programming, which is a widely used technique for finding optimal solutions to such problems. In this sense 'programming' is used in its broad sense of 'planning' and has nothing to do with computer programming.

The characteristic approach of linear programming (LP) is illustrated by an example of production planning. This highlights the assumptions made as well as the general methodology.

The usual stages in tackling a linear programming problem are:

- formulation (getting the problem in the right form);
- solution (finding an optimal solution to the problem);
- sensitivity analysis (seeing what happens when the problem is changed slightly or the solution is adjusted).

For real problems, formulation is usually the most difficult stage, especially as reliable data is often difficult to find. Solutions to small problems can be found using a graphical approach, but computers must be used for problems of any size. Output from one LP package is described here. There are several aspects to sensitivity analysis and in this chapter we will concentrate on the use of marginal values (or shadow prices).

It is possible to adopt a very rigorous mathematical approach to LP, but this is rather demanding and often tedious. This chapter will illustrate concepts by reference to examples.

OBJECTIVES

After reading this chapter and doing the numerical exercises you should be able to:

- understand the concept of constrained optimization;
- formulate linear programmes in algebraic terms;
- recognize the assumptions that are made in these formulations;
- use graphical methods to solve linear programmes with two decision variables;
- calculate the effect of changes in the objective function;
- calculate shadow prices and the ranges over which these apply;
- assess the value of introducing additional products;
- appreciate the ways in which larger problems can be solved;
- interpret the results obtained from a computer package;
- recognize some extensions to linear programming.

6.1   INTRODUCTION

Managers are often faced by problems of achieving some objective subject to constraints on the availability of scarce resources. An operations manager might devise a production plan which maximizes the number of units made with the limited resources available to him. A marketing manager might plan an advertising campaign to maximize the impact on potential customers without exceeding a specified budget. A finance manager might maximize return on investment of a limited amount of funds. These problems are concerned with 'constrained maximization' and linear programming (LP) is one method which has proved successful in their solution.

Suppose a manager must decide the number of units of a particular item to make next month. If the profit is £10 on each unit and he decides to make X units, the profit in the month will be $10 * X$. This does not, however, take into account any constraints on the system which must inevitably limit the value of X. The profit will only be $10 * X$ if enough raw materials are available, there is enough equipment and the demand is high enough. Figure 6.1 shows an idealized system (with inputs, processing and outputs) and constraints must operate somewhere or the system would be uncontrolled. These constraints could be on inputs (perhaps shortages of raw materials or skilled workers), processing (with maximum capacity of equipment, buildings, etc.) or output (maximum sales, available transport, etc.).

Figure 6.1 Diagram of an idealized system.

Managers often work with explicit objectives and constraints but, because of uncertainties in plans and operations, decisions are often phrased in terms such as, 'We want to make as much as possible within the limits of production capacity and sales. We will plan 1000 units of item 1 and 2000 units of item 2: this should use 90% of available capacity and if there is any spare we will make more of item 2'. Linear programming helps in such decisions by allowing rational analysis of problems, suggesting solutions and calculating the consequences of alternative plans.

Linear programming was developed in the 1950s, when 'programming' was not used to mean 'computer programming', and the name is derived from the more general meaning of 'planning'. Although it is widely used for production planning, this is not its only use and there are applications in oil and chemical industries, agriculture, financial institutions, food industries, public utilities and many other sectors of industry.

In summary
Linear programming is a method of finding optimal solutions to problems of constrained optimization.

6.2   AN INTUITIVE APPROACH TO PRODUCTION PLANNING

Many of the ideas in this chapter are developed by reference to a simple problem of production planning. We will begin by introducing this problem, which is a typical example of constrained optimization.

A small factory produces two types of liquid fertilizer 'Growbig' and 'Thrive'. These are made by similar processes, using the same equipment for blending raw materials, distilling the mix and finishing (bottling, testing, weighing, etc.). Because the factory has a limited amount of equipment, there are constraints on the total time available for each process (see Figure 6.2). In particular no more than 40 hours of blending is available in a week, 40 hours of distilling and 25 hours of finishing. We will assume that these are the only constraints operating and there are none on, say, sales or availability of raw materials.

The fertilizers are made in batches of 1000 litres and each batch requires the following times on each process.

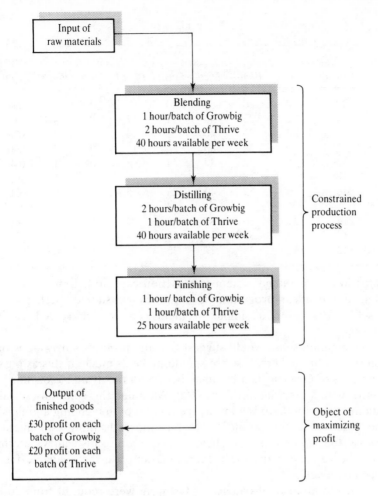

Figure 6.2 The constrained manufacturing process for Growbig and Thrive.

	Growbig	*Thrive*
Blending	1 hour	2 hours
Distilling	2 hours	1 hour
Finishing	1 hour	1 hour

If the factory makes a net profit of £30 on each batch of Growbig and £20 on each batch of Thrive how many batches of each should it make a week?

This problem is clearly one of optimizing an objective (maximizing

Table 6.1

Batches		Hours used			Hours spare			
Growbig	Thrive	Blend	Distl	Finsh	Blend	Distl	Finsh	Profit
20	0	20	40	20	20	0	5	600
19	2	23	40	21	17	0	4	610
18	4	26	40	22	14	0	3	620
17	6	29	40	23	11	0	2	630
16	8	32	40	24	8	0	1	640
15	10	35	40	25	5	0	0	650
14	11	36	39	25	4	1	0	640
13	12	37	38	25	3	2	0	630
12	13	38	37	25	2	3	0	620

profit) in a constrained system (production capacity). Before we look in detail at the linear programming approach we should, perhaps, satisfy ourselves that even a simple problem can not be solved easily by intuition.

Common sense would suggest that the profit on Growbig is higher than the profit on Thrive, so we should make as much of this as possible. 20 batches of Growbig can be made before all the available distilling time is used, with a resulting profit of £600. Although this solution uses all the distilling capacity there is a lot of free time in both blending and finishing. One reaction to this would be to buy more distilling equipment and remove the bottleneck. A cheaper and more satisfactory alternative would be to change the production plan and use the available facilities more effectively.

If the number of batches of Growbig were reduced from 20 to 19 the amount of distilling needed would fall from 40 hours to 38 hours, while the profit would fall by £30. The spare capacity introduced would be enough to make 2 batches of Thrive before distilling again becomes limiting. These two batches would generate profit of £40, increasing total profit for the week by £10.

This intuitive approach could be continued by iteratively decreasing the number of batches of Growbig and increasing the batches of Thrive to give the results in Table 6.1.

The profit rises linearly until it reaches £650 and then decreases linearly, with the optimal solution of about 15 batches of Growbig and 10 batches of Thrive. At the optimal solution the limiting constraint changes from distilling to finishing. This is not coincidence, but we will return to this point later.

Such intuitive analyses could take a lot of effort (although the arithmetic can be done using a spreadsheet package) but there are other weaknesses. To start the process we guessed an initial solution and had no way of judging its quality. The product mix was then changed, using common sense arguments, to see if machine utilization and profit could be increased. This process could be very tedious and there is no means of guaranteeing that the final results are optimal. There would clearly be advantages in using a more formal solution procedure which reduces effort and guarantees optimal solutions, and this is provided by linear programming.

In summary

Intuitive approaches to problems of constrained maximization are unreliable. LP provides a way of ensuring optimal solutions with a reasonable effort.

6.3   FORMULATION OF LINEAR PROGRAMMING PROBLEMS

For the example above we want to determine the optimal number of batches of Growbig and Thrive, so these are the decision variables which can be represented by G and T.

Let G be the number of batches of Growbig made in a week

and

let T be the number of batches of Thrive made in a week.

Obviously, any other name could be used, such as $X1$ and $X2$, GROWBIG and THRIVE or even NumBatGro and NumBatThr. Although there are advantages to each of these we will stick to the single letters.

Consider the blending constraint first. Each batch of Growbig uses one hour of blending, so G batches use $1 * G$ hours of blending. Similarly, each batch of Thrive uses two hours of blending, so T batches use $2 * T$ hours. Adding these together gives the total amount of blending time used as $1 * G + 2 * T$. The maximum amount of blending time available is 40 hours, so the time used must be less than, or at worst equal to, this and we have the first constraint of:

$1 * G + 2 * T \leq 40$ blending constraint

Turning to the distilling constraint, each batch of Growbig uses two hours of distilling, so G batches use $2 * G$ hours. Similarly, each batch of Thrive uses one hour of distilling, so T batches use $1 * T$ hours. Adding these together gives the total amount of distilling used and this must be less than, or at worst equal to, the amount of distilling available (40 hours). This is the second constraint:

$$2 * G + 1 * T \leq 40 \qquad \text{distilling constraint}$$

Similarly, the finishing constraint has the total time used for finishing ($1 * G$ for batches of Growbig plus $1 * T$ for batches of Thrive) less than or equal to the time available (25 hours) to give:

$$1 * G + 1 * T \leq 25 \qquad \text{finishing constraint}$$

These are the three constraints for the process, but there is an additional implicit constraint that the number of batches of Growbig and Thrive must both be positive (the company can not make a negative number of batches). This non-negativity constraint is a standard feature of linear programmes.

$$G \geq 0 \quad \text{and} \quad T \geq 0 \qquad \text{non-negativity constraints}$$

Now the constraints have been developed we can turn to the objective function. In this case the objective will be to maximize the profit. If £30 is made on each batch of Growbig and G batches are made the profit is $30 * G$: if £20 is made on each batch of Thrive and T batches are made the profit is $20 * T$. Adding these gives the total profit to be maximized.
Maximize:

$$30 * G + 20 * T \qquad \text{objective function}$$

The linear programming formulation (or mathematical model) of this problem is now complete with descriptions of:

- problem variables;
- an objective function which is linear with respect to these variables;
- a set of constraints which are linear with respect to the variables;
- a non-negativity constraint.

Maximize:
$$30 * G + 20 * T$$
Subject to:
$$1 * G + 2 * T \leq 40$$
$$2 * G + 1 * T \leq 40$$
$$1 * G + 1 * T \leq 25$$
with $G \geq 0$ and $T \geq 0$

This formulation has made a number of assumptions, two of which are implicit in all LPs. Firstly, it is assumed that the use of resources is proportional to the quantity being produced: if production is doubled the use of resources is doubled, and so on. There are a number of reasons why this assumption may not be valid. Increased production may, for example, use longer batch runs and reduce set-up times for equipment and running-in problems. Conversely, higher production may mean faster throughput with higher rates of scrap and rejects. In linear programmes it is assumed that such affects are included in the coefficients chosen and that the 'proportionality assumption' is valid (at least as a reasonable approximation).

A second assumption is that adding the resources used for each product gives the total amount of resources used. Again there are reasons why this assumption may not be valid. Consider a craft manufacturer where the most skilled craftsmen are used for more complex jobs. If no complex jobs are made in one period the skilled craftsmen will be used on less complex jobs, which will then be done better or faster than usual. Again LP assumes that such interactions are included in the data used and the 'additivity assumption' is valid (at least as a reasonable approximation).

One significant problem with LP may be inferred from these assumptions. A lot of data is required and this must allow for real constraints and be adjusted to ensure the proportionality and additivity assumptions are valid. As with any quantitative analysis, some data will be approximate and may contain errors. As LP uses a lot of data it is sometimes vulnerable to such uncertainties.

WORKED EXAMPLE 6.1

A political campaign wants to acquire enough photocopying machines to provide leaflets for a local election. There are two suitable machines which can be leased for the necessary time. ACTO costs £120 a month to rent, occupies 2.5 square metres of floor space and can produce 15,000 copies a day. ZENMAT costs £150 a month to rent, occupies 1.8 square metres of floor space and can produce 18,500 copies a day. The campaign has allowed up to £1200 a month for copying machines which will be put in a room of 19.2 square metres.

What are the problem variables, objective function and constraints for this problem?

SOLUTION

The problem variables are the things we can vary, which are the number of ACTO and ZENMAT machines leased. The objective is to produce as many copies as possible with constraints on floor space and costs.

Let A be the number of ACTO machines rented and Z the number of ZENMAT machines.

Maximize:

$15{,}000 * A + 18{,}500 * Z$ objective function

Subject to:

$120 * A + 150 * Z \leq 1200$ cost constraint

$2.5 * A + 1.8 * Z \leq 19.2$ space constraint

with

$A \geq 0$ and $Z \geq 0$ non-negativity constraint

WORKED EXAMPLE 6.2

An investment trust has £1 million to invest. After consultation with its financial advisers it decides that there are six possible investments with the characteristics shown in Table 6.2.

Table 6.2

Investment	% risk	% dividend	% growth	Rating
1	18	4	22	4
2	6	5	7	10
3	10	9	12	2
4	4	7	8	10
5	12	6	15	4
6	8	8	8	6

The trust wants to invest the £1 million with minimum risk, but with a dividend of at least £70,000 a year, average growth of at least 12% and average rating of at least 7. Formulate this problem as a linear programme.

SOLUTION

The decision variables are the amount of money put into each investment.

Let $X1$ be the amount of money put into investment 1
$X2$ be the amount of money put into investment 2 and so on.

The objective is to minimize risk.

Minimize:

$0.18 * X1 + 0.06 * X2 + 0.10 * X3 + 0.04 * X4 + 0.12 * X5 + 0.08 * X6$

Constraints are on the amount of money:

$$X1 + X2 + X3 + X4 + X5 + X6 = 1,000,000$$

dividend:

$$0.04 * X1 + 0.05 * X2 + 0.09 * X3 + 0.07 * X4 + 0.05 * X5$$
$$+ 0.08 * X6 \geq 70,000$$

average growth:

$$0.22 * X1 + 0.07 * X2 + 0.12 * X3 + 0.08 * X4 + 0.15 * X5 + 0.08 * X6$$
$$\geq 120,000$$

and rating:

$$4 * X1 + 10 * X2 + 2 * X3 + 10 * X4 + 4 * X5 + 6 * X6 \geq 7,000,000$$

The non-negativity constraints $X1$, $X2$, $X3$, $X4$, $X5$ and $X6 \geq 0$ complete the formulation.

WORKED EXAMPLE 6.3

A local authority is planning to build a number of blocks of flats in an inner city area. Five blocks have been designed, containing flats of four categories (senior citizens, single person, small family and large family). The number of flats in each block, and other relevant information is given in Table 6.3:

Table 6.3

Type of block	No. of flats in each category				No. of storeys	Plan area	Cost per block (£'000)
	1	2	3	4			
A	1	2	4	0	3	5	208
B	0	3	6	0	6	5	320
C	2	2	2	4	2	8	300
D	0	6	0	8	8	6	480
E	0	0	10	5	3	4	480

The council wants to build a total of 500 flats with at least 40 in category 1 and 125 in each of the other categories. In the past, high-rise flats have proved unpopular and the council wants to limit the number of storeys in the development. In particular, the average number of storeys must be at most five and at least half the flats must be in blocks of three or fewer storeys. An area of 300 units has been set aside for the development and any spare land will be used as a park.

Formulate this problem as a linear programme.

237

SOLUTION

The decision variables are the number of blocks of each type to be built.

Let A be the number of blocks of type A built, B the number of blocks of type B and so on.

The objective is to minimize the total cost of the development.
Minimize:

$$208 * A + 320 * B + 300 * C + 480 * D + 480 * E$$

There must be a total of 500 flats, so adding the number of flats in each block gives:

$$7 * A + 9 * B + 10 * C + 14 * D + 15 * E = 500$$

The minimum numbers of flats in each category is specified, so adding the number of flats of category 1 gives:

$$1 * A + 0 * B + 2 * C + 0 * D + 0 * E \geq 40$$

and similarly for the other categories

$$2 * A + 3 * B + 2 * C + 6 * D + 0 * E \geq 125$$
$$4 * A + 6 * B + 2 * C + 0 * D + 10 * E \geq 125$$
$$0 * A + 0 * B + 4 * C + 8 * D + 5 * E \geq 125$$

The average number of storeys in the development must be at most five. This gives the constraint

$$\text{average number of storeys} = \frac{\text{total number of storeys}}{\text{number of blocks}} \leq 5$$

or

$$\frac{3 * A + 6 * B + 2 * C + 8 * D + 3 * E}{A + B + C + D + E} \leq 5$$
$$3 * A + 6 * B + 2 * C + 8 * D + 3 * E \leq 5 * (A + B + C + D + E)$$
$$2 * A - 1 * B + 3 * C - 3 * D + 2 * E \geq 0$$

At least half the flats must be in blocks of three or fewer storeys. Blocks of types A, C and E have three or fewer storeys and the total number of flats is 500, so this constraint can be written as:

$$7 * A + 10 * C + 15 * E \geq 250$$

Finally the area available is limited so

$$5 * A + 5 * B + 8 * C + 6 * D + 4 * E \leq 300$$

The non-negativity condition that A, B, C, D and E are all greater than or equal to zero completes the formulation.

6.1 What is the purpose of linear programming?

6.2 What are the drawbacks of using intuition to solve problems of constrained optimization?

6.3 What are the main assumptions behind linear programming?

6.4 What is meant by a linear programming 'formulation' and what are the components which make up such a formulation?

6.4 GRAPHICAL SOLUTIONS TO LINEAR PROGRAMMES

For most problems of any size the formulation stage is the most difficult, while actually solving the problem can be relatively straightforward. LP problems are almost inevitably solved by computers using a procedure called Simplex and there are many software packages available for this. Here we will not go into the details of the Simplex procedure but will illustrate some general principles. This is not because the process is difficult (it is, in fact, rather straightforward) but it relies on a lot of arithmetic manipulation which is, at best, tedious to do by hand. Later in the chapter we will look at the output from a typical LP package, but here we will use the previous Growbig and Thrive example to illustrate some general principles about the representation of LP problems as graphs.

The blending constraint has $1 * G + 2 * T \leq 40$. The strict equality $1 * G + 2 * T = 40$ can be drawn as a straight line on a graph of G against T as shown in Figure 6.3. (The easiest way to draw lines of this

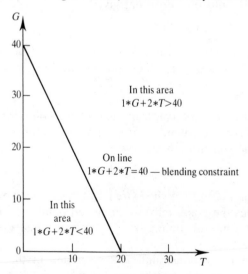

Figure 6.3 Graph of blending constraint.

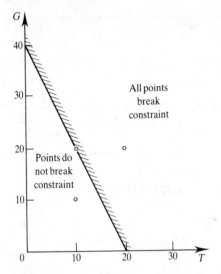

Figure 6.4 Blending constraint divides graph into two areas.

type is to take two convenient points and draw a straight line through them.) Setting, for example, $G = 0$ means that $2 * T = 40$ or $T = 20$: similarly, setting $T = 0$ gives $1 * G = 40$. The constraint line can then be drawn passing through the points $G = 0$, $T = 20$ and $G = 40$, $T = 0$.)

An important observation is that the blending constraint will be broken for any point above this line, while for any point on or below the line the blending constraint will hold. This can be checked by taking any random point. The point $G = 10$, $T = 10$, for example, is below the line and substitution into the constraint gives:

$$1 * 10 + 2 * 10 \leq 40$$

which is true and the constraint is not broken. Conversely the point $G = 20$, $T = 20$ is above the line and substitution gives:

$$1 * 20 + 2 * 20 \leq 40$$

which is not true and the constraint is broken. Points which are actually on the line satisfy the equality, for example the point $G = 20$, $T = 10$ is on the line and substitution gives:

$$1 * 20 + 2 * 10 \leq 40$$

which is true and represents the extreme values allowed by the constraint. The line divides the graph into two areas: all points above the line break the constraint while all points on or below the line do not break the constraint (see Figure 6.4).

The other two constraints can be added in the same way. The distilling constraint is the straight line through $G = 20$, $T = 0$ and $G = 0$,

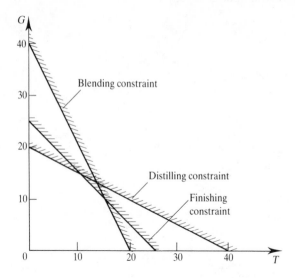

Figure 6.5 Three constraints added to the graph.

$T = 40$. As before, any point above the line breaks the constraint while any point on or below it does not break the constraint and is acceptable for the solution. The Finishing constraint is the straight line through the points $G = 0$, $T = 25$ to $G = 25$, $T = 0$ and again any point above the line will break the constraint and be unacceptable (see Figure 6.5).

Any point which is below all three of the constraint lines represents a valid, feasible solution, but if the point is above any of the lines it will break at least one of the constraints and will not represent a feasible solution. Finally, adding the non-negativity constraints limits feasible solutions to the positive quadrant of the graph and defines a 'feasible region' which represents the area in which all feasible solutions must lie. Any point inside the feasible region represents a valid solution to the problem while any point outside breaks at least one of the constraints (see Figure 6.6).

The next stage of the solution procedure is to examine all feasible solutions and identify the optimal one. This is where the objective function is used.

For this problem the objective function to be maximized is

profit $= 30 * G + 20 * T$

This line can be plotted on the graph of G against T in the same way as the constraints. Although we do not know the optimal value of the profit we could start looking at an arbitrary value of, say, £600. The graph of $30 * G + 20 * T = 600$ can be drawn as before (through two convenient points, say $G = 0$, $T = 30$ and $G = 20$, $T = 0$). Similar lines could be

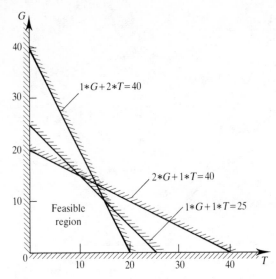

Figure 6.6 Three constraints for the problem (with non-negative conditions) define a feasible region.

drawn for a number of other arbitrary values for profit with the results shown in Figure 6.7.

The lines for different profits are all parallel and the further they are from the origin the higher is the value of the objective function (see Figure 6.8). This observation shows how we can find an optimal solution for the problem. An objective function line can be superimposed on the

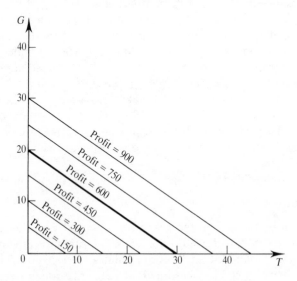

Figure 6.7 Objective function lines for different values of profit.

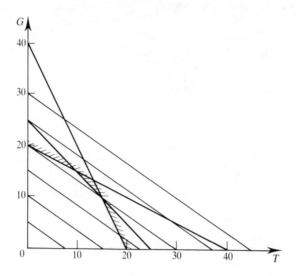

Figure 6.8 Superimposing objective function lines on the constraint graph.

graph of constraints so that it passes through the feasible region. This line is then moved away from the origin and the further it moves the higher is the profit. As the objective function line is moved further out there will come a point where it only just passes through the feasible region and eventually just passes through a single point. This single point is the optimal solution (see Figure 6.9).

The optimal solution can be read from the graph as the point $G = 15$, $T = 10$. This is the point where the distilling constraint crosses the finishing constraint and these are the active constraints which limit production. There must be spare capacity in blending and this constraint does not limit production. The optimal solution can be found more accurately by solving the simultaneous equations of the limiting constraints.

Limiting constraints are:

$2 * G + 1 * T = 40$ distilling

$1 * G + 1 * T = 25$ finishing

which can be solved as simultaneous equations to confirm the optimal solution is $G = 15$ and $T = 10$.

Substituting these values into the objective function gives:

$30 * G + 20 * T = 30 * 15 + 20 * 10 = 650$

as the maximum value for profit.

Substituting $G = 15$ and $T = 12$ into the constraints gives:

Blending: time available = 40 hours

time used $= 1 * G + 2 * T = 1 * 15 + 2 * 10 = 35$

243

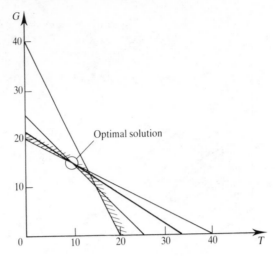

Figure 6.9 Optimal solution is the last point of the feasible region.

spare capacity = 5 hours

Distilling: time available = 40 hours

time used = $2 * G + 1 * T = 2 * 15 + 1 * 10 = 40$

spare capacity = 0

Finishing: time available = 25 hours

time used = $1 * G + 1 * T = 1 * 15 + 1 * 10 = 25$

spare capacity = 0

This effectively solves the linear programme and defines the optimal production plan for the company.

In summary
Constraints can be drawn on a graph to identify a feasible region. An objective function line can be superimposed on this graph. Moving the objective function line away from the origin increases its value and the maximum value is the last point in the feasible region through which the objective function line passes. Moving the objective function line towards the origin decreases its value and the minimum value is the last point in the feasible region through which the objective function line passes.

WORKED EXAMPLE 6.4

Find the optimal solution to the following linear programme.

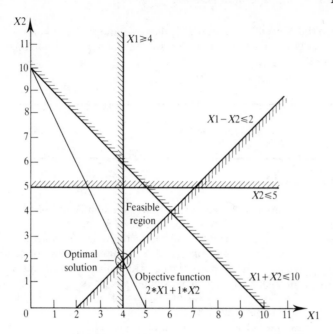

Figure 6.10 Graph for Worked example 6.4.

Minimize $2 * X1 + 1 * X2$

Subject to: $1 * X1 + 1 * X2 \leq 10$ (1)

              $1 * X1 - 1 * X2 \leq 2$ (2)

              $1 * X1 \qquad\qquad \geq 4$ (3)

              $\qquad\quad 1 * X2 \leq 5$ (4)

with $X1$ and $X2$ greater than or equal to zero.

SOLUTION

The formulation for this problem is already complete so we can immediately draw a graph of the problem as shown in Figure 6.10. Sometimes it may not be obvious if a constraint restricts solutions to points above the line or below it (constraint 2, for example). In these cases random points on either side of the line can be taken and those which break the constraint identified.

The objective function is to be minimized so it should be pulled as close to the origin as possible. As the line moves towards the origin the last point it passes through in the feasible region is the point where constraints (2) and (3) cross. Here:

$1 * X1 - 1 * X2 = 2$ (2)

and $1 * X1 \qquad\qquad = 4$ (3)

These can be solved to give the optimal solution of $X1 = 4$ and $X2 = 2$. Substituting these values into the objective function gives a minimum value of $2 * 4 + 1 * 2 = 10$.

WORKED EXAMPLE 6.5

Weekly production schedules are needed for the manufacture of two products X and Y. Each unit of X uses one component made in the factory, while each unit of Y uses two of the components, and the factory has a maximum output of 80 components a week. Each unit of X and Y requires 10 hours of subcontracted work and agreements have been signed with subcontractors for a minimum weekly usage of 200 hours and a maximum weekly usage of 600 hours. The marketing department says that all production of Y can be sold but there is a maximum demand of 50 units of X, despite a long term contract to supply 10 units of X to one customer. The net profit on each unit of X and Y is £200 and £300 respectively.

SOLUTION

The decision variables in this problem are the numbers of units of X and Y which should be made a week.

Let X be the number of units of product X made a week

and let Y be the number of units of product Y made a week.

The formulation then becomes:

Maximize: $200 * X + 300 * Y$

Subject to:

$1 * X + 2 * Y \leq 80$		component availability
$10 * X + 10 * Y \geq 200$		minimum subcontracted
$10 * X + 10 * Y \leq 600$		maximum subcontracted
$1 * X \leq 50$		maximum sales of X
$1 * X \geq 10$		long term contract
$X, Y \geq 0$		non-negativity

This formulation is drawn on the graph shown in Figure 6.11. When the objective function is added and moved as far away from the origin as possible the last point it passes through in the feasible region is about $X = 40$ and $Y = 20$, where the component availability and maximum subcontractor hours constraints are active.

$1 * X + 2 * Y = 80$ component availability

and $10 * X + 10 * Y = 600$ maximum subcontracted

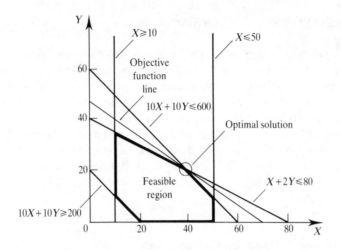

Figure 6.11 Graph for Worked example 6.5.

Solving these simultaneous equations confirms the optimal solution read from the graph and substitution gives a maximum weekly profit of $200 * 40 + 300 * 20$ = £14,000.

A useful observation from these examples is that the feasible region is always convex (that is, it is a polygon without any indentations) and the optimal solution always occurs at a corner or extreme point. This is not a coincidence but is a fundamental property of all linear programmes.

> If an optimal solution exists for a linear programme it will be at an extreme point of the feasible region.

This is a very useful property as it shows how computers can tackle large problems. Essentially they search extreme points around the feasible region until an optimal is found.

SELF ASSESSMENT QUESTIONS

6.5 What is the feasible region for a problem?

6.6 What is the role of the objective function in a LP model?

6.7 What is meant by an extreme point of a feasible region and what is its significance?

6.8 How can the optimal solution be identified on a graph?

6.5   SENSITIVITY ANALYSIS

Before managers implement the optimal solution to a constrained optimization problem they may modify it in the light of their experiences, non-quantifiable factors, assumptions made in the model, and so on. One point which is particularly important concerns the data used in the model. We have already said that linear programmes use a lot of data and this will inevitably include some approximations. We might then ask how sensitive the optimal solution is to such approximations or errors. Sensitivity or post-optimal analysis attempts to answer this question using the solution already found rather than re-solving a modification of the original problem.

6.5.1 Changes in contribution to profit

Returning to the original problem of making Growbig and Thrive we have:

$$\text{Maximize:} \quad 30 * G + 20 * T$$

$$
\begin{array}{llr}
\text{Subject to:} & 1 * G + 2 * T \le 40 & \text{blending} \\
& 2 * G + 1 * T \le 40 & \text{distilling} \\
& 1 * G + 1 * T \le 25 & \text{finishing}
\end{array}
$$

with $G \ge 0$ and $T \ge 0$

Suppose a new accounting convention adjusts the profits to £20 for each batch of Growbig and £30 for each batch of Thrive. The graph of constraints is exactly the same as before and the feasible region is unchanged, but adding the new objective function line and moving it as far away from the origin as possible identifies a new optimal solution.

This is illustrated in Figure 6.12.

The revised optimal solution is the point $G = 10$, $T = 15$, where the blending constraint crosses the finishing constraint. These are the active constraints which limit production and there must be spare capacity in distilling which does not limit production. These results can be confirmed by solving the equations algebraically as before.

Limiting constraints are:

$$
\begin{array}{lr}
1 * G + 2 * T = 40 & \text{blending} \\
1 * G + 1 * T = 25 & \text{finishing}
\end{array}
$$

which give $G = 10$ and $T = 15$ as the optimal solution. Substituting these values into the objective function gives a profit of $20 * 10 + 30 * 15 =$ £650.

Suppose the new accounting convention gave the profit on both

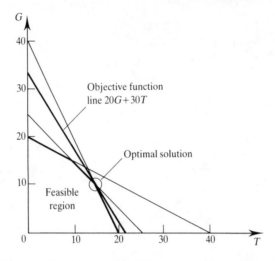

Figure 6.12 Solution for objective function $20G + 30T$.

Growbig and Thrive as £30 a batch. This objective function line can again be superimposed on the feasible region as shown in Figure 6.13.

In this case the line of the objective function does not leave the feasible region at a single point. It is parallel to one of the limiting constraints and leaves the feasible region along one edge. When this happens any point along the edge is optimal and gives the same profit. This can be demonstrated by taking arbitrary points along the edge.

At one extreme point of the edge $G = 15$, $T = 10$
profit $= 30 * 15 + 30 * 10 = £750$

At the other end of the edge $G = 10$ and $T = 15$
profit $= 30 * 10 + 30 * 15 = £750$

In the middle of the edge $G = 12.5$ and $T = 12.5$
profit $= 30 * 12.5 + 30 * 12.5 = £750$
(assuming there are no disadvantages with part batches).

We can summarize these findings by saying:

- an optimal solution lies at an extreme point where two constraints cross;
- the gradient of the objective function has a value between the gradients of the two limiting constraints;
- if the gradient of the objective function changes so that it is no longer between these gradients the optimal solution moves from one extreme point to another.

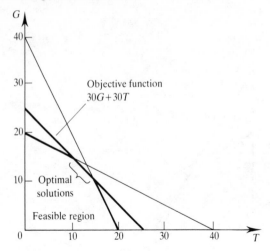

Figure 6.13 Multiple solutions for objective function.

For equations expressed as $a * G + b * T = c$ the gradient of the line is $-b/a$. (This assumes G is the vertical axis, otherwise the gradient is $-a/b$ when T is the vertical axis.) In the example, the gradients of objective function and limiting constraints are:

objective function $= -0.667$
distilling $\qquad = -0.5$
finishing $\qquad = -1.0$

If the gradient of the objective falls below -1.0 or rises above -0.5, the vertex of the optimal solution will change. Keeping the coefficient of G constant while varying the coefficient of T (so the objective function is $30 * G + b * T$), will make the optimal solution change to another vertex when:

either $-b/30 \leq -1.0$ $\qquad$ i.e. $b \geq 30$
or $\quad -b/30 \geq -0.5$ $\qquad$ i.e. $b \leq 15$

Similarly, keeping the coefficient of T constant (so the objective function is $a * G + 20 * T$) would mean the vertex changes when:

either $-20/a \leq -1.0$ $\qquad$ i.e. $a \leq 20$
or $\quad -20/a \geq -0.5$ $\qquad$ i.e. $a \geq 40$

6.5.2 Changes in resource availability

Returning to the original statement of the problem, the limiting constraints were distilling and finishing and the optimal solution was found by solving:

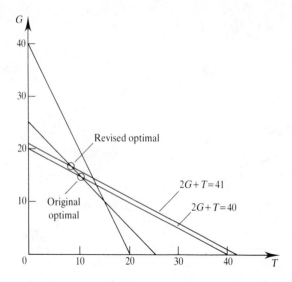

Figure 6.14 Showing the effect of an additional hour of distilling.

$$2 * G + 1 * T = 40 \qquad \text{distilling constraint}$$
$$1 * G + 1 * T = 25 \qquad \text{finishing constraint}$$

If some extra capacity for distilling could be bought, how much would it be worth? The answer to this can be found by calculating a marginal value for distilling (that is, the value of one additional hour) by replacing the original constraint

$$2 * G + 1 * T \le 40$$

by $\quad 2 * G + 1 * T \le 41$

and resolving the problem. In practice, the expansion of the feasible region is so small that it is not worth plotting a new graph (see Figure 6.14).

Provided the increase in resources is small, we can be confident that the same constraints will be limiting and the optimal solution will remain at the same extreme point of the feasible region. A revised optimal solution can then be found by simply solving the equations:

$$2 * G + 1 * T = 41 \qquad \text{distilling constraint}$$
$$1 * G + 1 * T = 25 \qquad \text{finishing constraint}$$

to give values of $G = 16$ and $T = 9$. Substitution of these in the objective function gives an maximum profit of $30 * 16 + 20 * 9 = £660$. This is a rise of £10 from the previous optimal solution and suggests that distilling has a marginal value of £10 an hour. In LP this marginal value is usually

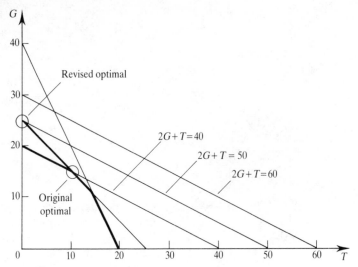

Figure 6.15 Revised optimal solution when distilling is not limiting.

called a 'shadow price' which is an upper bound on the amount which should be paid for one extra unit of a resource.

A similar argument shows that the shadow price is also the cost of losing one hour of distilling capacity and if, for example, equipment broke down for a short time the cost of the stoppage is found by multiplying its duration by the shadow price.

The shadow price is only valid for small additions to capacity. We found that an extra hour of distilling is worth £10, but there are limits and an extra 1000 hours would certainly not be worth £10,000. If an extra 20 hours of distilling becomes available the constraint $2 * G + 1 * T \le 60$ would replace $2 * G + 1 * T \le 40$, as shown in Figure 6.15.

Distilling now has so much capacity that it is no longer limiting and the production is only limited by finishing. The graph shows that distilling ceases to be limiting when the amount available is increased beyond 25 hours and any increase beyond this adds spare capacity. Hence, it is worthwhile paying £10 for each extra hour of distilling up to a maximum of 25 hours.

This analysis of shadow prices can be repeated for finishing, where the value of an extra hour is found by replacing the original limiting constraints by:

$$2 * G + 1 * T = 40 \qquad \text{distilling constraint}$$
$$1 * G + 1 * T = 26 \qquad \text{new finishing constraint}$$

These equations can be solved to give $G = 14$ and $T = 12$. Substitution into the objective function gives an optimal value of £660 which is an

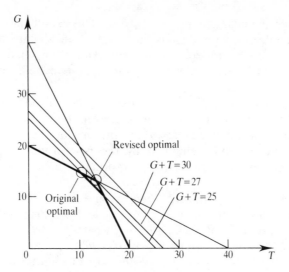

Figure 6.16 Revised optimal solution when finishing is not limiting.

increase of £10 over the original optimal solution. The shadow price for finishing, that is, the maximum amount which should be paid for an extra hour of capacity, is £10. (It is simply coincidence that this is the same as the shadow price for distilling.) This value holds for small changes, but if the capacity for finishing were increased beyond 26.7 hours it would no longer be limiting and there would be no advantage in further increases (see Figure 6.16).

Obviously, if a process already has spare capacity there would be no benefit in increasing the capacity further, so the shadow prices of non-limiting resources are zero. In this example there is spare capacity in blending so the shadow price is zero.

The shadow prices for the three processes have now been calculated separately as:

blending = £0 an hour

distilling = £10 an hour

finishing = £10 an hour.

It would be useful to see what happens if several resources are increased at the same time. The value of an extra hour of both distilling and finishing, for example, is found by replacing the original constraints by

$$2 * G + 1 * T = 41 \qquad \text{new distilling constraint}$$
$$1 * G + 1 * T = 26 \qquad \text{new finishing constraint}$$

Solving these gives $G = 15$ and $T = 11$ and substitution in the objective function gives a maximum profit of £670. This is £20 more than the original optimal solution and is also the sum of the shadow prices when the increases were considered separately. Thus, for small changes in resources the total benefit is the sum of the separate benefits of increasing each resource separately.

One application of this principle is the introduction of new products to compete for resources with existing ones. The total cost of reducing the resources available to existing products can be compared with the increased profit generated by the new product. If the profit generated is greater than the cost the new product should be added to the solution.

Suppose a new fertilizer, Vegup, could be made in addition to Growbig and Thrive. Vegup uses two hours of blending, two hours of distilling and two hours of packing for each batch and contributes £50 to profits. Should this new product be introduced?

If one batch of Vegup is made the cost of reduced production of Growbig and Thrive is found by multiplying the reduction in available capacity for each process by the shadow price. Vegup uses two hours of blending with a shadow price of £10 an hour, so this would cost £20. The total cost of producing one batch of Vegup is then:

Process	Hours used	Shadow price	Total cost
Blending	2	0	0
Distilling	2	10	20
Finishing	2	10	20
Total			40

The total cost of reducing existing production is £40 while increased profit from a batch of Vegup is £50, so the new product should be manufactured. The next obvious question is how much Vegup should be made. Unfortunately, this can not be found from the original solution and a revised problem must be solved. As there are now three variables to consider we could try to draw three-dimensional graphs but the Simplex procedure is a much more efficient algebraic procedure. This is relatively straightforward, but it involves a lot of arithmetical manipulation of matrices which is done much more conveniently on a computer. As we mentioned earlier, the computer will search the extreme points of the feasible region until it finds an optimal value. Later in this chapter will look at larger problems and illustrate the kind of results which can be obtained from standard software.

WORKED EXAMPLE 6.6

An engineering company manufactures two gear boxes, 'Manual' and 'Automatic'. There are four stages in the production of these, with details of required times and weekly availabilities given in Table 6.4. The company makes a profit of £64 on each Manual sold and £100 on each Automatic.

Table 6.4

Stage in manufacture	Time required (hours per unit)		Time available (hours a week)
	Manual	Automatic	
Foundry	3	5	7,500
Machine Shop	5	4	10,000
Assembly	2	1	3,500
Testing	1	1	2,000

(a) Formulate this profit maximization problem as a linear programme.
(b) Use a graphical method to find the optimal solution.
(c) Find the spare capacities in each manufacturing stage.
(d) Calculate the shadow prices of each manufacturing stage.
(e) A new 'Semi-automatic' gear box is proposed which needs 4, 4, 1 and 1 hours respectively in each manufacturing stage and gives a profit of £80 a unit. Should the company make the semi-automatic gear box?

SOLUTION

(a) Let M be the number of Manual gear boxes made a week and let A be the number of Automatic gear boxes made a week.
   The formulation becomes:

Maximize: $64 * M + 100 * A$

Subject to:
$$3 * M + 5 * A \leq 7500 \qquad \text{foundry}$$
$$5 * M + 4 * A \leq 10{,}000 \qquad \text{machine shop}$$
$$2 * M + 1 * A \leq 3500 \qquad \text{assembly}$$
$$1 * M + 1 * A \leq 2000 \qquad \text{testing}$$
$$M, A \geq 0 \qquad \text{non-negativity}$$

(b) The graph of this problem is shown in Figure 6.17.
   The optimal solution occurs where the foundry and testing constraints are limiting, so solving

$$3 * M + 5 * A = 7500$$

and $\quad 1 * M + 1 * A = 2000$

255

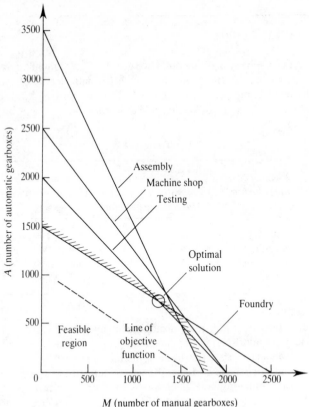

Figure 6.17   Graph for Worked example 6.6.

gives the optimal solution of $M = 1250$ and $A = 750$ with a profit of $1250 * 64 + 750 * 100 = £155,000$ a week.

(c) The availability of foundry and testing are limiting so they have no spare capacity, but there is spare capacity in the machine shop and assembly. Time used in the machine shop is $1250 * 5 + 750 * 4 = 9250$ hours and there is 750 hours of spare capacity. Time used in assembly is $1250 * 2 + 750 * 1 = 3250$ hours and there is 250 hours of spare capacity.

(d) Since both the machine shop and assembly have spare capacity their shadow price is zero. The shadow prices of the other stages in manufacturing are found by increasing the availability of each by one hour. With one extra hour of foundry time the new optimal solution is found by solving:

$$3 * M + 5 * A = 7501 \qquad \text{new foundry constraint}$$

$$\text{and} \quad 1 * M + 1 * A = 2000 \qquad \text{testing constraint}$$

to give $M = 1249.5$ and $A = 750.5$. The profit is then $1249.5 * 64 + 750.5 * 100 = £155,018$. This is an increase of £18 which is the shadow price of foundry time.

With one extra hour of testing the new optimal solution is found by solving:

$$3 * M + 5 * A = 7500 \qquad \text{foundry constraint}$$

and $\quad 1 * M + 1 * A = 2001 \qquad \text{new testing constraint}$

to give $M = 1252.5$ and $A = 748.5$. The profit is then $1252.5 * 64 + 748.5 * 100 = £155{,}010$. This is an increase of £10 which is the shadow price of testing.

(e) The new Semi-automatic gear box needs:

4 hours of foundry at a cost of £18 an hour = £72

4 hours of machine shop costing £0 an hour = £ 0

1 hour of assembly costing £0 an hour = £ 0

1 hour of testing costing £10 an hour = £10

The total cost of making one gear box is £82 while the profit is £80. This means there would be a loss of £2 on every unit made and the company should not start making the Semi-automatic gear box.

WORKED EXAMPLE 6.7

An importer buys two versions of a computer board, one from the Far East and one from South America. The boards are delivered in bulk and the wholesaler tests them and repackages them to sell to a number of small manufacturers. Each board from the Far East takes two hours to test and two hours to repackage, while each board from South America takes three hours to test and one hour to repackage. The importer has enough facilities to provide up to 8000 hours a week for testing and 4000 hours a week for repackaging. If there are maximum sales of 1500 a week for the board from the Far East and each board gives a profit of £10 when sold, what is the optimal mix of boards for the importer?

- How does this optimal mix vary with changing profits on each board?
- What are the shadow prices on each resource and over what ranges are these valid?
- If another version of the board becomes available from Europe, which takes two hours of testing, one hour of repackaging and yields a profit of £10, should this new board be imported?

SOLUTION

Let FE be the number of boards imported from the Far East and SA be the number imported from South America. The formulation then becomes:

Maximize: $\quad 10 * FE + 10 * SA$

Subject to: $\quad 2 * FE + 3 * SA \le 8000 \qquad \text{testing}$

$\qquad\qquad\quad 2 * FE + 1 * SA \le 4000 \qquad \text{repackaging}$

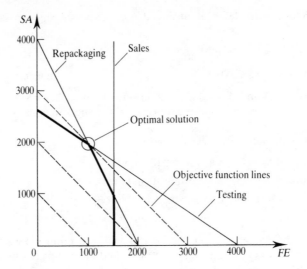

Figure 6.18 Graph for Worked example 6.7.

$$1 * FE \qquad \leq 1500 \qquad\qquad \text{sales}$$

with $FE \geq 0$ and $SA \geq 0$.

It can be seen from Figure 6.18 that the optimal solution occurs where the testing and repackaging constraints are limiting, so solving

$$2 * FE + 3 * SA = 8000$$
$$2 * FE + 1 * SA = 4000$$

gives the optimal solution of $FE = 1000$ and $SA = 2000$ with a profit of £30,000 a week.

The gradient of the objective function and limiting constraints are:

objective function $= -1.0$

testing constraint $= -0.667$

repackaging constraint $= -2.0$

For small changes in the gradient of the objective function the optimal solution will remain at the same extreme point. If the gradient of the objective function moves outside the range -0.667 to -2.0 the optimal solution will move to another vertex. Thus, if the gradient decreases until the objective function is parallel to the repackaging constraint the optimal solution will change to the extreme point $FE = 1500$ and $SA = 1000$. This happens when:

$$- \frac{\text{profit per unit of } SA}{\text{profit per unit of } FE} \geq -2.0$$

If the gradient of the objective function increases until it is parallel to the testing constraint the optimal solution will change to the extreme point $FE = 0$ and $SA = 2667$ (see Figure 6.19). This happens when:

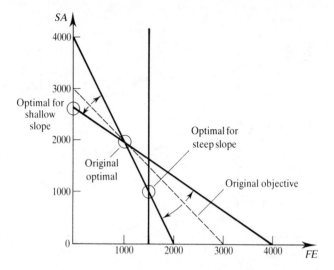

Figure 6.19 Showing effects of changing objective gradient.

$$- \frac{\text{profit per unit of } SA}{\text{profit per unit of } FE} \leq \frac{-2}{3}$$

The revised profit is found from:

1000 * profit per unit of *FE* + 2000 * profit per unit of *SA*

The shadow price of repackaging is found by solving:

2 * *FE* + 3 * *SA* = 8000	testing
2 * *FE* + 1 * *SA* = 4001	repackaging

which gives *FE* = 1000.75, *SA* = 1999.5 and a profit of £30,002.50. Thus the shadow price for repackaging is £2.50. This is valid until there is so much repackaging capacity that it is no longer limiting. Figure 6.20(a) shows that when this occurs the constraints on testing and sales become limiting and the optimal solution moves to *FE* = 1500 and *SA* = 1667. This mix would need 2 * 1500 + 1 * 1667 = 4667 hours of repackaging and any capacity above this would be spare.

The shadow price for testing is found by solving:

2 * *FE* + 3 * *SA* = 8001	testing
2 * *FE* + 1 * *SA* = 4000	repackaging

which gives *FE* = 999.75, *SA* = 2000.5 and a profit of £30,002.50. The shadow price for testing is £2.50. This is valid until there is so much testing capacity that it is no longer limiting. Figure 6.20(b) shows that when this occurs repackaging is limiting and the new optimal solution is *FE* = 0 and *SA* = 4000. This mix would need 3 * 4000 = 12,000 hours of testing and any capacity above this would be spare.

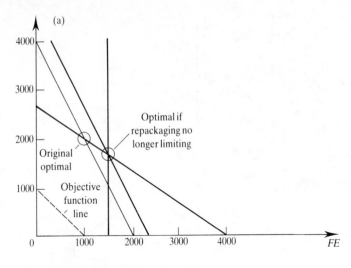

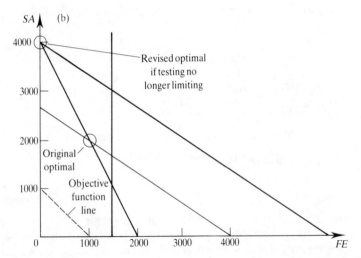

Figure 6.20 Effect of slackening constraints in Worked example 6.7: (a) with repackaging no longer limiting; (b) with testing no longer limiting.

Importing one unit of the European board would use two hours of testing and one hour of repackaging. The cost of reduced capacity for the existing boards is $2 * 2.50 + 1 * 2.50 = £7.50$. As the profit generated is £10 the European board should be imported. The revised problem must be solved to find how many boards should be imported from Europe.

SELF ASSESSMENT QUESTIONS

6.9 What is meant by 'sensitivity analysis' in LP problems?

6.10 Why might it be useful to look at the effect of altering some data used in an LP model?

6.11 Within what limits can the coefficients of the objective function vary without affecting the position of the optimal solution?

6.12 What are 'shadow prices' in linear programming?

6.13 Within what limits are the shadow prices valid?

6.6 COMPUTER SOLUTIONS TO LARGER LINEAR PROGRAMMES

We have already suggested a method by which computers might find solutions to linear programmes. This was based on the observation that the feasible region for LPs is always convex and that an optimal solution will lie at one of the extreme points of the feasible region. The solution procedure is to examine the extreme points and select the best. This is the basis of the Simplex procedure which is used by most computer packages.

Although packages vary in detail they have many common features and we will look at the output which might come from a typical package. The Simplex procedure is iterative as it searches the extreme points for an optimal and some packages print a 'progress report' at each iteration. We will only look at the information which might be given once an optimal solution is found.

Throughout this chapter we have done calculations on the production planning problem of Growbig and Thrive. It would be interesting to confirm these calculations by looking at a computer solution to this problem. The formulation is:

$$
\begin{aligned}
\text{Maximize:} \quad & 30 * G + 20 * T \\
\text{Subject to:} \quad & 1 * G + 2 * T \le 40 \\
& 2 * G + 1 * T \le 40 \\
& 1 * G + 1 * T \le 25 \\
\text{with } & G \ge 0 \text{ and } T \ge 0
\end{aligned}
$$

```
Max  +30.0000G    +20.0000T
Subject to
(1)   +1.00000G    +2.00000T    ≤ +40.0000
(2)   +2.00000G    +1.00000T    ≤ +40.0000
(3)   +1.00000G    +1.00000T    ≤ +25.0000
```

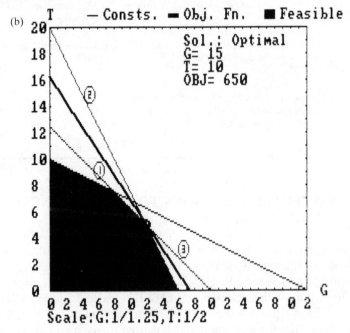

(b)

— Consts. ■ Obj. Fn. ■ Feasible

Sol.: Optimal
G= 15
T= 10
OBJ= 650

Scale:G:1/1.25,T:1/2

(c)

Summarized Results for Fertiliser Page : 1						
Variables No. Names	Solution	Opportunity Cost	Variables No. Names		Solution	Opportunity Cost
1 G	+15.000000	0	4 S2		0	+10.000000
2 T	+10.000000	0	5 S3		0	+10.000000
3 S1	+5.0000000	0				
Maximum value of the OBJ = 650 Iters. = 2						

(d)

Sensitivity Analysis for OBJ Coefficients Page : 1							
C(j)	Min. C(j)	Original	Max. C(j)	C(j)	Min. C(j)	Original	Max. C(j)
C(1)	+20.000000	+30.000000	+40.000000	C(2)	+15.000000	+20.000000	+30.000000

(e)

Sensitivity Analysis for RHS Page : 1							
B(i)	Min. B(i)	Original	Max. B(i)	B(i)	Min. B(i)	Original	Max. B(i)
B(1)	+35.000000	+40.000000	+ Infinity	B(3)	+20.000000	+25.000000	+26.666666
B(2)	+35.000000	+40.000000	+50.000000				

Figure 6.21 Results from running an LP package: (a) input to program; (b) graphical output from program; (c) summary of results from output; (d) effects of changing the objective function; (e) effect of changing the constraints.

Many packages require data to be presented as a matrix so we could rewrite this as:

		G	T		
Maximize:		30	20		
Subject to:		1	2	≤	40
		2	1	≤	40
		1	1	≤	25

This data was input to a package written in BASIC available on any microcomputer and run with the results shown in Figure 6.21.

This output is fairly straightforward but one or two comments can be made. The first output shows the data input to confirm it was entered correctly. This is followed by a graph of the problem, which is the same as Figure 6.9 but with the axes transposed. The table of summarized results (Figure 6.21(c)) shows the optimal values for G and T (15 and 10) in the 'solution' column. The variables $S1$, $S2$ and $S3$ (with values 5, 0 and 0) are the spare capacities for each constraint. The 'opportunity cost' is another name for the shadow price (this is also called the dual price), so constraints 2 and 3 have shadow prices of £10 each. The optimal value of the objective function is £650 and this solution took two iterations to find.

Figure 6.21(d) shows the sensitivity for objective function coefficients. This shows, for each coefficient, the original value and the minimum and maximum value which the coefficient can take without moving the optimal solution to another vertex. These values assume that only one coefficient is varied and the other remains unchanged. Thus, the original profit on each batch of Growbig is £30 but this can vary between £20 and £40 without changing the location of the optimal solution (provided the profit on each batch of Thrive remains at £20). Similarly the profit on each batch of Thrive can vary between £15 and £30 without changing the location of the optimal solution (provided the profit on each batch of Growbig remains at £30).

Figure 6.21(e) shows the sensitivity of the righthand side of constraints. For each constraint the original righthand side value is given together with the maximum and minimum values for which the relevant shadow costs are valid. Thus constraint 2 (distilling) has a shadow price of £10 provided the availability (given in the righthand side of the constraint) is between 35 and 50 hours. Similarly the shadow price of Blending is zero provided the availability remains above 35 hours.

WORKED EXAMPLE 6.8

West Coast Wood Products Ltd make four types of pressed panels from pine and spruce. Each sheet of panel must be cut and pressed. Table 6.5 shows the hours needed to produce a batch of each type of panel and the hours available each week.

Table 6.5

Panel type	Hours of cutting	Hours of pressing
Classic	1	1
Western	1	4
Nouveau	2	3
East Coast	2	2
Available	80	100

There is also a limited amount of suitable wood available. The amounts needed for each type of panel and maximum weekly availability are given below.

Panel	Classic	Western	Nouveau	East Coast	Availability
Pine	50	40	30	40	2500
Spruce	20	30	50	20	2000

The net profit on each batch of panel is estimated to be £40 for Classic, £110 for Western, £75 for Nouveau and £35 for East Coast.

(a) Formulate this as a linear programme.
(b) A computer program gave the results for this problem shown in Figure 6.22. Interpret these results.

SOLUTION

(a) Define the decision variables as the number of batches of each type of panelling made a week (Clas, West, Nouv and East). The formulation can then be represented by the following matrix:

	Clas	West	Nouv	East			
Maximize:	40	110	75	35			
Subject to:	50	40	30	40	≤	2500	pine
	20	30	50	20	≤	2000	spruce
	1	1	2	2	≤	80	cutting
	1	4	3	2	≤	100	pressing

with Clas, West, Nouv and East ≥ 0.

(a)

```
                    Input Data of The Problem Wood      Page  1

Max   +40.0000Clas+110.000West+75.0000Nouv+35.0000East
Subject to
(1)   +50.0000Clas+40.0000West+30.0000Nouv+40.0000East≤ +2500.00
(2)   +20.0000Clas+30.0000West+50.0000Nouv+20.0000East≤ +2000.00
(3)   +1.00000Clas+1.00000West+2.00000Nouv+2.00000East≤ +80.0000
(4)   +1.00000Clas+4.00000West+3.00000Nouv+2.00000East≤ +100.000
```

(b)

Variables No. Names	Solution	Opportunity Cost	Variables No. Names	Solution	Opportunity Cost
1 Clas	+37.500000	0	5 S1	0	+.31250000
2 West	+15.625000	0	6 S2	+781.25000	0
3 Nouv	0	+7.4999986	7 S3	+26.875000	0
4 East	0	+26.250000	8 S4	0	+24.375000

Maximum value of the OBJ = 3218.75   Iters. = 3

(c)

	Sensitivity Analysis for OBJ Coefficients					Page : 1	
C(j)	Min. C(j)	Original	Max. C(j)	C(j)	Min. C(j)	Original	Max. C(j)
C(1)	+27.500000	+40.000000	+137.50000	C(3)	- Infinity	+75.000000	+82.500000
C(2)	+100.00000	+110.00000	+160.00000	C(4)	- Infinity	+35.000000	+61.250000

(d)

	Sensitivity Analysis for RHS					Page : 1	
B(i)	Min. B(i)	Original	Max. B(i)	B(i)	Min. B(i)	Original	Max. B(i)
B(1)	+1000.0000	+2500.0000	+3933.3333	B(3)	+53.125000	+80.000000	+ Infinity
B(2)	+1218.7500	+2000.0000	+ Infinity	B(4)	+50.000000	+100.00000	+250.00000

Figure 6.22 Results for Worked example 6.8: (a) data input; (b) summary of
results; (c) sensitivity of objective function; (d) sensitivity of constraints.

(b) The summarized results show that the optimal solution is to make 37.5 batches of Classic a week, 15.6 batches of Western and none of the others. This gives a profit of £3218.75. If a batch of Nouveau is made it would reduce profit by £7.50 while making a batch of East Coast would reduce profit by £26.25.

The limiting constraints are pine and pressing, with spare capacity in spruce (781.25) and cutting (26.88 hours). This will remain true while the constraint on spruce remains over 1218.75 and the amount of cutting remains above 53.13 hours. The shadow price of pine is £0.31 (valid for amounts between 1000 and 3933) and of pressing is £24.38 (valid for between 50 and 250 hours).

The profit for each batch of Classic could vary between £27.50 and £137.50 without changing the position of the optimal solution (provided the profits on the other panels remain unchanged). Similar ranges are given over which profit can vary on Western, Nouveau and East Coast without affecting the location of the optimal solution (between £100.00 and £160.00, below £82.50 and below £61.25 respectively).

WORKED EXAMPLE 6.9

A manufacturer produces four models of metal filing cabinet. Each of these has four stages in manufacturing: cutting, stamping, assembly and packing. The times needed for each stage, together with the times available each week are given in Table 6.6.

Table 6.6

Model	Hours per unit A	B	C	D	Number of machines	Hours available per machine per week
Cutting	2	3	4	4	10	40
Stamping	1	2	2	3	6	36
Assembly	3	3	2	4	12	38
Packing	2	3	3	3	8	40

The fixed cost of production is £30,000 a year. Selling prices are £25, £28, £34 and £40 respectively for each cabinet with direct costs of £16, £18, £22 and £25 respectively. On average the cutting machines need 10% of their total time for maintenance, stamping machines need 16.667%, assembly machines 25% and packing machines 10%. The company works a standard 48 week year.

(a) Formulate a linear programme for this problem.
(b) The solution to this problem is given in Figure 6.23. Interpret these results.
(c) How would you interpret a solution which included non-integer values for the number of cabinets to be made?
(d) Why does the company not produce any of cabinet model B?

(a)

```
                    Input Data of The Problem Cabinets    Page  1

Max  +9.00000A   +10.0000B   +12.0000C   +15.0000D
Subject to
(1)  +2.00000A   +3.00000B   +4.00000C   +4.00000D   ≤ +360.000
(2)  +1.00000A   +2.00000B   +2.00000C   +3.00000D   ≤ +180.000
(3)  +3.00000A   +3.00000B   +2.00000C   +4.00000D   ≤ +342.000
(4)  +2.00000A   +3.00000B   +3.00000C   +3.00000D   ≤ +288.000
```

(b)

Variables No. Names	Solution	Opportunity Cost	Variables No. Names	Solution	Opportunity Cost
1 A	+74.571434	0	5 S1	+25.714277	0
2 B	0	+2.8571429	6 S2	0	+1.2857142
3 C	+33.428577	0	7 S3	0	+.85714287
4 D	+12.857138	0	8 S4	0	+2.5714285

Summarized Results for Cabinets   Page : 1

Maximum value of the OBJ = 1265.143   Iters. = 3

(c)

Sensitivity Analysis for OBJ Coefficients   Page : 1

C(j)	Min. C(j)	Original	Max. C(j)	C(j)	Min. C(j)	Original	Max. C(j)
C(1)	+7.0000000	+9.0000000	+10.500000	C(3)	+8.3999996	+12.000000	+14.000000
C(2)	− Infinity	+10.000000	+12.857143	C(4)	+13.200000	+15.000000	+19.500000

(d)

Sensitivity Analysis for RHS   Page : 1

B(i)	Min. B(i)	Original	Max. B(i)	B(i)	Min. B(i)	Original	Max. B(i)
B(1)	+334.28574	+360.00000	+ Infinity	B(3)	+252.00003	+342.00000	+420.00000
B(2)	+162.00000	+180.00000	+225.00000	B(4)	+241.20000	+288.00000	+310.50000

Figure 6.23 Results for Worked example 6.9: (a) data input; (b) summary of results; (c) sensitivity of objective function; (d) sensitivity of constraints.

267

(e) What would be the effect on the company's profit if maintenance requirements were reduced to 10% of available machine time?

SOLUTION

(a) Let A be the number of filing cabinets of type A made each week, B be the number of filing cabinets of type B made each week and so on.

The profit on each cabinet is:

Model	A	B	C	D
Selling price	25	28	34	40
Direct costs	16	18	22	25
Profit	9	10	12	15

Weekly time available for each process is:

	Machines	Hours	Use	Net hours/week
Cutting	10	40	0.9	360
Stamping	6	36	0.833	180
Assembly	12	38	0.75	342
Packing	8	40	0.9	288

The formulation then becomes:

Maximize: $9 * A + 10 * B + 12 * C + 15 * D$

Subject to:

$$2 * A + 3 * B + 4 * C + 4 * D \leq 360 \quad \text{cutting}$$
$$1 * A + 2 * B + 2 * C + 3 * D \leq 180 \quad \text{stamping}$$
$$3 * A + 3 * B + 2 * C + 4 * D \leq 342 \quad \text{assembly}$$
$$2 * A + 3 * B + 3 * C + 3 * D \leq 288 \quad \text{packing}$$

with A, B, C and $D \geq 0$.

(b) The summary of results show that the company should make 74.57 cabinets of type A a week, 33.43 of type C and 12.86 of type D. No cabinets of type B should be made. The resulting profit is £1265.14 a week or £60,726.72 in a 48 week year, from which fixed costs of £30,000 have to be subtracted.

This solution has 25.71 hours of spare cutting, but all other processes are fully used with shadow prices of 1.28, 0.86 and 2.57 respectively.

The computer took three iterations to find this solution.

(c) The optimal solution calls for 74.57 cabinets of type A to be made a week. This could be done simply by leaving a cabinet partly finished at the end of a week. Alternatively there may be enough flexibility in the system to allow 74 cabinets to be made in one week and 75 the next so that, on average, the optimal number are made. If this is unsatisfactory the problem can be defined as an 'integer linear programme', which will be mentioned in section 6.7.

(d) If one cabinet of type B is made it would reduce profits by £2.86. This can be confirmed by finding the cost of the resources needed to make one unit and subtracting the profit (see Table 6.7).

Table 6.7

Process	Hours	Shadow price	Cost
Cutting	3	0	0
Stamping	2	1.29	2.58
Assembly	3	0.86	2.58
Packing	3	2.57	7.71
Total cost			12.87

Subtracting the profit of £10 from this gives the reduction in profits for each unit of B made (allowing for rounding errors when working to 2 places of decimals).

(e) There are already 25.71 spare hours of cutting so reducing the maintenance requirement there would have no effect. The other three processes are all fully used and additional capacity would increase profits.

Reducing the maintenance requirements for stamping would increase weekly availability by $6 * 36 * (0.9 - 0.83) = 14.5$ hours. Stamping has a shadow price of 1.29 so the extra weekly profit would be $1.29 * 14.5 = £18.71$ a week.

Similarly, reduced maintenance for assembly would give extra profit of $12 * 38 * (0.9 - 0.75) * 0.86 = £58.82$. Packing already has maintenance of 10% so no change would be made there. These effects are additive so the overall effect would be an increase in profit of £77.53 a week or about 6%.

SELF ASSESSMENT QUESTIONS

6.14 Why are computers usually used to solve LPs?

6.15 What information might be given in a computer print-out for the solution of an LP?

6.7 EXTENSIONS TO LINEAR PROGRAMMING

The arithmetic needed to solve linear programmes can be very tedious and it is certainly advisable to use a computer for even small problems. There are several possible extensions to linear programming which generally require even more arithmetic and should certainly not be tackled by hand. Here we will mention one or two of these extensions.

A fundamental requirement of linear programming is that both the objective function and constraints are linear with respect to the decision variables. Removing this constraint allows the formulation of non-linear programmes. For these the feasible region need no longer be convex and some solution procedure other than Simplex is needed. Such problems are very difficult to solve and optimal solutions can only be guaranteed for a few specific types.

There has been more success with integer (linear) programming. Many types of problem can be formulated with linear constraints and objective, but with some decision variables constrained to take integer values. We might, for example, be looking for the optimal number of machines to be bought in which case an answer of 2.6 machines would be meaningless. An obvious approach would be to solve a standard LP with continuous variables and then simply round these to the nearest integer. There are circumstances in which this does not give optimal (or even good) results and the only way in which an optimal solution can be guaranteed is to use a procedure specifically designed for integer variables. 'Branch-and-bound' methods are generally used for this and although reasonably sized problems can be tackled the amount of computation is considerable.

One specific type of integer programming is zero–one programming where variables are limited to taking the values zero or one. This is useful for determining whether, for example, a piece of equipment should be used or not, or whether a vehicle should travel between two towns or not. Again, the amount of computation needed for such problems can become excessive for even small problems.

Finally we will mention goal programming, where a single objective function is replaced by several goals. A production plan might, for example, have goals of satisfying customer demand, minimizing costs, limiting hours of overtime and achieving specified productivity. Weights can be given to these goals and the problem is to find a solution which minimizes deviations from the goals.

Perhaps it is worth emphasizing that all mathematical models contain assumptions and approximations. They are not meant to duplicate reality but aim to help in decision making, so using a larger or more complex model does not necessarily give better or more useful solutions.

WORKED EXAMPLE 6.10

A company is about to buy some production machines and has a choice of two alternatives. Each machine of type A costs £20,000, can make 9000 units and needs 40 hours of maintenance a month. Each machine of type B costs £10,000,

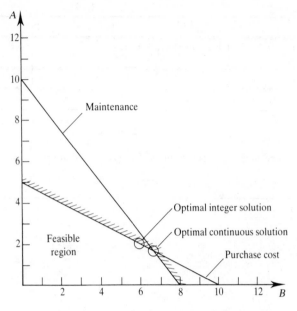

Figure 6.24 Solution for Worked example 6.10.

can make 7000 units and needs 50 hours of maintenance a month. The company has 400 hours of maintenance available each month and has allocated £100,000 for the machines. What mix of machines should they buy?

SOLUTION

With A as the number of machines of type A bought and B as the number of machines of type B, the formulation for this problem is:

Maximize: $9000 * A + 7000 * B$

Subject to:
$20 * A + 10 * B \leq 100$	purchase cost
$40 * A + 50 * B \leq 400$	maintenance
$A, B \geq 0$	non-negativity

This could be solved graphically (Figure 6.24) to give the solution $A = 1.67$ and $B = 6.67$ with a production of 61,667 units a month.

Although this solution would be satisfactory in many circumstances, it is nonsensical to suggest buying 1.67 machines. The results could be rounded, but setting $A = 2$ and $B = 7$ would break the constraints. A more reliable method would be to define A and B as integers in the formulation. The problem could then be solved using an integer linear programming package. Figure 6.25 illustrates the results from one such package, where the optimal solution is identified as $A = 2$ and $B = 6$ with a production of 60,000 units a month.

Summary of Results for Machines					Page : 1	
Variables No. Names	Solution	Obj. Fnctn. Coefficient	Variables No. Names	Solution	Obj. Fnctn. Coefficient	
1 A	+2.0000000	+9000.0000	2 B	+6.0000000	+7000.0000	
Maximum value of the OBJ = 60000 Total iterations = 3						

Figure 6.25 Integer solution for Worked example 6.10.

CONCLUSIONS

This chapter has described linear programming, which is a widely used quantitative technique. Many situations can be described by constrained optimization models. For some of these the objective function and constraints are linear with respect to the decision variables and then LP can be used to find optimal solutions.

The stages in the solution of such problems are:

- formulation
- solution
- post-optimal analysis.

The formulation stage is often the most difficult.

Problems with two (or maybe three) variables can be solved graphically. For any reasonably sized problem a numerical procedure must be used and Simplex is the most common. A computer is almost essential for any real problem.

Some of the assumptions made in a model are almost inevitably open to interpretation, and the data may contain approximations and errors. Sensitivity analysis can be used to see how sensitive the optimal solution is to such factors. In practice computers allow large problems to be solved, often with thousands of constraints and variables.

There are several extensions to linear programming, with integer programming being the most useful.

PROBLEMS

6.1   Two additives X1 and X2 can be used to increase the octane number of petrol. One pound of X1 in 500 gallons of petrol will increase the octane number by 10, while one pound of X2 in 500 gallons will increase the octane number by 20. The total additives must increase the octane number by at least 5, but a total of no more than half a pound can be added to 500 gallons and the amount of X2 plus twice the amount of X1 must be at least half a pound. If X1 costs £30 a pound and X2 costs £40 a pound, formulate this problem as a linear programme.

6.2   A diet is required to give a daily intake of at least 3000 calories and 160 units of protein. Four basic foods can be used in the diet with characteristics as shown in Table 6.8.

Table 6.8

Food	Calories per pound	Protein per pound	Cost (pence per pound)
1	600	4	40
2	50	16	20
3	500	20	50
4	800	6	60

Formulate this as a linear programme.

6.3   Use a graphical method to find an optimal solution to the formulation in problem 6.1.

6.4   Novacook Ltd makes two types of cooker, one electric and one gas. There are four stages in the production of each of these, with details given in Table 6.9.

The electric cooker has variable costs of £200 a unit and a selling price of £300 while the gas cooker has variable costs of £160 and a selling price of £240 a unit. Fixed overheads are estimated at £60,000 a week and the company works a 50-week year.

The marketing department suggest maximum sales of 800 electric and 1250 gas cookers a week.

Table 6.9

Manufacturing stage	Time required (hours per unit)		Total time available (hours per week)
	Electric	Gas	
Forming	4	2	3,600
Machine shop	10	8	12,000
Assembly	6	4	6,000
Testing	2	2	2,800

- Formulate this as a profit maximizing linear programme.
- Use a graphical method to find an optimal product mix for the company. What is the expected annual profit?
- Find the use and spare capacity of each manufacturing stage.
- Calculate the shadow price of each manufacturing stage.
- An outside consultant offers his testing services to the company. What price should Novacook be willing to pay for this service and how many hours should they buy a week?
- A new cooker is planned which would use the manufacturing stages for four, six, six, and two hours respectively. At what selling price would it be advantageous to make this cooker if the other variable costs are £168 a unit?

6.5 A manufacturer of electrical components produces two types of tester, Standard and Normal. The production time (in hours per hundred units) of each type and the capacity of each production process are given below. All testers made can be sold and the profits on each unit of Standard and Normal are £6 and £8 respectively.

	Standard	Normal	Capacity (hours per month)
Pressing	2	4	160
Wiring	6	2	240
Assembly	4	4	200

- Formulate the problem of maximizing monthly profit as a linear programme.
- Use a graphical method to determine the optimal solution to this problem.
- Find the spare capacity in production facilities.
- Calculate the shadow prices of production facilities.
- It has been suggested that the selling price of the Standard tester

be raised. To what level could the profit be raised without changing the pattern of production found above?

- A new tester is planned which could go through Pressing, Wiring and Assembly at a rate of 200 units an hour on each process. What profit is needed before it becomes advantageous to manufacture the new tester?

6.6 Figure 6.26 shows the printout from a linear programming package. What information can be found from this?

```
                    Input Data of The Problem Planning     Page  1

Max   +10.0000X1   +20.0000X2   +15.0000X3   +20.0000X4
Subject to
 (1)   +4.00000X1   +2.00000X2   +6.00000X3   +4.00000X4   ≤ +15.0000
 (2)  +10.0000X1   +10.0000X2   +20.0000X3   +20.0000X4   ≤ +75.0000
 (3)   +6.00000X1   +8.00000X2   +3.00000X3   +7.00000X4   ≤ +30.0000
 (4)  +15.0000X1   +10.0000X2   +12.0000X3   +20.0000X4   ≤ +100.000
```

Summarized Results for Planning				Page : 1			
Variables No. Names	Solution	Opportunity Cost		Variables No. Names	Solution	Opportunity Cost	
1 X1	0	+8.5714283		5 S1	0	+1.4285715	
2 X2	+3.2142856	0		6 S2	+14.285714	0	
3 X3	+1.4285715	0		7 S3	0	+2.1428571	
4 X4	0	+.71428573		8 S4	+50.714283	0	
Maximum value of the OBJ = 85.71429 Iters. = 2							

Sensitivity Analysis for OBJ Coefficients							Page : 1
C(j)	Min. C(j)	Original	Max. C(j)	C(j)	Min. C(j)	Original	Max. C(j)
C(1)	- Infinity	+10.000000	+18.571428	C(3)	+13.333333	+15.000000	+60.000000
C(2)	+19.000000	+20.000000	+40.000000	C(4)	- Infinity	+20.000000	+20.714285

Sensitivity Analysis for RHS							Page : 1
B(i)	Min. B(i)	Original	Max. B(i)	B(i)	Min. B(i)	Original	Max. B(i)
B(1)	+7.5000000	+15.000000	+19.615385	B(3)	+7.5000000	+30.000000	+60.000000
B(2)	+60.714287	+75.000000	+ Infinity	B(4)	+49.285717	+100.00000	+ Infinity

Figure 6.26 Solution to LP problem 6.6.

6.7 Figure 6.27 shows the printout from a linear programming package. What information can be found from this?

```
                Input Data of The Problem Product Mix      Page  1

Max   +120.000Time+110.000Spac+240.000Mach+178.000Manp+96.0000Cost
      +45.0000Sale
Subject to
  (1)   +12.0000Time+17.0000Spac+20.0000Mach+25.0000Manp+42.0000Cost
        +17.0000Sale≤ +450.000
  (2)   +25.0000Time+40.0000Spac+50.0000Mach+50.0000Manp+50.0000Cost
        +30.0000Sale≤ +1000.00
  (3)   +1.00000Time+1.00000Spac+1.00000Mach+2.00000Manp+2.00000Cost
        +2.00000Sale≤ +40.0000
  (4)   +110.000Time+150.000Spac+120.000Mach+90.0000Manp+100.000Cost
        +130.000Sale≤ +4000.00
  (5)   +10.0000Time+10.0000Spac+10.0000Mach+10.0000Manp+10.0000Cost
        +10.0000Sale≤ +800.000
  (6)   +240.000Time+200.000Spac+300.000Mach+250.000Manp+180.000Cost
        +200.000Sale≤ +12000.0
  (7)   +5.00000Time+6.00000Spac+4.00000Mach+3.00000Manp+5.00000Cost
        +7.00000Sale≤ +180.000
  (8)   +8.00000Time+7.00000Spac+9.00000Mach+6.00000Manp+8.00000Cost
        +8.00000Sale≤ +400.000
```

	Summarized Results for Product Mix				Page : 1	
Variables No. Names		Solution	Opportunity Cost	Variables No. Names	Solution	Opportunity Cost
1	Time	0	0	8 S2	0	+4.8000002
2	Spac	0	+82.000000	9 S3	+20.000000	0
3	Mach	+20.000000	0	10 S4	+1599.9999	0
4	Manp	0	+61.999989	11 S5	+600.00000	0
5	Cost	0	+144.00000	12 S6	+6000.0005	0
6	Sale	0	+99.000008	13 S7	+100.00000	0
7	S1	+49.999992	0	14 S8	+220.00000	0

Maximum value of the OBJ = 4800 (multiple sols.)   Iters. = 1

	Sensitivity Analysis for OBJ Coefficients				Page : 1	
C(j)	Min. C(j)	Original	Max. C(j)	C(j)	Min. C(j)	Original	Max. C(j)
C(1)	- Infinity	+120.00000	+120.00000	C(4)	- Infinity	+178.00002	+240.00000
C(2)	- Infinity	+110.00000	+192.00000	C(5)	- Infinity	+96.000000	+240.00000
C(3)	+240.00000	+240.00000	+ Infinity	C(6)	- Infinity	+45.000000	+144.00000

	Sensitivity Analysis for RHS				Page : 1	
B(i)	Min. B(i)	Original	Max. B(i)	B(i)	Min. B(i)	Original	Max. B(i)
B(1)	+400.00000	+450.00000	+ Infinity	B(5)	+200.00000	+800.00000	+ Infinity
B(2)	0	+1000.0000	+1125.0000	B(6)	+5999.9995	+12000.000	+ Infinity
B(3)	+20.000000	+40.000000	+ Infinity	B(7)	+80.000000	+180.00000	+ Infinity
B(4)	+2400.0000	+4000.0000	+ Infinity	B(8)	+180.00000	+400.00000	+ Infinity

Figure 6.27 Solution to LP problem 6.7.

6.8 An emergency ambulance service has found the minimum number of ambulance crews needed in each four-hour period of the day as shown in Table 6.10.

Each crew works a continuous eight hour shift. Show how the problem of scheduling crews to meet requirements can be expressed as an integer linear programme.

Table 6.10

Time period	Crews needed
midnight–4am	12
4–8 am	8
8–12am	28
12–4 pm	16
4–8 pm	24
8pm–midnight	32

CASE STUDY – SMITHERS ENGINEERING COMPANY

In the 1930s George Smithers started to supply parts to the car plants opening around the West Midlands. His company prospered and Smithers Engineering Company opened new factories to expand capacity. Over time a number of other companies were taken over to expand the product range. John Smithers took control of the company when his father retired in the mid 1960s. Everything continued to run smoothly until the early 1970s when the economy began to decline and the traditional engineering centres of the West Midlands were badly affected by recession. Smithers closed several of their older factories and concentrated on production of a few of their most successful products. The company hoped to survive this period of entrenchment and be able to take advantage of any future upturn in the economy. Things continued badly for the company until the late 1980s when the period of continuous contraction seemed to be ending. The company could now do some serious planning for the future.

Strategic planning within Smithers concentrated on the period between one and five years in the future and was done by a group of five executive directors, including three members of the Smithers family. In the mid 1970s a small tactical planning group was formed to bridge the gap between these strategic plans and daily operations. This group was made up of three people, but they could only begin to do useful work now that conditions were more stable. Three more people were added to the group and they were given their first job of coordinating proposed production, marketing and distribution policies.

The main aim of the tactical planning group was to design an annual plan for their eight main products which were made in three factories and sold in seven regional markets. Essentially they wanted to find how much of each product should be made at each factory and transported to each market.

The first consideration was that available production resources be used efficiently. Because they had dramatically reduced production in their factories there was some free space available but this was kept in mothballs and was not normally maintained. If sales increased beyond base production capacities this space could be used (with higher associated costs), and they would also have to increase employment, increase overtime and consider subcontracting.

The long term difficulties faced by Smithers had left them with an appreciation for the need of effective marketing. Sales were influenced by advertising and pricing policies, and increased profits depended on their ability to generate extra sales as much as their ability to manufacture efficiently.

The most relevant variables for the annual plan appeared to be:

- the quantity of each product to make at each factory destined for each market;
- the extent to which higher cost capacity should be used at each factory;
- the advertising budget which should be allocated to each product;
- the price level for each product.

The tactical planning group was anxious to establish their credentials and decided to build a linear programming model of the system. They hoped to demonstrate a basic version of the model for the current year and expand the model later so that subsequent years' plans would be more detailed. One part of the group started to build a model while the other part collected data.

The modelling group soon established a series of rules, including the following.

- A reasonable objective is the maximization of total profit. This is found from:

      selling price − material and manufacturing cost − cost of transport − cost of selling

- Production levels for each product in each factory must lie between upper and lower limits.
- Total capacity (including use of higher cost expansions) at each factory must not be exceeded.

- Deliveries between factories and markets must not exceed transport availability.

- Sales of each product in each market must lie between upper and lower limits.

- Total sales must not exceed total production (including that from higher cost expansions).

- Total production of any product must not exceed maximum possible sales for that product.

- Advertising expenditure must not exceed budget limits.

- Cash required for advertising and expanding production facilities must not exceed working capital available.

Unfortunately the data collection did not go well. After a considerable effort information had only been collected from one factory making four products and for one market. A summary of this data follows.

Production

Four products A, B, C and D are made on two assembly lines in the factory: A and B are made on the first line while C and D are made on the second. The standard capacity of the factory can be increased by incurring higher costs.

Production line	Standard cost per unit	Standard capacity per year	Increased cost per unit	Increased capacity per year
1	16.00	2000	18.40	600
2	12.00	1800	14.00	400

Product	A	B	C	D
Material cost per unit	64	84	72	28

Marketing

Each £20,000 spent on advertising increases sales of products by the percentages shown below. Estimates were also made of the effect of selling price on forecast sales (Table 6.11).

Product	A	B	C	D
Percentage increase in demand for £20,000 in advertising	1.0	7.0	0.4	8.0

Table 6.11

Product	Selling price	Estimated annual sales
A	120	64,000
B	120	18,000
	130	11,000
C	120	30,000
D	70	60,000
	80	90,000

The total advertising budget for the year was £140,000 of which at most £20,000 could be spent on product C.

Although there was considerably less data than expected the group felt it could still present a convincing case by:

- describing a linear programming formulation which would have given results for this year's tactical plan if adequate data had been available;
- demonstrating this formulation with the limited data available;
- describing plans for expanding the model in future years.

SOLUTIONS TO SELF ASSESSMENT QUESTIONS

6.1 Linear programming is a means of tackling constrained optimization problems. Problems of this type are commonly faced by management and the aim of LP is to suggest solutions which optimize a stated objective and demonstrate the consequences of using other policies.

6.2 The main assumption is that the problem tackled is one of constrained optimization with linear constraints and objective function. Other assumptions common to all linear programming models include proportionality, additivity and non-negativity of problem variables. There must also be a number of assumptions about the availability and reliability of data.

6.3 Intuition is unreliable, it does not guarantee an optimal (or even good) solution and can take a lot of effort.

6.4 A linear programming formulation is an algebraic statement of a problem: it is a mathematical model stated in a specific form. The components of a formulation are variables, constraints and an objective function.

6.5 The feasible region for a problem

represents those solutions which satisfy all constraints, including the non-negativity conditions.

6.6 The objective function supplies the measure by which solutions are judged and hence allows an optimal solution to be identified.

6.7 The feasible region is always convex and is surrounded by straight lines: the corners or vertices of the feasible region are the extreme points. The significance of the extreme points is that an optimal solution will always be found at an extreme point.

6.8 The line of the objective function is superimposed on the graph of the constraints. As this line moves away from the origin its value increases and the maximum value is at the last point it passes through in the feasible region. As the line moves in towards the origin its value decreases and the minimum value is at the last point it passes through in the feasible region.

6.9 Sensitivity, or post-optimal, analysis looks at the way an optimal solution varies with changing data. The effect of varying levels of resource or changing objective function can be assessed from the optimal solution without resolving the whole problem.

6.10 There are two main reasons for this. Firstly, some data may be approximate and it is useful to see how sensitive the final solution is. Secondly, some values may be changed (advertising can increase sales, overtime payments can increase capacity and so on) and it would be useful to compare results for different levels of resource allocation.

6.11 The gradient of the objective function line is between the gradients of the two limiting constraints. If this gradient $(-b/a)$ rises or falls until it is no longer between the gradients of these two constraints, the optimal solution moves to another extreme point.

6.12 Shadow prices measure the rate of change of the objective function with changes in resource levels. They are equivalent to the marginal value of a resource.

6.13 The shadow prices are valid until so many resources become available that the constraint is no longer limiting (or resources are reduced until a new constraint becomes limiting).

6.14 Graphical solutions can only be used with two (or at best three) variables. For larger problems the Simplex procedure is used. This involves a lot of simple arithmetic on matrices which can be done easily and reliably on computers.

6.15 Many kinds of information can be given, but the most usual are:

- a copy of the problem solved;
- details of the optimal solution;
- limiting constraints and unused resources;
- shadow prices and ranges over which these are valid;
- variations in the objective function which will not change the position of the optimal solution.

REFERENCES FOR FURTHER READING

Early work

Dantzig G. B. (1963). *Linear Programming and Extensions* New Jersey: Princeton University Press

Garvin W. W. (1960). *Introduction to Linear Programming* New York: McGraw-Hill

Hadley G. (1962). *Linear Programming* Reading: Addison-Wesley

Later books

Anderson D. R., Sweeney D. J. and Williams T. A. (1974). *Linear Programming for Decision Making* St Paul: West Publishing

Bradley S. P., Hax A. C. and Magnanti T. L. (1977). *Applied Mathematical Programming* Reading: Addison-Wesley

Bunday B. (1984). *Basic Linear Programming*

London: Edward Arnold

Cooper L. and Steinberg D. (1974). *Methods and Applications of Linear Programming* Philadelphia: W. B. Saunders

Hayhurst G. (1976). *Mathematical Programming for Management and Business* London: Edward Arnold

Kolman B. and Beck R. (1980). *Elementary Linear Programming with Applications* New York: Academic Press

Luenberger D. G. (1973). *Introduction to Linear and Non-Linear Programming*

Reading: Addison-Wesley

Rothenberg R. I. (1979). *Linear Programming* New York: Elsevier North-Holland

Schrage L. (1984). *Linear, Integer and Quadratic Programming with LINDO* Palo Alto: Scientific Press

Shapiro R. O. (1984). *Optimisation for Planning and Allocation* New York: John Wiley

Wu N. and Coppins R. (1981). *Linear Programming and Extensions* New York: McGraw-Hill

Chapter 7

Sequencing, scheduling and routing

SYNOPSIS

The aim of this chapter is to describe some sequencing, scheduling and routing problems and suggest ways in which these can be solved. Such problems are closely related and generally require the best sequence to be found for a set of 'activities'. Typical examples of these are the determination of the best order for jobs to be processed on a machine, the best route for a bus to take between towns and the best assignment of operators to machines. Although such sequencing problems are common, they are usually difficult to solve and significant progress has only been made in a few specific areas.

In essence, sequencing is concerned with finding an optimal order for activities; scheduling is concerned with the timing of activities; routing problems determine the sequence in which a set of customers should be visited. These terms are often not used specifically and 'scheduling' is generally used to describe all activities of this type. There are many different types of scheduling problems, so here we will concentrate on a few of the most important.

The chapter starts by discussing the nature of sequencing and scheduling problems. In most scheduling problems the number of possible combinations and permutations of activities make the problems very complex. Although linear programming formulations can be used for some scheduling problems, they are usually very cumbersome and their use is restricted to very small problems. Other approaches are needed for realistically sized problems and here we are helped by a number of specialized solution procedures.

Many scheduling rules have been devised to give reasonable solutions to problems where jobs queue to be processed on a single machine. Some of these are described and the results compared. Similar rules are available for flow shops with two machines, so the total time in the system can be minimized. Unfortunately, there are no simple rules for larger problems.

The assignment problem is considered next, where a number of operators are assigned to machines. Although this can be solved as a linear programme, simpler algorithms exist. Similarly, the transportation problem, where goods are moved between a number of sources and destinations, can be described as a linear programme but a much simpler algorithm has been developed.

The last type of problem considered involves calculations on a network. Specifically we will look at problems of finding the shortest paths from one node to every other node in a network and problems of finding the maximum flow through a network. These network problems are indirectly related to the project networks drawn in Chapter 5.

OBJECTIVES

After reading this chapter and doing the numerical exercises you should be able to:

- appreciate the nature of scheduling problems;
- identify a number of different situations which can be characterized as scheduling;
- use permutations and combinations to calculate the number of possible sequences;
- appreciate the difficulty of obtaining optimal solutions to scheduling problems;
- use a variety of scheduling rules to achieve different objectives when a number of jobs have to be processed on a single machine;
- use Johnson's rule for a flow shop with two machines;
- formulate assignment problems as zero–one integer linear programmes;
- use the assignment algorithm;
- formulate transportation problems as linear programmes;
- use the transportation algorithm;
- calculate the shortest paths between one node and all the other nodes in a network;
- calculate the maximum flow through a network.

7.1 BACKGROUND TO SEQUENCING PROBLEMS

Sequencing problems occur in a very wide range of circumstances. A train or bus schedule shows one possible sequence of stops and illustrates a solution to one specific problem (presumably the sequence is aimed at minimizing travel time or maximizing revenue), but related problems arise in many other situations. In essence, sequencing problems have a number of activities which may be performed in different orders. Often the order in which the activities are taken will affect the overall performance. The time taken for a bus to travel between a suburb and a city centre, for example, depends on the sequence in which specified stops are visited. The time taken to process a number of jobs on a machine will depend on the adjustments needed to the machine between each job, and hence on the order in which the jobs are taken. The number of people employed by a restaurant depends on their availability and hence the order in which they are assigned to shifts, days off and holidays.

Strictly speaking there is a difference between sequencing and scheduling although the two terms are often used to mean the same thing.

Sequencing is the determination of the order in which activities are performed.

Scheduling is the determination of times for each activity.

Determining the order in which a bus visits stops is a sequencing problem while determining the times when it arrives at each is a scheduling problem.

The main difficulty with problems of this type is the large number of possible sequences which have to be considered. If we need to sequence n activities we can select the first as any one of the n. The second activity selected can be any one of the remaining $(n - 1)$, so there are $n * (n - 1)$ possible sequences for the first two activities. The third selected can be any one of the remaining $(n - 2)$, the fourth any of $(n - 3)$ and so on. Then the total number of sequences for n activities is:

$$\text{Number of sequences} = n * (n - 1) * (n - 2) * (n - 3) \ldots$$
$$* 3 * 2 * 1$$
$$= n!$$

Even a small problem with, say, 15 activities has $15! = 1.3 * 10^{12}$ possible sequences. It is obviously impossible to list all possible sequences, evaluate each and select the best, so algorithms are needed to find optimal, or at least good, solutions.

Two important calculations for sequencing problems are concerned with 'permutations' and 'combinations'. These determine the number of ways in which groups of r things can be selected from n things. Suppose we have n things which are distinct (that is, we can tell the difference between them) and we want to select r of these. In how many ways can this be done?

If we are *not* interested in the order in which the r things are selected the answer is the *combination* of r things from n, which is written as ^nC_r.

The number of ways r things can be selected from n, regardless of the order of selection, is given by:

$$^nC_r = \frac{n!}{r! * (n - r)!}$$

If there is a pool of 10 cars and three customers arrive to use them there are $^{10}C_3$ ways of allocating cars to customers.

$$^{10}C_3 = \frac{10!}{3! * (10 - 3)!} = 120$$

If we *are* interested in the order in which the r things are selected the answer is the *permutation* of r things from n, which is written as ^nP_r.

The number of ways r things can be selected from n, when the order of selection is important, is given by:

$$^nP_r = \frac{n!}{(n - r)!}$$

Suppose there are 10 applicants for a social club's committee consisting of a chairman, deputy chairman, secretary and treasurer. We are interested in selecting a group of four from 10, but the order in which they are selected is important (corresponding to the different jobs). Then the number of ways in which the committee of four can be chosen is

$$^nP_r = \frac{n!}{(n - r)!} = \frac{10!}{(10 - 4)!}$$
$$= 5040$$

If four ordinary committee members were to be selected (that is, with no differentiation in job description and hence no importance to the order in which the people were chosen) we would be interested in the combinations of four from 10. The number of ways of selecting the members is:

$$^nC_r = \frac{n!}{r! * (n - r)!} = \frac{10!}{4! * (10 - 4)!}$$
$$= 210$$

Permutations depend on order of selection and combinations do not, so there are always a lot more permutations than combinations (any particular combination of r things from n can be arranged in a large number of permutations). The number of combinations of four letters of the alphabet is $26!/(4! * 22!) = 14{,}950$. One combination is the letters A, B, C and D, but these can be arranged in 24 different ways (ABCD, ABDC, ACBD etc.). The number of permutations of four letters from the alphabet is $26!/22! = 358{,}800$.

WORKED EXAMPLE 7.1

(a) A company has eight applicants to fill eight different jobs. In how many different ways can it assign applicants to jobs?

(b) There is a sudden reorganization in the company and the number of available jobs falls to six. In how many different ways can the jobs be filled with the eight applicants?

(c) Suppose the reorganization leads to a reclassification of jobs and the six jobs are now identical. In how many different ways can they be filled?

SOLUTION

(a) This essentially asks, 'How many different ways can eight things be sequenced' and the answer is 8!. The applicants can be assigned to jobs in $8! = 40,320$ different ways.

(b) This asks the number of ways in which six things can be selected from eight. As the jobs are different we are interested in the order of selection and the number of ways six different jobs can be filled from eight applicants is:

$$^nP_r = \frac{n!}{(n-r)!} = \frac{8!}{(8-6)!}$$
$$= 20,160$$

(c) This again asks the number of ways in which six things can be selected from eight, but now the jobs are identical so the order of selection is not important. The number of ways six identical jobs can be filled from eight applicants is:

$$^nC_r = \frac{n!}{r! * (n-r)!} = \frac{8!}{6! * (8-6)!}$$
$$= 28$$

Note that this problem could be looked at from the other viewpoint of finding how many ways two applicants could be rejected from eight. Then with $r = 2$ we have:

$$^nC_r = \frac{n!}{r! * (n-r)!} = \frac{8!}{2! * (8-2)!}$$
$$= 28$$

WORKED EXAMPLE 7.2

Twelve areas in the North Sea become available for oil exploration and Government policy of encouraging competition limits the allocation of these to at most one area for any exploration company.

(a) If 12 exploration companies bid for the areas in how many ways can the areas be allocated?

(b) Initial forecasts show that each area is equally likely to produce oil and they can, therefore, be considered equally attractive. If 20 exploration companies put in bids for areas how many ways are there of allocating areas to companies?

(c) A last minute report shows the probabilities of major oil discoveries in each area. Based on this four companies withdraw their bid. If the areas are now allocated randomly, in how many ways can this allocation be done?

SOLUTION

(a) There are 12 companies receiving one area each so the companies can be sequenced in 12! possible ways, or $4.79 * 10^8$.

(b) Here there are 20 companies, only 12 of whom will be selected. As each area is equally attractive it does not matter in which order the companies are selected, so the number of possible combinations is:

$$^nC_r = \frac{n!}{r! * (n-r)!} = \frac{20!}{12! * (20-12)!}$$

$$= 125{,}970$$

(c) Now the areas are different and we are interested in the orders in which the remaining 16 companies can be selected. This is given by:

$$^nP_r = \frac{n!}{(n-r)!} = \frac{16!}{(16-12)!}$$

$$= 8.72 * 10^{11}$$

In summary

- There are $n!$ possible sequences of n different things.
- If the order of selection is *not* important r things can be selected from n in ^nC_r different ways.
- If the order of selection *is* important r things can be selected from n in ^nP_r different ways.
- $^nC_r = \dfrac{n!}{r! * (n-r)!}$ and $^nP_r = \dfrac{n!}{(n-r)!}$

SELF ASSESSMENT QUESTIONS

7.1 What is the difference between sequencing and scheduling?

7.2 In how many ways can n different activities be sequenced?

7.3 What is the difference between a permutation and a combination?

7.4 When selecting r things from n are there

(a) more combinations than permutations

(b) less combinations than permutations

(c) the same number of combinations and permutations

(d) either more or less combinations than permutations?

7.2 SCHEDULING JOBS ON MACHINES

One of the most common scheduling problems can be characterized by jobs queueing to be processed on machines. Consider a process which has different items passing through a piece of equipment (different blends of whisky passed through the same bottling machine, different material printed on the same press, etc.). Ordinarily, a number of units of each item are formed into a batch so that set-up costs are reduced. The determination of batch sizes has been described in Chapter 3 on inventory control, but here we will look at another aspect of the problem, which is to determine the sequence in which the batches should be scheduled on the equipment (see Figure 7.1).

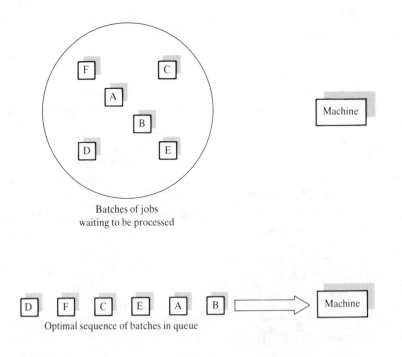

Figure 7.1 Sequencing jobs for processing.

We will start by assuming the set-up time for each batch is constant, regardless of the item which was processed previously. This implies that the total time needed to process all jobs will remain constant whichever order they are taken. There are, however, a number of other considerations which may be important. If stocks of one item are low, this item could be given a high priority; having a small number of jobs in the queue or a short average queueing time may also be important. A number of simple scheduling rules have been developed to deal with problems of this kind.

Perhaps the most widely used scheduling rule is based on the urgency with which a batch of items is needed:

> To minimize stock-outs:
> schedule items in order of increasing runout time (that is, most urgent first).

The runout time for an item is the length of time existing stocks will last.

$$\text{Runout time} = \frac{\text{current stock level}}{\text{average demand}}$$

If there are currently 100 units of an item in stock and average demand is 20 units a week the runout time is five weeks.

WORKED EXAMPLE 7.3

Six items are made in batches on the same piece of equipment. At some point, average weekly demands, current stock levels and times to produce a batch of each item are as follows:

Item	A	B	C	D	E	F
Average demand	10	4	26	34	7	3
Current stock	72	21	48	92	28	23
Production time	2.0	1.5	0.5	0.5	1.0	1.5

Design a schedule for making one batch of each item and say whether there will be any stock-outs.

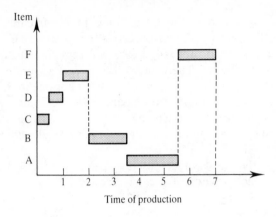

Figure 7.2 Gantt chart for production schedule in Worked example 7.3.

SOLUTION

The runout time for each item is calculated by dividing the current stock by the average demand, and items are scheduled in order of increasing runout time (C, D, E, B, A and F).

Taking the start time for the first batch as time 0, a batch of item C will be finished at time 0.5. A batch of item D can then be started and finished 0.5 later at time 1.0, then a batch of E can be started and finished at time 2.0, and so on. By noting the finish time for each batch, a check can be made to ensure no item will run out of stock before its next batch is finished.

Item	C	D	E	B	A	F
Runout time	1.85	2.71	4.00	5.25	7.20	7.67
Start production	0	0.5	1.0	2.0	3.5	5.5
Production time	0.5	0.5	1.0	1.5	2.0	1.5
Finish production	0.5	1.0	2.0	3.5	5.5	7.0

This is illustrated in Figure 7.2.

The rule 'schedule in order of increasing runout time' is typical of the simple scheduling rules which can be applied to jobs waiting at a single processor. Different rules can be used to achieve different objectives, but before describing some of these we should draw a clear distinction between processing time and time in the system.

- Processing time is the time a job is actually worked on by the equipment.
- Time in the system is the sum of the processing time and the time the job waits before processing starts.

> Time in the system = processing time + queueing time

If a job needs two days on a piece of equipment but arrives for processing and has to wait in a queue for three days before processing starts:

- processing time = 2 days
- time in the queue = 3 days
- time in the system = 5 days.

Suppose a string of jobs has different processing times. If the objective is to minimize the average time in the system the rule is:

> To minimize average time in the system:
> sequence the jobs in order of increasing length (that is, shortest first)

As the time each job spends in the queue is determined by the time taken by preceding jobs, taking the shortest jobs first will minimize the average waiting time and hence the average time in the system.

Jobs may have some date when they are due to be finished, and if they are not ready by this due date they are late. A reasonable objective is to minimize the average lateness of jobs. This leads to another scheduling rule.

> To minimize average lateness:
> sequence jobs in order of earliest due date first

WORKED EXAMPLE 7.4

Eight jobs are waiting to be processed on a single machine, with processing times as follows:

Job	A	B	C	D	E	F	G	H
Processing time	2	5	3	8	4	7	2	3

(a) What sequence of jobs will minimize the mean queueing time?

(b) If jobs have the following due dates, what order will minimize the average lateness?

Job	A	B	C	D	E	F	G	H
Due date	13	7	8	30	14	20	2	36

SOLUTION

(a) Mean queueing time is minimized when jobs are taken in order of increasing duration (when several jobs have the same processing time they can be taken in arbitrary order). This gives the sequence A, G, C, H, E, B, F and D. Setting the start time for the first job as 0, the start and finish times of other jobs are as follows:

Job	A	G	C	H	E	B	F	D
Duration	2	2	3	3	4	5	7	8
Start processing	0	2	4	7	10	14	19	26
Processing time	2	2	3	3	4	5	7	8
Finish processing	2	4	7	10	14	19	26	34

The average waiting time is found by adding the start times and dividing by 8, to give 82/8 = 10.25.

(b) Mean lateness is minimized by taking jobs in order of increasing due date (G, B, C, A, E, F, D and H).

Job	G	B	C	A	E	F	D	H
Due date	2	7	8	13	14	20	30	36
Start processing	0	2	7	10	12	16	23	31
Processing time	2	5	3	2	4	7	8	3
Finish processing	2	7	10	12	16	23	31	34
Lateness	–	–	2	–	2	3	1	–

The mean lateness is (2 + 2 + 3 + 1)/8 = 1 day.

Although both of these rules give the same total processing time of 34 days they have different characteristics. The first solution has an average wait of 10.25 days, while the second has 101/8 = 12.625 days. The second has four jobs late and an average lateness over all jobs of one day. If the same due dates are used for the first sequence, there are four jobs late (B, D, F and G), with an average lateness of (12 + 4 + 6 + 2)/8 = 3 days.

Rather than minimize the average lateness, it may be useful to minimize the number of jobs which are late. There is a simple extension of the 'earliest due date' rule which achieves this, with the following five steps.

(1) Use the earliest due date rule to find an initial sequence of jobs. If no job is late this is the optimal solution, otherwise move on to step 2.

(2) Identify the first late job in the schedule.

(3) Identify the longest job preceding (and including) the job identified in step 2.

(4) Remove this longest job from the schedule and update the times for the other jobs. If there are still late jobs go to step 2, otherwise continue to step 5.

(5) Add the jobs removed in step 4 to the end of the schedule.

WORKED EXAMPLE 7.5

Take the eight jobs described in worked example 7.4 and find the sequence which minimizes the number of late jobs.

SOLUTION

The jobs are:

Job	A	B	C	D	E	F	G	H
Processing time	2	5	3	8	4	7	2	3
Due date	13	7	8	30	14	20	2	36

(1) Taking them in order of due date gives the solution:

Job	G	B	C	A	E	F	D	H
Due date	2	7	8	13	14	20	30	36
Start processing	0	2	7	10	12	16	23	31
Processing time	2	5	3	2	4	7	8	3
Finish processing	2	7	10	12	16	23	31	34
Late			*		*	*	*	

(2)   The first late job in the schedule is C.

(3)   The longest job up to and including C is B with a processing time of 5.

(4)   Removing job B from the schedule and updating the times of the other jobs gives:

Job	G	C	A	E	F	D	H
Due date	2	8	13	14	20	30	36
Start processing	0	2	5	7	11	18	26
Processing time	2	3	2	4	7	8	3
Finish processing	2	5	7	11	18	26	29

(5)   There are no jobs late now so we add the deleted job to the end of the schedule.

Job	G	C	A	E	F	D	H	B
Due date	2	8	13	14	20	30	36	7
Start processing	0	2	5	7	11	18	26	29
Processing time	2	3	2	4	7	8	3	5
Finish processing	2	5	7	11	18	26	29	34

Now there is only one job late, the average queueing time is 98/8 = 12.25 and the average lateness is 27/8 = 3.375 days.

There are many such scheduling rules to cater for different circumstances and objectives. We will not go into details of these, but a few rules take jobs in order of:

- arrival time (that is, first come first served)
- least slack time (time to due date − processing time)

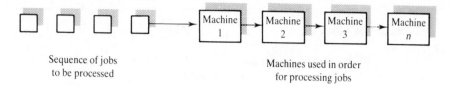

Figure 7.3 Schematic of a flowshop.

- most nearly finished
- fewest remaining operations before completion
- shortest queue at next operation
- lowest critical ratio (time to due date divided by total time needed to finish job)
- highest priority

  and

- least changeover cost.

The rules described so far have assumed jobs are queueing at a single piece of equipment. One useful extension would be to look at problems where jobs are processed on several pieces of equipment. This is typical of a 'flowshop', where jobs use the same set of machines in the same order (see Figure 7.3). The problem here is to determine the best sequence of jobs through the flowshop.

We will consider a small flowshop where jobs are processed on two machines (machine 1 followed by machine 2). The jobs are put into a sequence and this sequence is used for both machine 1 and machine 2. We will assume the best sequence is the one which minimizes total time spent in the system (that is, the time between the first job starting on machine 1 and the last job finishing on machine 2). To find this we can use 'Johnson's Rule' which has the following steps.

(1) List the jobs and their processing time on each machine.

(2) Find the job with the next smallest processing time on either machine.

(3) If this time is on machine 1 sequence the job as early as possible: if it is on machine 2 sequence the job as late as possible.

(4) Do not consider the job put into the sequence again, but repeat steps 2 and 3 (working inwards from the ends of the sequence) until all jobs have been scheduled.

WORKED EXAMPLE 7.6

Seven jobs are to be processed on machine 1 followed by machine 2. The time needed by each job on each machine is as follows:

Job	A	B	C	D	E	F	G
Machine 1	2	5	10	8	4	12	9
Machine 2	14	7	3	10	5	6	6

What sequence of jobs would maximize the machine utilizations?

SOLUTION

If jobs spend as short a time as possible in the system it follows that the machines are used as fully as possible. Thus we can use Johnson's Rule to find the best sequence.

(1) The processing times are given in the table above.
(2) The shortest processing time is 2, which is the time job A spends on machine 1.
(3) This time is on machine 1, so we will schedule the job as early as possible (in this case first).

      Sequence: A . . .

(4) There are still jobs left unscheduled

(2) The shortest remaining processing time is 3, which is the time job C takes on machine 2.
(3) This time is on machine 2, so we will schedule the job as late as possible (in this case last).

      Sequence: A . . . C

(4) There are still jobs left unscheduled.

(2) The shortest remaining processing time is 4, which is the time job E takes on machine 1.
(3) This time is on machine 1, so we will schedule the job as early as possible (in this case after A).

      Sequence: A E . . . C

Repeating this procedure until all jobs have been allocated to the sequence (in the order B, F then G).

      Sequence: A E B G F C

In summary
There are many rules for achieving different objectives when scheduling jobs on one machine, including:

- scheduling shortest first minimizes waiting time
- scheduling earliest due date first minimizes average lateness.

Johnson's Rule can be used to find the best sequence through two machines.

SELF ASSESSMENT QUESTIONS

7.5 What is a 'scheduling rule'?

7.6 In what order should jobs be sequenced through a single machine to minimize average waiting time?

7.7 In what order should jobs be sequenced through a single machine to minimize average lateness?

7.8 When is Johnson's Rule used?

7.3 THE ASSIGNMENT PROBLEM

The problems we have looked at so far have found the best sequence of jobs through equipment. An associated problem is the allocation of operators to the equipment, which is formalized as the assignment problem. Different people have different skills and the total cost and efficiency of an operation will depend on the way in which operators are assigned to equipment. Similar situations are met when, for example, the output from a factory is assigned to a particular market, books are assigned to editors, or warehouses are assigned to cover geographical areas.

The starting point for this analysis is a table of costs for each combination of operator and equipment. For convenience we will talk in terms of 'operators' being assigned to 'machines' and define $C(i,j)$ as the cost of assigning operator i to machine j. For the assignment problem each operator is assigned to only one machine, while each machine has only one operator assigned to it. This allows a linear programming formulation based on a variable $X(i,j)$ which can only take the values zero and one.

$X(i,j) = 1$ if operator i is assigned to machine j
$\quad\quad\quad = 0$ otherwise.

A valid allocation of operators to machines can be represented by the following table of $X(i,j)$.

| | Machine | | | | | |
	1	2	3	4	5	6
Operator 1	0	1	0	0	0	0
2	0	0	0	1	0	0
3	1	0	0	0	0	0
4	0	0	0	0	0	1
5	0	0	0	0	1	0
6	0	0	1	0	0	0

Here operator 1 is assigned to machine 2, operator 2 is assigned to machine 4 and so on. The important thing to notice in this matrix is that every row and column has a single '1' and the rest of the entries are zero. This suggests constraints for the linear programme of the form:

- there is only one entry in each row:

$$\sum_{i=1}^{n} X(i,j) = 1 \qquad \text{for } j = 1, \ldots n$$

- and one entry in each column:

$$\sum_{j=1}^{n} X(i,j) = 1 \qquad \text{for } i = 1, \ldots n$$

The cost of an assignment is only incurred when the assignment is actually used, so the cost of any particular assignment is $X(i,j) * C(i,j)$. If an assignment is made $X(i,j)$ has the value 1 and the cost is $C(i,j)$: if the assignment is not made $X(i,j)$ has the value 0 and the cost is 0. The objective function will complete the LP formulation, with:

$$\text{Minimize} \quad \sum_{i=1}^{n} \sum_{j=1}^{n} X(i,j) * C(i,j)$$

with $C(i,j) \geq 0$ for $i = 1, \ldots n$ and $j = 1, \ldots n$.

This illustrates a type of integer programming, called zero–one programming, which has been mentioned in Chapter 6. Unfortunately, such problems are difficult to solve and solutions can only be found for small problems. Another solution procedure, called the 'Hungarian Method', has been developed specifically for the assignment problem and this is much easier than zero–one programming.

The Hungarian method starts with the cost matrix $C(i,j)$ and uses the following iterative procedure.

(1) Form a cost matrix with number of rows equal to number of columns.

(2) Reduce the matrix (that is, subtract the smallest element in each row from all elements in the row: then subtract the smallest element in each column from all elements in the column). There should now be at least one zero in each row and one in each column.

(3) Cross out all the zeros with the minimum number of straight lines. (Use only lines through rows and columns but not diagonal lines.) If this minimum number of lines equals the number of rows an optimal solution has been found, go to step (5). Otherwise continue to step (4).

(4) Find the smallest uncovered (that is not crossed out) element and subtract this from all uncovered elements and add it to those elements which have been crossed out twice. Go to step (3).

(5) Identify the optimal assignment from the position of the zeros. (If there are several alternatives start with rows and columns which only contain a single zero which must form part of the solution).

This perhaps seems a strange process, but there is a genuine theoretical basis for the steps and we can illustrate the procedure by the following example.

WORKED EXAMPLE 7.7

Five ships of different types are to be unloaded at berths. There are five berths available, each with different facilities, and the costs of unloading are given below (in thousands of pounds). What assignment of ships to berths would minimize total costs?

		Berths			
	1	2	3	4	5
1	8	10	9	3	6
2	7	8	11	2	9
Ships 3	2	4	6	4	4
4	7	7	5	2	7
5	10	8	10	3	11

SOLUTION

Following the steps described in the Hungarian method:

(1) The cost matrix has already been defined.

	1	2	3	4	5
1	8	10	9	3	6
2	7	8	11	2	9
3	2	4	6	4	4
4	7	7	5	2	7
5	10	8	10	3	11

(2) Reduce the matrix by subtracting the smallest element in each row from all elements in the row.

	1	2	3	4	5	Smallest
1	8	10	9	3	6	3
2	7	8	11	2	9	2
3	2	4	6	4	4	2
4	7	7	5	2	7	2
5	10	8	10	3	11	3

Then subtract the smallest element in each column from all elements in the column.

	1	2	3	4	5
1	5	7	6	0	3
2	5	6	9	0	7
3	0	2	4	2	2
4	5	5	3	0	5
5	7	5	7	0	8
Smallest	0	2	3	0	2

This gives the following reduced cost matrix.

	1	2	3	4	5
1	5	5	3	0	1
2	5	4	6	0	5
3	0	0	1	2	0
4	5	3	0	0	3
5	7	3	4	0	6

(3) The next step is to cross all the zeros out with the minimum number of

straight (either horizontal or vertical) lines. In this case the minimum number of lines is three. This does not equal the number of rows so we proceed to step 4.

	1	2	3	4	5
1	5	5	3	0	1*
2	5	4	6	0	5
3	0	0	1	2	0
4	5	3	0	0	3
5	7	3	4	0	6

(4)   The smallest number not crossed out is identified (1 in row 1 column 5). This is subtracted from all other numbers which have not been crossed out and added to all numbers which have been crossed out twice. Then return to step 3.

	1	2	3	4	5
1	4	4	2	0	0
2	4	3	5	0	4
3	0	0	1	3	0
4	5	3	0	1	3
5	6	2*	3	0	5

(3)   The minimum number of straight lines needed to cross out all the zeros is now 4. This is not equal to the number of rows so we find the smallest number not crossed out (2 in row 5 column 2). This is subtracted from all numbers not crossed out and added to those crossed out twice.

	1	2	3	4	5
1	4	4	2	2	0
2	2	1	3	0	2
3	0	0	1	5	0
4	5	3	0	3	3
5	4	0	1	0	3

(4)   This time there are five lines needed to cross out all the zeros. This means an optimal solution has been found so we move to step 5 to identify this optimal.

	1	2	3	4	5
1	4	4	2	2	0
2	2	1	3	0	2
3	0	0	1	5	0
4	5	3	0	3	3
5	4	0	1	0	3

(5) The optimal assignment of ships to berths is identified by the zeros. There are eight zeros, so we must find the five which identify an optimal. Each ship must be assigned to a berth and each berth must have a ship assigned to it, so there must be one zero in each row and each column. To identify these zeros we start with the rows and columns with only a single zero. Ship 1 must be assigned to berth 5, ship 2 must be assigned to berth 4 and ship 4 must be assigned to berth 3. Similarly berth 1 must have ship 3 assigned to it. This leaves ship 5 which might be assigned to berth 2 or 4, but ship 2 is already assigned to berth 4, so ship 5 must be assigned to berth 2.

	1	2	3	4	5
1	4	4	2	2	0*
2	2	1	3	0*	2
3	0*	0	1	5	0
4	5	3	0*	3	3
5	4	0*	1	0	3

The cost of this assignment is found by substitution in the original cost matrix $(6 + 2 + 5 + 8 + 2 = 23)$.

The Hungarian method is straightforward except for the identification of the optimal solution which might be awkward, particularly with large problems or large numbers of zeros in the solution. In worked example 7.7 we used a sensible argument, but a more formal approach can be used.

(1) Starting with the first row of the matrix and working down, find the rows with only one zero. Mark these zeros with an asterisk (showing that they form part of the optimal assignment) and cross out all other zeros in the same columns.

(2) Starting with the first column and working across, find the columns with only one zero. Mark these zeros with an asterisk (showing that they form part of the optimal assignment) and cross out all other zeros in the same rows.

(3) Repeat steps 1 and 2 until no more zeros can have an asterisk or be crossed out. If there are still unmarked zeros arbitrarily mark one of them with an asterisk and repeat steps 1 to 3 until all zeros either have an asterisk or are crossed out. Those zeros with an asterisk mark the optimal solution.

WORKED EXAMPLE 7.8

A sales manager has six salesmen who must be assigned to six different territories. Because they have different contacts and techniques the expected monthly sales (in thousands of pounds) are shown in the following table. What assignment would maximize the monthly income?

		Territory					
		1	2	3	4	5	6
Salesman	1	17	24	41	19	33	28
	2	22	22	31	14	27	26
	3	9	33	25	26	30	31
	4	29	43	45	8	22	20
	5	39	19	17	30	32	30
	6	31	37	27	23	37	10

SOLUTION

(1) The Hungarian method will only deal with minimizing problems, so this maximizing problem must first be transformed. This is done by calculating an opportunity cost for each element. For this the largest element in the matrix is found and all other elements are subtracted from it. Here the largest element is 45 and subtracting each entry in the original matrix from this gives a new cost matrix.

		Territory					
		1	2	3	4	5	6
Salesman	1	28	21	4	26	12	17
	2	23	23	14	31	18	19
	3	36	12	20	19	15	14
	4	16	2	0	37	23	25
	5	6	26	28	15	13	15
	6	14	8	18	22	8	35

Repeating the steps described for the Hungarian method gives the following results.

(2) Reducing the matrix by subtracting the smallest element in each row:

	1	2	3	4	5	6	Smallest
1	28	21	4	26	12	17	4
2	23	23	14	31	18	19	14
3	36	12	20	19	15	14	12
4	16	2	0	37	23	25	0
5	6	26	28	15	13	15	6
6	14	8	18	22	8	35	8

(2) Then subtracting the smallest element in each column:

	1	2	3	4	5	6
1	24	17	0	22	8	13
2	9	9	0	17	4	5
3	24	0	8	7	3	2
4	16	2	0	37	23	25
5	0	20	22	9	7	9
6	6	0	10	14	0	27
Smallest	0	0	0	7	0	2

(3)–(4) Giving the reduced matrix. In this all zeros can be crossed out by four straight lines.

	1	2	3	4	5	6
1	24	17	0	15	8	11
2	9	9	0	10	4	3
~~3~~	~~24~~	~~0~~	~~8~~	~~0~~	~~3~~	~~0~~
4	16	2*	0	30	23	23
~~5~~	~~0~~	~~20~~	~~22~~	~~2~~	~~7~~	~~7~~
~~6~~	~~6~~	~~0~~	~~10~~	~~7~~	~~0~~	~~25~~

(3)–(4) Subtracting the smallest uncovered element (2) from all other elements and adding it to those crossed out twice.

	1	2	3	4	5	6
1	22	15	0	13	6	9
2	7	7	0	8	2	1*
~~3~~	~~24~~	~~0~~	~~10~~	~~0~~	~~3~~	~~0~~
4	14	0	0	28	21	21
~~5~~	~~0~~	~~20~~	~~24~~	~~2~~	~~7~~	~~7~~
~~6~~	~~6~~	~~0~~	~~12~~	~~7~~	~~0~~	~~25~~

This time five lines are needed to cross out all the zeros.

(3)–(4) Repeating this procedure gives the final matrix, which needs six lines to cross out all the zeros.

	1	2	3	4	5	6
1	21	15	0	12	5	8
2	6	7	0	7	1	0
3	24	1	11	0	3	0
4	13	0	0	27	20	20
5	0	21	25	2	7	7
6	6	1	13	7	0	25

(5) Determine the optimal assignment.

	1	2	3	4	5	6
1	21	15	0*	12	5	8
2	6	7	0	7	1	0*
3	24	1	11	0*	3	0
4	14	0*	1	28	21	21
5	0*	21	25	2	7	7
6	6	1	13	7	0*	25

The optimal solution is shown by the asterisks and expected sales are found by substitution (41 + 26 + 26 + 43 + 39 + 37 = 212).

In summary

- The Assignment Problem looks for the lowest cost of assigning operators to facilities.
- This can be found by zero–one linear programming, but the Hungarian method is much more straightforward.
- Benefits can be maximized using a relative cost matrix (subtracting all elements from the largest entry in the original matrix).

SELF ASSESSMENT QUESTIONS

7.9 What is the 'Assignment Problem'?

7.10 Linear programming can be used to solve the assignment problem. Is this:

(a) true
(b) false
(c) partly true?

7.11 How is the optimal solution identified in the Hungarian method?

7.12 How are maximizing assignments found?

7.4   THE TRANSPORTATION ALGORITHM

The transportation problem considers the movement of goods between a number of sources and a number of destinations. Typically, factories at several locations have to supply enough goods to meet demands at warehouses in several other locations. In the basic version each source has a known capacity it can supply, each destination has a known demand, and there is a fixed cost of moving one unit of goods between any source and destination. The problem can be represented by a cost matrix of the form shown below and the objective is to minimize the total cost of transportation.

		Destinations						
		1	2	3	.	.	n	Supply
Sources	1	.	.	.				$S(1)$
	2	.	.					$S(2)$
	3	.		costs	$C(i,j)$			.
	.							
	.							.
	m							$S(m)$
Demand		$D(1)$	$D(2)$	.	.	.	$D(n)$	Total

$S(i)$ = supply of goods from source i

$D(j)$ = demand for goods at destination j

$C(i,j)$ = cost of transporting one unit of goods from source i to destination j

Like the assignment problem, this can be solved by zero–one linear programming. Defining $X(i,j)$ as the amount transported from source i to destination j gives an objective function as:

$$\text{Minimize } \sum_{i=1}^{m} \sum_{j=1}^{n} X(i,j) * C(i,j)$$

Subject to a supply constraint:

$$\sum_{j=1}^{n} X(i,j) = S(i) \quad \text{for } i = 1 \text{ to } m$$

and a demand constraint:

$$\sum_{j=1}^{m} X(i,j) = D(j) \qquad \text{for } j = 1 \text{ to } n$$

with $X(i,j) \geq 0$ for $i = 1 \ldots n$ and $j = 1 \ldots n$.

We can again avoid using standard linear programming with an alternative, specialized algorithm called the transportation algorithm. This is based on an iterative procedure, rather like the Simplex method.

The transportation algorithm is in two parts which:

- find an initial feasible solution
- keep iteratively improving this solution until an optimal is reached.

There are many methods of finding an initial solution. Here we will use Vogel's approximation method (VAM) which generally gives initial solutions which are close to optimal. This should reduce the effort needed in the second part of the algorithm. VAM is based on the idea that if the cheapest option is not used in any row or column then, at best, the second cheapest must be used and there is a consequent penalty cost. This penalty is at least as big as the difference between the cheapest and second cheapest element in the row or column. In detail, the procedure is as follows:

(1) Describe the problem in terms of a cost matrix (with the format illustrated above).

(2) Calculate the penalty cost for each row as the difference between lowest cost in the row and the second lowest cost.

(3) Calculate the penalty cost for each column as the difference between the lowest cost in the column and the second lowest cost.

(4) Find the maximum value for this penalty cost and identify the element in the chosen row or column which has the lowest cost.

(5) Assign as much as possible to this element (limited by the minimum of available supply or remaining demand).

(6) Adjust the unmet supply and demand by subtracting the amount assigned in this round. Then exclude from further consideration any column with no remaining demand or row with no remaining supply.

(7) Repeat this process until all supply has been used and all demands met.

This procedure seems quite complicated when it is written down, but is quite straightforward in practice, as demonstrated by the following example.

WORKED EXAMPLE 7.9

Use Vogel's approximation method to find an initial solution to the following transportation matrix.

		To destination				Supply
		1	2	3	4	
From	1	10	12	20	10	60
source	2	16	6	10	22	30
	3	18	14	10	16	25
	4	2	16	18	14	45
Demand		40	40	40	40	160

SOLUTION

Calculate the penalty cost for each row and column, by subtracting the lowest cost from the second lowest in each row, and the lowest cost from the second lowest in each column.

		To destination				Supply	Penalty cost
		1	2	3	4		
From	1	10	12	20	10	60	0
source	2	16	6	10	22	30	4
	3	18	14	10	16	25	4
	4	2	16	18	14	45	12 <
Demand		40	40	40	40	160	
Penalty cost		8	6	0	4		

The highest penalty cost is 12 in row 4. The lowest cost in row 4 is 2 in column 1. The maximum which can be assigned to this element is the minimum of remaining supply in row 4 (45) and demand in column 1 (40). Thus 40 is assigned to travel between source 4 and destination 1 (this value can be entered in the appropriate element with an asterisk to show it is not a cost but an assignment). The remaining supply in row 4 is reduced to 5 and the demand in column 1 to zero. Column 1 is removed from further consideration and the process is repeated.

		To destination 1	2	3	4	Remaining supply	Penalty cost
From source	1		12	20	10	60	2
	2		6	10	22	30	4
	3		14	10	16	25	4
	4	40*	16	18	14	5	2
Unmet demand		0	40	40	40	120	
Penalty cost		−	6	0	4		
			∧				

This time the highest penalty cost is 6 for column 2. As much as possible is assigned to the lowest cost in column 2, so 30 units are transported from source 2 to destination 2 (limited by supply from source 2). The supply and demand are updated and row 2 is eliminated from further consideration.

		To destination 1	2	3	4	Remaining supply	Penalty cost
From source	1		12	20	10	60	2
	2		30*			0	−
	3		14	10	16	25	4
	4	40*	16	18	14	5	2
Unmet demand		0	10	40	40	90	
Penalty cost		−	2	8	4		
				∧			

Iteratively repeating this process gives the following tables.

		To destination 1	2	3	4	Remaining supply	Penalty cost
From source	1		12	20	10	60	2
	2		30*			0	−
	3			25*		0	−
	4	40*	16	18	14	5	2
Unmet demand		0	10	15	40	65	
Penalty cost		−	4	2	4		
			∧				

		To destination 1	2	3	4	Remaining supply	Penalty cost
From source	1		10*	20	10	50	10 <
	2		30*			0	–
	3			25*		0	–
	4	40*		18	14	5	4
Unmet demand		0	0	15	40	55	
Penalty cost		–	–	2	4		

		To destination 1	2	3	4	Remaining supply	Penalty cost
From source	1		10*	20	40*	10	–
	2		30*			0	–
	3			25*		0	–
	4	40*		18		5	–
Unmet demand		0	0	15	0	15	
Penalty cost		–	–	2	–		

Penalty cost: ∧ (under column 3)

		To destination 1	2	3	4	Remaining supply
From source	1		10*	10*	40*	0
	2		30*			0
	3			25*		0
	4	40*		5*		0
Unmet demand		0	0	0	0	0

This gives an initial feasible solution. The total cost of this can be found by substituting values from the original matrix.

$$(10 * 12) + (10 * 20) + (40 * 10) + (30 * 6) + (25 * 10) + (40 * 2)$$
$$+ (5 * 18) = 1320$$

The next stage in the transportation algorithm is to use an iterative procedure to improve this initial solution. This procedure is based on the calculation of a shadow price for each blank entry in the matrix. This shadow price can be interpreted as the cost we should be prepared to pay to transfer goods between two points. If the actual cost is more than this, goods should not be transported: if the actual cost is less than this goods should be transported.

The information available so far can be put into a single matrix as shown below. The figures in the body of each box are the amounts transported, while the figures in the top right hand corner are the costs.

	1	2	3	4	Supply
1	10 0	12 10	20 10	10 40	60
2	16 0	6 30	10 0	22 0	30
3	18 0	14 0	10 25	16 0	25
4	2 40	16 0	18 5	14 0	45
Demand	40	40	40	40	160

Now we can calculate the shadow prices which we should be prepared to pay for transport. Suppose, for every element of the matrix which has a positive amount transported, we separate the cost of going between i and j, $C(i,j)$, into two elements; a cost $u(i)$ of coming from i and a cost $v(j)$ of going to j. Then for every element of the matrix with a positive amount transported:

$$C(i,j) = u(i) + v(j)$$

We know $C(i,j)$ for every entry, so if we know either $u(i)$ or $v(j)$ we can find a value for the other. To start the process we will arbitrarily set $u(1)$ as 0. Taking the first element with a positive amount transported:

$$C(1,2) = 12$$

We define $\quad C(1,2) = u(1) + v(2)$

and have set $\quad u(1) = 0$

So: $\qquad C(1,2) = 12 = u(1) + v(2) = 0 + v(2)$

$$v(2) = 12$$

Moving to the next element with a positive entry:

$$C(1,3) = 20 = u(1) + v(3) = 0 + v(3)$$
$$v(3) = 20$$

Similarly $\quad C(1,4) = 10 = u(1) + v(4) = 0 + v(4)$

$$v(4) = 10$$

Then $\qquad C(2,2) = 6 = u(2) + v(2) = u(2) + 12$

$$u(2) = -6$$
$$C(3,3) = 10 = u(3) + v(3) = u(3) + 20$$
$$u(3) = -10$$

Continuing this process will give values to every $u(i)$ and $v(j)$. Sometimes the process stops before all values can be found, in which case another $u(i)$ is arbitrarily set to zero.

	1		2		3		4		Supply	$u(i)$
		10		12		20		10		0
1	0		10		10		40		60	
		16		6		10		22		−6
2	0		30		0		0		30	
		18		14		10		16		−10
3	0		0		25		0		25	
		2		16		18		14		−2
4	40		0		5		0		45	
Demand	40		40		40		40		160	
$v(j)$	4		12		20		10			

Now we can calculate a shadow price for each element of the matrix which has nothing transported. The price we should be willing to pay to use the element is the sum of the relevant $u(i)$ and $v(j)$ found in the last stage. For every element of the matrix with nothing transported we define the shadow price as:

$$C'(i,j) = u(i) + v(j)$$

Starting at the top we have:

$$C'(1,1) = u(1) + v(1)$$

but we know that $u(1) = 0$ and $v(1) = 4$, so:

$$C'(1,1) = u(1) + v(1) = 0 + 4 = 4$$

Similarly

$$C'(2,1) = u(2) + v(1) = -6 + 4 = -2$$
$$C'(2,3) = u(2) + v(3) = -6 + 20 = 14$$

etc.

These figures are added to the top lefthand corners of the elements in the matrix.

	1	2	3	4	Supply	u(i)
1	4 · 10 · 0	12 · 10	20 · 10	10 · 40	60	0
2	−2 · 16 · 0	6 · 30	14 · 10 · 4 · 0	22 · 0	30	−6
3	−6 · 18 · 0	2 · 14 · 0	10 · 0 · 25	0 · 16 · 0	25	−10
4	40	2 · 10 · 16 · 0	18 · 8 · 5	14 · 0	45	−2
Demand	40	40	40	40	160	
v(j)	4	12	20	10		

315

The elements with no goods transported now have two costs; an actual cost which we are asked to pay, $C(i,j)$, and a cost we would be prepared to pay, $C'(i,j)$. If we are asked to pay more than we are prepared to pay, we will not transport goods using the element. If we are prepared to pay more than we are asked to pay, we may want to transport as much as possible using it. The next step in the algorithm is to identify the element where we are prepared to pay most above the actual price (i.e. the maximum value of $C'(i,j) - C(i,j)$). In this example there is only one element (2,3) where $C'(i,j)$ is greater than $C(i,j)$, so we now arrange to transport as much as possible using this.

Suppose an amount X is moved from source 2 to destination 3. Other changes must be made or we would have $30 + X$ coming from source 2 and $40 + X$ going to destination 3. The amounts already transported from source 2 and to destination 3 must be reduced by X as shown below.

	1	2	3	4	Supply	$u(i)$
1	4 | 10 0	12 10	20 $10 - X$	10 40	60	0
2	−2 | 16 0	6 | 14 $30 - X$	10 | 4 X	22 0	30	−6
3	−6 | 18 0	2 | 14 0	10 | 0 25	16 0	25	−10
4	2 | 10 40	16 0	18 | 8 5	14 0	45	−2
Demand	40	40	40	40	160	
$v(j)$	4	12	20	10		

Unfortunately this does not completely solve the problem as now row 1 and column 2 do not add properly and there is a deficit of X in both. If, however, we added an amount X transported from source 1 to destination 2 the sums now add properly.

	1	2	3	4	Supply	u(i)
1	4 10 0	12 10 + X	20 10 − X	10 40	60	0
2	−2 16 0	6 14 30 − X	10 4 22 X	 0	30	−6
3	−6 18 0	2 14 0	10 25	0 16 0	25	−10
4	2 10 40	16 0	18 8 5	14 0	45	−2
Demand	40	40	40	40	160	
v(j)	4	12	20	10		

We should emphasize that after adding X to the initial element, all other changes are made to elements which already have some goods assigned to them; only elements with positive values are changed. The changes made form a circuit through the matrix, and the rows and columns still add properly because an equal amount has been added to and subtracted from each column and row.

The last step is to see how big X should be. We want to make it as large as possible but there is a restriction that the amounts of goods transported cannot be negative. This means we must look at those elements where X is subtracted from the amount already transported and the value of X must still leave these non-negative. In this case if X is more than 10 the entry in (1,3) will go negative. Setting X to 10 gives the revised transport plan shown in the following matrix.

This has completed one iteration of the algorithm and substitution shows that the cost has been reduced to 1280. To find an optimal solution the process must be repeated until the amount we are asked to pay is more than we are willing to pay for every element.

Subsequent iterations are exactly the same as the first. Calculating values for $u(i)$ and $v(j)$ from the elements with positive amounts transported, and calculating new values for $C'(i,j)$ for elements where no goods are transported, gives the last matrix in this section.

Table 1

	1	2	3	4	Supply
1	10 / 0	12 / 20	20 / 0	10 / 40	60
2	16 / 0	6 / 20	10 / 10	22 / 0	30
3	18 / 0	14 / 0	10 / 25	16 / 0	25
4	2 / 40	16 / 0	18 / 5	14 / 0	45
Demand	40	40	40	40	160

Table 2

	1	2	3	4	Supply	$u(i)$
1	4 · 10 / 0	12 / 20	16 · 20 / 0	10 / 40	60	0
2	−2 · 16 / 0	6 / 20	10 / 10	4 · 22 / 0	30	−6
3	−6 · 18 / 0	6 · 14 / 0	10 / 25	4 · 16 / 0	25	−6
4	2 / 40	14 · 16 / 0	18 / 5	12 · 14 / 0	45	2
Demand	40	40	40	40	160	
$v(j)$	0	12	16	10		

Here every value for the actual price is higher than the price we are prepared to pay so an optimal solution has been found, identified by the figures in the body of the boxes. The cost of this solution is found by adding individual transport costs:

$$(20 * 12) + (40 * 10) + (20 * 6) + (10 * 10) + (25 * 10)$$
$$+ (40 * 2) + (5 * 18) = 1280$$

In summary
The transportation algorithm has the following steps.

(1) Construct a cost matrix with supply equal to demand.

(2) Find a feasible initial solution (using, say, Vogel's approximation method).

(3) Define a set of values $u(i)$ and $v(j)$ which are the costs of leaving source i and arriving at destination j. Arbitrarily set $u(1)$ to zero then the others are defined by $C(i,j) = u(i) + v(j)$ for all elements with positive entries.

(4) Find the shadow prices for all elements with no goods transported with $C'(i,j) = u(i) + v(j)$.

(5) Find the maximum value for $C'(i,j) - C(i,j)$. If this is negative an optimal solution has been found. Otherwise goods should be transferred to this element.

(6) To find the maximum amount which can be assigned to the element form a circuit through elements with positive values, and ensure any changes keep these values non-negative.

WORKED EXAMPLE 7.10

Find the minimum cost of transporting goods between sources and destinations when the costs, supplies and demands are described by the following matrix.

		To destination			Supply
		1	2	3	
From source	1	10	8	9	100
	2	8	10	11	150
	3	6	7	9	200
Demand		50	225	175	450

SOLUTION

Firstly, we use Vogel's approximation method to find an initial solution. The arithmetic for this is given in the following tables.

Calculate $u(i)$ and $v(j)$:

		To destination 1	2	3	Remaining supply	Penalty cost
From source	1	10	8	9	100	1
	2	8	10	11	150	2
	3	6	7	9	200	1
Unmet demand		50	225	175	450	
Penalty cost		2	1	0		

$\wedge$

Assign 50 from source 3 to destination 1:

		To destination 1	2	3	Remaining supply	Penalty cost
From source	1		8	9	100	1
	2		10	11	150	1
	3	50*	7	9	150	2 <
Unmet demand		0	225	175	400	
Penalty cost		–	1	0		

Assign 150 from source 3 to destination 2:

		To destination 1	2	3	Remaining supply	Penalty cost
From source	1		8	9	100	1
	2		10	11	150	1
	3	50*	150*		0	–
Unmet demand		0	75	175	250	
Penalty cost		–	2	2		

$\wedge$

Assign 75 from source 1 to destination 2:

		To destination 1 2 3	Remaining supply	Penalty cost
From source	1	75* 9	25	–
	2	11	150	–
	3	50* 150*	0	–
Unmet demand		0 0 175	175	
Penalty cost		– – 2		

$\wedge$

Assign 25 from source 1 to destination 3, which gives the initial solution:

		To destination 1 2 3	Remaining supply
From source	1	75* 25*	0
	2	150*	0
	3	50* 150*	0
Unmet demand		0 0 0	175

Now the iterative procedure is used to improve this initial solution. For the first iteration the values for $u(i)$, $v(j)$ and $C'(i,j)$ are given in the following matrix.

	1	2	3	Supply	$u(i)$
1	7 ⌐ 10 ¬ 0	8 75 − X	9 25 + X	100	0
2	9 ⌐ 8 0 + X	10 ⌐ 10 0	11 150 − X	150	2
3	6 50 − X	7 ⌐ 150 + X	8 ⌐ 9 0	200	−1
Demand	50	225	175	450	
$v(j)$	7	8	9		

321

Some goods should be transported from source 2 to destination 1, where we are prepared to pay more than we are asked. Transporting X on this route leads to adjustments in other amounts transported. The circuit needed to ensure all rows and columns add up properly is a little more complex, remembering it must be made using only elements with positive entries. The maximum which can be transported is 50 (set by the quantity from 3 to 1) and the revised matrix is shown below.

	1	2	3	Supply	$u(i)$
1	6 10 0	8 25	9 75	100	0
2	8 10 50	10 0	11 100	150	2
3	5 6 0	7 8 200	9 0	200	−1
Demand	50	225	175	450	
$v(j)$	6	8	9		

The asking price is now always greater than the price we are prepared to pay, so an optimal solution has been found. The cost of this is:

$$(25 * 8) + (75 * 9) + (50 * 8) + (100 * 11) + (200 * 7) = 3775$$

SELF ASSESSMENT QUESTIONS

7.13 What are the characteristics of a transportation problem?

7.14 What is the penalty cost in Vogel's approximation method?

7.15 In the transportation algorithm does the relationship

$$\text{actual cost} = C(i,j) = u(i) + v(j)$$

hold for:

(a) all elements
(b) all elements with positive entries
(c) all elements with zero entries
(d) a mixture of elements with positive and zero entries?

7.16 In the transportation algorithm does the relationship

cost prepared to pay
$$= C'(i,j) = u(i) + v(j)$$

hold for:

(a) all elements
(b) all elements with positive entries

(c) all elements with zero entries
(d) a mixture of elements with positive and zero entries?

7.17 How is an optimal solution to a transportation problem identified?

7.5 SHORTEST PATHS THROUGH A NETWORK

The transportation problem deals with the movement of goods from sources to destinations, and starts with the assumption that a valid cost matrix is available. In some cases this cost matrix may be difficult to find. Suppose, for example, the sources and destinations are connected by a complex network of roads. How could the shortest path through a network between a specified source and destination be found? A useful algorithm for this has similarities with project networks described in Chapter 5, with most of the work done on the network itself. This algorithm (which is sometimes called a labelling algorithm) is demonstrated by the following example.

Figure 7.4 represents a road network where the nodes are towns or intersections and the numbers on the lines are distances. We will define the road length between nodes i and j as $L(i,j)$. The object of this problem is to find the shortest path between node 1 and every other node.

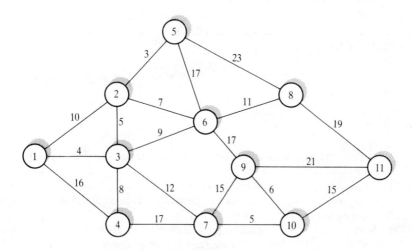

Figure 7.4 Road network with shortest distance needed from node 1 to all other nodes.

The algorithm works by giving each node a label which identifies the shortest distance found to it and the previous node on the route. The label $[D(j),n]$ on node j would show the shortest route found so far between nodes 1 and j is $D(j)$ and the previous node on the route is node n. Initially, temporary labels are assigned, the algorithm iteratively improves these until the optimal distance is found and the labels are made permanent (shown by adding an asterisk).

The steps of the algorithm are as follows.

(1) Put the permanent label $[0,s]$ on the starting node and the temporary labels $[T,-]$ on all other nodes.

(2) Find the nodes directly connected to the starting node and put the label $[L(1,j),1]$ on each. Make the label on the node nearest to the starting node permanent (by adding an asterisk).

(3) Find all the nodes, j, which can be reached directly from the new permanently labelled node, i (excluding permanently labelled nodes). For each of these find the minimum of the existing distance and the distance through i

$$MIN[D(j), D(i) + L(i,j)].$$

If the distance through node i is lower, change the label to $[D(i) + L(i,j),i]$.

(4) Find the temporary label with the lowest distance $D(j)$ and make the node permanent.

(5) If all nodes have permanent labels the optimal solution has been found. Otherwise go to step 3.

WORKED EXAMPLE 7.11

Find the shortest path between node 1 and every other node in the network shown in Figure 7.5.

SOLUTION

(1) Put the permanent label $[0,s]$ on node 1 and temporary labels $[T,-]$ on all other nodes.

(2) There are two nodes reached directly from node 1. The labels [20,1] and [15,1] are put on nodes 2 and 3 respectively. As node 3 is closer to node 1 this label is made permanent.

(3) Nodes 4 and 6 can be reached directly from node 3 (which is the node with a new permanent label). The shortest known route to both of these comes through node 3, so they are labelled [25,3] and [21,3] respectively.

(4) Nodes 2, 4 and 6 have temporary labels. The label on node 2 has the shortest distance and this is made permanent.

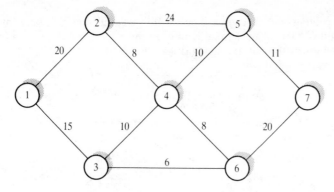

Figure 7.5   Network for Worked example 7.11.

(5)   Four nodes are still not permanently labelled so the algorithm returns to step 3.

(3)   Nodes 4 and 5 can be reached directly from node 2. The distance to node 5 through node 2 is 44 so the label is changed to [44,2]. The distance to node 4 through node 2 is 32 and as this is greater than the distance on the existing label is it not changed.

(4)   Nodes 4, 5 and 6 have temporary labels and the shortest distance in these is 21 on node 6, so the label is made permanent.

(3)   Nodes 4 and 7 can be reached directly from node 6. The label on node 7 is changed to [41,6] while the label on node 4 is not changed (as the distance through node 6 is 29).

(4)   Nodes 4, 5 and 7 have temporary labels and the distance to 4 is least so it is made permanent.

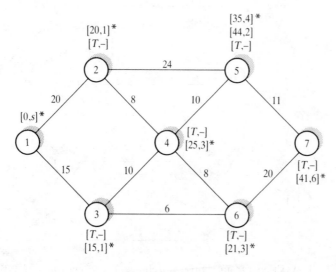

Figure 7.6   Solution to Worked example 7.11.

Repeating this procedure twice more gives all nodes permanent labels. The shortest distances can then be read from the nodes, and the routes found by tracing backwards through the network (see Figure 7.6).

Node	Shortest distance from Node 1	Route
2	20	1–2
3	15	1–3
4	25	1–3–4
5	35	1–3–4–5
6	21	1–3–6
7	41	1–3–6–7

WORKED EXAMPLE 7.12

Figure 7.7 shows the travel times between a central warehouse (1) and a number of customers. What is the shortest travel time from the central warehouse to all customers?

SOLUTION

Following the procedure described above the labels on the network are developed as shown in Figure 7.8.

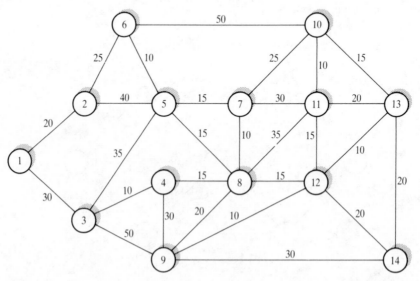

Figure 7.7 Travel times from central warehouse (1) to customers for Worked example 7.12.

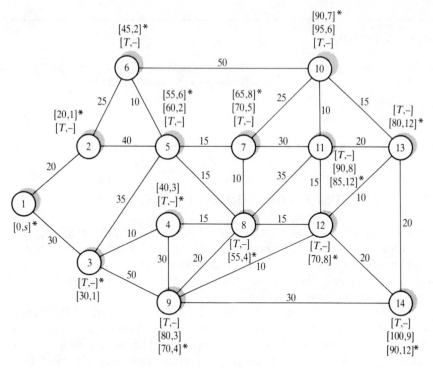

Figure 7.8 Solution to network in Worked example 7.12.

The nodes are permanently labelled in the order:

1, 2, 3, 4, 6, 5, 8, 7, 9, 12, 13, 11, 10, 14

and the solution is

Node	Shortest distance	Route
2	20	1–2
3	30	1–3
4	40	1–3–4
5	55	1–2–6–5
6	45	1–2–6
7	65	1–3–4–8–7
8	55	1–3–4–8
9	70	1–3–4–9
10	90	1–3–4–8–7–10
11	85	1–3–4–8–12–11
12	70	1–3–4–8–12
13	80	1–3–4–8–12–13
14	90	1–3–4–8–12–14

7.18 What does the label $[D(j),n]$ mean in a shortest path labelling algorithm?

7.19 How does a labelling algorithm find the nodes which are on the shortest paths?

7.20 How might the shortest path between any two nodes in a network be found?

7.6 MAXIMUM FLOW THROUGH A NETWORK

When flows are scheduled through a network (traffic along roads, gas or oil through pipelines, telephone calls along conductors, goods through lines in a factory, etc.) there may be an upper limit on the capacity of the links. A problem, then, is to determine the maximum possible flow between two points in a network.

The basic maximum flow problem assumes a network of links each with a finite capacity and an objective of determining the maximum amount which can flow between two points. The approach to this is similar to the shortest path labelling algorithm described above in that labels are put on nodes until a continuous flow through the network is identified. The algorithm is also iterative, as once a flow is identified it is subtracted from the available capacities and the process is repeated.

In this case the labels put on nodes are the flow into a node and the previous node from which this flow comes. Thus the label $[F,n]$ represents a node with a flow of F coming in from node n.

The steps in the algorithm are as follows.

(1) Label the source $[\infty,s]$

(2) Select any labelled node, i and examine the unlabelled nodes, j, which can be reached directly from it.

(3) For each unlabelled node j calculate the maximum flow which can go between i and j. This is the minimum of the capacity of the link between i and j, and the amount which is flowing into i. Call this flow F and label the nodes j $[F,i]$.

If no flows are possible between labelled and unlabelled nodes, an optimal solution has been found: go to step 5.

(4) If the terminal node is not labelled go to step 2. If the terminal node is labelled calculate the additional flow through the network. Subtract this amount from the link capacities and go to step 1.

(5) The maximum flow through the network is found by adding the separate flows identified in step 4.

WORKED EXAMPLE 7.13

Figure 7.9 shows a network of connected pipes with the capacity given on each section. What is the maximum possible flow between nodes 1 and 7?

SOLUTION

(1) Label the source node [∞,*s*].

(2) There is only one labelled node (1) so consider the unlabelled nodes which can be reached directly from this, i.e.nodes 2 and 3.

(3) The maximum amount which can flow from 1 to 2 is 18 and from 1 to 3 is 10 (both determined by the capacity of the connecting pipes). Thus these are labelled [18,1] and [10,1] respectively.

(4) The terminal node (7) is not labelled so we return to step 2.

(2) Taking the labelled node 2 and considering unlabelled nodes connected directly to this (i.e. 4 and 5).

(3) The maximum flow from 2 to 4 is 7, and the maximum flow from 2 to 5 is 6, both determined by the capacity of the connecting pipes. Label nodes 4 and 5 [7,2] and [6,2] respectively. The terminal node is not labelled so we return to step 2.

(2) Taking the labelled node 5 and considering the unlabelled nodes connected directly to this (i.e. 6 and 7).

(3) The maximum flow from 5 to 6 is 6 and from 5 to 7 is 6, both determined by the flow into 5. Labels [6,5] are put on both nodes 6 and 7. The terminal node has now been labelled, so move on to step 4.

(4) A flow of 6 has been defined through the path 1–2–5–7 (see Figure 7.10). The capacity of the pipes is reduced by this amount and the process is repeated starting at step 1.

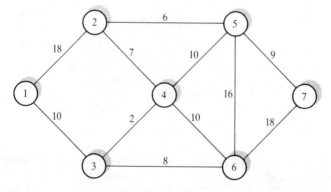

Figure 7.9 Capacities on links for Worked example 7.13.

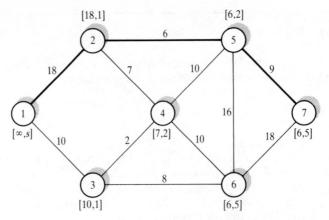

Figure 7.10 The first iteration for Worked example 7.13 identifies a flow of 6 on the path 1–2–5–7.

Repeating this process (see Figure 7.11) gives, in order:

flow of 3 through 1–2–4–5–7
flow of 8 through 1–3–6–7
flow of 4 through 1–2–4–6–7
flow of 2 through 1–3–4–6–7

After this the labelling cannot reach the terminal node and the optimal solution has been found. The labels on the pipes after the final iteration show the spare capacities and the maximum flow is is found by adding the flows calculated in steps 4. The maximum flow from node 1 to node 7 is 23, with flows in each link shown in Figure 7.12.

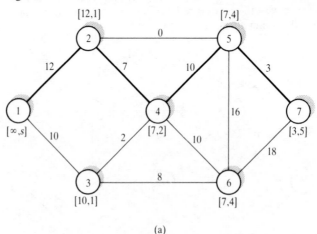

(a)

Figure 7.11 Iterations of maximum flow algorithm for Worked example 7.13: (a) flow of 3 on path 1–2–4–5–7; (b) flow of 8 on path 1–3–6–7; (c) flow of 4 on path 1–2–4–6–7; (d) flow of 2 on path 1–3–4–6–7; (e) final iteration which cannot complete labelling (values on pipes are spare capacities).

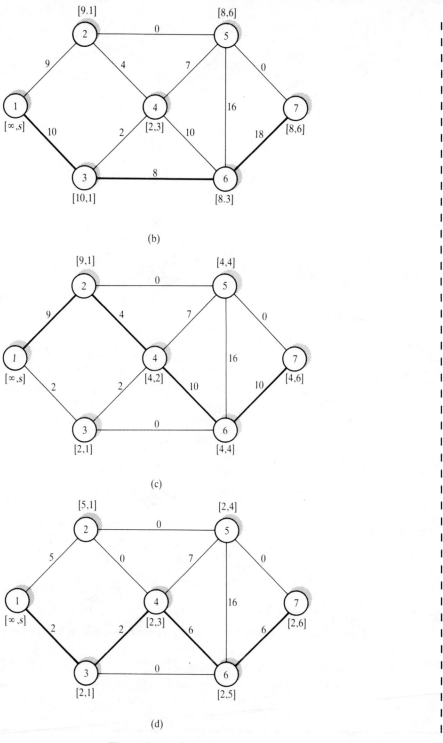

(b)

(c)

(d)

Figure 7.11 (cont.)

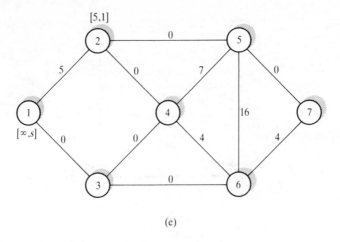

(e)

Figure 7.11   (cont.)

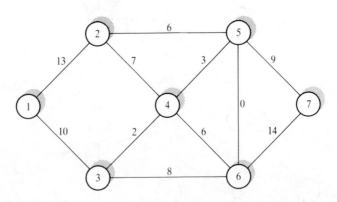

Figure 7.12   Optimal solution for maximum flows of 23 in Worked example 7.13.

WORKED EXAMPLE 7.14

The roads between a city centre and airport can be represented by the network shown in Figure 7.13. If the number on each link is the maximum number of cars (in thousands per hour) which can use a road, what is the maximum number of vehicles which can travel between the city centre and airport?

SOLUTION

Using the procedure described above identifies the following separate flows in the network (see Figure 7.14).

      flow of 7 through 1–2–5–9
      flow of 4 through 1–4–7–8–9
      flow of 4 through 1–3–6–9
      flow of 2 through 1–2–5–6–9
      flow of 1 through 1–2–3–6–9
      flow of 1 through 1–4–3–7–8–9

The maximum number of cars is the sum of these flows which is 19,000 an hour.

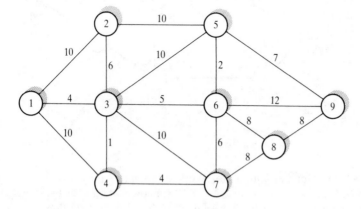

Figure 7.13 Road network between city centre (1) and airport (9) for Worked example 7.14.

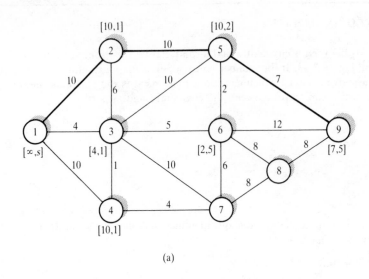

(a)

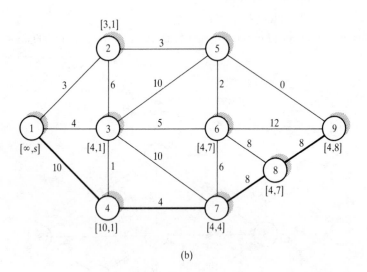

(b)

Figure 7.14 Optimal solution for Worked example 7.14: (a) flow of 7 on path 1–2–5–9; (b) flow of 4 on path 1–4–7–8–9; (c) flow of 4 on path 1–3–6–9; (d) flow of 2 on path 1–2–5–6–9; (e) flow of 1 on path 1–2–3–6–9; (f) flow of 1 on path 1–4–3–7–8–9; (g) final iteration which cannot complete labelling (values on links are spare capacities); (h) flows in each link to give maximum of 19 from 1 to 9.

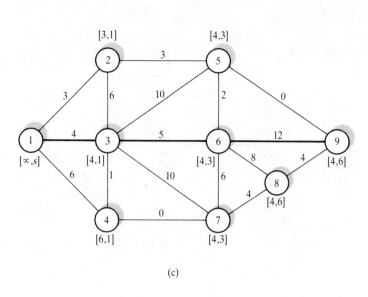

(c)

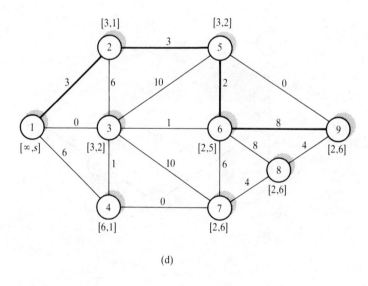

(d)

Figure 7.14 (cont.)

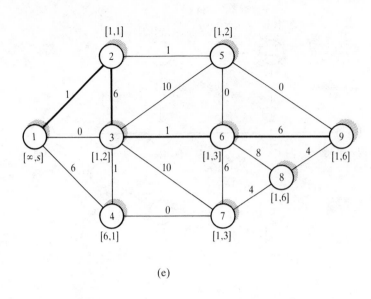

(e)

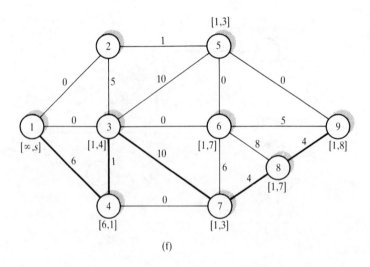

(f)

Figure 7.14 (cont.)

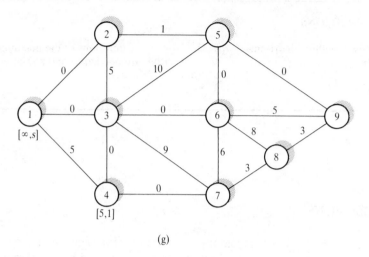

(g)

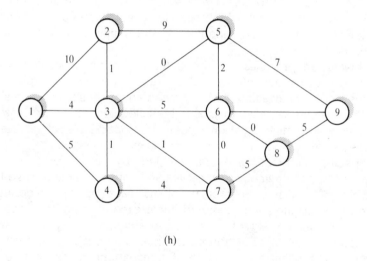

(h)

Figure 7.14 (cont.)

SELF ASSESSMENT QUESTIONS

7.21 In a maximum flow labelling algorithm what does the node label $[F,n]$ signify?

7.22 How many iterations of the maximum flow algorithm are needed to find an optimal solution?

CONCLUSIONS

In this chapter we have considered a number of scheduling problems. These are concerned with finding the best order in which a series of activities should be taken. Strictly speaking, determining this order is a sequencing problem while scheduling finds the timing of the operations. This type of problem is one of the most commonly met in business and in spite of the different forms taken, there are many common characteristics.

The fundamental problem with scheduling is the large number of possible solutions. Relevant calculations for this include combinations (if the order of selection is not important) and permutations (if the order of selection is important).

Specific approaches to scheduling jobs on machines were considered. A number of scheduling rules are widely applied to problems with jobs waiting to be processed on a single processor. Johnson's Rule may be used for jobs to be scheduled on two processors. Unfortunately such rules have only been developed for small problems and there is little guidance for larger problems.

Specific problems may be tackled by linear programming formulations, but the number of variables and constraints often make this impossible in practice. Several problems have specific algorithms designed to avoid the use of standard linear programming procedures.

The assignment algorithm is used to assign jobs to machines (or any analogous situation). The transportation algorithm is a more complex procedure for minimizing the costs of transporting goods between a number of sources and destinations. Both of these algorithms depend on iterative manipulation of a matrix to find optimal solutions.

An alternative approach uses network models. Two such 'labelling' algorithms were described where labels are put on nodes to build a solution. The first problem looked for the shortest distance between a starting node and every other node in a network. The second problem found the maximum possible flow through a network of connected links.

PROBLEMS

7.1   (a)   Part of a stockroom has eight bins to hold eight different items. In how many ways can the items be assigned to bins?

In how many ways can the items be assigned if the number of available bins is increased to 11?

(b)   An open plan office has 10 desks. If 10 clerks work in the area, how many different seating arrangements are there?

If two of the clerks leave, how many seating arrangements are there?

How many different arrangements are there for the two empty desks?

7.2   Seven items are made in batches on a machine. Current stocks, average demands and production times are given below. Develop a schedule for the machine which ensures no item runs out of stock.

Item	A	B	C	D	E	F	G
Average demand	20	15	10	4	15	25	14
Current stock	72	20	50	24	32	100	68
Production time	1	1.5	0.5	1	0.5	1.0	0.5

7.3   Seven jobs are waiting to be processed on a single machine with processing times as follows.

Job	A	B	C	D	E	F	G
Processing time	20	17	6	30	25	12	34

(a)   What sequence of jobs minimizes the mean queueing time?

(b)   If each job has the following due date, what order will minimize the average lateness?

Job	A	B	C	D	E	F	G
Due date	48	80	45	25	130	120	70

(c)   What sequence minimizes the number of late jobs?

7.4   Ten jobs are to be processed on machine 1 followed by machine 2 with expected times as follows. In what sequence should the jobs be processed to maximize machine utilization?

Job	A	B	C	D	E	F	G	H	I	J
Machine 1	14	19	24	22	6	40	20	4	1	25
Machine 2	2	10	8	32	35	18	30	6	35	28

7.5   The costs of assigning 7 tasks to equipment are given in the following table. Find the cost minimizing assignment.

		Equipment						
		1	2	3	4	5	6	7
	1	68	48	57	48	84	10	77
	2	14	64	71	50	24	10	84
	3	54	10	54	13	8	9	8
Tasks	4	15	12	55	54	46	45	87
	5	55	78	12	84	84	54	48
	6	19	8	48	54	84	62	45
	7	44	12	48	77	43	46	52

7.6   Solve the transportation problem described by the following matrix.

		Demand							Supply
		1	2	3	4	5	6	7	
	1	41	62	84	12	55	30	50	150
	2	44	46	83	91	10	90	71	200
	3	55	31	10	15	51	47	47	200
Supply	4	64	49	21	29	27	73	50	350
	5	80	19	46	56	68	70	46	150
	6	71	18	82	46	28	55	49	50
	7	76	38	42	67	13	49	86	50
Demand		75	225	175	275	125	150	125	1150

7.7   Figure 7.15 shows a network of roads with distances marked on links. Find the shortest distance from node 1 to all other nodes.

7.8   Figure 7.16 shows a network of pipes with maximum capacities marked on each link. Find the maximum flow between nodes 1 and 14.

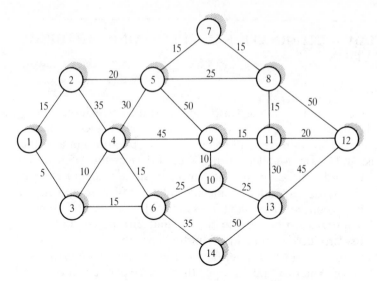

Figure 7.15 Road network for problem 7.7 (distances marked on links).

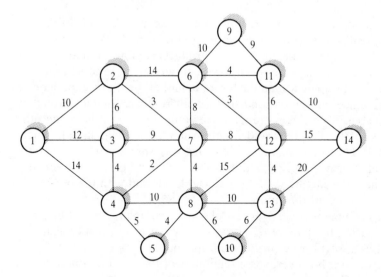

Figure 7.16 Pipe network for problem 7.8 (maximum flows marked on links).

CASE STUDY – INTERNATIONAL ELECTRONIC TRADING CORPORATION

Background

International Electronic Trading Corporation (IETC) is a large trading company with headquarters in the USA. It has wholly owned subsidiary companies in over 30 countries and has marketing operations in a further 90 countries. IETC was founded on the West Coast of the USA during the late 1920s and started by manufacturing cash registers. Later the range of products was expanded to include related office equipment. In recent years it has concentrated on various kinds of electronic equipment.

IETC continued to be, primarily, a manufacturing company until the 1960s. Its production remained centred on the West Coast of America, but with a number of other factories nearer the main markets of the East Coast of America and Europe. Its range expanded to cover all office requirements and it had established markets in most areas of the world. In the 1960s changes were noticed, particularly with the development of computers and the growth of the Far East as a manufacturing centre for electronics. Competition was increasing, not only from old established rivals, but also from new companies based in Japan and Singapore.

A major change in direction was made in the mid 1970s. The company realized that it could not continue to make items in its traditional locations and compete with products coming from areas where labour and other costs were much lower. It decided to become more of a trading company than a manufacturer. It had 50 years of experience in marketing office equipment and had a well respected name throughout the world. Based on these strengths the company started licensing other companies in the Far East and South America to build its equipment. This had IETC brand names added and was shipped to the lucrative markets of North America and Europe. Production was continued in some of the older factories, but at reduced levels and with the prospect of further reductions in the future.

This change was very successful for the company and, after a drop in profits during the late 1970s, the company began to prosper again. By the late 1980s world wide profits were increasing by an average of 7% a year. There were, however, some reminders of the previous operations of the company. These were most obvious in the distribution system.

Current distribution system

Because it originally considered itself a manufacturing company IETC set up its marketing function in offices around the factories. Then all products were made in a factory and passed to an adjacent 'central finished goods warehouse' which was run by marketing. Any imported items for the local market were brought to the same warehouse. Customers were served from a number of regional warehouses. Any goods for the domestic market were transported from the central warehouse to one of the regional ones. Goods for export were sent to a central warehouse if there was one, or directly to a regional warehouse.

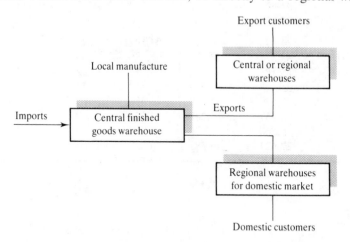

This pattern of movements was still the company's declared intent, but with the change in emphasis within the company it was clear that there was no need to move all goods through central warehouses and it was often more convenient to move things directly to regional warehouses. Shortcuts were often taken without explicit company approval. In those countries where there were more than one manufacturing plant, there were more than one central warehouse and the movements through each became confused. Conversely countries without factories often had goods sent first to another country with a central warehouse before they were passed on. There was considerable confusion in the distribution and it was becoming clear that some action was needed to improve the efficiency.

It was suggested that the West European division look at the pattern of goods moved during the past year to see where improvements could be made. This division manufactured at three factories in Peterborough in the United Kingdom, Toulouse in France, and Bruxelles in Belgium. Something over 3000 tonnes of goods were made in these factories, while almost 1800 tonnes of equipment were imported. Goods flowing into Europe, both imported and manufactured, were shipped to 17 countries.

Company records were searched to find the total weights moved in the past year between manufacturing plants, central warehouses and regional warehouses in each country. These are given in Tables 7.5–7.8 (weights in kg). They should, however, be viewed with some caution. There is no guarantee that historic movements will give an accurate

Table 7.5

To From	Central warehouses			Regional w'house	
	Peterborough	Toulouse	Bruxelles	Austria	Belgium
Peterborough	520,002	65,712	261,081	1,645	0
Toulouse	103,676	351,772	171,734	637	216,090
Bruxelles	187,134	7,078	0	0	0
USA West Coast	124,279	306,111	103,692	1,295	0
USA North East	285,572	70,124	36,746	760	0
USA South East	125,184	30,064	69,950	22	0
USA Central	25,644	10,549	7,519	344	0
Japan	107,570	2,450	350	0	0
Brazil	3,557	25,282	19,023	0	0
Mexico	5,860	0	0	0	0
Canada	27,622	46,287	20,326	0	0

Table 7.6

To From	Regional warehouses					
	Denmark	Finland	France	Germany	Greece	Holland
Peterborough	10,563	22,013	0	118,855	7,966	44,948
Toulouse	10,727	9,494	0	18,212	487	64,767
Bruxelles	160	3,228	736,439	1,713	4,300	1,432
USA West Coast	7,770	21,916	0	52,453	1,482	22,599
USA North East	12,409	2,675	0	6,460	1,467	5,933
USA South East	570	7,000	0	3,084	16	8,719
USA Central	5	327	0	3,511	20	1,161
Japan	225	350	0	992	0	10,257
Brazil	1,056	470	0	41	1,172	0
Mexico	0	0	0	0	0	0
Canada	2,547	3,100	0	1,709	863	5,952

picture of future movements, particularly as markets for office equipment change very rapidly. The sales of office equipment are always higher in countries which have a stronger technological base and economic growth is a major factor in sales. More important are the serious inconsistencies found in the figures with many shipments clearly not recorded in the company's files. Although these figures are the best available they should, perhaps, be considered approximations.

The amounts shipped between, say, Peterborough and Peterborough refer to the amounts shipped between the factory and the central warehouse on the same site. All other entries are shipments from the central warehouse to regional warehouses.

Table 7.7

To From	Iceland	Italy	Regional warehouses Luxembourg	Norway	Portugal
Peterborough	3,196	126,891	0	19,861	12,067
Toulouse	5	10,376	3,684	5,802	20
Bruxelles	210	3,727	0	128	316
USA West Coast	0	4,956	0	3,482	1,593
USA North East	484	4,874	22	151	1,386
USA South East	2	2,418	0	879	84
USA Central	0	16,370	0	3,415	1,029
Japan	0	0	1,164	0	0
Brazil	0	269	0	293	0
Mexico	0	0	0	0	0
Canada	0	1,552	0	1,120	0

Table 7.8

To From	Spain	Sweden	Regional warehouses Switzerland	UK	Rest of World
Peterborough	39,037	33,957	42,724	950,631	2,260,427
Toulouse	6,348	10,910	30,126	0	248,334
Bruxelles	61	2,624	2,999	0	237,591
USA West Coast	1,139	6,599	15,560	0	438,564
USA North East	4,265	7,167	12,375	0	383,132
USA South East	847	2,734	4,629	0	322,219
USA Central	1,039	905	527	0	134,337
Japan	0	7,583	5,228	0	37,479
Brazil	0	940	0	0	169,914
Mexico	0	0	0	0	111,350
Canada	1,743	1,408	0	0	107,242

Transport mode

Over 1700 tonnes of goods were imported to Europe by air. Although more expensive than sea, IETC liked the speed of service and felt the additional cost was a relatively small part of overall price. They also argued that stock levels could be reduced with shorter lead times. Cargo ships move frequently between Europe and most other parts of the world, but some journeys are difficult. The delivery time from USA East Coast is 11 to 17 days, but from Brazil is 21 to 28 days. A comparison of average costs of transport to European destinations is given in Table 7.9.

Table 7.9

Source	Cost (US $/kg)	
	Air	Surface
USA West Coast	3.30	0.75
USA North East	2.40	0.45
USA South East	2.40	0.45
USA Central	2.50	0.52
Japan	8.79	0.67
Brazil	4.88	0.85
Mexico	3.30	0.75
Canada	2.74	0.60

Transport within Europe causes few problems as there is a well developed road haulage system which moves 90% of IETC goods. This provides fast reliable service at reasonable cost. It is difficult to be specific about freight rates as these can either be negotiated for long term contracts or they can be agreed for individual jobs. IETC had long term arrangements with several haulage contractors, but they frequently used other companies which gave cheaper rates for a particular delivery. The typical range of quotations from different haulage companies for delivery from Peterborough to regional warehouses is given in Table 7.10 (values in US cents per kg). Transport costs between other locations are not known, but may be approximated, either using this data or from prevailing transport rates.

Table 7.10

Destination	Minimum rate	Maximum rate
Austria	32.0	139.9
Belgium	18.4	76.2
Denmark	28.8	133.5
France	20.8	99.7
Germany	25.9	129.0
Holland	14.9	92.1
Italy	26.4	158.0
Norway	18.7	211.1
Portugal	40.0	176.7
Spain	40.0	190.4
Sweden	16.0	198.2
Switzerland	28.8	101.7
UK	3.7	33.7

Location of logistics centres

As distribution is now less closely linked to production it would seem logical for IETC to look at the possibility of closing down central warehouses near factories. One interesting alternative would be to replace these by a small number (between one and three) of large European logistics centres. Then all production from European factories and all imports would be sent to these centres and either passed on to regional warehouses within Europe or exported to markets outside.

There are many possible locations for warehouses within Europe. Such logistics centres should be convenient for factories within Europe, imported goods and near to main markets. Availability of suitable transport is obviously a major consideration. Another factor is the operating costs within different areas.

IETC could decide to use a single logistics centre. There is currently space to spare at the Peterborough site and this could be used with no additional cost. At Bruxelles there is some room which could be converted to a warehouse, but extra facilities would have to be built at an estimated annual cost of of $80,000 a year. Similarly Toulouse would need expansion at a cost of $120,000 a year. There is no need for the IETC to build distribution centres near its existing factories. It could build a centre at a new site, but then completely new facilities would have to be provided. If this were done attractive alternatives for location would be Amsterdam (with annual cost of $330,000 a year), Southampton ($430,000 a year), Hamburg ($560,000 a year) or Genoa ($460,000 a year). The cost of operating the centre (wages, overheads etc.) would be added to these costs, but could be balanced by the savings in no longer using Central warehouses.

If IETC used two distribution centres the annual costs of each location would be about 35% less than the cost of running the single centre. Similarly if they used three centres the cost of each would be about 50% less than running the single centre.

Suggested questions

- Is IETC really a trading company rather than a manufacturer (what are the differences)?
- What are the likely long term changes in patterns of freight movement within the company?
- How reliable is the data collected?
- How effective is the current logistics system (what are its strengths and weaknesses)?
- Should the company change its modes of transport?
- What would be the benefits of setting up a European Logistics Centre?

SOLUTIONS TO SELF ASSESSMENT QUESTIONS

7.1 Strictly speaking there is a difference between sequencing and scheduling, although the two terms are often used to mean the same thing. Sequencing is the determination of the order in which activities are performed. Scheduling is the determination of times for each activity.

7.2 $n!$

7.3 If the order of selection is not important we are considering combinations, if the order of selection is important we are considering permutations.

7.4 **(b)** less combinations than permutations.

7.5 A simple heuristic rule which determines the sequence in which jobs should be processed to achieve some objective.

7.6 In order of increasing duration (that is, shortest first).

7.7 In order of increasing due date (that is, most urgent first).

7.8 When there is a flow shop with two machines and the object is to minimize total time in the system.

7.9 Assigning 'operators' to 'equipment' (or equivalent problems) with minimum cost. One operator is assigned to each piece of equipment and each piece of equipment has one operator assigned to it.

7.10 **(c)** partly true. Ordinary linear programming can not be used, but zero–one programming can be.

7.11 There is one zero in each row and one in each column which identify the optimal assignment.

7.12 By transforming the benefits into relative costs by subtracting every entry in the original matrix from the largest entry in the matrix.

7.13 The transportation problem has a number of demands to be met from a number of sources. In the basic version each source has a known capacity it can supply, each destination has a known demand and there is a fixed cost of moving one unit of goods between any two points. The objective is to minimize total transportation costs.

7.14 VAM is based on the idea that if the cheapest option is not used in any row or column then, at best, the second cheapest must be used and there is a consequent penalty cost. This penalty is at least as big as the difference between the cheapest and second cheapest element in the row or column.

7.15 **(b)** all elements with positive entries.

7.16 **(c)** all elements with zero entries.

7.17 When all values for $C'(i,j)$ (the amount we are prepared to pay) are less than corresponding $C(i,j)$ (the amount we are asked to pay).

7.18 $D(j)$ is the shortest path found so far to node j and n is the previous node in the path to j.

7.19 Each node is labelled with the previous node in the path, so working backwards through the sequence of nodes allows paths to be identified.

7.20 The algorithm described finds the shortest path from one node (s) to all others nodes, so repeating the algorithm setting s to all nodes in turn will allow a complete shortest distance matrix to be formed.

7.21 F is the maximum flow into a node on this iteration and n is the node from which this flow comes.

7.22 This varies from problem to problem and there is no set number.

REFERENCES FOR FURTHER READING

Baker K. R. (1974). *Introduction to Sequencing and Scheduling* New York: John Wiley

Bazarra M. S. and Jarvis J. J. (1977). *Linear Programming and Network Flows* New York: John Wiley

Bradley S. P., Hax A. C. and Magnanti T. L. (1977). *Applied Mathematical Programming* Reading: Addison Wesley

Fitzsimmons J. A. and Sullivan R. S. (1982). *Service Operations Management* New York: McGraw-Hill

Fogarty D. F. and Hoffman T. R. (1983). *Production and Inventory Management* Ohio: South-West Publishing

Ford L. R. and Fulkerson D. R. (1962). *Flows and Networks* New Jersey: Princeton University Press

Jemsen P. and Barnes J. W. (1980). *Network Flow Programming* New York: John Wiley

Kwak N. K. (1973). *Mathematical Programming with Business Applications* New York: McGraw-Hill

Minieka E. (1978). *Optimisation Algorithms for Networks and Graphs* New York: Marcel Dekker

Chapter 8

Probability and probability distributions

SYNOPSIS

This chapter introduces some basic concepts of statistics. It is not meant to give an exhaustive coverage of the subject (which would be a major undertaking) but presents some important ideas which are used in later chapters. It is important to understand the contents of this chapter as the rest of the book assumes they are reasonably familiar.

For those who have no background in statistics this chapter can be used as a self-contained introduction. Statistics are met in many different areas and a lot of people will already have some knowledge of the subject. In this case you may find the chapter reinforces ideas you have already met and focuses on specific applications in business. Anyone wanting to pursue the subject in more detail should read a fuller text, many of which are available. Some useful references are listed at the end of the chapter.

The chapter starts by introducing the idea of data reduction with graphical and numerical representation of data. Then, concentrating on numerical representation, it describes measures for the average and spread of data.

Relative frequencies may be described as probabilities. Some properties of these are outlined and calculations for independent events are considered. Conditional probabilities are described, with updating by Bayes' theorem.

The idea of frequency distributions is extended to probability distributions. Three widely used standard distributions, the Binomial, Poisson and Normal are described.

The ideas developed in this chapter will be applied to a variety of business situations in Chapter 9.

OBJECTIVES

After reading this chapter and doing the numerical exercises you should be able to:

- appreciate the need for data reduction;
- calculate the mean, median and mode of a set of data;
- calculate the range, mean absolute deviation, variance and standard deviation of a set of data;
- calculate probabilities and appreciate their meaning;
- know how to multiply and add probabilities for independent events;
- understand and calculate conditional probabilities;
- use Bayes' theorem and draw probability trees;
- develop probability distributions for sets of data;
- understand when and how to use the Binomial distribution;
- understand when and how to use the Poisson distribution;
- understand when and how to use the Normal distribution.

8.1 DATA DESCRIPTION

A distinction can be drawn between data and information. Data is generally taken to be raw numbers or facts which are processed to give information which is in a useable form. Thus 78, 64, 36, 70 and 52 are data which might be processed to give the useful information that the average mark of five students sitting an exam is 60%.

We continuously collect data from many sources, and much of this is numerical. Provided it comes in small quantities there is little difficulty understanding it. We can happily say 'petrol costs £2.10 a gallon', 'a Member of Parliament had a majority of 10,547', 'the family next door has three cars', and so on. Problems begin when there is a lot of data and we are swamped with detail. Then it is impossible to get an intuitive 'grasp' of its meaning and we need some means of summarizing it. A list giving the number of children in each family in a city would have little meaning, but if the data were summarized we could accept that the average number of children in a family is 1.9. The general term for summarizing raw data and presenting it in forms which allows underlying patterns to be identified is 'data reduction'.

The advantages of condensing large quantities of raw data are:

- results are shown in a compact form
- it is easy to understand
- graphical or pictorial representations are possible
- overall patterns can be seen
- comparisons can be made
- quantitative measures can be used.

Conversely, the disadvantages are:

- details of original data are lost
- the process is irreversible.

Data can be reduced and presented either graphically (using a bar chart, histogram, pictograph or some other pictorial means) or numerically. Graphical representations of data are important, but they have limited scope. This chapter concentrates on more useful numerical descriptions.

In summary
Raw data must be processed to give useful information. The aim of data reduction is to organize and present raw data so that underlying patterns are revealed.

SELF ASSESSMENT QUESTIONS

8.1 What is the difference between data and information?

8.2 Why is data reduction necessary?

8.3 What are the two main methods of presenting statistical data?

8.2 MEASURES FOR AVERAGE AND SPREAD

There are many ways of summarizing data, but the most widely used is to calculate the mean (or arithmetic average). For a set of n values, x_i, the mean is calculated by:

$$\text{mean} = \frac{\sum_{i=1}^{n} x_i}{n}$$

This usually gives a reasonable measure and has the advantages of:

- being easy to calculate
- being easy to understand
- using all the data
- being objective
- being useful in other calculations.

Sometimes the mean does not give an accurate picture and there would be advantages is using some other measures. The two most common alternatives are median and mode.

- If observations are arranged in order of magnitude the middle observation is the **median**.
- The **mode** is the value of the observation which occurs most frequently.

WORKED EXAMPLE 8.1

The number of visitors received by a hospital patient in five consecutive days were four, two, one, seven and one. What are the mean, median and mode of numbers visiting?

SOLUTION

The mean is found by adding the numbers and dividing by 5:

mean = (4 + 2 + 1 + 7 + 1)/5 = 15/5 = 3

The median is found by arranging the numbers in order and selecting the middle one (the third number in this case):

1, 1, 2, 4, 7   median = 2

The mode is the value which occurs most frequently, which is 1.

These three measures show the average or 'usual' values of a set of data, but they do not give a complete picture. Suppose two doctors and three receptionists work in a village health centre. Last year the gross annual pays earned by these five were £42,000, £38,000, £14,000, £8000 and £8000. When discussing this year's pay with the local health authority it could truthfully be said that the mean pay is £22,000 a year, the median is £14,000 and the mode is £8000. Unfortunately, statistics are often used selectively to support previously adopted positions rather than to present facts and clarify complex situations. The mean, median and mode all have distinct meanings and care should be taken in their use.

The difficulty with average values is that they give no indication of the 'spread' of the data. Records from a local authority for the past two years show the mean number of people attending a Consumer Advice Centre is 100 a week. This is useful information, but it would be even more useful to know how the numbers fluctuated. They could show little variation from, say, 95 on quiet weeks to 105 on busy weeks: alternatively they could show large variations and range between 0 and 500. The centre would clearly have to be organized differently to meet a steady demand than to cope with a widely fluctuating one.

The 'range' used above is a simple measure but is of limited use.

$$\text{range} = \text{maximum observation} - \text{minimum observation}$$

A more useful alternative is the mean absolute deviation from the mean (MAD) which was used in Chapter 4 to judge the quality of forecasts.

$$\text{MAD} = \frac{\sum_{i=1}^{n} \text{ABS}\,[x_i - \mu]}{n}$$

Where: x_i = the observations

μ = mean value of observations

n = number of observations

$\text{ABS}[y]$ = the absolute value of y (i.e. ignoring sign)

The absolute value is taken so that positive and negative variations do not cancel each other. This measure is relatively easy to calculate, but has limitations which begin to appear when statistical analyses are extended. An alternative measure which is equally simple and does not have these limitations is the variance. Instead of taking absolute values of deviation from the mean, the variance uses the squares. This is equivalent to the mean squared error (MSE) discussed in Chapter 4 and again stops positive and negative variations cancelling.

$$\text{Variance} = \frac{\sum\limits_{i=1}^{n} (x_i - \mu)^2}{n}$$

The units of variance are the square of the units of the original observations. If, for example, the original units of observations were tonnes the variance would have the meaningless units of tonnes^2. To return them to normal the square root of the variance can be used and the result is called the standard deviation.

$$\text{Standard deviation} = \sqrt{\text{variance}}$$

The units are now correct and we have a useful measure of spread. One comment at this point is that variances may sometimes be added together, but standard deviations can never be simply added.

In summary

The 'average' of a set of data can be described by its mean, median or mode. The 'spread' can be measured by its range, variance or standard deviation.

WORKED EXAMPLE 8.2

Worked example 8.1 described a hospital patient receiving four, two, one, seven and one visitors on consecutive days. The mean number of visitors was three a day. How can the spread of this data be calculated?

SOLUTION

The range is found as the difference between the largest and smallest values.

range $= 7 - 1 = 6$

Mean absolute deviation is found from:

$$\text{MAD} = \frac{\sum_{i=1}^{n} \text{ABS}[x_i - \mu]}{n}$$

$$= \{\text{ABS}[4 - 3] + \text{ABS}[2 - 3] + \text{ABS}[1 - 3] + \text{ABS}[7 - 3] + \text{ABS}[1 - 3]\}/5$$

$$= 10/5$$

$$= 2$$

Variance is found from:

$$\text{Variance} = \frac{\sum_{i=1}^{n} (x_i - \mu)^2}{n}$$

$$= \{(4 - 3)^2 + (2 - 3)^2 + (1 - 3)^2 + (7 - 3)^2 + (1 - 3)^2\}/5$$

$$= 26/5$$

$$= 5.2$$

Standard deviation is the square root of variance

$$\text{Standard deviation} = \sqrt{5.2}$$

$$= 2.28$$

WORKED EXAMPLE 8.3

A hotel is concerned about the number of people who book rooms by telephone but do not actually turn up. Over the past few weeks it has kept records of the number of people who do this, as shown below. How can this data be summarized?

Day	1	2	3	4	5	6	7	8	9	10	11	12	13	14	15
No-shows	4	5	2	3	3	2	1	4	7	2	0	3	1	4	5

Day	16	17	18	19	20	21	22	23	24	25	26	27	28	29	30
No-shows	2	6	2	3	3	4	2	5	6	3	3	2	4	3	4

Day	31	32	33	34	35	36	37	38	39	40	41	42	43	44	45
No-shows	5	2	4	3	3	1	4	5	3	6	4	3	1	4	5

SOLUTION

These values can be summarized by adding the number of times each no-show number occurs, as shown in the following table.

No-shows	0	1	2	3	4	5	6	7
No. of days	1	4	8	12	10	6	3	1

Then several pictorial representations could be used including a line graph, histogram, cumulative frequency diagram or pie chart (see Figure 8.1).

Numerical descriptions of the data are given below.
Measures of average:

Mean $\quad$ = sum/no. of observations = 151/45 = 3.356

Median = 23rd observation = 3

Mode $\quad$ = most frequent observation = 3

Measures of spread:

Range $\qquad\qquad\qquad$ = 7

Mean absolute deviation = 1.240

Variance $\qquad\qquad\quad$ = 2.320

Standard deviation $\qquad$ = 1.523

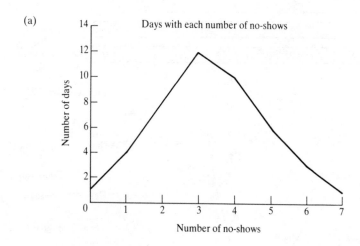

Figure 8.1 Graphical representations of no-show rates for Worked example 8.3: (a) line graph; (b) histogram; (c) relative frequency shown as horizontal bar chart; (d) pie chart.

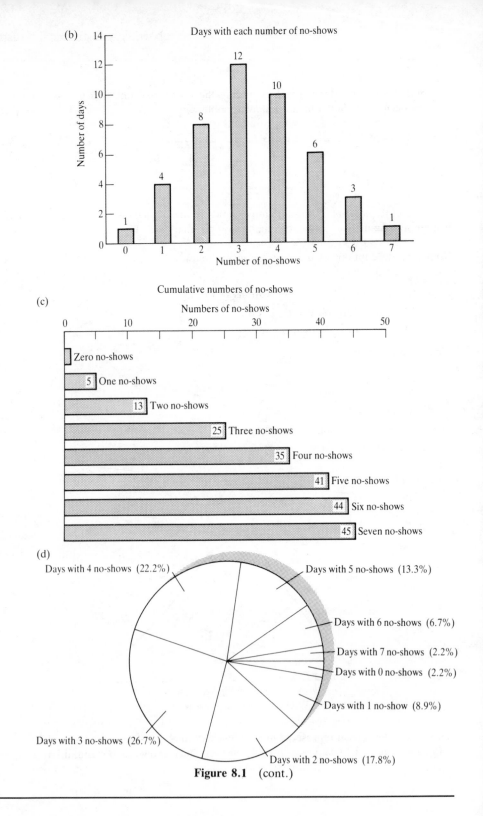

Figure 8.1 (cont.)

WORKED EXAMPLE 8.4

The mean weight and standard deviation of airline passengers are known to be 72 kg and 6 kg respectively. What will be the mean weight and standard deviation of total passenger weight carried by a 200-seat airplane?

SOLUTION

The mean weight of 200 passengers is found by multiplying the mean weight of each passenger by the number of passengers:

$$\text{mean} = 200 * 72 = 14{,}400 \text{ kg.}$$

We mentioned above that standard deviations can not be added, but variances can. Thus, the variance in weight of 200 passengers is found by multiplying the variance in weight of each passenger by the number of passengers.

$$\text{variance} = 200 * 6^2 = 7200 \text{ kg}^2$$

The standard deviation is then $\sqrt{7200} = 84.85$ kg.

SELF ASSESSMENT QUESTIONS

8.4 Define three measures for the average of a set of data.

8.5 Define four measures for the spread of a set of data.

8.3   PROBABILITY

In Section 8.1 we looked at ways of reducing data and describing it. Here we are going to move on from descriptions of a set of data to making inferences about its general characteristics, and we will start by considering the **probability** of an event as a measure of its relative frequency, or likelihood of occurrence.

Experience leads us to believe that when a fair coin is tossed it will come down heads half the time and tails half the time. This observation allows the rather more formal statement that 'the probability of a fair coin coming down heads is 0.5'. This intuitive judgement is made by defining the probability of an event as the proportion of times the event occurs.

There are 52 cards in a pack and if we chose one at random there is a probability of 1/52 that it will be the ace of hearts (or any other specified card). In the last 500 days the train to work has broken down 10 times, so the probability of it breaking down on any day is 10/500 or 0.02. For 200 of the last 240 trading days the Toronto Stock Exchange has had more advances than declines, so there is a probability of 200/240 or 0.83 that the stock exchange advances on a particular day. This idea of probabilities as relative frequencies means that values are only defined in the range 0 to 1.

> - probability = 0 means the event will *never* occur
> - probability = 1 means the event will *always* occur
> - probability between 0 and 1 gives relative frequency
> - probabilities outside the range 0 to 1 have no meaning

An event with a probability of 0.8 is quite likely (it will happen eight times out of 10), while one with a probability of 0.2 is quite unlikely.

There are essentially two ways in which probabilities can be found. Theoretical argument can be used to give 'a priori' probabilities, or historical data can be used to give empirical values. The probability that a husband and wife share the same birthday is 1/365 (ignoring leap years). This is an *a priori* probability calculated by saying there are 365 days on which the second partner can have a birthday and only one of these corresponds to the birthday of the first partner. The last 100 times a football team has played at home it has attracted crowds of more than 20,000 on 62 occasions. This gives an empirical probability of 62/100 = 0.62 that next week's game will have a crowd of more than 20,000 (all other things being equal).

In summary
The probability of an event is the likelihood that the event will occur, or its relative frequency. This is measured on a scale of 0 to 1 with:

probability = 0 meaning there is no chance of the event happening

probability = 1.0 meaning it is certain to happen.

WORKED EXAMPLE 8.5

A magazine advertised that it would run a prize draw with one first prize, five second prizes, 100 third prizes and 1000 fourth prizes. The prizes would be drawn at random from entries for the competition and after each draw the winning ticket would be returned to the draw. By the closing date there were 10,000 entries and at the draw no entry won more than one prize. What is the probability that a given individual won first prize or that they won any prize?

SOLUTION

There are 10,000 entries and one first prize, so the probability of a given individual winning first prize is 1/10,000.

Similarly there are 5 second prizes, so the probability of winning one of these is 5/10,000. The probabilities of winning third or fourth prizes are 100/10,000 and 1000/10,000 respectively.

There were a total of 1106 prizes so the probability of winning one of these was 1106/10,000. Conversely the probability of not winning a prize was 8894/10,000.

8.4   CALCULATING PROBABILITIES FOR INDEPENDENT EVENTS

If the occurrence of one event does not effect the occurrence of a second event, the two events are said to be independent. Using the notation:

$P(a)$ = the probability of event a

$P(a/b)$ = the probability of event a given that b has already occurred

$P(a/\underline{b})$ = the probability of event a given that b has *not* occurred

Two events, a and b, are independent if

$$P(a) = P(a/b) = P(a/\underline{b})$$
and $$P(b) = P(b/a) = P(b/\underline{a})$$

For example, the probability that a person buys a particular newspaper is independent of the probability that they suffer from hay fever. Then

$$P(\text{buys } The\ Times) = P(\text{buys } The\ Times/\text{suffers from hay fever})$$
$$= P(\text{buys } The\ Times/\text{does not suffer from hay fever})$$

Another important concept is 'mutually exclusive' events. This

363

means that if one event happens the other event cannot happen (if a coin is tossed the event that it comes down heads is mutually exclusive with the event that it comes down tails).

With these definitions we can look at some properties of probability. For independent, mutually exclusive events the probabilities of one *or* another happening is found by adding the separate probabilities.

$$P(a \text{ OR } b) = P(a) + P(b)$$
$$P(a \text{ OR } b \text{ OR } c) = P(a) + P(b) + P(c)$$

and so on

> OR means ADD probabilities

An illustration of this was given in worked example 8.5 where the probability a particular individual won a magazine prize draw was calculated as 1106/10,000. The probability that they did not win was 8894/10,000. This could have been found by saying that an entry *must* win or lose so:

$$P(\text{win}) + P(\text{lose}) = 1$$
or $\quad P(\text{lose}) = 1 - P(\text{win})$

WORKED EXAMPLE 8.6

A company makes 40,000 washing machines a year. Of these 10,000 are for the home market, 8000 are exported to North America, 7000 to Europe, 5000 to South America, 4000 to the Far East, 3000 to Australasia and 3000 to other markets.

(a) What is the probability that a particular machine is sold on the home market?
(b) What is the probability that a machine is exported?
(c) What is the probability that a machine is exported to either North or South America?
(d) What is the probability that a machine is sold in either the home market or Europe?

SOLUTION

The probability that a machine is sold on the home market is:

$$P(\text{home}) = \frac{\text{number on home market}}{\text{number sold}} = \frac{10,000}{40,000} = 0.25$$

All events are independent and mutually exclusive, so the probability a machine is exported is found by adding the total number of machines which are exported and dividing this by the total machines made.

$$P(\text{exported}) = 30,000/40,000 = 0.75$$

Alternatively we could use the observation that all machines made are sold somewhere, so the probability that a machine is sold is 1.0. It is either sold on the home market or exported so:

$$P(\text{sold}) = 1 = P(\text{exported}) + P(\text{home})$$

Hence $P(\text{exported}) = 1 - P(\text{home})$

$$= 1 - 0.25$$

$$= 0.75$$

$$P(\text{North America OR South America}) = P(\text{North America})$$
$$+ P(\text{South America})$$

$$= 8000/40,000 + 5000/40,000$$

$$= 0.2 + 0.125 = 0.325$$

$$P(\text{home OR Europe}) = P(\text{home}) + P(\text{Europe})$$
$$= 10,000/40,000 + 5000/40,000$$
$$= 0.25 + 0.125 = 0.375.$$

A second rule for probabilities is relevant when a number of separate events all occur. For independent events the probability of one *and* another happening is found by multiplying the probabilities of the separate events.

$$P(a \text{ AND } b) = P(a) * P(b)$$
$$P(a \text{ AND } b \text{ AND } c) = P(a) * P(b) * P(c)$$
$$\text{and so on}$$

AND means MULTIPLY probabilities

WORKED EXAMPLE 8.7

A workshop combines two parts, an 'inner' and an 'outer', into a final assembly. This is tested and an average of 10% of inners are found to be defective and 5% of outers. If defects on inners and outers are independent, what is the probability that a final assembly has both a defective inner and outer?

SOLUTION

For independent events

P(inner defective AND outer defective)

$= P(\text{inner defective}) * P(\text{outer defective})$

$= 0.1 * 0.05$

$= 0.005$

Similarly

P(inner defective AND outer not defective) = 0.095

P(inner not defective AND outer defective) = 0.045

P(inner not defective AND outer not defective) = 0.855

The probabilities of these four combinations add to 1.

WORKED EXAMPLE 8.8

A warehouse classifies its stock into three different categories. On all category A items it promises a service level of 97% (in other words there is a probability of 0.97 that the warehouse can meet demand immediately from stock). On category B and C items it promises service levels of 94% and 90% respectively. If service levels are independent, what are the probabilities that the warehouse can immediately supply an order for:

    (a)   one item of category A and one item of category B

    (b)   one item from each category

    (c)   two different items from A, one from B and three from C

    (d)   three different items from each category?

SOLUTION

(a)   As the events are independent the probabilities can be multiplied to give:

P(one A AND one B) $= P(\text{one A}) * P(\text{one B})$

$= 0.97 * 0.94$

$= 0.912$

(b) $\quad P(\text{one A AND one B AND one C}) = P(\text{one A}) * P(\text{one B}) * P(\text{one C})$

$$= 0.97 * 0.94 * 0.90$$

$$= 0.821$$

(c) $\quad P(\text{two A AND one B AND three C}) = P(\text{two A}) * P(\text{one B}) * P(\text{three C})$

This must be broken down further by noting that the probability of two items of category A is the probability the first is there AND the second is there. In other words

$$P(\text{two A}) = P(\text{one A AND one A})$$

$$= P(\text{one A}) * P(\text{one A})$$

$$= P(\text{one A})^2$$

Similarly

$$P(\text{three C}) = P(\text{one C})^3$$

Then the answer becomes $P(\text{one A})^2 * P(\text{one B}) * P(\text{one C})^3$

$$= 0.97^2 * 0.94 * 0.9^3$$

$$= 0.645$$

(d) $\quad P(\text{three A AND three B AND three C})$

$$= P(\text{one A})^3 * P(\text{one B})^3 * P(\text{one C})^3$$

$$= 0.97^3 * 0.94^3 * 0.9^3$$

$$= 0.553$$

In summary

For independent, mutually exclusive events:

- OR means ADD probabilities

$$P(a \text{ OR } b) = P(a) + P(b)$$

- AND means MULTIPLY probabilities.

$$P(a \text{ AND } b) = P(a) * P(b)$$

SELF ASSESSMENT QUESTIONS

8.6 What is meant by the probability of an event?

8.7 What are independent events?

8.8 What are mutually exclusive events?

8.9 How could you determine the probability of one of several events occurring?

8.10 How could you determine the probability of all of several events occurring?

8.5 CONDITIONAL PROBABILITIES FOR DEPENDENT EVENTS

The addition and multiplication of probabilities described in the last section can only be done if events are independent. This is not always true and we will now look at events where the occurrence of one directly effects the occurrence of the other. For example, the probability that a person is employed in one of the professions is not independent of their having a university degree. The probability that a machine will break down this week is not independent of its age.

The most important thing to understand for conditional probabilities is a general rule which says that the probability of two dependent events occurring is the probability of the first, multiplied by the conditional probability that the second occurs given the first has already occurred. This rather clumsy statement can be formulated as:

$$P(a \text{ AND } b) = P(a) * P(b/a)$$

Where: $P(a \text{ AND } b)$ = probability that both a and b occur

$P(a)$ = probability that a occurs

$P(b/a)$ = probability that b occurs given that a has already occurred.

This can be extended to give the obvious result:

$$P(a \text{ AND } b) = P(a) * P(b/a) = P(b) * P(a/b)$$

Taking the second two terms and rearranging them gives:

$$P(a/b) = \frac{P(b/a) * P(a)}{P(b)}$$

This is known as Bayes' theorem and is the basis of most updating of conditional probabilities.

WORKED EXAMPLE 8.9

The students in a class can be classified as follows:

	home	overseas
male	66	29
female	102	3

(a) If a student is selected at random from the class what is the probability that they will be from overseas?

(b) If the student selected is female what is the probability that she is from overseas?

(c) If the student selected is male what is the probability that he is from overseas?

(d) If the student is from overseas what is the probability that they are male?

(e) Confirm the relationship $P(a \text{ AND } b) = P(a) * P(b/a)$ for several combinations of sex and origin.

SOLUTION

(a) $P(\text{overseas})$ $\quad = $ number from overseas/number of students

$= 32/200 = 0.16$

(b) $P(\text{overseas/female})$ $\quad = $ no. overseas females/no. females

$= 3/105 = 0.029$

This could also be calculated from

$\quad P(\text{overseas/female})$ $\quad = P(\text{overseas AND female})/P(\text{female})$

$= 0.015/0.525 = 0.029$

(c) $P(\text{overseas/male})$ $\quad = $ no. overseas males/no. males

$= 29/95 = 0.305$

This could also be calculated from

$\quad P(\text{overseas/male})$ $\quad = P(\text{overseas AND male})/P(\text{male})$

$= 0.145/0.475 = 0.305$

(d) $P(\text{male/overseas})$ $\quad = $ no. overseas males/no. overseas

$= 29/32 = 0.906$

This could also be calculated from

$\quad P(\text{male/overseas})$ $\quad = P(\text{male AND overseas})/P(\text{overseas})$

$= 0.145/0.16 = 0.906$

(e) This relationship has already been demonstrated in sections (a) to (d) and can be tested further using any other combinations. For example,

$\quad P(\text{home AND male})$ $\quad = P(\text{home}) * P(\text{male/home})$

$= 0.84 * 0.393 = 0.330$

(compare this with $66/200 = 0.33$)

$\quad P(\text{female AND overseas})$ $\quad = P(\text{female}) * P(\text{overseas/female})$

$= 0.525 * 0.029 = 0.015$

(compare this with $3/200 = 0.015$)

WORKED EXAMPLE 8.10

Two machines make identical parts which are combined on a production line. The older machine makes 40% of the units, of which 85% are of satisfactory quality. The newer machine makes 60% of the units, of which 92% are of satisfactory quality. A random check further down the production line shows an unusual fault which suggests the machine which made the unit needs some adjustment. What is the probability that the older machine made the unit?

SOLUTION

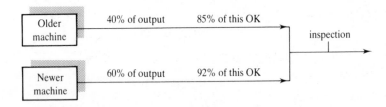

Using the abbreviations O for the older machine, N for the newer machine, OK for good units and F for faulty ones, we want $P(O/F)$ and this can be found using Bayes' theorem:

$$P(a/b) = \frac{P(b/a) * P(a)}{P(b)} \text{ or } P(O/F) = \frac{P(F/O) * P(O)}{P(F)}$$

$P(O) = 0.4$ and $P(F/O) = 0.15$. The remaining value we need is $P(F)$, the probability a unit is faulty. This is calculated from:

$$P(F) = P(F/O) * P(O) + P(F/N) * P(N)$$

In other words, the probability that a unit is faulty is found by adding the probability that it is faulty and comes from the older machine to the probability it is faulty and comes from the newer machine.

Substitution then gives:

$$P(O/F) = \frac{0.15 * 0.4}{0.15 * 0.4 + 0.08 * 0.6} = \frac{0.06}{0.108} = 0.556$$

For confirmation of this we could calculate:

$$P(N/F) = \frac{P(F/N) * P(N)}{P(F)} = \frac{0.08 * 0.6}{0.108} = 0.444$$

As the unit must have come from either the older or newer machine the fact that these two probabilities add to one confirms the result.

The arithmetic in this worked example is straightforward but could be tedious if there were several calculations to do. An obvious solution is to use a computer, but there is an easy mechanical procedure which will usually make this unnecessary. This procedure starts by drawing a matrix of the known probabilities.

	faulty	OK	
older machine	0.15	0.85	0.4
newer machine	0.08	0.92	0.6

The lefthand box of figures give the conditional probabilities as they are known. Thus, $0.15 = P(F/O)$, $0.08 = P(F/N)$, etc. The box to the right gives the values of $P(O)$ and $P(N)$.

We can form a third box by multiplying each conditional probability in the lefthand box by the probability on the same line in the righthand box. Thus $0.15 * 0.4 = 0.060$, $0.08 * 0.06 = 0.048$, etc. Adding the columns of the third box gives the values under each column. Thus $0.060 + 0.048 = 0.108$, which is the probability a unit is faulty: $0.340 + 0.552 = 0.892$, which is the probability a unit is OK.

	faulty	OK		faulty	OK
older machine	0.15	0.85	0.4	0.060	0.340
newer machine	0.08	0.92	0.6	0.048	0.552
				0.108	0.892

Finally, dividing every element in the third box by the column totals gives the element in a bottom box. Thus $0.340/0.892 = 0.381$, $0.060/0.108 = 0.556$, etc. This last result is the one found above and indicates we have found the conditional probabilities we are looking for, that is, $P(O/F)$, $P(N/OK)$, etc.

	faulty	OK		faulty	OK
older machine	0.15	0.85	0.4	0.060	0.340
newer machine	0.08	0.92	0.6	0.048	0.552
				0.108	0.892
older machine				0.556	0.381
newer machine				0.444	0.619

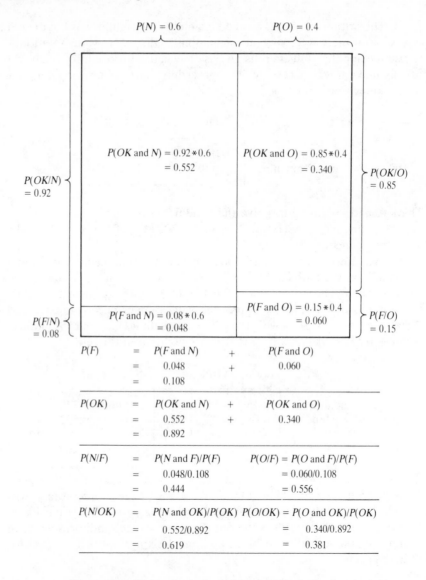

Figure 8.2 Illustrating calculations for Worked example 8.10.

Although the description of this procedure may seem a bit strange, comparison with the equation for Bayes' theorem shows that we are simply repeating the calculations described there.

The probabilities for this example are illustrated in the diagram shown in Figure 8.2.

It is sometimes easier to visualize conditional probabilities on a 'probability tree'. These are drawn from left to right with branches

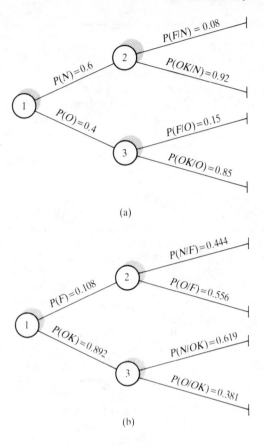

Figure 8.3 Probability trees for the original and updated probabilities in Worked example 8.10.

representing possible events. Figure 8.3(a) shows a probability tree for this example. Node 1 represents the start and there are two possibilities:

- a part comes from the older machine
- a part comes from the newer machine.

From both nodes 2 and 3 there are two possibilities:

- a part is faulty
- a part is OK.

The updated probabilities for this example, found using Bayes' theorem, are shown in Figure 8.3(b).

373

WORKED EXAMPLE 8.11

Secondhand cars may be classified as either good buys or bad buys. Among good buys 70% have low oil consumption and 20% have medium oil consumption. Among bad buys 50% have high oil consumption and 30% have medium oil consumption. A test was done on a secondhand car and showed a low oil consumption. If 60% of secondhand cars are good buys, what is the probability that a particular car is a good buy?

SOLUTION

We can start by defining the abbreviations GB and BB for 'good buy' and 'bad buy'; HOC, MOC and LOC for high, medium and low oil consumption. The known values could be substituted into the equation for Bayes' theorem, but we can use the mechanical procedure to ease calculation.

	HOC	MOC	LOC		HOC	MOC	LOC
GB	0.1	0.2	0.7	0.6	0.06	0.12	0.42
BB	0.5	0.3	0.2	0.4	0.20	0.12	0.08
					0.26	0.24	0.50
			GB		0.23	0.5	0.84
			BB		0.77	0.5	0.16

From this table (and Figure 8.4), the probability that a car with a low oil consumption is a good buy is 0.84. The table also shows that the probability of a low oil consumption is 0.5 (compared with 0.26 for a high oil consumption).

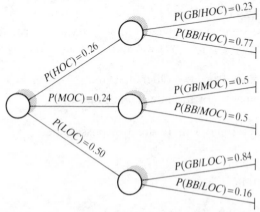

Figure 8.4 Probability tree for Worked example 8.11.

SELF ASSESSMENT QUESTIONS

8.11 What is meant by conditional probability?

8.12 What is Bayes' theorem and when is it used?

8.6 PROBABILITY DISTRIBUTIONS

One method of describing data graphically is to draw a frequency distribution. We know that probabilities can be considered as relative frequencies, so combining these two ideas leads to the description of a set of data by a 'probability distribution' where each value is plotted against the probability of its occurrence.

In worked example 8.1, the numbers of visitors to a hospital patient in five consecutive days were four, two, one, seven and one. A frequency diagram for this data is shown in Figure 8.5(a). Calculating the probability of each number of visitors gives the following results.

Number of visitors	1	2	3	4	5	6	7
Frequency	2	1	0	1	0	0	1
Probability	0.4	0.2	0.0	0.2	0.0	0.0	0.2

Then replacing the frequency by the probability gives the probability distribution histogram shown in Figure 8.5(b).

Similarly the data described in worked example 8.3 shows the number of people who booked rooms in a hotel but did not turn up. Adding the number of nights with various numbers of no-shows gives a frequency distribution. Dividing these numbers by the total number of observations gives a relative frequency or probability distribution.

No-shows	0	1	2	3	4	5	6	7
Frequency	1	4	8	12	10	6	3	1
Probability	0.02	0.09	0.18	0.27	0.22	0.13	0.07	0.02

This probability distribution histogram is shown in Figure 8.6.

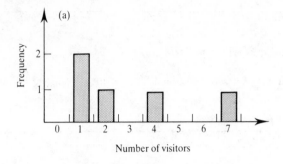

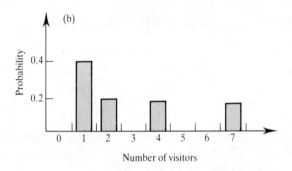

Figure 8.5 (a) Frequency diagram for the number of visitors a day; (b) probability distribution for numbers of visitors.

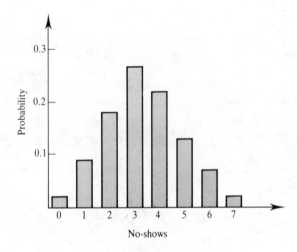

Figure 8.6 Probability distribution histogram for no-shows.

These two probability distributions are specific to the examples, but there are several distributions which are more generally applicable. We are going to look at three of these:

- Binomial distribution
- Poisson distribution
- Normal (or Gaussian) distribution.

8.7 BINOMIAL DISTRIBUTION

The Binomial distribution is used when a series of 'trials' have the following characteristics:

- each trial has two possible outcomes (conventionally called success and failure)
- the two outcomes are mutually exclusive
- there is a constant probability of success, p, and failure, $q = 1 - p$
- the outcomes of successive trials are independent.

Tossing a coin is a standard illustration of a Binomial process.

Consider the Binomial process of inspecting a batch of some item to see how many are defective. If the batch contains n units, what is the probability that exactly r of the units will be defective? In the conventional terminology for Binomial distributions a defective unit would be a 'success'. The probability of exactly r successes can then be found by the following argument.

$$P(\text{exactly } r \text{ successes}) = P(r \text{ successes and } n - r \text{ failures})$$

The probability of the first r units being successes is p^r. The probability of the next $n - r$ units being failures is $q^{(n-r)}$. Then the probability of the first r units being successes and the next $n - r$ units being failures is $p^r * q^{(n-r)}$.

This is the probability of one sequence of r successes and $(n - r)$ failures, and we must find how many other possible sequences there are. In Chapter 7 we showed how the number of sequences of r things chosen from a population of n is:

$$^nC_r = \frac{n!}{r! * (n - r)!}$$

Using this argument, there must be ^nC_r possible sequences of r successes and $n - r$ failures, each with probability $p^r * q^{(n-r)}$. The total probability of r successes is found by multiplying the probability of any one such sequence by the number of possible sequences. Hence the probability of r successes in n trials is:

$$P(r \text{ successes in } n \text{ trials}) = {}^{n}C_r * p^r * q^{(n-r)}$$

This is the Binomial probability distribution.

WORKED EXAMPLE 8.12

A salesman knows that in the long term he has a 50% chance of making a sale when calling on a customer. One morning he arranges six calls.

(a) What is the probability of making exactly three sales?
(b) What are the probabilities of making other numbers of sales?
(c) What is the probability of making fewer than three sales?

SOLUTION

The problem is a Binomial process with probability of success, making a sale, of $p = 0.5$. The probability of failure, not making a sale, is $q = 0.5$. The number of trials, n, is 6.

(a) The probability of making exactly three sales (i.e. $r = 3$) is given by:

$P(r \text{ successes in } n \text{ trials}) = {}^{n}C_r * p^r * q^{(n-r)}$

$P(3 \text{ successes in } 6 \text{ trials}) = {}^{6}C_3 * 0.5^3 * 0.5^{(6-3)}$

$$\frac{6!}{3!3!} * 0.125 * 0.125$$

$$= 0.3125$$

(b) Similarly substituting other values for r gives the values

r	0	1	2	3	4	5	6
$P(r$ successes in 6 trials)	0.0156	0.0938	0.2344	0.3125	0.2344	0.0938	0.0156

These are drawn in the probability distribution shown in Figure 8.7.

(c) The probability of making fewer than three sales is the sum of the probabilities of making 0, 1 and 2 sales.

$P(\text{fewer than 3 sales}) = P(0 \text{ sales}) + P(1 \text{ sale}) + P(2 \text{ sales})$

$$= 0.0156 + 0.0938 + 0.2344$$

$$= 0.3438$$

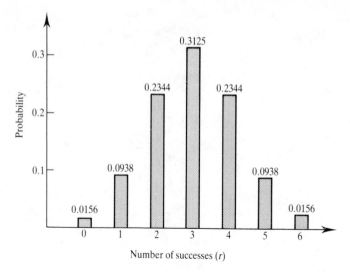

Figure 8.7 Probability distribution for Binomial process with $n = 6$ and $p = 0.5$.

The shape of the Binomial distribution varies with p and n. For small values of p the distribution is asymmetrical and the peak occurs to the left of centre. As p increases the peak moves to the centre of the distribution and with $p = 0.5$ the distribution is symmetrical. As p increases further the distribution again becomes asymmetrical but this time the peak is to the right of centre. For larger values of n the distribution is flatter and broader. Some typical binomial distributions are shown in Figure 8.8.

Whatever the values of n and p the mean, variance and standard deviation of a binomial distribution are calculated from:

$$\text{mean} \qquad\qquad = \mu = n * p$$
$$\text{variance} \qquad\quad = \sigma^2 = n * p * q$$
$$\text{standard deviation} = \sigma = \sqrt{n * p * q}$$

The calculations of probabilities are fairly simple, but standard tables have been prepared for many values of n and p. Appendix B illustrates some of these tables.

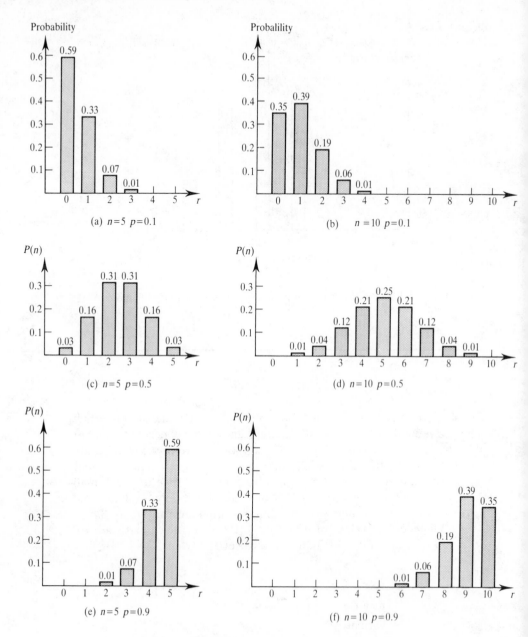

Figure 8.8 Typical Binomial distributions for varying values of n and p.

In summary

The Binomial distribution is used when an event has two mutually exclusive outcomes, success and failure.

$$P(r \text{ successes in } n \text{ trials}) = {}^nC_r * p^r * q^{(n-r)}$$

WORKED EXAMPLE 8.13

A market researcher is asked to visit 12 houses in a given area between 7.30 and 9.30 one evening. Previous calls have suggested that there will be someone at home in 85% of houses.

(a) Describe the probability distribution of the number of houses with people at home.
(b) What is the probability that the researcher will find someone at home in exactly nine houses?
(c) What is the probability there will be someone at home in exactly seven houses?
(d) What is the probability there will be someone at home in at least 10 houses?

SOLUTION

(a) The process is binomial with $n = 12$, $p = 0.85$ and $q = 0.15$.

Mean number of houses with people at home $= n * p$

$$= 12 * 0.85$$
$$= 10.2$$

variance $= n * p * q = 12 * 0.85 * 0.15 = 1.53$

standard deviation $= \sqrt{1.53} = 1.24$

(b) Let $P(9)$ be the probability that there is someone at home in exactly 9 houses. Then:

$$P(9) = {}^{12}C_9 * 0.85^9 * 0.15^3$$
$$= 220 * 0.2316169 * 0.003375$$
$$= 0.172$$

(c) $\quad P(7) = {}^{12}C_7 * 0.85^7 * 0.15^5$
$$= 792 * 0.320577 * 0.000076$$
$$= 0.0193$$

These figures could be found in the tables in Appendix B. Values are only given for p up to 0.5, so we need to redefine 'success' as finding a house with no one at home. Then $p = 0.15$ and $r = 5$. Looking at the entry for $n = 12$, $p = 0.15$ and $r = 3$ (finding nine houses with someone at home is the same as finding three

381

houses with no-one at home) gives the value 0.1720 while $r = 5$ gives the value 0.0193.

(d) We want

$$P(\text{at least } 10) = P(10) + P(11) + P(12)$$

Again using 'success' as finding no-one at home, the tables can be used to give:

$$P(\text{at least } 10) = 0.2924 + 0.3012 + 0.1422$$
$$= 0.7358$$

Even with such tables and use of computers the arithmetic can, in certain circumstances, become intractable. Consider the following example where n is very large.

> The accounts department of a company sends out 10,000 invoices a month and on average five of these are returned with some error. What is the probability that exactly five invoices will be returned in a given month?

This is a typical application for Binomial distributions, but as soon as we try to do the arithmetic we run into difficulties. Substituting known values gives

$$n = 10,000 \quad r = 5 \quad p = 5/10,000 \quad q = 9995/10,000$$

$$P(r \text{ returns}) = \frac{n!}{r!(n - r)!} * p^r * q^{(n-r)}$$

$$= \frac{10,000!}{5! * 9995!} * (5/10,000)^5 * 9995/10,000^{9995}$$

Although this calculation may be tackled, it does not seem reasonable to raise figures to the power of 9995 or to contemplate 10,000 factorial. Fortunately, there is an alternative calculation. When n, the number of trials, is large and p, the probability of success, is small the Binomial distribution can be approximated by the Poisson distribution. This is described in Section 8.8.

SELF ASSESSMENT QUESTIONS

8.13 In what circumstances can a Binomial distribution be used?

8.14 How are the mean and variance of a Binomial distribution calculated?

8.15 Find, from the tables in Appendix B, the probability of two successes from seven trials, when the probability of success is 0.2.

8.8 POISSON DISTRIBUTION

The Poisson distribution is a close relative of the Binomial distribution and can be used to approximate it when:

- the number of trials, n, is large (say greater than 20)
- the probability of success, p, is small (say $n * p$ is less than 5).

As n gets larger and p gets smaller the approximation becomes better.

The Poisson distribution is also useful in its own right for solving problems where events occur at random. The number of accidents each month in a factory, the number of defects in a metre of cloth and the number of phone calls received each hour in an office each follow a Poisson distribution.

The main difference between the Binomial and Poisson distributions is that the former needs both the number of successes and failures, while the latter needs only the number of successes. p is small, so the number of failures is large and we are looking for a few successes in a continuous background of failures. The number of spelling mistakes in a long report, the number of faults in a pipeline or the number of accidents in a month all look for the number of 'successes' and do not bother with the large number of events which are conventionally called failures.

The Poisson distribution is described by the equation

$$P(r \text{ successes}) = \frac{e^{-\mu} * \mu^r}{r!}$$

where: e = exponential constant = 2.7183

μ = mean number of successes

We can illustrate the use of the Poisson distribution by the Binomial example which we did not finish above.

The accounts department of a company sends out 10,000 invoices a month and on average five of these are returned with some error. What is the probability that exactly five invoices will be returned in a given month?

Here n is large, $n * p = 5$ (fairly high but the result should still be reasonable) and we can use the Poisson approximation to the Binomial. The variables are $r = 5$ and $\mu = n * P = 5$.

$$P(r \text{ successes}) = \frac{e^{-\mu} * \mu^r}{r!}$$

$$P(5 \text{ successes}) = \frac{e^{-5} * 5^5}{5!}$$

$$= (0.0067 * 3125)/120$$

$$= 0.1755$$

WORKED EXAMPLE 8.14

In a large office complex there have been 40 accidents which lead to absence from work in the past 50 weeks. In what proportion of weeks would you expect 0, 1, 2, 3 and more than 4 accidents?

SOLUTION

A small number of accidents occur, presumably at random, over time. We are not interested in the number of accidents which did *not* occur, so the process can be described by a Poisson distribution.

The mean number of accidents a week is 40/50 = 0.8

$$P(r \text{ successes}) = \frac{e^{-\mu} * \mu^r}{r!}$$

Substituting $\mu = 0.8$ and $r = 0$ gives:

$$P(0) = \frac{e^{-0.8} * 0.8^0}{0!} = 0.4493$$

Similar substitution of $r = 1$ etc. gives:

$$P(1) = \frac{e^{-0.8} * 0.8^1}{1!} = 0.3595$$

$$P(2) = \frac{e^{-0.8} * 0.8^2}{2!} = 0.1438$$

$$P(3) = \frac{e^{-0.8} * 0.8^3}{3!} = 0.0383$$

$$P(4) = \frac{e^{-0.8} * 0.8^4}{3!} = 0.0077$$

Then $P(>4) = 1 - P(\leq 4)$

$$= 1 - P(0) - P(1) - P(2) - P(3) - P(4)$$

$$= 1 - 0.4493 - 0.3593 - 0.1438 - 0.0383 - 0.0077$$

$$= 0.0014$$

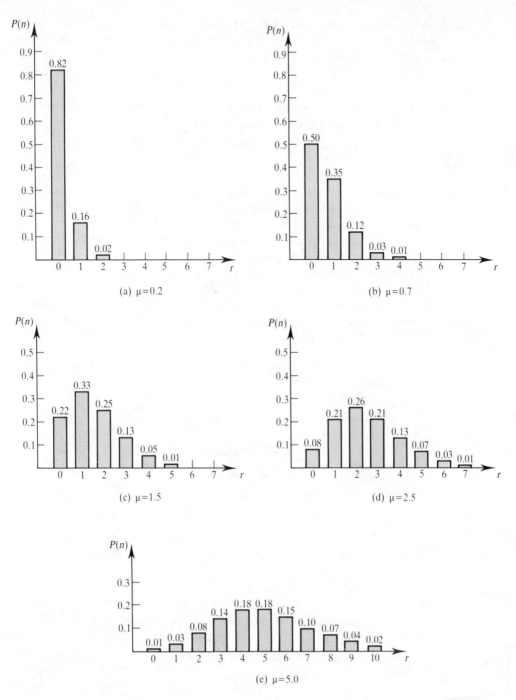

Figure 8.9 Typical Poisson distributions for varying values of μ.

When events occur at random a Poisson distribution can often be used, but strictly speaking there are a number of other requirements. In particular a Poisson process needs:

- occurrences of events which are independent;
- the probability of an event happening in an interval is proportional to the length of the interval;
- in theory, an infinite number of events should be possible in an interval.

The mean of a Poisson distribution is μ and may be calculated from $n * p$, and the variance is also μ. This is an example of a probability distribution whose shape and position is determined by a single parameter, in this case μ. For small μ the distribution is asymmetrical with a peak to the left of centre. Then as μ increases the curve becomes more symmetrical. This is illustrated for some values in Figure 8.9.

The arithmetic for calculating probabilities is straightforward, but could be rather time consuming if a large number of values are to be found. A computer could help, but standard tables have again been prepared. An example of these is given in Appendix C.

In summary

The Poisson distribution can be used as an approximation to the Binomial distribution when the probability of success is small, or to describe random events.

$$P(r \text{ successes}) = \frac{e^{-\mu} * \mu^r}{r!}$$

WORKED EXAMPLE 8.15

During a test to see if a road intersection should be improved it was found that cars arrived randomly at the intersection at an average rate of five cars every 10 minutes.

(a) What is the probability that during a ten-minute period exactly three cars will arrive?

(b) What is the probability that more than five cars will arrive in a ten minute period?

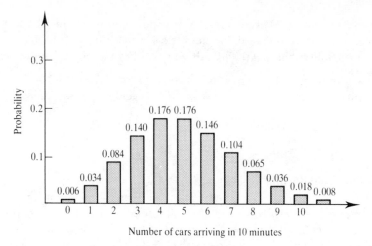

Figure 8.10 Probability distribution of number of cars arriving at intersection in 10 minutes.

SOLUTION

(a)   Here random arrivals over time imply a Poisson process. The mean number of successes (i.e. cars arriving at the intersection in ten minutes) is $\mu = 5$. Then the probability of exactly three cars arriving can be found from:

$$P(3) = \frac{e^{-5} * 5^3}{3!} = 0.1404$$

This value could also be found from the tables in Appendix C. Looking up the value for $\mu = 5$ and $r = 3$ also gives 0.1404.

(b)   To find the probability that more than five cars will arrive at the intersection in a ten minute period we need to calculate:

$$P(>5) = 1 - P(5 \text{ or less})$$
$$= 1 - P(0) - P(1) - P(2) - P(3) - P(4) - P(5)$$

These values can either be calculated or looked up in tables to give:

$$P(>5) = 1 - 0.0067 - 0.0337 - 0.0842 - 0.1404 - 0.1755 - 0.1755$$
$$= 0.384$$

This is also illustrated in Figure 8.10.

Even with appropriate tables there may be difficulties with the calculations for Poisson distributions. Consider the following example.

A motor insurance policy is only available to drivers with low risk of accidents. 100 drivers holding the policy in a certain area would expect an average of 0.2 accidents each a year. What is the probability that less than 15 drivers will have accidents in one year?

This is a Binomial process with mean $= n * p = 100 * 0.2 = 20$. The probability that less than 15 drivers will have accidents in the year is given by:

$$\sum_{r=1}^{15} {}^{20}C_r * 0.2^r * 0.8^{100-r}$$

This is difficult to evaluate so we would look for a Poisson approximation. Unfortunately $n * p$ is 20 which does not meet the requirement that $n * p$ be less than 5. Another approach is needed, and this time we will use the most common probability distribution of all. When n is large and $n * p$ is greater than 5 the Binomial distribution can be approximated by the Normal distribution. This is described in Section 8.9.

SELF ASSESSMENT QUESTIONS

8.16 In what circumstances can a Poisson distribution be used?

8.17 How are the mean and variance of a Poisson distribution calculated?

8.18 The average number of defects per square yard of material is 0.8. Use the tables in Appendix C to find the probability that a square yard has exactly two defects.

8.19 In what circumstances can a Poisson distribution be used as an approximation for a Binomial distribution?

8.9   NORMAL DISTRIBUTION

This is a bell shaped curve which describes a very wide range of applications. Many natural phenomena such as the heights of trees, harvest from an acre of land or daily temperature, follow a precise curve which is so widely used that it has become known as the 'Normal' distribution. Many business functions are also described by this curve, such as daily takings in a shop, number of customers a week and production in a factory. The distribution is so common that the rule of thumb, 'For large numbers of observations use the Normal distribution' is quite defensible (see Figure 8.11).

The first thing to notice about the Normal distribution is that is continuous. So far in this chapter we have only considered data which is

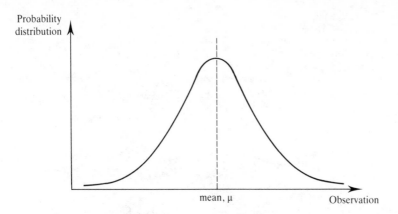

Figure 8.11 Normal distribution.

discrete (that is, comes in fixed quantities with an integer number of occurrences, such as defects or successes). This is our first venture in continuous data, which can take non-integer values (such as lengths or profits).

The Normal distribution curve has the properties:

- it is continuous
- it is symmetrical about the mean value, μ
- the mean, median and mode are all equal
- the total area under the curve equals 1
- in theory the curve extends to plus and minus infinity on the x-axis.

The equation for the Normal (sometimes called Gaussian) distribution is rather complex. The height of the curve at any point is given by:

$$f(x) = \frac{1}{\sqrt{2\pi}\sigma} e^{-(x-\mu)^2/2\sigma^2}$$

where: x = value of interest

  μ = mean value

  σ = standard deviation

  π, e = constants taking their conventional values of 3.14159 and 2.71828 respectively.

Fortunately we do not have to worry about this equation as it is hardly ever used. With continuous data the height of the curve at any specific point does not have much value, but probabilities are calculated from the area under the curve.

Suppose a factory makes boxes of chocolates with a mean weight

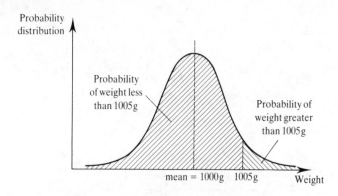

Figure 8.12 Distribution of weights for chocolate boxes (probabilities given by areas under curve).

of 1000 g. There will be small variations in the weight of each box, and if a large number of boxes are made the weights will follow a Normal distribution. Management of the factory will not be interested in the number of boxes which weigh exactly 1005.0000 g, say, but they could well be interested in the number of boxes which weigh more than 1005 g. This is represented by the area under the right hand tail of the distribution (see Figure 8.12).

There are two ways of finding the area under the tail of the distribution. Either we could integrate the curve between 1005.0 and infinity (which would be rather tedious) or we could look up the values in standard tables. The latter is obviously preferable and we will always use tables for such calculations.

The two factors which affect the position and shape of the Normal curve are the mean and standard deviation. In this case the mean weight of a box of chocolates is 1000 g, and we will assume the standard deviation is 3 g. To look up the area under the tail of the probability distribution in standard tables we need to calculate the number of standard deviations the point of interest (1005 g) is away from the mean. This is usually called Z.

Z = number of standard deviations from the mean

$$= \frac{\text{value} - \text{mean}}{\text{standard deviation}}$$

$$= \frac{1005 - 1000}{3}$$

$$= 1.6$$

A table of areas under the normal curve is given in Appendix D, and looking up 1.6 in this gives a value of 0.0548. This is the probability

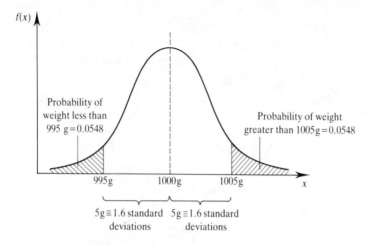

Figure 8.13 Symmetrical distribution for weights of chocolate boxes.

that a box will weigh more than 1005 g. (Tables of Normal curves have slight differences so care must be taken that the value given is the one actually wanted.)

Because the Normal distribution curve is symmetrical about the mean, we could do some other calculations. The probability, for example, that a box of chocolates weighs less than 995 g is the same as the probability it weighs more than 1005 g and has been calculated as 0.0548 (see Figure 8.13).

The Normal distribution is always symmetrical, so the two factors which affect its shape (the mean and the standard deviation) only affect its height and position. The larger the standard deviation the greater will be the spread, while the mean determines the position of the distribution, as illustrated in Figure 8.14.

Generally about 68% of observations will be within one standard deviation of the mean, 95% will be within two standard deviations and 99.7% will be within three standard deviations (see Figure 8.15).

In summary

Large numbers of observations often follow a Normal distribution. Probabilities are invariably found from standard tables.

A practical introduction to management science

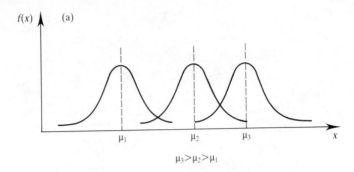

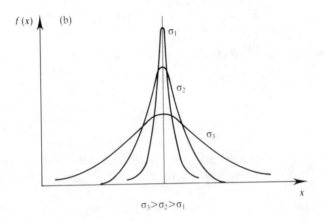

Figure 8.14 Showing the way Normal distributions vary with mean and standard deviation: (a) Normal distributions with same standard deviations but different means; (b) Normal distributions with same mean but different standard deviations.

WORKED EXAMPLE 8.16

Figures kept by an auctioneer for the past five years show that the weight of beef cattle brought to market has a mean of 950 kg and a standard deviation of 150 kg. What proportion of these have weights:

(a) more than 1250 kg
(b) less than 850 kg
(c) between 1100 kg and 1250 kg
(d) between 800 kg and 1300 kg?

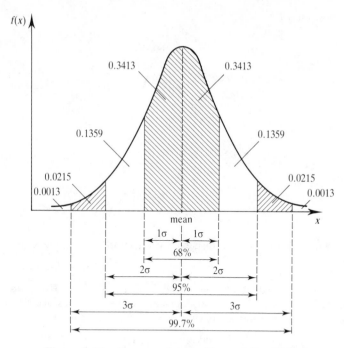

Figure 8.15 Areas under the Normal distribution.

SOLUTION

In this example there are presumably a large number of cattle brought to market so we can assume a Normal distribution with $\mu = 950$ and $\sigma = 150$.

(a) The probability of weight greater than 1250 kg is found as follows.

Z = number of standard deviations from the mean

$\quad = (1250 - 950)/150$

$\quad = 2.0$

Looking this value up in the table in Appendix D gives a value of 0.0228, which is the required probability (see Figure 8.16).

(b) The probability of weight less than 850 kg is found in the same way.

$Z = (850 - 950)/150$

$\quad = -0.67$

The table only shows positive values, but as the distribution is symmetrical we can use the value for +0.67, which is 0.2514. This is the area under the tail of the curve and is the required probability.

Because the table only shows probabilities under the tail of the

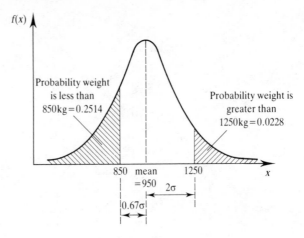

Figure 8.16 Normal distribution for Worked example 8.16.

distribution some juggling of the values is often needed. There are several different ways of doing the following calculations and the ones described are the most convenient. Any valid alternative can, of course, be used.

(c)   The calculation that the weight is between 1100 kg and 1250 kg relies on the relationship

$$P(\text{between 1100 kg and 1250 kg}) = P(\text{greater than 1100 kg})$$
$$- P(\text{greater than 1250 kg})$$

For weight above 1100 kg: $Z = (1100 - 950)/150 = 1$
probability $= 0.1587$

For weight above 1250 kg: $Z = (1250 - 950)/150 = 2$
probability $= 0.0228$

Therefore the probability that the weight is between these two is $0.1587 - 0.0228 = 0.1359$ (see Figure 8.17).

(d)   The calculation that the weight is between 800 kg and 1300 kg relies on the relationship

$$P(\text{between 800 kg and 1300 kg}) = 1 - P(\text{less than 800 kg})$$
$$- P(\text{greater than 1300 kg})$$

For weight below   800 kg: $Z = (800 - 950)/150 = -1$
probability $= 0.1587$

For weight above 1300 kg: $Z = (1300 - 950)/150 = 2.33$
probability $= 0.0099$

Therefore the probability that the weight is between these two is $1 - 0.1587 - 0.0099 = 0.8314$. This is illustrated in Figure 8.18.

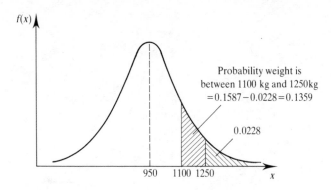

Figure 8.17   Calculations for Worked example 8.16.

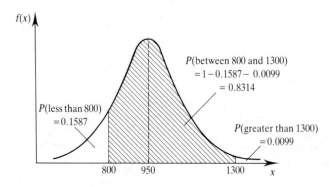

Figure 8.18   Calculations for Worked example 8.16.

WORKED EXAMPLE 8.17

The Poisson distribution was inappropriate for the example of motor insurance described previously, where a motor insurance policy is only available to drivers with low risk of accidents. 100 drivers holding the policy in a certain area would expect an average of 0.2 accidents each a year. Use a Normal distribution to find the probability that less than 15 drivers will have accidents in a year? How might the integer number of accidents be taken into account?

SOLUTION

This is a Binomial process with $n = 100$ and $p = 0.2$, so the mean $= n * p = 100 * 0.2 = 20$. The standard deviation of a Binomial distribution is

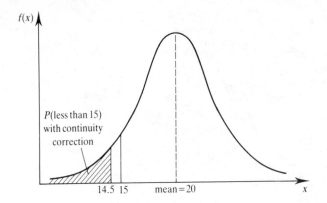

Figure 8.19 Normal distribution with continuity correction for Worked example 8.17.

$\sqrt{n*p*q} = \sqrt{16} = 4$. To find the probability of less than 15 drivers having an accident

$$Z = (15 - 20)/4 = -1.25$$
$$\text{probability} = 0.1056$$

Because the number of accidents is discrete a 'continuity correction' is sometimes applied. We are looking for the probability of less than 15 accidents but it is clearly impossible to have *between* 14 and 15 accidents. An allowance can be added to interpret 'less than 15' as 'less than 14.5' (see Figure 8.19).
This continuity correction for integer values then gives:

$$Z = (14.5 - 20)/4 = -1.375$$
$$\text{probability} = 0.0846$$

If the question had asked for '15 or less' accidents the continuity correction might have been applied to interpret this as 'less than 15.5'. Then:

$$Z = (15.5 - 20)/4 = -1.125$$
$$\text{probability} = 0.1303$$

WORKED EXAMPLE 8.18

On average a supermarket sells 500 pints of milk a day with a standard deviation of 50 pints.

(a) If the supermarket has 600 pints in stock at the beginning of a day what is the probability that it will sell out of milk?
(b) What is the probability that demand is between 450 and 600 pints?

(c)   How many pints should the supermarket stock if it wants the probability of running out to be 0.05?

(d)   How many should it stock if it wants the probability of running out to be 0.01?

SOLUTION

(a)   With 600 pints: $Z = (600 - 500)/50 = 2.0$

$$\text{probability} = 0.0228$$

This is illustrated in Figure 8.20.

(b)   The probability of demand greater than 600 is 0.0228. For demand less than 450 pints:

$Z = (450 - 500)/50 = -1.0$

probability $= 0.1587$

Therefore the probability of demand between 450 and 600 is:

$1 - 0.0228 - 0.1587 = 0.8185$

(c)   For probability $= 0.05$, $Z = 1.645$ (look up 0.05 in the body of the table and this is mid-way between 1.64 and 1.65).

1.645 standard deviations is $1.645 * 50 = 82.25$ pints from the mean. Therefore the supermarket needs to have $500 + 83 = 583$ pints at the beginning of the day (rounding up to ensure a maximum probability of stock-outs of 0.05).

(d)   For probability 0.01, $Z = 2.33$. This is $2.33 * 50 = 116.5$ pints from the mean. Therefore the supermarket needs to have $500 + 117 = 617$ pints at the beginning of the day (see Figure 8.21).

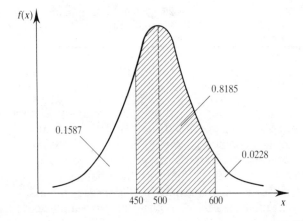

Figure 8.20   Normal distribution for Worked example 8.18.

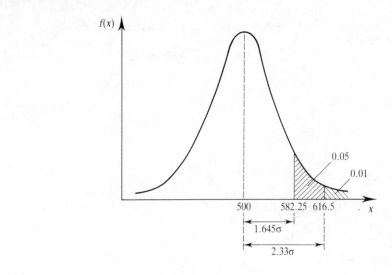

Figure 8.21   Probabilities of stock-out for Worked example 8.18.

SELF ASSESSMENT QUESTIONS

8.20   In what circumstances can a Normal distribution be used?

8.21   What is the most obvious difference between a Normal distribution and a Binomial or Poisson distribution?

8.22   What two factors affect the shape of a Normal distribution?

8.23   In what circumstances can a Normal distribution be used as an approximation to a Binomial distribution?

8.24   If the mean of a set of observations is 100 and the standard deviation is 10, what proportion of observations will be between 90 and 110?

8.25   What is a 'continuity correction' for discrete data?

CONCLUSIONS

The purpose of this chapter is to provide an overview of some important statistical concepts. The approach is not mathematical but uses examples to illustrate the main points.

   The chapter started by considering the need to reduce raw data and the ways in which summarized information can be presented. Essentially graphical or numerical methods are available. We have concentrated on numerical methods, starting with measures for averages and spread.

   Probabilities were then described in terms of the likelihood of an event or its relative frequency. Rules were developed for calculating probabilities for independent events.

Not all events are independent and some results for conditional probabilities were described, particularly Bayes' theorem.

Using the concept of probabilities as relative frequencies, the idea of probability distributions was outlined. Three widely used probability distributions were described in more detail. The Binomial distribution was used for trials which ended in either success or failure. The Poisson distribution was used for random occurrences. The Normal distribution was used to describe large numbers of observations.

The ideas developed here will be used to build probabilistic models in the following chapters.

PROBLEMS

8.1 Show how the data in Table 8.1 can be represented graphically.

Table 8.1

14	21	35	24	18	40	18	22	15	31
16	19	23	15	23	17	22	30	24	20
24	18	38	20	25	21	25	23	17	19
23	35	23	37	26	30	19	24	25	23
38	16	20	24	23	26	22	15	27	22
24	37	23	25	19	23	24	23	28	24
16	14	21	24	29	21	27	31	25	23
39	19	36	29	17	26	32	23	22	16
23	18	20	21	26	20	26	18	31	20
22	34	35	22	24	16	33	19	28	21
17	20	28	41	27	27	28	22	25	25
40	33	21	29	42	22	32	17	23	19

(a) Calculate the mean, median and mode for this data.

(b) What are the range, variance and standard deviation?

8.2 There are five equally likely outcomes to a trial, A, B, C, D and E.

(a) What is the probability of C occurring?

(b) What is the probability of A or B or C occurring?

(c) What is the probability that neither A nor B occur?

8.3 Four mutually exclusive, independent events A, B, C and D have probabilities of 0.1, 0.2, 0.3 and 0.4 respectively. What are the probabilities of:

(a) A and B occurring
(b) A or B
(c) neither A nor B
(d) A and B and C
(e) A or B or C
(f) none of A, B or C?

8.4 If $P(a) = 0.4$ and $P(b/a) = 0.3$, what is $P(a$ AND $b)$? If $P(b) = 0.6$ what is $P(a/b)$?

8.5 The probabilities of two events X and Y are 0.4 and 0.6 respectively. The conditional probabilities of three other events A, B and C occurring, given that X or Y has already occurred, are given in the following table.

	A	B	C
X	0.2	0.5	0.3
Y	0.6	0.1	0.3

What are the conditional probabilities of X and Y occurring given that A, B or C has already occurred?

8.6 A Binomial process has a probability of success of 0.15. If eight trials are run what is the mean number of successes and the standard deviation? What is the probability of:

(a) two successes in the eight trials
(b) seven successes
(c) at least six successes?

8.7 100 trials are run for a Poisson process. If the probability of a success is 0.02, what is the mean number of successes and the standard deviation? What is the probability of:

(a) exactly 2 successes
(b) exactly seven successes
(c) at least six successes?

8.8 Some observations follow a Normal distribution with mean 40 and standard deviation 4. What proportion of observations have values:

(a) greater than 46
(b) less than 34
(c) between 34 and 46
(d) between 30 and 44
(e) between 43 and 47?

SOLUTIONS TO SELF ASSESSMENT QUESTIONS

8.1   Data is raw numbers or facts. This must be processed to put it in a useful form, which is then information.

8.2   If there is a lot of data it is easy to get swamped with detail and not appreciate the overall picture (trends, average, spread and so on). The main aim of data reduction is to organize and present raw data so that the underlying patterns are revealed.

8.3   If there is a lot of data it can be reduced and presented either graphically (using a bar chart, histogram, or some other pictorial means) or numerically.

8.4   For n observations, x_i, the mean is calculated by:

$$\text{mean} = \frac{\sum\limits_{i=1}^{n} x_i}{n}$$

If observations are arranged in order of magnitude the middle observation is the median.
The mode is the value which occurs most frequently.

8.5   range = maximum observation − minimum observation

$$\text{MAD} = \frac{\sum\limits_{i=1}^{n} \text{ABS}[x_i - \mu]}{n}$$

$$\text{Variance} = \frac{\sum\limits_{i=1}^{n} (x_i - \mu)^2}{n}$$

Standard deviation = $\sqrt{\text{variance}}$

8.6   The probability of an event can be considered as a measure of its likelihood: it is the relative frequency with which it occurs.

8.7   For independent, mutually exclusive events the rule 'OR means ADD' can be used and the separate probabilities are added.

8.8   Two events are independent if the probability of one occurring is not affected by whether or not the other occurs.

8.9   Two events are mutually exclusive if they cannot both occur.

8.10   For independent events the rule 'AND means MULTIPLY' can be used and the probabilities are multiplied together.

8.11   If two (or more) events are not independent, conditional probabilities are used. These take the form $P(a/b)$ to represent the probability of event a occurring given that event b has already occurred.

8.12   Bayes' theorem is used for calculating conditional probabilities. In particular it states:

$$P(a/b) = \frac{P(b/a) * P(a)}{P(b)}$$

8.13   The Binomial distribution can be used when a series of 'trials' have the following characteristics:

- each trial has two possible outcomes (conventionally called success and failure)
- the two outcomes are mutually exclusive
- there is a constant probability of success, p, and failure, $q = 1 - p$
- the outcomes of successive trials are independent.

8.14   For the Binomial distribution:

mean   = $\mu = n * p$

variance = $\sigma^2 = n * p * q$

standard deviation = $\sigma = \sqrt{n * p * q}$

8.15   Looking at the entry in Appendix B under $n = 12$, $p = 0.2$ and $r = 2$ gives the probability of 0.2835.

8.16   The Poisson distribution describes events which occur infrequently and at random. Other requirements include:

- occurrences of events are independent
- the probability of an event happening in an interval is proportional to the length of the interval
- in theory an infinite number of events should be possible in an interval.

8.17 The mean of a Poisson distribution is μ and may be calculated from $n * p$. The variance is also μ.

8.18 $\mu = 0.8$ so looking up the value for $r = 2$ in the tables in Appendix C gives a value of 0.1438.

8.19 A Poisson distribution can be used to approximate a Binomial distribution when the number of events, n, in the Binomial process is large and the probability of success is small, with $n * p$ less than 5.

8.20 The Normal distribution can be used in a wide range of applications when there is a large number of observations.

8.21 The Binomial and Poisson distributions are for discrete data (that is, values which can only take integer values) while the Normal distribution describes continuous data (which can take any value).

8.22 The mean determines the location of the distribution and the standard deviation determines its spread.

8.23 The Normal distribution can be used as an approximation for the Binomial distribution when the number of events, n, is large and the probability of success is relatively large (with $n * p$ greater than 5).

8.24 About 68% of observations are within one standard deviation of the mean.

8.25 Because the Normal distribution describes continuous data a small correction can be used for discrete data. Questions which ask for the probability of, for example, 'between 3 and 6 people (inclusively)' could use a correction to make this 'between 2.5 and 6.5 people'. This correction is usually small, but may sometimes be important.

REFERENCES FOR FURTHER READING

Daniel W. W. and Terrell J. C. (1986). *Business Statistics* Boston: Houghton Mifflin Company

Freund J. E. and Williams F. J. (1984). *Elementary Business Statistics: the modern approach* 4th edn. New Jersey: Prentice Hall

Greensted C. S., Jardine A. K. S. and Macfarlane J. D. (1978). *Essentials of Statistics in Marketing* 2nd edn. London: Heinemann

Harper W. M. (1982). *Statistics* 4th edn. London: Macdonald & Evans

Huff D. (1973). *How to Lie with Statistics* Harmondsworth: Penguin Books

Kazmier L. J. (1976). *Schaum's Outline of Theory & Problems of Business Statistics* New York: McGraw-Hill

Kennedy G. (1983). *Invitation to Statistics* Oxford: Martin Robertson

Moroney M. J. (1951). *Facts from Figures.* Harmondsworth: Penguin Books

Reichmann W. J. (1962). *Use and Abuse of Statistics* London: Chapman & Hall

Rowntree, D. (1981). *Statistics Without Tears: a primer for non-mathematicians* Harmondsworth: Penguin Books

Spiegel M. R. (1972). *Schaum's Outline of Theory and Problems of Statistics* New York: McGraw-Hill

Walpole W. (1982). *Introduction to Statistics* 3rd edn. Collier Macmillan

Wonnacott T. H. and Wonnacott R. J. (1977). *Introductory Statistics* 3rd edn. New York: John Wiley

Chapter 9

Statistical models in business

SYNOPSIS

The first part of this book described a number of quantitative models where the values taken by variables were known exactly and there was no uncertainty. These situations are generally called 'deterministic'. Chapter 8 described a number of statistical ideas. These ideas can be incorporated into models where variables have values which are not known exactly but can be described by some probability distribution. These situations are called 'probabilistic' or 'stochastic'.

In this chapter we are going to describe stochastic models for a number of business situations. These illustrate potential application areas and the chapter can be considered as a link between Chapter 8 and the more detailed applications in Chapters 10 and 11.

The first model extends the description of project network analysis given in Chapter 5. There, activity durations were known exactly, while this section describes how uncertainty in durations can be dealt with. In a similar way, Chapter 3 described some deterministic models for inventory control, where the demand was known with certainty. This chapter expands these analyses by describing approaches to probabilistic demands.

The next section looks at reliability of systems and considers the age at which equipment should be replaced. A number of models are developed to suggest ways in which statistical ideas can be used to calculate reliabilities or compare different replacement policies.

Sometimes a specific bit of information is needed from a large number of sources. The mean weight of a particular item, for example, can be found by weighing all units of the item produced. Often it is impractical or impossible to collect information from *all* sources and a sample is taken. This is the basis of sampling theory.

Finally the chapter looks at one aspect of hypothesis testing. Here a hypothesis is made about a population and a sample is taken to see if the evidence supports this hypothesis.

OBJECTIVES

After reading this chapter and doing the numerical exercises you should be able to:

- appreciate ways in which probabilistic values can be used in models;
- use three estimates of activity durations in PERT networks;
- calculate a safety stock when lead time demand is normally distributed;
- solve the 'Newsboy problem';
- do an ABC analysis of inventory items;
- use statistical ideas to solve problems with the reliability of equipment;
- calculate the reliability of a system of components;
- consider some problems with replacement of equipment that deteriorates;
- understand why and how sampling is used;
- use a sampling distribution of the mean;
- calculate confidence limits for a population mean from a sample;
- appreciate the approach of hypothesis testing;
- test hypotheses about population values found from samples.

9.1 PROGRAMME EVALUATION AND REVIEW TECHNIQUE

Chapter 5 described project network analysis, where projects are represented by a network of alternating activities and events. Such networks can be analysed and timings found for activities, with the objectives of organizing projects on a rational basis, using resources efficiently and avoiding potential difficulties. If you are unsure about any aspect of network analysis it would be useful to review Chapter 5 before continuing.

Chapter 5 described the critical path method (CPM) where each activity is given a single estimate for duration. A useful extension to this deals with uncertainty in activity durations. This extension constitutes the main difference between CPM and PERT (programme evaluation and review technique) which we will now discuss.

It is often difficult to forecast the precise time needed to complete an activity and there is almost inevitably some uncertainty in the duration. One common way of allowing for this is to use three estimates:

- an optimistic duration (*OD*) which is the shortest time an activity would take if everything goes smoothly and without any difficulties;
- a most likely duration (*MD*) which is the most likely duration for the activity under normal conditions;
- a pessimistic duration (*PD*) which is the time needed if there are significant problems and delays.

Typically we might express the finish time for an activity in terms such as, 'we should finish the foundations in five days, but might manage it in four if there are no difficulties, or we could take 12 days if the weather gets worse'.

Experience has suggested that activity durations can usually be described by a Beta distribution. We need not go into the details of this distribution (which looks something like a skewed Normal distribution), but need only note that the three estimates of duration (*OD*, *MD* and *PD*) allow an 'expected duration' to be calculated with uncertainty expressed by a variance. The expected project duration and its variance are calculated from the 'rule of sixths':

$$\text{Expected duration} = \frac{OD + 4 * MD + PD}{6}$$

$$\text{Variance} = \frac{(PD - OD)^2}{36}$$

Suppose the duration of a particular activity is uncertain but can be assigned an optimistic duration of four days, a most likely duration of five days and a pessimistic duration of 12 days (see Figure 9.1). Assuming a Beta distribution for duration:

$$\text{Expected duration} = \frac{OD + 4 * MD + PD}{6}$$
$$= (4 + 4 * 5 + 12)/6$$
$$= 6$$

$$\text{Variance} = \frac{(PD - OD)^2}{36}$$
$$= (12 - 4)^2/36$$
$$= 1.78$$

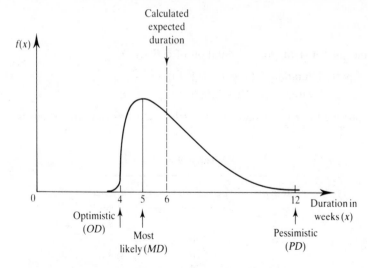

Figure 9.1 A typical Beta distribution of activity duration (OD = 4, MD = 5, PD = 12).

Expected durations can be used in the network for analysis of timings in the same way as the single estimate of CPM.

WORKED EXAMPLE 9.1

A network consists of nine activities with dependencies and estimated activity durations shown in Table 9.1. Draw the network, identify the critical path and estimate the overall duration of the project.

Table 9.1

Activity	Depends on	Optimistic	Duration Most likely	Pessimistic
A	–	2	3	10
B	–	4	5	12
C	–	8	10	12
D	A, G	4	4	4
E	B	3	6	15
F	B	2	5	8
G	B	6	6	6
H	C, F	5	7	15
I	D, E	6	8	10

SOLUTION

Using the rule of sixths for the duration of activity A:

$$\text{expected duration} = (2 + 4 * 3 + 10)/6 = 4$$
$$\text{variance} = (10 - 2)^2/36 \qquad = 1.78$$

Then repeating these calculations for the other activities gives the results in Table 9.2.

Table 9.2

Activity	Expected duration	Variance
A	4	1.78
B	6	1.78
C	10	0.44
D	4	0
E	7	4.00
F	5	1.00
G	6	0
H	8	2.78
I	8	0.44

The network for this problem is drawn in Figure 9.2.

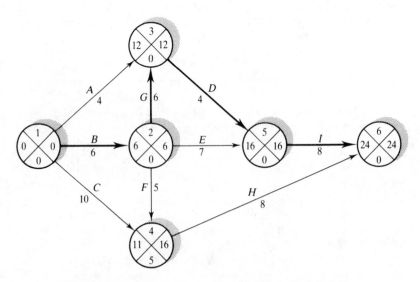

Figure 9.2 Network for Worked example 9.1.

The critical path for the project is B, G, D and I which has an expected duration of 24, and the analysis of times can be done as described in Chapter 5. For this you need to remember the definitions used:

(a) $ET(i)$ and $LT(i)$ are the earliest and latest times for event i;
(b) $ES(k)$ and $EF(k)$ are the earliest start and finish times for activity k which is between events i and j;
(c) $D(i,j)$ is the duration of activity k;

$$ES(k) = ET(i)$$
$$EF(k) = ES(k) + D(i,j)$$

(d) $LF(k)$ and $LS(k)$ are the latest finish and start of activity k.

$$LF(k) = LT(j)$$
$$LS(k) = LF(k) - D(i,j)$$

(e) The definitions of total, free and independent floats for activity k are:

$$TF(k) = LT(j) - ET(i) - D(i,j)$$
$$FF(k) = ET(j) - ET(i) - D(i,j)$$
$$IF(k) = ET(j) - LT(i) - D(i,j)$$

If you are unsure about any of these terms it would be sensible to look them up in Chapter 5.

Table 9.3 gives the analysis of activity times.

Table 9.3

Activity	Expected duration	ES	EF	LS	LF	Float Total	Float Free	Float Indep.	
A	4	0	4	8	12	8	8	8	
B	6	0	6	0	6	0	0	0	*
C	10	0	10	6	16	6	1	1	
D	4	12	16	12	16	0	0	0	*
E	7	6	13	9	16	3	3	3	
F	5	6	11	11	16	5	0	0	
G	6	6	12	6	12	0	0	0	*
H	8	11	19	16	24	5	5	0	
I	8	16	24	16	24	0	0	0	*

The duration of the critical path is the sum of the durations of activities making up that path. If there is a large number of activities on the path, and if the duration of each activity is independent of the others, the overall duration of the project will follow a Normal distribution. This distribution has:

• a mean equal to the sum of the expected durations of activities on the critical path;

409

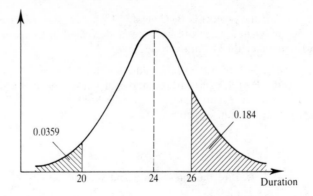

Figure 9.3 Normal distribution of project duration for Worked example 9.1.

- a variance equal to the sum of the variances of activities on the critical path.

In the example above, the critical path is B, G, D and I with expected durations of 6, 6, 4 and 8 respectively and variances of 1.78, 0, 0 and 0.44 respectively. Although the number of activities on the critical path is quite small it is still reasonable to assume the overall duration of the project is Normally distributed. The expected project duration then has mean $6 + 6 + 4 + 8 = 24$ and variance $1.78 + 0 + 0 + 0.44 = 2.22$.

This is illustrated in Figure 9.3.

We can now do some other calculations on the overall project duration. The probability that it will not be finished before 26, for example, can be found using Normal distribution tables with Z as the number of standard deviations the point of interest is away from the mean:

$Z = (26 - 24)/\sqrt{2.22} = 1.34$

probability $= 0.0901$

Similarly the probability it will be finished before 20 is:

$Z = (20 - 24)/\sqrt{2.22} = -2.68$

probability $= 0.0037$

WORKED EXAMPLE 9.2

A project is represented by Table 9.4 which shows the dependency of activities and three estimates of durations.

(a) What is the probability that the project will be completed before 17?
(b) By what time is there a probability of 0.95 that the project will be finished?

Table 9.4

Activity	Depends on	Optimistic	Duration Most likely	Pessimistic
A	–	1	2	3
B	A	1	3	6
C	B	4	6	10
D	A	1	1	1
E	D	1	2	2
F	E	3	4	8
G	F	2	3	5
H	D	7	9	11
I	A	0	1	4
J	I	2	3	4
K	H, J	3	4	7
L	C, G, K	1	2	7

SOLUTION

Using the rule of sixths to determine the expected duration and variance for activity A gives:

$$\text{expected duration} = (1 + 4*2 + 3)/6 = 2$$
$$\text{variance} = (3 - 1)^2/36 = 0.11$$

Repeating these calculations for the other activities gives the results in Table 9.5.

Table 9.5

Activity	Expected duration	Variance
A	2.00	0.11
B	3.17	0.69
C	6.33	1.00
D	1.00	0.00
E	1.83	0.03
F	4.50	0.69
G	3.17	0.25
H	9.00	0.44
I	1.33	0.44
J	3.00	0.11
K	4.33	0.44
L	2.67	1.00

The network for this project is shown in Figure 9.4.

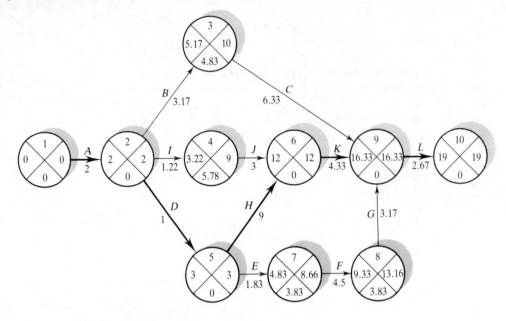

Figure 9.4 Network for Worked example 9.2.

The critical path is A, D, H, K and L. Adding the expected durations and variances for these activities shows the overall duration of the project has a mean of 19 with variance of 1.99 and standard deviation of 1.41.

The probability the project is finished before 17 is given by:

$$Z = (19 - 17)/1.41 = -1.42$$
$$\text{probability} = 0.0778$$

To get a 95% chance of completion Z must be 1.64 and the point of interest is $1.64 * 1.41 = 2.31$ from the mean. There is a 95% chance that the project will be finished by time 21.31.

In summary

PERT is an extension to CPM which allows for uncertainty in activity durations. Expected activity durations and variances can be found using the rule of sixths. The overall project duration is Normally distributed with mean and variance found by adding values for activities on the critical path.

9.1 What is the main difference between CPM and PERT?

9.2 What is the 'rule of sixths' and when is it applied?

9.3 How could you calculate the expected duration of a project and its standard deviation? What assumptions are made in this calculation?

9.2 INVENTORY CONTROL MODELS WITH PROBABILISTIC DEMAND

Chapter 3 described a number of models for inventory control but these all assumed a deterministic demand. In other words, the future demand for an item is known with certainty. This is rarely the case in practice where future demand is usually forecast from historic figures. Fortunately such forecasts are fairly accurate and inventory models are insensitive to the parameters, so the models are useful for a wide range of applications. Sometimes, however, the variability of demand is too great for deterministic models to work and other stochastic models must be used. A range of these has been developed, but they are often complicated. This section will consider two of the more straightforward approaches.

9.2.1 Safety stocks

When developing the economic order quantity in Chapter 3, it was suggested that an order of size Qo should be placed whenever stock fell to a reorder level, ROL. In the classic analysis this meant:

$$Qo = \text{economic order quantity} = \sqrt{2 * RC * D/HC}$$
$$ROL = \text{lead time demand} = LT * D$$

with RC = reorder cost

HC = holding cost

D = demand per unit time

LT = lead time

The effect of using the classic analysis is shown in Figure 9.5.

This strategy works well when the demand is fairly stable, but when the demand has significant variation weaknesses of the analysis appear. If, for example, the supply is delayed or demand in the lead time is heavier than expected, stock will run out. The resulting shortages can incur high costs from lost profit, lost goodwill, interrupted production in a factory which has run out of components, and so on.

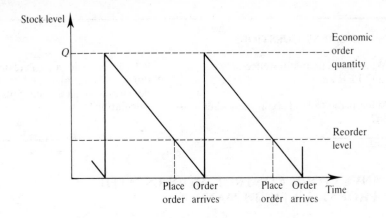

Figure 9.5 Stock level using the 'classic analysis' for economic order quantity.

Although it is difficult to find accurate values for stock-out costs, they are usually high in relation to stock holding costs. This means that companies are willing to hold additional stocks, above their perceived needs, to add a margin of safety. These 'safety stocks' are available when the normal working stock has been exhausted (see Figure 9.6). The question we can now ask is, 'How much safety stock should be held?'

It is possible, at least in principle, to calculate the cost of stock-outs and balance them with the cost of holding stock. Unfortunately, this is rather difficult in practice. Stock-out costs are notoriously difficult to find and are often little more than informed guesses. For this reason analyses based on shortage costs are often considered unreliable. An alternative approach is based more directly on management judgement with the setting of a 'service level'. This specifies the probability that a demand should be met directly from stock (and conversely the maximum acceptable probability of being out of stock).

The selection of an appropriate service level is a policy decision. If demand varies widely, very high safety stocks would be needed to ensure a service level near to 100%. This may be prohibitively expensive and companies will usually set a lower level, typically around 95%. The company then ensures 95% of orders are met directly from stock, implying a probability of 0.05 that a demand cannot be met from stock.

There are several ways of measuring service level (proportion of orders completely satisfied from stock, proportion of units demanded which are delivered, proportion of time there is stock on the shelves, etc.) and care should be taken to define the meaning used. In this chapter we will use 'cycle service level', which sets the probability that all demand in a single stock cycle will be met.

Consider a company which experiences demand for an item which is not known exactly but is known to be Normally distributed with a mean

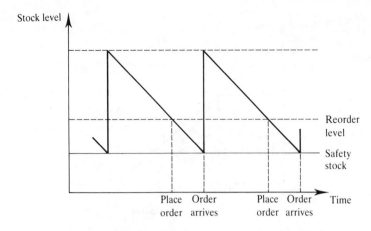

Figure 9.6 Stock levels when a safety stock is added.

of D per unit time and a standard deviation of σ. If the lead time is constant at LT, the mean lead time demand is $LT * D$, variance of lead time demand is $\sigma^2 * LT$ and the standard deviation is $\sigma * \sqrt{LT}$. This is a standard result which comes from the observation that variances (but not standard deviations) can be added. If the demand has a variance of σ^2 in one period, it has a variance of $2 * \sigma^2$ over two periods, $3 * \sigma^2$ over 3 periods, and $LT * \sigma^2$ over the lead time.

In Chapter 3 we used $LT * D$ as a reorder level, but this assumed that the demand was constant. If lead time demand is Normally distributed, it will be greater than the mean value on half of occasions and there will be stock-outs in 50% of stock cycles (see Figure 9.7). If we specify a maximum acceptable probability for a stock-out (presumably greater than 0.5) we need to add a safety stock and the associated reorder level is:

reorder level = lead time demand + safety stock

The size of the safety stock depends on the service level specified: the higher the service level the higher the safety stock needed to support it. We can do a calculation to demonstrate this by assuming the lead time demand is Normally distributed. Then the service level can be translated into a value for Z (from Normal tables) which allows:

safety stock = Z * standard deviation of lead time demand

$\qquad = Z * \sigma * \sqrt{LT}$

where Z is the number of standard deviations away from the mean (see Figure 9.8).

Thus, $Z = 1$ means a stock-out will occur on average 15.9% of stock cycles, $Z = 2$ means stock-outs will occur on 2.3% of stock cycles, $Z = 3$ means that stock-outs will occur on 0.1% of stock cycles and so on.

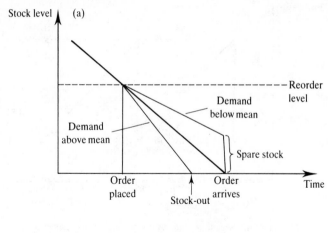

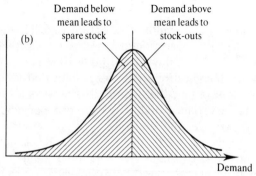

Figure 9.7   Illustrating the probability of 0.5 of stock-out if lead time demand is normally distributed and no safety stock is held: (a) lead time demand higher than mean gives stock-outs, lower than mean gives spare stock; (b) normal distribution of lead time demand.

In summary

For normally distributed demand during lead time a reorder level can be set as:

$$ROL = \text{lead time demand} + \text{safety stock}$$
$$= LT * D + Z * \sigma * \sqrt{LT}$$

WORKED EXAMPLE 9.3

A company advertises a 95% service level for all items it stocks. Stock is replenished from a single supplier who guarantees a lead time of 4 weeks. What

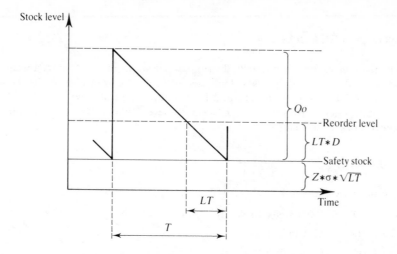

Figure 9.8   Stock cycle with safety stock.

reorder level should the company adopt for an item which has a Normally distributed demand with mean of 1000 units a week and standard deviation of 100 units? What would the reorder level be if a 98% service level were adopted?

SOLUTION

The reorder level is found from:

$$ROL = LT * D + \text{safety stock}$$
$$= 4 * 1000 + \text{safety stock}$$
$$= 4000 + \text{safety stock}$$

For a service level of 95%, the number of standard deviations from the mean, Z, equals 1.64. Then:

$$\text{safety stock} = Z * \sigma * \sqrt{LT}$$
$$= 1.64 * 100 * \sqrt{4}$$
$$= 328$$

and the reorder level is 4328 units.

If the service level is increased to 98%, $Z = 2.05$ and:

$$\text{safety stock} = 2.05 * 100 * \sqrt{4}$$
$$= 410$$

and the reorder level is 4410 units.

WORKED EXAMPLE 9.4

Demand for an item is normally distributed with a mean of 100 units a week and standard deviation of 20 units. Unit cost is £1 and reorder cost is £10. Holding costs are 30% of value a year and lead time is fixed at 3 weeks. Describe an ordering policy which will give a 95% service level. What is the cost of holding the safety stock in this case?

SOLUTION

Listing the values we know:

$$D = 100 \text{ a week } (\sigma = 20)$$
$$UC = £1 \text{ a unit}$$
$$RC = £10 \text{ an order}$$
$$HC = 0.3 \text{ of value held a year}$$
$$LT = 3 \text{ weeks}$$

Substitution of these gives:

$$Qo = \sqrt{2 * RC * D/HC}$$
$$= \sqrt{2 * 10 * 100 * 52/0.3}$$
$$= 589 \text{ (rounded to the nearest integer)}$$

$$ROL = LT * D + \text{safety stock}$$
$$= 300 + \text{safety stock}$$

For a 95% service level $Z = 1.64$ standard deviations from the mean. Then:

$$\text{safety stock} = Z * \sigma * \sqrt{LT}$$
$$= 1.64 * 20 * \sqrt{3}$$
$$= 56.8$$

The ordering policy is to order 589 units whenever stock declines to 357 units. Orders should arrive, on average, when there are 57 units remaining.

The expected cost of the safety stock is:

$$= \text{safety stock} * \text{holding cost}$$
$$= 56.8 * 0.3$$
$$= £17.04 \text{ a year.}$$

SELF ASSESSMENT QUESTIONS

9.4 What is safety stock?

9.5 How is the reorder level calculated when lead time demand is Normally distributed?

9.2.2 Newsboy problem

A second model for stochastic demand is not based on a service level, but assumes known probabilities for discrete demands. The 'Newsboy problem' is phrased in terms of a newsboy who buys papers at a unit cost of UC and sells them at the higher price of S each. Problems of this type occur in a range of circumstances, but we will stick to the original terminology.

[The following derivation is a bit messy so you may prefer to skip the details and follow the general argument.]

Suppose the demand for newspapers follows a known probability distribution, with demand for x papers being $P(x)$.

Demand	0	1	2	3	4	5	. . .
Probability	$P(0)$	$P(1)$	$P(2)$	$P(3)$	$P(4)$	$P(5)$	. . .

If the newsboy buys N papers and the demand, x, is less than N, the newsboy will not sell all of his papers and will make a profit of:

$$\text{income} - \text{expenditure} = x * S - N * UC$$

(assuming unsold papers have no value).

If the demand is greater than or equal to N the newsboy will sell all his papers and make a profit of:

$$\text{income} - \text{expenditure} = N * (S - UC)$$

This gives the demands and associated profits and probabilities in Table 9.6.

Table 9.6

Demand (x)	Profit	Probability
0	$0 - N * UC$	$P(0)$
1	$1 * S - N * UC$	$P(1)$
2	$2 * S - N * UC$	$P(2)$
.	.	.
.	.	.
$N - 1$	$(N - 1) * S - N * UC$	$P(N - 1)$
N	$N * (S - UC)$	$P(N)$
$N + 1$	$N * (S - UC)$	$P(N + 1)$
.	.	.
∞	$N * (S - UC)$	$P(\infty)$

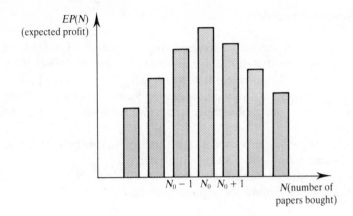

Figure 9.9 Expected profit for the Newsboy Problem with $EP(N_0 + 1) - EP(N_0) < 0 < EP(N_0) - EP(N_0 - 1)$.

The expected overall profit is the sum of the profits multiplied by their probabilities. Hence the expected profit if the newsboy buys N papers is:

$$EP(N) = \text{sum of (profit * probability)}$$
$$= \Sigma(\text{probable profits} + \Sigma(\text{probable profits}$$
$$\text{when } x < N) \qquad \text{when } x \geq N)$$

$$EP(N) = \sum_{x=0}^{N} (x * S - N * UC) * P(x) + \sum_{x=N+1}^{\infty} N * (S - UC) * P(x)$$

$$= S * \{\sum_{x=0}^{N} x * P(x) + N * \sum_{x=N+1}^{\infty} P(x)\} - N * UC$$

Substituting $N - 1$ for N gives the expected profit if the newsboy buys $N - 1$ papers:

$$EP(N - 1) = S * \{\sum_{x=0}^{N-1} x * P(x) + (N - 1) * \sum_{x=N}^{\infty} P(x)\} - (N - 1) * UC$$

Subtracting the second of these from the first and doing some rearrangement gives:

$$EP(N) - EP(N - 1) = S * \{\sum_{x=N}^{\infty} P(x) - UC/S\}$$

This can now be used to give a guideline for an optimal number of newspapers:

- if $EP(N) - EP(N - 1)$ is positive the profit is still increasing with additional papers

- if $EP(N) - EP(N - 1)$ is negative the profit is decreasing with additional papers.

N should be chosen so that the profit would begin to decline if another unit were bought and:

$$EP(N) - EP(N - 1) > 0$$
$$EP(N + 1) - EP(N) < 0$$

or $EP(N + 1) - EP(N) < 0 < EP(N) - EP(N - 1)$

Substituting the derived value for $EP(N) - EP(N - 1)$ into these expressions gives:

$$EP(N) - EP(N - 1) = S * \{ \sum_{x=N}^{\infty} P(x) - UC/S \}$$

so we want:

$$S * \{ \sum_{x=N+1}^{\infty} P(x) - UC/S \} < 0 < S * \{ \sum_{x=N}^{\infty} P(x) - UC/S \}$$

or

$$\boxed{\sum_{x=N+1}^{\infty} P(x) < UC/S < \sum_{x=N}^{\infty} P(x)}$$

This gives the general rule that the value of N is chosen to make

$$\sum_{x=N}^{\infty} P(x)$$

as near UC/S as possible.

WORKED EXAMPLE 9.5

In mid December the owner of a conifer plantation employs a contractor to cut down enough trees to meet the expected demand for Christmas trees. He supplies these to a local wholesaler in batches of 100. Over the past few years the demand has been as follows:

Batches	1	2	3	4	5	6	7	8
Probability	0.05	0.1	0.15	0.2	0.2	0.15	0.1	0.05

If it costs £8 to cut and trim a tree which sells for £12, how many trees should be cut down?

SOLUTION

In this example $UC = 800$ (for each batch of trees) and $S = 1200$. Then $UC/S = 800/1200 = 0.67$.

The rule derived above suggests we choose N so that

$$\sum_{x=N}^{\infty} P(x)$$

is as near UC/S as possible. Substituting values for N gives the results in Table 9.7.

Table 9.7

N	$\Sigma P(x)$
8	0.05
7	0.15
6	0.30
5	0.50
4	0.70
3	0.85

The nearest $\Sigma P(x)$ comes to 0.67 is when $N = 4$ and we would suggest cutting down 400 Christmas trees.

Checking this value in the relationship:

$$\sum_{x=N+1}^{\infty} P(x) < UC/S < \sum_{x=N}^{\infty} P(x)$$

gives:

$$0.5 < 0.67 < 0.7$$

which is true and the optimal answer is confirmed.

WORKED EXAMPLE 9.6

A tour operator is going to book a number of hotel rooms in anticipation of future bookings for holidays. The number of holidays actually booked is equally likely to be any number between 0 and 99 (for simplicity rather than reality). Each hotel room booked costs the operator £150 while the selling price of each room is £250. How many rooms should the operator book?

SOLUTION

Although this is phrased differently, the characteristics of this problem are the same as the Newsboy problem with $UC = 150$ and $S = 250$, that is, $UC/S = 0.6$. As each number of bookings between 0 and 99 is equally likely $P(i) = 0.01$ for $i = 0$ to 99.

Then we choose N so that:

$$\sum_{x=N+1}^{\infty} P(x) < 0.6 < \sum_{x=N}^{\infty} P(x)$$

Then

$$\sum_{x=N}^{\infty} P(x) = 0.6 \quad \text{or} \quad \sum_{x=0}^{N-1} P(x) = 0.4$$

This occurs when $N = 40$ and the optimal policy is to book 40 rooms.

SELF ASSESSMENT QUESTIONS

9.6 What are the main assumptions in the Newsboy problem?

9.7 What is the optimal number of purchases in the Newsboy problem?

9.2.3 ABC analysis for inventory control

The inventory control models described here and in Chapter 3 make it clear that even simple models can involve some effort. Most inventory control systems are computerized, but someone must still input data, check values, update supplier details, forecast demand, and so on. For some items, especially cheap ones, this effort will not be worthwhile. Conversely, some other items might be very expensive and require special care (above routine calculations). An ABC analysis is one way of putting items into categories which reflect the amount of effort worth expending on inventory control. This kind of analysis is sometimes called a Pareto analysis or the 'rule of 80/20' (as a frequent observation is that 80% of results come from 20% of the effort while the remaining 20% of results need 80% of the effort). The basis of ABC analysis is:

- A items are expensive and need special care
- B items are ordinary ones needing standard care
- C items are cheap and need little care.

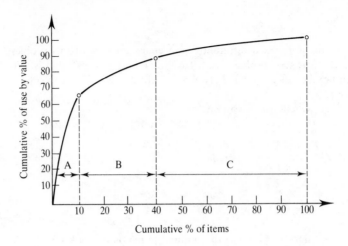

Figure 9.10 Cumulative annual use versus cumulative percentage of items.

To start the ABC analysis we need to calculate the total annual use of stock items in terms of value. This is found by multiplying the number of units used in a year by the unit cost. Usually there will be a few expensive items which account for a lot of use and many cheap ones which account for little use. If we list the items in order of decreasing annual use by cost, A items are at the top of the list and C items are at the bottom. We might typically find:

Category	% of items	Cumulative % of items	% of use by value	Cumulative % of use by value
A	10	10	70	70
B	30	40	20	90
C	60	100	10	100

Plotting the cumulative percentage of annual use against the cumulative percentage of items gives the graph shown in Figure 9.10.

WORKED EXAMPLE 9.7

A small store consists of ten categories of product with the following costs and annual demands:

Product	X1	X2	X3	Y1	Y2	Y3	Z1	Z2	Z3	Z4
Cost (£)	20	25	30	1	4	6	10	15	20	22
Annual demand ('00s)	3	2	2	10	8	7	30	20	6	4

Do an ABC analysis of these items. If resources for inventory control are limited, which items should be given least attention?

SOLUTION

The annual use of X1 in terms of value is $300 * 20 = £6000$. If this calculation is repeated for the other items and they are sorted into order of decreasing annual use by value we get the figures in Table 9.8. The boundaries between categories of items may be unclear, but Z1 and Z2 are clearly A items and the Y group are clearly C items (see Figure 9.11). The C items account for only 8% of annual use by value and these should be given least attention if resources are limited.

Table 9.8

Product	Z1	Z2	Z3	Z4	X1	X3	X2	Y3	Y2	Y1
Cumulative % of items	10	20	30	40	50	60	70	80	90	100
Annual use ('00s)	300	300	120	88	60	60	50	42	32	10
Cumulative annual use	300	600	720	808	868	928	978	1020	1052	1062
Cumulative % annual use	28	56	68	76	82	87	92	96	99	100
Category	<----A---->		<------------B------------>				<--------------C-------------->			

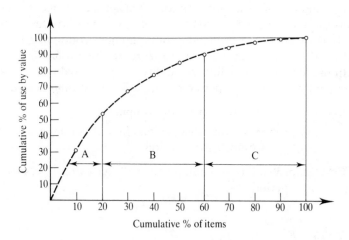

Figure 9.11 Cumulative percentage annual use versus cumulative percentage of items.

9.3 RELIABILITY AND REPLACEMENT

When we buy something like a car or television, one of our main concerns is that it be reliable. If it breaks down or develops a fault it can be inconvenient and expensive. Companies with large investments in equipment are even more concerned about its reliability. If part of a production line breaks down the consequences can be very expensive. In more extreme cases, such as heart pacemakers, helicopter rotors or space capsules, the reliability of equipment is even more important.

Unfortunately almost all equipment can fail. These failures are generally random and will probably occur at an inconvenient time (that is, when the equipment is actually operating). The purpose of studying reliability is to assess the probability of equipment continuing to operate properly and see what can be done to increase this probability.

Intuitively, we can define 'reliability' as the probability that a piece of equipment continues to operate during a specified time period. Then:

R = the reliability of a piece of equipment

= the probability that the equipment will continue to operate during a specified time period

F = the probability the equipment will fail within the specified time period

and

$$R = 1 - F$$

This concept, together with the probability distributions described in Chapter 8, can be used to solve a range of problems about reliability.

WORKED EXAMPLE 9.8

A railway goods yard has ten elderly shunting engines which are used on weekdays. At the weekend a maintenance crew does routine maintenance and any necessary repairs to the engines. During the past 12 weeks records show that there have been 12 occasions on which an engine has broken down during the week and been unable to continue work. The goods yard needs at least eight engines to be operating at any time.

(a)   What is the reliability of the engines measured on a weekly basis?
(b)   What is the probability that at least eight engines will continue to operate throughout the week?

SOLUTION

This is a Binomial process where 'success' is an engine continuing to operate throughout a week and 'failure' is an engine not operating throughout the week.
   The probability an engine breaks down during a week is:

F = number of breakdowns/number of operating weeks

   = 12/120

   = 0.1

Then the reliability is:

$R = 1 - F$

   = 0.9

   The probability that at least eight engines operate throughout a week is:

$P(\geq 8 \text{ work}) = P(8 \text{ work}) + P(9 \text{ work}) + P(10 \text{ work})$

These values can either be looked up in Binomial tables or calculated from:

$P(r) = p^r * q^{n-r} * {}^nC_r$

$P(8) = \dfrac{0.9^8 * 0.1^2 * 10!}{8! * 2!} = 0.1937$

Similarly

$P(9) = 0.3874$ and $p(10) = 0.3487$

The probability that at least 8 engines will continue working is 0.1937 + 0.3874 + 0.3487 = 0.9298.

WORKED EXAMPLE 9.9

In the last 100 working days a bulk mining excavator had 160 breakdowns.

(a) What is the expected distribution of days with each number of breakdowns?

(b) It takes an average of four man hours and costs £200 in parts to make each repair. How could the annual maintenance costs for the excavator be calculated?.

SOLUTION

Random events, such as breakdowns, follow a Poisson distribution. Here the mean number of breakdowns in a working day is 1.6 and the probability distribution of breakdowns can be found from Poisson tables. Multiplying the probabilities by the number of days in a year gives the expected number of days in a year with each number of breakdowns as shown in Table 9.9.

Table 9.9

Number of breakdowns	Probability	Number of days in year with this number	Total number of breakdowns
0	0.2019	73.69	0
1	0.3230	117.90	117.90
2	0.2584	94.32	188.64
3	0.1378	50.30	150.90
4	0.0551	20.11	80.44
5	0.0176	6.42	32.10
6	0.0047	1.72	10.32
7	0.0011	0.40	2.80
8	0.0002	0.07	0.56

The mean number of breakdowns in a year is $1.6 * 365 = 584$. Each of these takes four man hours or 2336 hours a year. This is around 1.5 full-time men whose related costs can be estimated from payroll data. In addition there are material costs of $£200 * 584 = £116,800$.

WORKED EXAMPLE 9.10

A small steam turbine has three sets of blades. Each of these has a working life which is normally distributed with mean 15,000 hours and standard deviation 3000 hours. Failure of any one set of blades means all sets of blades must be replaced.

(a) How often should the blades be replaced to ensure the probability of failure during operation is less than 0.1?

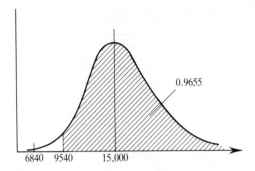

Figure 9.12 Distribution of working life of turbine blades (Worked example 9.10).

(b) What is the annual cost of maintaining the turbine if it is run for an average of 7000 hours a year and new blades for the turbine cost £10,000?

(c) What is the cost of improving the reliability of the turbine to 0.99?

SOLUTION

(a) If R is the probability that one set of blades does not fail between replacements, we want the probability that none of the three sets of blades fails to be $R^3 = 0.9$. Thus $R = 0.9655$.

From Normal tables this corresponds to $Z = 1.82$ standard deviations from the mean. Then the age at replacement is $15,000 - 1.82 * 3000 = 9540$ hours (see Figure 9.12).

(b) The expected number of replacements of blades in a year is $7000/9540 = 0.7338$. Each of these costs £10,000 so the maintenance cost is £7338 a year. To this should be added an allocation for repairing the turbine on those 10% of occasions when it fails during operation.

(c) To raise the reliability to 0.99 would have $R^3 = 0.99$, or $R = 0.9967$. This corresponds to $Z = 2.72$ and the time for replacement should be $15,000 - 2.72 * 3000 = 6840$ hours.

The expected number of replacements of blades each year is $7000/6840 = 1.0234$ so the annual maintenance cost is £10,234. This would be offset by the reduced cost of failures during operation.

9.3.1 Reliability of components

Sometimes a single piece of equipment can be considered as a number of connected components. (There is a trend towards 'modular' construction so that when one part fails it can be replaced easily and quickly by

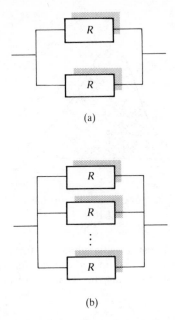

Figure 9.13 Reliability of identical components in parallel: (a) reliability of two identical components in parallel is $(1 - F^2)$; (b) reliability of n identical components in parallel is $(1 - F^n)$.

another complete module.) Back-up components can be added to the equipment to increase its reliability. These backups are not ordinarily used, but when a normal component fails they start working to ensure continued operation (like the spare wheel in a car). Skiing competitions, for example, usually have a main timing system with a backup which automatically takes over if the main timer fails.

The reliability of a system of components depends not only on the reliability of each individual component but also on their arrangement. If a single component has a reliability of R, putting two such components in parallel will have an increased reliability. The assumption is that the second component will only start to operate when the first fails and that the system can work adequately with only one of the components operating. Adding more components in parallel increases reliability as a system only fails if *all* components fail.

Consider a system of 2 identical components in parallel with the reliability of each component $R = 1 - F$. Then the probability that both components fail is F^2 so the reliability of the system (which is the probability that at least one of the components is operating) $= 1 - F^2$. Similarly, the probability that n identical components in parallel will all fail is F^n. Then the reliability of the system is $1 - F^n$. It follows that any system of parallel components is more reliable than the individual components (see Figure 9.13).

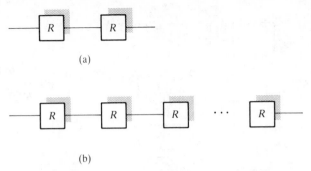

(a)

(b)

Figure 9.14 Reliability of components in series: (a) reliability of two identical components in series is R^2; (b) reliability of n identical components in series is R^n.

If additional components are added in series the reliability of the system is reduced. This is because a system with components in series only works if all separate components are working. Consider two components in series. If the reliability of each is R, the reliability of the two is the probability that both are working, which is R^2. If there are n components in series their reliability is R^n. Thus, a system of components in series is less reliable than the individual components (see Figure 9.14).

The reliability of complex systems of components can be found by reducing them to simpler forms, as illustrated in worked example 9.11.

WORKED EXAMPLE 9.11

The independent reliability of each component in three electronic circuits is shown below. In each case the circuit will operate properly as long as there is one functioning route from input (I) to output (O). What is the reliability of each circuit?

(a)

(b)
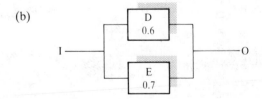

(c)

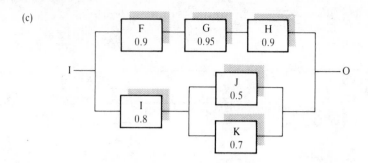

SOLUTION

(a)   The components are in series, so the circuit only works if all the components are operating. The probability that A and B and C continue working is $0.9 * 0.95 * 0.85 = 0.727$.

(b)   The components are in parallel, so the circuit fails if both components fail. The probability that D fails is $1 - 0.6 = 0.4$ and the probability that E fails is $1 - 0.7 = 0.3$. The probability that both D fails and E fails is $0.3 * 0.4 = 0.12$. It follows that the probability that at least one route is functional is $1 - 0.12 = 0.88$.

(c)   In this case we can not solve the problem straight away but must take the circuit in sections and simplify each part.

Firstly, consider components J and K which are in parallel. For this section of the circuit to fail both J and K must fail. The probability of this is $(1 - 0.5) * (1 - 0.7) = 0.15$, so the reliability of this section of the circuit is 0.85.

Similarly we can take the three components F, G and H which are in series. The reliability of this section of the circuit is $0.9 * 0.95 * 0.9 = 0.77$.

We have now simplified the circuit to:

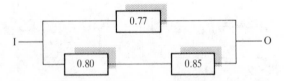

Taking the bottom two elements, which are in series, the reliability is the probability that they both continue to function, which is $0.8 * 0.85 = 0.68$. Then the circuit is simplified to:

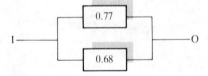

The probability that these two components in parallel both fail is $(1 - 0.77) * (1 - 0.68) = 0.07$, Then the overall reliability of the circuit $= 1 - 0.07 = 0.93$.

WORKED EXAMPLE 9.12

The diagram below shows the layout of a shop floor which consists of three parallel production lines A, B and C. The output of the shop is 50,000 units a week when all three lines are functioning, with the output from A being twice that from each of B and C. The diagram shows the reliability of each machine and if a line fails during the week all its production during the week is lost.

(a) Find the reliability of each line.
(b) Construct a table to show the possible outputs from the shop and the probability of each output.
(c) What is the expected average output of the shop?
(d) The company plans to expand production facilities either by providing one more production line of type A (cost £50,000), or two lines of type B (cost £30,000 each). Which is the more cost effective plan and what will be the expected increase in weekly production?

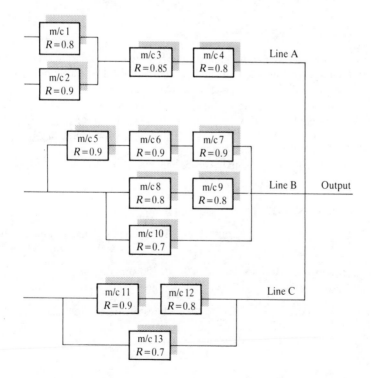

SOLUTION

(a) The solution to this problem is found by simplifying the diagram into separate bits. Let R_1 be the reliability of machine 1 and F_1 the probability it fails in a week. The reliability of Line A is found from:

$$R_A = (1 - F_1 * F_2) * R_3 * R_4$$
$$= (1 - 0.2 * 0.1) * 0.85 * 0.8$$
$$= 0.666$$

The reliability of line B is found from:

$$F_B = (1 - R_5 * R_6 * R_7) * (1 - R_8 * R_9) * (1 - R_{10})$$
$$= (1 - 0.9 * 0.9 * 0.9) * (1 - 0.8 * 0.8) * (1 - 0.7)$$
$$= 0.029$$
$$R_B = 1 - F_B$$
$$= 1 - 0.029$$
$$= 0.971$$

The reliability of line C is found from:

$$F_C = (1 - R_{11} * R_{12}) * (1 - R_{13})$$
$$= (1 - 0.9 * 0.8) * (1 - 0.7)$$
$$= 0.084$$
$$R_C = 1 - F_C$$
$$= 1 - 0.084$$
$$= 0.916$$

(b) We know the output of A is twice that of either B or C. As the overall output is 50,000 the output from A must be 25,000, with 12,500 from each of B and C. The production can be found by taking various combinations of lines failing and calculating the overall output. If lines A and B failed while line C continued the output would be 12,500. This has a probability of $F_A * F_B * R_C$ = 0.334 * 0.029 * 0.916 = 0.009.

Similarly, the other values can be calculated as shown in Table 9.10.

(c) The average production is:

$$25,000 * R_A + 12,500 * (R_B + R_C) = 40,238$$

(d) The better value can be found by dividing the expected production by the amount invested. Then:

For line A 25,000 * 0.666/50,000 = 0.333 units per £

For line B 12,500 * 0.97/30,000 = 0.404 units per £

Line B is more cost effective and with two lines of this kind expected production would rise by 2 * 12,500 * 0.971 = 24,275.

Table 9.10

Production	Probability
0	$F_A * F_B * F_C = 0.001$
12,500	$F_A * F_B * R_C$ $+ \quad F_A * R_B * F_C = 0.036$
25,000	$R_A * F_B * F_C$ $+ \quad F_A * R_B * R_C = 0.299$
37,500	$R_A * R_B * F_C$ $+ \quad R_A * F_B * R_C = 0.072$
50,000	$R_A * R_B * R_C = 0.592$

In summary

The reliability of a system of components depends on both the reliability of individual components and the configuration of the system.

- Putting components in parallel increases the reliability of the system.
- Putting components in series decreases the reliability of the system.

SELF ASSESSMENT QUESTIONS

9.10 What is meant by 'reliability'?

9.11 If a number of components are put in parallel is the reliability of the system

(a) increased
(b) decreased
(c) either increased or decreased?

9.3.2 Replacement of items which deteriorate over time

The first analyses in this section were based on items that either fail or continue to operate as usual. Experience suggests that the performance of almost everything declines with age. A useful analysis would include an increased probability of failure with age or an increased cost of operation.

The last two examples in this section look at the replacement of items which deteriorate over time. The first example shows how probability trees can be used to look at items which have an increased probability of failure over time (light bulbs are a classic illustration of this). The second example shows how increased costs can be taken into account.

Detailed models for replacement can be built, but the mathematics becomes quite complex. One way around this is to consider a number of discrete alternatives, cost them and select the cheapest. Rather than build a detailed model for, say, light bulb replacement, the costs of routinely replacing bulbs every one, two, three or four years might be found and a reasonably good policy identified.

WORKED EXAMPLE 9.13

An office block has 100 identical detectors for smoke and heat. A signal light shows when a detector stops working and a maintenance team is sent to replace it at an average cost of £100 each. The probability that a detector is working properly declines over time as shown in the following table.

Age	0	1	2	3	4
Probability of detector working	1.0	0.8	0.4	0.1	0.0

The company is now considering a replacement policy where all 100 detectors are routinely replaced at regular intervals. This would reduce the costs of each replacement to £50. Special calls to replace failed units would be eliminated, but annual inspection would replace any which failed between block replacements at the standard cost of £100. What would be a good policy for the company for replacing detectors?

SOLUTION

The above table of survivors at various ages can be redrawn as a table of probabilities of detectors failing within any year:

Year	1	2	3	4
Probability of failing in year	0.2	0.4	0.3	0.1

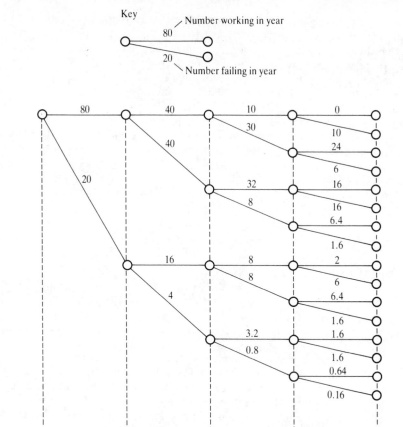

Figure 9.15 Failure tree for Worked example 9.13.

If the current ad hoc replacement of detectors is continued 20% will fail within one year, 40% within two years, 30% within three years and the remaining 10% within four years. Assuming detectors fail, on average, mid way through the year, the expected life is:

$$0.2 * 0.5 + 0.4 * 1.5 + 0.3 * 2.5 + 0.1 * 3.5 = 1.8 \text{ years}$$

As there are 100 detectors the average number to be replaced each year is $100/1.8 = 55.56$. Each of these costs £100 so the average annual cost is £5556.

Using a block replacement policy, the number to be replaced each year can be shown in a kind of probability tree, which is called a failure tree. The failure tree for this example is given in Figure 9.15.

In this the horizontal lines show the number of units which are still working, while diagonal lines show those which fail in the specified year. With 100 units starting, 20 will fail within the first year. 20% of these replacements will fail within the second year and so on. The number of detectors failing or working in any year must obviously add up to 100, and the number of failures in any year can be found by adding the numbers on diagonal lines of Figure 9.15.

If a block replacement is done every year there would be no annual inspections. If the block replacement is done every two years, 20 detectors would be replaced at the intermediate annual inspection. If the block replacement is done every three years, 20 detectors would be replaced at the first annual inspection and 44 at the second. These figures can be summarized in Table 9.11.

Table 9.11

Block replacement at end of year	Cost of block replacement	Cost of annual inspections	Total cost	Average cost per year
1	5,000	0	5,000	5,000
2	5,000	2,000	7,000	3,500 *
3	5,000	6,400	11,400	3,800
4	5,000	11,080	16,080	4,020

The average cost per year rises if block replacements are made less frequently than every two years. This trend would continue, so we need not draw any more of the table. The best policy is to replace the detectors in a block every two years with an annual inspection at the end of alternate years to replace the expected 20 defective units. This has a cost of £3500 a year compared with £5556 for the current arrangements.

WORKED EXAMPLE 9.14

A grinder is set to finish a cylindrical shaft to a size of 10.00 cm +/− 0.01 cm. Any shaft outside the range 9.99 cm to 10.01 cm is rejected at a cost of £10. When the grinder is set to produce a size μ it actually produces shafts which are normally distributed with mean μ and standard deviation 0.004 cm. The grinder produces 1000 units a shift but at the end of the shift its diameter has been reduced by an average of 0.001 cm. This means that any subsequent production has its mean size increased by this amount, while the standard deviation remains unaltered. A new grinding wheel costs £800, and fitting costs £200 in labour and lost production. How often should the grinding wheel be replaced?

SOLUTION

The cost of wear of the grinding wheel is in two parts: the direct cost of replacement and the cost of units rejected. A wheel should be replaced when the sum of these costs per good unit produced is minimized. The related calculations are shown in Tables 9.12 and 9.13. The probability of rejection because shafts are outside the acceptable range are found from Normal tables.

Table 9.12

Number of shifts since last replacement	Mean size of production	Probability of rejection		Expected number of rejects per shift
		too large	too small	
0	10.000	0.0062	0.0062	12.4
1	10.001	0.0122	0.0030	15.2
2	10.002	0.0228	0.0013	24.1
3	10.003	0.0401	0.0006	40.7
4	10.004	0.0668	0.0002	67.0

The expected cost of rejects is added to the cost of replacing the wheel and dividing this total by the number of good units produced gives a cost per unit. With replacement every shift the cost of rejects (12.4 * 10) is added to the cost of a new wheel (800 + 200) and divided by the number of good units (1000 − 12.4) to give a cost of 1.14 per unit produced. The alternatives can be compared as shown in Table 9.13.

Table 9.13

Replace after shift	Average cost of replacement per unit produced	Average cost of rejects per unit produced	Total cost per unit produced
1	1.01	0.13	1.14
2	0.51	0.14	0.65
3	0.34	0.18	0.52
4	0.26	0.24	0.50 *
5	0.21	0.33	0.54

The optimal policy is to replace the grinding wheel every four shifts, with a total maintenance cost of £0.50 per good unit produced.

In summary

The performance of almost everything deteriorates with age. Models can be developed which include an increasing probability of failure or increased costs with age.

SELF ASSESSMENT QUESTIONS

9.12 In what ways might the performance of equipment deteriorate over time?

9.13 It is always cheaper to use regular block replacement of units which fail (such as light bulbs) with intermediate inspections to correct individual faults. Is this statement:

(a) true
(b) false
(c) partly true?

9.4 SAMPLING

9.4.1 Sampling distributions

All quantitative models need reliable data and here we are going to look at one aspect of data collection. Sampling attempts to get reliable data by looking at a few units rather than all available units, and hence reduce data collection costs. We might, for example, decide to assess the quality of a product by examining 10% of output rather than examining all units made.

In many circumstances it is not practical to collect all possible information and some kind of sampling procedure must be used. Suppose a political party is running an election campaign and wants to know how many votes it will get at a forthcoming election. There are two ways it can find this:

- it can ask every person eligible to vote in the constituency what their intentions are, or
- it can take a sample of eligible people, ask them their intentions and then estimate the voting intentions of the population as a whole.

The second approach has a number of advantages. Firstly, information is expensive to collect, so the more people who are surveyed the more it will cost; using a sample will significantly reduce costs. Secondly, there are circumstances in which all of a population can not be tested. It would be senseless to find the mean life of light bulbs produced by a factory by testing the entire output until they failed. A sample is the only realistic way of getting results. Thirdly, there may be an infinite number of tests to perform. A new drug may claim to cure some disease: it can either be tested on a sample of people in particular circumstances, or it could be tested on everybody in all possible circumstances (which gives a virtually infinite number of combinations).

Of course, sampling also has the disadvantage of needing a reliable sample which fairly represents the whole population. Notice that we are using the term 'population' to refer to all things which could be examined rather than its more general use for populations of people. We will talk of a sample being taken from a population. The purpose of sampling, then, is to take a sample of units from the population, measure the desired property (weight, length, etc.) and hence estimate the value of the property for the population as a whole. 'Population' is used to describe all the things which could be tested while 'sample' is used to describe those which actually are tested.

The sample chosen must reflect the population as a whole. We want a fair sample and a convenient way of ensuring fairness is to take samples at random. For this we require two things:

- a method of selecting a random sample
- the size of sample to be selected (large enough to ensure it is fair and representative of the population, yet small enough to be reasonable and cost effective).

The method of selecting a random sample varies according to circumstances, but one common way is to use random numbers. Suppose, for example, we are interested in the number of people travelling in each car on a particular stretch of road. The cars might be travelling too quickly to count the number of occupants in each, so we would select a sample. This can be done using random numbers. Tables of random numbers are readily available (see Appendix E) and selecting a string of numbers from such tables gives 836351847101. Using this we may decide to look at the eighth car, then the third after that, the sixth after that and so on. We will return to the idea of random sampling when looking at simulation in Chapter 11.

Now we can turn to the effect of sample size. If we take any population and look at samples from it, we would expect some variation from sample to sample. If, for example, we know that apples being delivered to a jam factory are supposed to have a mean weight of 4 ozs, we could take a sample of 100 apples a day and weigh them. We would expect the mean weight in the samples to be about 4 ozs, but would not be surprised by small variations. It might be that samples over consecutive days have mean weights of 4.03 ozs, 3.96 ozs, 4.01 ozs and so

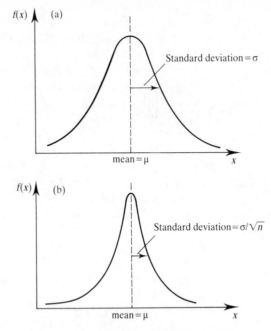

Figure 9.16 Comparing the sampling distribution of the mean, shown in (b), with the population, shown in (a).

on. Taking a series of samples and calculating the mean value of some variable in each gives a distribution of values, and this distribution is called the 'sampling distribution of the mean'. This has two useful properties.

- The mean of the sampling distribution of the mean equals the mean of the population.
- The variance of the sampling distribution of the mean is less than the variance of the population and decreases as the sample size increases.

This second property is fairly obvious as it implies that larger samples give more reliable results.

Suppose a large population has mean μ and standard deviation σ. Taking samples of size n will give a sampling distribution of the mean which also has mean μ but the standard deviation is reduced to $\sigma/\sqrt{n}$. If the population is Normally distributed the sampling distribution of the mean is also Normally distributed, but provided the sample size is large (say more than 30) the sampling distribution of the mean is always normally distributed, regardless of the population distribution (see Figure 9.16). These observations are given without proof, but anyone interested can find them in specialized texts on statistics.

In summary

If samples of size n are taken from a large population with mean μ and standard deviation σ:

- the mean of all sample means is equal to μ
- the standard deviation of all sample means is equal to $\sigma/\sqrt{n}$
- if the sample size is large the distribution of sample means is Normal.

WORKED EXAMPLE 9.15

A production line makes units with a mean length of 60 cm and standard deviation of 1 cm. What is the probability that a sample of 36 units taken from a large population has a mean length of less than 59.7 cm?

SOLUTION

With samples of size 36 the sampling distribution of the mean is Normally distributed with mean μ and standard deviation $\sigma/\sqrt{n}$. Therefore:

mean length $= \mu = 60$ cm

standard deviation $= \sigma/\sqrt{n} = 1/\sqrt{36} = 0.167$ cm.

To find the area under the tail of the distribution we need to find the number of standard deviations the point of interest (59.7) is away from the mean.

$$Z = (59.7 - 60)/0.167 = -1.80$$

Looking this up in Normal tables gives the probability of 0.0359, so we would expect 3.59% of samples to have a mean length of less than 59.7 cm.

This is illustrated in Figure 9.17.

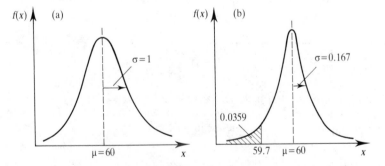

Figure 9.17 Population, (a), and sampling distribution of the mean, (b), for Worked example 9.15.

WORKED EXAMPLE 9.16

Soft drinks are put into cans which hold a nominal 200 ml, but the filling machine introduces a standard deviation of 10 ml. These cans are packed into cartons of 25 and exported to a market which requires the mean weight of a carton to be at least the quantity specified by the manufacturer. To ensure this happens, the canner sets the machine to fill cans to 205 ml. What is the probability that a carton chosen at random will not pass the quantity test?

SOLUTION

The mean volume per can is set at 205 ml and has a standard deviation of 10 ml. Taking a random sample of 25 cans gives a sampling distribution of the mean with mean 205 ml (per can) and standard deviation of $10/\sqrt{25} = 2$ ml (again per can). The case will fail the quantity test if the average quantity per can is less than 200 ml. That is:

$$Z = (200 - 205)/2 = -2.5$$
$$\text{probability} = 0.0062$$

About six cases in a thousand will fail the test.

9.4.2 Confidence interval

These two worked examples show how point estimates for sample means can be found, but it is often more useful to know the range in which a value lies. This range is called the 'confidence interval'. We might want to say, for example, that we are 95% confident that the actual value lies within a specified range. The calculation for this comes from the work we have already done, as demonstrated in the following example.

WORKED EXAMPLE 9.17

A machine produces parts which have a standard deviation in length of 1.4 cm. A random sample of 100 parts has a mean length of 80 cm. What is the 95% confidence interval for the true mean length of the parts?

SOLUTION

A sample of 100 units from a large population has mean 80 cm and will have a standard deviation of $1.4/\sqrt{100} = 0.14$ cm. 95% of observations for a Normal

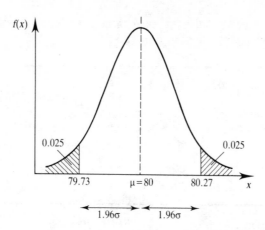

Figure 9.18 Confidence limits from the sampling distribution.

distribution are within 1.96 standard deviations of the mean. Thus, we would expect 95% of observations to be within the range μ +/− (1.96 * 0.14).

Although we do not know μ the best estimate we can get is 80 cm, so the 95% confidence interval is 80 +/− 0.27 i.e. the range 79.73 cm to 80.27 cm.

This is illustrated in Figure 9.18.

WORKED EXAMPLE 9.18

A security company employs night watchmen to patrol warehouses and they want to find the average time needed to patrol warehouses of a certain size. On a typical night records were kept of the time to patrol 40 similar warehouses. These showed the mean time to be 76.4 minutes, and the standard deviation is known to be 17.2 minutes. What are the 95% and 99% confidence intervals on the true mean?

SOLUTION

Unfortunately, we do not know the mean of the population, but the best estimate we have is 76.4 minutes from the sample. Provided the sample size is large (more than 30) it is reasonable to use this as an estimate for the population.

Then the standard deviation of all samples is:

$17.2/\sqrt{40} = 2.72$ mins.

95% confidence interval: 76.4 +/− 1.96 * 2.72 = 71.07 to 81.73

99% confidence interval: 76.4 +/− 2.58 * 2.72 = 69.38 to 83.42

Obviously the more confident we want to be that the true mean lies within a specified range the wider the range must be.

In summary
The sampling distribution of the mean allows point estimates and confidence intervals to be found for a population mean using a reliable sample.

SELF ASSESSMENT QUESTIONS

9.14 What is the purpose of sampling?

9.15 What is the sampling distribution of the mean?

9.16 Describe the shape of the sampling distribution of the mean.

9.17 What is the 95% confidence interval for a value?

9.5 HYPOTHESIS TESTING

In the last section we used data from a sample to estimate values for a population. Here we will extend this idea a little and test whether a population parameter is equal to some prescribed value.

Suppose we have some pre-conceived idea about the parameters of a situation (that is a hypothesis), we could take a sample from the population and use it to judge if our hypothesis is correct. The formal process for this is:

- define a simple precise statement about the situation;
- test to see if the data supports the statement or if it is highly improbable;
- if the statement is highly improbable decide the original hypothesis is untrue, otherwise accept it.

We can illustrate this process by an example. Suppose bottles are filled with a nominal 400 g of fluid. Small deviations occur from this nominal amount and the actual weights are normally distributed with a standard deviation of 20 g. Periodic samples are taken to ensure the mean weight is still 400 g. A sample is found to contain 446 g. Are the bottles now being overfilled?

An initial hypothesis is that the mean weight of bottles is still

400 g. This can be tested as follows. From the distribution of weights we can see that:

$$Z = (446 - 400)/20 = 2.3$$

which has probability = 0.01

The occurrence of a bottle weighing 446 g is highly improbable (1% of occasions). We can reject as untrue the initial statement that the mean content is 400 g as we now believe the bottles are being overfilled.

This is an illustration of hypothesis testing. The original statement is the hypothesis (sometimes called the null hypothesis). Unfortunately hypothesis testing is not foolproof and there are two types of error which can occur

- we can accept a hypothesis which is not true
- we can reject a hypothesis which is true.

| | | Hypothesis is actually | |
		True	False
Decision	Accept	correct	Type II error
	Reject	Type I error	correct

Because hypothesis testing needs a precise definition of the hypothesis to be tested, this is almost inevitably phrased in terms of one thing equalling another. We might have a null hypothesis that the mean weight is 1.5 kg and an alternative that the mean weight is not 1.5 kg. A null hypothesis might be that average salaries are £16,000 while the alternative hypothesis could be that they are lower than this.

WORKED EXAMPLE 9.19

The mean wage in a certain industry is said to be £300 a week with a standard deviation of £60. There is a feeling that this is no longer true and a random sample of 36 wages is checked. The null hypothesis is rejected if the sample of wages has a mean less than £270 or greater than £330. What are the probabilities of making Type I and Type II errors?

SOLUTION

We can start by defining a null hypothesis that the mean wage is £300, and the alternative hypothesis that the mean wage is not £300.

The standard deviation of the sampling distribution of the mean for samples of size 36 is $60/\sqrt{36} = 10$.

The probability that a sample of 36 wages is greater than £330 is found from Normal tables with $Z = (330 - 300)/10 = 3$. The probability of this is 0.0013. By symmetry the probability that a sample has a mean of less than £270 is also 0.0013.

With rejection levels outside £270 − £330 there is a chance of $0.0013 + 0.0013 = 0.0026$ that the hypothesis is rejected even though it is actually true.

WORKED EXAMPLE 9.20

A city takes a survey of monthly food and shelter costs for a particular type of family. It is suggested that the mean cost is £160 with a standard deviation of £48.90. A sample of 100 families was taken and found to have an average expenditure of £171.25. Is the suggested value of £160 true?

SOLUTION

The null hypothesis is that the monthly cost of food and shelter equals £160 while the alternative hypothesis is that it does not equal £160.

Calculating the standard deviation for a sample of 100 gives $48.90/\sqrt{100} = 4.89$.

Then:

$$Z = (171.25 - 160)/4.89 = 2.3$$

There is a likelihood of less than 0.0107 that this will happen so we would say the outcome is extremely unlikely, reject the null hypothesis and accept the alternative hypothesis.

9.5.1 Significance level

In the last example we considered a probability of 0.0107 as unlikely, but this was only an opinion. Such judgements can be formalized into a 'significance level', which is defined as the minimum acceptable probability that an observation is a random sample from the hypothesized population (see Figure 9.19). If we set a 5% significance level, we will accept a null hypothesis if there is a probability greater than 5% that an observation comes from a population with the specified value. Conversely, if there is a probability of less than 5% that the observation came from such a population we will reject the null hypothesis. Although

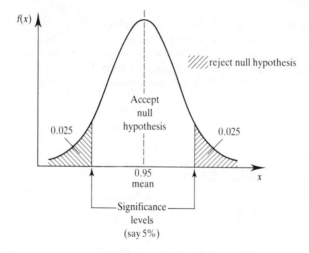

Figure 9.19 Illustrating acceptance and rejection regions for hypothesis tests (5% significance level).

significance levels can take any value, 5%, 1% and 0.1% are conventionally the most frequently used. The smaller the significance level selected the stronger will be the evidence needed to reject the null hypothesis.

In summary

The overall approach for significance testing is:

- adopt a suitable null and alternative hypothesis;
- choose a suitable significance level;
- calculate the probability of obtaining the observed results as random samples from the hypothesized population;
- if this probability is less than the significance level reject the null hypothesis and say 'this result is significant at the chosen significance level';
- if the probability is greater than the significance level accept the null hypothesis.

WORKED EXAMPLE 9.21

A management consultant has introduced new procedures to a reception office. The receptionist should not do more than 10 minutes of paperwork in each hour,

449

with a standard deviation of 3 minutes. A check is made on 40 random hours of operation and the mean time spent on paperwork is 11.25 minutes. Based on these figures, can the assumption that the new procedures meet specifications be rejected at the 1% level of significance?

SOLUTION

The null hypothesis is that paperwork takes ten minutes an hour and the alternative hypothesis is that paperwork takes more than 10 minutes an hour. The significance level has been chosen as 1%.

The sampling distribution of the mean with sample size 40 has mean 10 minutes and standard deviation $3/\sqrt{40} = 0.47$ minutes.

The observed number of minutes of paperwork in each hour is 11.25. Then $Z = (11.25 - 10)/0.47 = 2.66$ which corresponds to a probability of 0.0039 or 0.39%.

This is less than the significance level so the null hypothesis can be rejected at the 1% level of significance and the alternative hypothesis that the paperwork takes more than ten minutes an hour is accepted.

Note that this example only used one tail of the distribution (in other words we were interested in whether the actual value was *greater than* the suggested value rather than was *different to* the suggested value).

WORKED EXAMPLE 9.22

A mail order company charges a flat rate for delivery based on a study several years ago when the mean weight of mail was 1.75 kg with a standard deviation of 0.5 kg. Postal charges now seem high and it is suggested that the mean weight is greater than 1.75 kg. A random sample of 100 packages has a mean weight of 1.84 kg. Does this support the view that the mean weight is more than 1.75 kg?

SOLUTION

The null hypothesis is that the mean weight of parcels is 1.75 kg and the alternative hypothesis is that the mean weight is more than 1.75 kg. The significance level has not been specified, so we will chose 5%.

The sampling distribution of the mean with sample size 100 has mean 1.75 kg and standard deviation $0.5/\sqrt{100} = 0.05$ kg.

The observed weight of parcels is 1.84 kg. Then $Z = (1.84 - 1.75)/0.05 = 1.8$ which corresponds to a probability of 0.0359 or 3.59%.

This is less than the significance level so the null hypothesis can be rejected at the 5% level of significance and the alternative hypothesis that the mean weight of parcels is more than 1.75 kg is accepted.

If we had chosen a 1% significance level the null hypothesis could not be

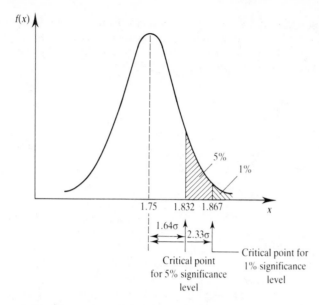

Figure 9.20 Illustrating the critical values for significance levels (Worked example 9.22).

rejected, illustrating the point that the more stringent the significance level the stronger is the evidence needed to reject the null hypothesis.

Again in this example (see Figure 9.20) we were only using one tail of the distribution (that is, finding the probability the mean weight was *greater* than the original value).

SELF ASSESSMENT QUESTIONS

9.18 What are the steps in testing a hypothesis?

9.19 What are Type I and Type II errors?

9.20 What is a significance level?

9.21 Is a 5% significance level

(a) more demanding
(b) less demanding
(c) either more or less demanding

than a 1% significance level?

CONCLUSIONS

The statistical ideas introduced in Chapter 8 can be incorporated into models of various situations where variables take values which are not known with certainty but can be described by some probability distribution. Such processes are called 'probabilistic' or 'stochastic' (in contrast to the deterministic processes described in previous chapters).

This chapter described a number of stochastic models to illustrate potential applications. It can be considered a link between Chapter 8 and the specific applications described in more detail in Chapters 10 and 11.

The first model extended the analysis of project network analysis described in Chapter 5 by adding uncertainty to activity durations (PERT). In essence, this took three estimates of duration and used the 'rule of sixths' to allow statistical analyses.

Chapter 3 described some deterministic models for inventory control, where the demand was known with certainty. This chapter extended these by describing an approach to probabilistic demands where a service level was defined to balance the costs of holding stock with the probability of stock-outs. An ABC or Pareto analysis was described to identify those stock items which need most attention.

The next section looked at reliability of systems and started by showing how probability distributions could be used to model a number of situations. The chapter then discussed the reliability of systems made up of components and saw how parallel back-up components could increase the reliability of a system. The performance of most things deteriorate over time and this section finished by showing how increasing probability of failure or increased operating costs could be incorporated in models.

Sometimes information is needed about a large number of units and it is either impossible or impractical to measure the property for every unit. In such cases a sample of units is taken and the property measured. This is the basis of sampling theory. The sampling distribution of the mean was described and point measures and confidence intervals for population values were calculated from samples.

Finally the chapter looked at hypothesis testing. This used a significance level to see if a null hypothesis could be supported or whether available evidence suggested it should be rejected.

PROBLEMS

9.1   A project is described by the dependence table in Table 9.14.

- Draw the network for this project.
- For each activity calculate the expected duration and its variance.
- Find the earliest and latest start and finish for each activity.
- Calculate the total, free and independent floats.
- What is the critical path?
- What is the expected duration of the project?

Table 9.14

| Activity | Depends on | Duration (in days) | | |
		Optimistic	Most likely	Pessimistic
A	–	4	6	8
B	A	1	2	2
C	B	2	4	10
D	B	3	3	3
E	A	6	10	16
F	C, D	5	6	8
G	C, D	4	4	5
H	D	3	5	7
I	D, E	2	3	4
J	D, E	4	6	8
K	F	10	12	14
L	G, H	14	15	18
M	I, J	8	12	18
N	K, L, M	5	6	6

- What are the probabilities that the project will finish by days 36, 40 and 43?
- By what days would you be 80%, 90% and 95% sure that the project will be finished?

9.2 An item of inventory has a unit cost of £20, reorder cost of £50 and holding cost of £0.5 a unit a week. Demand for the item has a mean of 100 a week with standard deviation of 10. Lead time is constant at 3 weeks. Devise an inventory policy for the item which will give a service level of 95%. How would this be changed to achieve a 90% service level? What are the costs of these two policies?

9.3 Each week a wholesaler replenishes stock of a perishable item which he buys for £150 a unit and sells for £250 a unit. Weekly demand over the last year has followed the following distribution.

Demand	1	2	3	4	5	6	7	8	9	10	11	12
Prob.	0	0.05	0.05	0.1	0.2	0.2	0.15	0.1	0.05	0.05	0.05	0

If unsold units of the item have no value at the end of the week, how many units should the wholesaler buy?

9.4 A store has 20 items with the following unit costs and annual demands. Do an ABC analysis for these items.

Item	1	2	3	4	5	6	7	8	9	10
Cost	10	15	20	1	50	1	15	80	60	30
Demand	10	60	30	100	20	200	20	20	15	30

Item	11	12	13	14	15	16	17	18	19	20
Cost	10	100	100	20	1	20	25	250	15	5
Demand	50	10	20	40	50	100	30	10	60	100

9.5(a) A shop floor has ten machines of which an average of 2 break down a week. What are the probabilities of 0, 1, 2 and 3 breaking down in a given week?

(b) A manufacturer of electric cable has an average of 1.5 faults in each 100 m of a low quality cable. What are the probabilities of 0, 1, 2 and 3 faults in a 100 m length?

9.6 The following diagram shows the reliability of each component in a network. What is the reliability of the network as a whole?

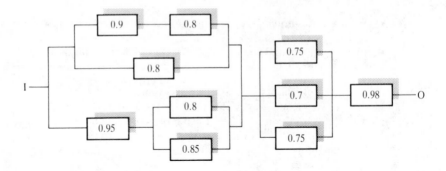

9.7 The probability that a piece of equipment fails in each year of operation is given below. A factory has 100 pieces of equipment of this type and they are currently replaced as soon as they fail at a cost of £150 a unit. A block replacement program is suggested, where all units are replaced after a fixed number of years of operation and with any units failing replaced at the end of the year. Block replacement would cost £100 a unit. Find the cost of alternative replacement programmes and identify the cheapest.

Year of operation	1	2	3	4
Probability of failing in year	0.1	0.3	0.4	0.2

9.8 A machine produces parts with a variance of 14.5 cm in length. A random sample of 50 parts is taken and has a mean length of 106.5 cm. What are the 95% and 99% confidence limits for the length of parts?

9.9 A food processor specifies the mean weight of a product as 200 g. The output is Normally distributed with a standard deviation of 15 g. A random sample of 20 has a mean of 195 g. Does this evidence suggest the mean weight is too low?

SOLUTIONS TO SELF ASSESSMENT QUESTIONS

9.1 The main difference is that CPM assumes each activity has a single estimate for duration, implying there is little uncertainty. PERT assumes there is more uncertainty in duration and uses three estimates to quantify this.

9.2 The rule of sixths assumes the duration of an activity can be described by a Beta distribution, in which case:

$$\text{Expected duration} = \frac{OD + 4 * MD + PD}{6}$$

$$\text{Variance} = \frac{(PD - OD)^2}{36}$$

9.3 The duration of a project is determined by its critical path. Assuming there are a large number of activities on the critical path and that the durations of these are independent, the duration of the project is Normally distributed. The mean of this distribution is the sum of the expected durations of activities on the critical path, while the variance is the sum of the variances of activities on the critical path. The standard deviation is the square root of the variance.

9.4 Safety stock is additional stock which is held to allow for unexpected variations in supply and demand. It is only used when demand is higher than usual or deliveries are delayed.

9.5 $ROL = LT * D + Z * \sigma * \sqrt{LT}$

9.6 Unit cost and selling price are known

exactly, with unsold units having no value. Demand is discrete and the probability distribution of demand is known.

9.7 The optimal number to be bought, N, has:

$$\sum_{x=N+1}^{\infty} P(x) < UC/S < \sum_{x=N}^{\infty} P(x)$$

9.8 Pareto analysis is a means of determining which items, functions, etc. are 'most important'. This is a formalized statement of the 80/20 rule which says 20% of effort is spent getting 80% of results and the remaining 80% of effort is spent getting the last 20% of results.

9.9 ABC analysis for inventory control is a way of categorizing items according to their importance and the effort which should be expended in controlling their stocks.

- A items are of major importance and need particular attention with management control.
- B items are of medium importance and could be dealt with automatically.
- C items are of minor importance, might be excluded from formal control and bought on an ad hoc basis.

9.10 Reliability is the probability that a piece of equipment continues to operate during a specified time period.

9.11 (a) increased

9.12   There are many ways of measuring the performance of equipment including increased operating cost, reduced output, more frequent breakdowns, reduced quality and so on.

9.13   **(b)** false. It may be cheaper to replace failures on an ad hoc basis than as a block. Some analysis is needed to identify the cheapest policy.

9.14   The purpose of sampling is to take a sample of units from the population, measure the desired property (weight, length, etc.) and hence estimate the value of the property for the population as a whole.

9.15   If we take any population and take samples from it we would expect some variation from sample to sample. If we take a series of samples and calculated the mean values of some variable this would follow some distribution. This distribution is the 'sampling distribution of the mean'.

9.16   If the sample size is greater than about 30 the sampling distribution of the mean is Normally distributed with mean μ and standard deviation $\sigma/\sqrt{n}$ (where σ and μ are

values for the population and n is sample size).

9.17   The range within which we are 95% confident the actual value lies.

9.18
   (1)   Define a simple precise statement about the situation;
   (2)   test to see if the data supports the statement or if it is highly improbable;
   (3)   if the statement is highly improbable decide the original hypothesis is untrue, otherwise accept it.

9.19

		Hypothesis is actually True	Hypothesis is actually False
Decision	Accept	correct	Type II error
	Reject	Type I error	correct

9.20   The minimum acceptable probability that an observation is a random sample from the hypothesized population.

9.21   **(b)** less demanding

REFERENCES FOR FURTHER READING

General

Daniel W.W. and Terrell J.C. (1986). *Business Statistics* Boston: Houghton Mifflin Company

Freund J.E. and Williams F.J. (1984). *Elementary Business Statistics: the modern approach* 4th edn. New Jersey: Prentice Hall

PERT

Battersby A. (1970). *Network Analysis for Planning and Scheduling* London: Macmillan

Harrison F.L. (1981). *Advanced Project Management* New York: Halsted

Meredith J.R. and Mantel S.J. (1985). *Project Management* New York: John Wiley

Weist J.D. and Levy F.K. (1977). *A Management Guide to PERT/CPM* 2nd edn. New Jersey: Prentice Hall

Inventory control

Buffa E.S. and Miller J.G. (1979). *Production-Inventory Systems: planning and control* 3rd edn. Homewood: Irwin

Silver E.A. and Peterson R. (1985). *Decision Systems for Inventory Management and Production Planning* 2nd edn. New York: John Wiley

Tersine R.J. (1982). *Principles of Inventory Management* 2nd edn. New York: North-Holland

Maintenance and replacement

Higgins L.R. (1977). *Maintenance Engineering Handbook* 3rd edn. New York: McGraw-Hill

Jardine A.K.S. (1970). *Operational Research in Maintenance* Manchester University Press

Jardine A.K.S. (1973). *Maintenance, Replacement and Reliability* New York: John Wiley

Moore J. (1978). *Developing a Preventive Maintenance Program* New York: Vantage

Sampling

Duncan A.J. (1974). *Quality Control and Industrial Statistics* 4th edn. Homewood: Irwin

Grant E.L. and Leavensworth R.S. (1980). *Statistical Quality Control* 5th edn. New York: McGraw-Hill

Jardine A.K.S., Macfarlane J.D. and Greensted C.S. (1975). *Statistical Methods for Quality Control* London: Heinemann

Chapter 10

Decision analysis

SYNOPSIS

This chapter introduces decision analysis, which takes a rational look at decision making and develops methods for improving decisions in a variety of circumstances. The chapter starts by emphasizing that managers, of various kinds, are employed to make decisions about the running of organizations. It then discusses ways in which these decisions may be improved.

Decisions are considered in situations of:

- certainty (selecting the best alternative)
- uncertainty (using decision criteria) and
- risk (using expected values and utilities).

As well as single decisions, series of sequential decisions are considered, emphasizing the use of decision trees.

As usual the methods are illustrated by examples rather than rigorous mathematics. Unfortunately, in decision analysis this often means that the illustrations are particularly simple and may lack realism. You should not, however, infer that more difficult, realistic problems can not be tackled. It is only the limitation on space which prohibits more realistic problems from being described. In practice the techniques described can be of significant benefit.

Some of the problems in this chapter use Bayes' theorem and it may be useful to revise this from Chapter 8.

By the end of the chapter you should be able to analyse problems of various types and suggest solutions based on rational argument rather than intuition and subjectivity.

OBJECTIVES

After reading this chapter and doing the numerical exercises you should be able to:

- appreciate the role of managers as decision makers;
- draw a map showing interactions for a decision situation;
- appreciate the characteristics of various decision situations;
- construct a payoff matrix;
- appreciate the way of making decisions under certainty;
- describe situations of uncertainty and use decision criteria to suggest policies;
- calculate a value for perfect information under uncertainty;
- describe situations of risk and use expected values to suggest policies;
- calculate a value for perfect information under risk;
- use Bayes' theorem to update conditional probabilities for decisions under risk;
- appreciate the use of utilities;
- draw decision trees to represent sequential decisions;
- analyse decision trees.

10.1 BACKGROUND TO DECISION ANALYSIS

Everybody has to make decisions. Which car is the best buy and when should we buy it; where should we eat; should we drive to work or go by train; which play should we go to; should we make tea or coffee. Such decisions come in a steady stream. Most of them are fairly unimportant and we use a combination of experience, intuition and subjectivity to decide what to do. Some decisions are more important and need a measure of care. Although we rarely think about the process involved in making these decisions, it can be quite complex. Fortunately many decisions share common characteristics and this chapter will give general guidelines for tackling problems in a variety of circumstances.

Long ago in mankind's development as a social creature he began to live in groups. Within these groups decisions became necessary which concerned the communal good, perhaps at the expense of certain individuals. Should, for example, the water supply of a city be improved by damming a river but at the expense of flooding agricultural land? A tradition grew whereby such decisions were put in the hands of experts (called pharaohs, kings, emperors, generals, etc.). This specialization

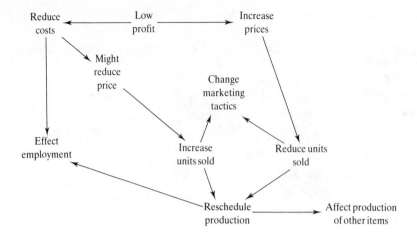

Figure 10.1 Illustrating part of a problem map.

generally brought better decisions as the decision makers gained experience and could bring objectivity to problems. Nowadays 'managers' of various kinds continue this tradition of specialized decision makers.

Many decisions are complex and involve a number of interactions. Suppose a company manufactures an item but finds its profitability is inadequate. It will look for ways of increasing the profit and two obvious alternatives are to reduce costs or increase the price. If the price is increased the demand may decline. Conversely, if costs are reduced the price may be reduced and demand may increase. If demand changes the factory may have to reschedule production and change marketing strategies. Changed production schedules could affect production of other items, change employment prospects and so on.

We could obviously continue with these more or less random thoughts for some time, but we would soon lose track of the main thrusts of argument. For this reason it is useful to devise a simple scheme which shows such interactions. One scheme for this is a 'problem map' and part of a map for the discussion above is given in Figure 10.1.

These maps are informal ways of representing a stream of connected ideas. They are useful as they sort out ideas and help clarify interactions and effects of decisions. They do not, however, directly help in decision making. For more formal aids to decisions we need to look more closely at the problems tackled.

Firstly we can start by listing the characteristics which make up a decision situation. These are:

- a decision maker who is responsible for making decisions;

- a number of alternatives are available to the decision maker, who must select one of them;
- the object of the decision maker is to select the best alternative;
- when the decision has been made an event occurs (over which the decision maker has no control and which may be considered an 'act of God');
- each combination of an alternative selected followed by an event happening leads to an outcome which has some measurable value.

To illustrate these, consider a house owner who is offered fire insurance at a cost of £200 a year. The decision maker is the person who owns the house. He or she will have an objective of minimizing costs and must select the better alternative from:

(1)   insure the house

(2)   do not insure the house.

Then an event happens, but the decision maker has no control over whether it is:

(1)   the house burns down, or

(2)   the house does not burn down.

This problem has obviously been simplified for convenience, and in reality there are a number of alternative insurance companies and policies, the house may be damaged but not destroyed by fire, and so on. Suppose the value of the house is £70,000 and the insurance company pays for all costs and inconvenience if the house burns down. We can summarize the combinations of alternatives, events and outcomes by the following table.

		Events	
		House burns down	House does not burn down
Alternatives	Insure house	£200	£200
	Do not insure house	£70,000	£0

The entries in this table show the cost to the house owner associated with every combination of alternative and event. This table is sometimes called a 'payoff matrix', 'reward matrix', 'standard decision format' or 'cost matrix'. It is important to remember that the alternatives (one of which has to be chosen) are listed down the lefthand side; the events (one of which will happen at some later time and over which the decision maker has no control) are listed across the top. The values of the outcomes given in the body of the matrix are in consistent units (here £s) and may be either costs or gains.

We have now used two distinct formats to describe situations: maps and payoff matrices. These are both useful as they add a structure to an otherwise unstructured and complex situation. Having added this structure, however, they do not suggest how decisions should be made. This is the step we are going to examine next, when we will consider situations of:

- decision making under certainty
- decision making under uncertainty
- decision making under risk
- sequential decisions under risk.

The degree of uncertainty in these situations refers to the events. If we know exactly which event will occur we are dealing with situations of certainty but if we do not know which event will occur we are dealing with uncertainty or risk.

In summary
Managers are often required to make decisions in complex situations. Maps and payoff matrices are ways of describing such situations and adding structure to problems. This structure is based on the identification of events, alternatives and outcomes.

10.2 DECISION MAKING UNDER CERTAINTY

The main characteristic of decision making under certainty is that we know, with certainty, which event will occur. We need only consider one event and the method of solution is obvious, in that all possible outcomes are listed and the alternative with the best outcome is selected.

Suppose we have £1000 to invest for a year. All other things being equal and assuming we are not interested in high risk ventures, we may describe the situation by the following payoff matrix.

		Event Gains interest to give at year end
	Bank	£1065
	Building society	£1075
Alternatives	Government stock	£1085
	Stock market	£1100
	Others	£1060

We have obviously simplified the original problem by using 'others' to describe a range of alternatives and using forecast returns from investments in the stock market. There is only one event 'receive interest', and by looking down the list of outcomes the best alternative can be identified. In this case we would invest in the stock market to give £1100 at the end of the year.

In many cases the outcomes are not so simple to evaluate. Would it be better, for example, to invest money in providing more kidney dialysis machines, giving nurses higher wages, doing open heart surgery, or providing more parking spaces at hospitals? Choosing the best site for a new warehouse would, in principle, need all possible alternatives to be listed. Simplifications often have to be made and a 'short-list' of reasonable alternatives prepared from an original 'long-list' of all possible alternatives.

WORKED EXAMPLE 10.1

A restaurant manager is given a booking for a large wedding banquet. He has a number of ways of providing staff with different associated costs. His most convenient alternatives are to pay full time staff to work overtime (costing £400), hire current part time staff for the day (£300), hire new temporary staff (£350) or use an agency (£550). Draw a payoff matrix for this decision and identify the alternative which minimizes costs.

SOLUTION

The cost matrix for this decision under certainty is:

		Event Pay staff
Alternatives	Pay full time staff for overtime	400
	Hire current part time staff	300
	Hire new temporary staff	350
	Use an agency	500

The lowest cost is £300 which is found by hiring current part time staff for the day. This is the solution which minimizes cost, but there are obviously other factors which might be used in such decisions.

SELF ASSESSMENT QUESTIONS

10.1 Why is it useful to consider representations of problem situations by maps and payoff matrices?

10.2 What are the five main characteristics of a decision process?

10.3 What is meant by 'decision making under certainty'?

10.3 DECISION MAKING UNDER UNCERTAINTY

Usually there are several events which may occur. Sometimes it is impossible to say which one actually will occur or even assign reliable probabilities. If, for example, a person decides to change their job a number of events may happen: they may not like the new job and quickly start looking for another, they may get the sack, they may like the job and stay, they might be moved by the company. These events are essentially outside the control of the person taking a new job and it is impossible to put reliable probabilities to them. Similarly, when buying motor insurance it is impossible to say in advance whether we will have an accident in the year or whether the car will get stolen or burnt. Sometimes figures are given which seem to be doing this, but they are usually global figures (that is, applying to a population but not necessarily to an individual) or are 'subjective' probabilities or guesses.

When no probabilities can be given to events we are dealing with strict uncertainty and the method of solution is to use 'decision criteria'. Decision criteria are simple rules which allow different alternatives to be compared in situations of uncertainty. Although there are many different criteria we will illustrate their use by three common ones.

10.3.1 Laplace decision criterion

As no probabilities can be given to events, Laplace suggests they should all be treated as equally likely and no more importance given to one event than to others. The method of determining the best alternative is:

(1) For each alternative find the mean value of the outcomes (i.e. find the average of each row);
(2) select the alternative with the best average outcome (i.e. lowest cost or highest gain).

WORKED EXAMPLE 10.2

Use the Laplace decision criterion on the example of house insurance described previously.

		Events	
		House burns down	House does not burn down
Alternatives	Insure house	£200	£200
	Do not insure house	£70,000	£0

SOLUTION

Following the steps described above:

(1) Find the mean value of outcomes for each alternative.
   (a) insure house. The average cost is $(200 + 200)/2 = £200$.
   (b) do not insure house. The average cost is $(70,000 + 0)/2 = £35,000$.
(2) Select the alternative with the best average outcome.

   The better of these is the lower average cost which is to insure the house.

WORKED EXAMPLE 10.3

A fruit retailer is going to set up a stall at a local gala. On the morning of the gala they visit the wholesale market and have to decide whether to buy a large, medium or small quantity of seasonal fruit. The profit they make depends on the number of people attending the gala and this is largely determined by the weather. The matrix of gains (in thousands of pounds) for different weather conditions is given below. The gains in this matrix were found by subtracting the costs of buying fruit and the cost of unsold fruit from the gross profit. What quantity of fruit should the retailer buy?

| | | Event | | |
		Weather good	Weather average	Weather poor
Alternatives	Large quantity	10	4	−2
	Medium quantity	7	6	2
	Small quantity	4	1	4

(Note that a negative profit is a loss.)

SOLUTION

(1) Taking the average value of outcomes for each alternative:

    (a) large quantity $(10 + 4 − 2)/3 = 4$
    (b) medium quantity $(7 + 6 + 2)/3 = 5$
    (c) small quantity $(4 + 1 + 4)/3 = 3$

(2) Select the best average outcome. As these figures are profits the best is the highest, which is to buy a medium quantity.

10.3.2 Wald decision criterion

Some alternatives appeal to people who like risks, as they could give a high gain but might also give a large loss. Most organizations have limited resources and are less keen to take risks. Although they would like to aim for the high gain, they can not afford to risk a large loss. This is the basis of the Wald decision, which assumes that decision makers are cautious (or even pessimistic) and want to avoid large potential losses. The steps are:

(1) For each alternative find the worst outcome.

(2) Select the alternative with the best of these worst outcomes.

With payoff matrices showing costs, this is sometimes known as the 'minimax cost' criterion as it looks for the maximum cost of each alternative and then selects the alternative with the minimum of these (i.e. the minimum[maximum cost] or minimax cost). With payoff matrices showing gains it is known as the 'maximin gain' criterion as it looks for the minimum gain for each alternative and selects the alternative with the highest of these.

We can demonstrate this criterion by the problems described in worked examples 10.2 and 10.3.

WORKED EXAMPLE 10.4

Use the Wald decision criterion for the example of house insurance described above.

| | | Events | |
		House burns down	House does not burn down
Alternatives	Insure house	£200	£200
	Do not insure house	£70,000	£0

SOLUTION

Following the steps described:

(1) The worst outcomes for each alternative are:

    (a) insure house   worst of 200 and 200
                                  = MAX[200, 200] = £200
    (b) do not insure house   worst of 70,000 and 0
                                  = MAX[70,000, 0] = 70,000

(2) The better of these is the lower worst cost

    = MIN[200, 70,000] = 200 from insuring the house.

WORKED EXAMPLE 10.5

Use the Wald decision criterion for the example of a fruit stall at a local gala described by the following gains matrix.

		Event		
		Weather good	Weather average	Weather poor
Alternatives	Large quantity	10	4	−2
	Medium quantity	7	6	2
	Small quantity	4	1	4

SOLUTION

(1) Taking the worst value of outcomes for each alternative:

   (a) large quantity   = MIN[10,4,−2] = −2

   (b) medium quantity = MIN[7,6,2] = 2

   (c) small quantity   = MIN[4,1,4] = 1

(2) Select the best of these worst outcomes. As the figures are profits the best is the highest, which comes from buying a medium quantity.

10.3.3 Savage decision criterion

Sometimes we are judged not by how well we actually did but how well we could possibly have done. A student who gets 70% in an exam might be judged by the fact that he did not get 100%. An investment broker who recommended a client to invest in platinum may be judged not by the fact that platinum rose 15% in value, but by the fact that gold rose 25%. This happens particularly when performance is judged by someone other than the decision maker.

In such cases there is a 'regret' which is the difference between actual outcome and best possible outcome. A student who gets 70% has a regret of 100 − 70 = 30%. An investor who gains 15% when they could have gained 25% has a regret of 25 − 15 = 10%. The Savage criterion is based on these regrets. It is essentially pessimistic (in the same way as Wald) and minimizes the maximum regret. The steps are:

(1) For each event find the best possible outcome (that is, find the best entry in each column).

(2) Find the regret for every other entry in the column, which is the difference between the best in the column and the entry.

(3) Put the regrets found in Step 2 into a 'regret matrix'. There should be at least one zero in each column and regrets are always positive.

(4) For each alternative find the highest regret (i.e. the largest number in each row).

(5) Select the alternative with the lowest value of these highest regrets.

Steps 4 and 5 apply the Wald minimax cost criterion to the regret matrix.

We can again demonstrate this procedure by reference to the previous worked examples.

WORKED EXAMPLE 10.6

Use the Savage decision criterion on the example of house insurance described above.

| | | Events | |
		House burns down	House does not burn down
	Insure house	£200	£200
Alternatives			
	Do not insure house	£70,000	£0

SOLUTION

Following the steps described above:

(1) The best outcomes for each event are:
  (a) house burns down   best of 200 and 70,000
                          = MIN[200, 70,000] = 200
  (b) house does not burn down   best of 200 and 0
                          = MIN[200, 0] = 0

The best outcome for each event is underlined in the cost matrix above.

(2) Now we can calculate the regret for not getting the best outcome for an event.

  (a) House burns down. The best alternative would have been to insure the house with a cost of £200. If we had done this there would be zero regret. If we had selected the other alternative of not insuring the house the cost would be £70,000 with a regret of $70,000 - 200 = £69,800$.

    (b) House does not burn down. The best alternative would have been to not insure the house with a cost of zero. If we had done this there would be no regret. If we had selected the other alternative of insuring the house the cost would be £200 with a regret of $200 - 0 = £200$.

(3) Putting these values into a regret matrix (which replaces the original values in the cost matrix by the regrets).

		Events	
		House burns down	House does not burn down
Alternatives	Insure house	<u>£0</u>	£200
	Do not insure house	£69,800	<u>£0</u>

(4) Finding the maximum regret for each alternative:

    (a) insure house   = MAX[0, 200] = 200

    (b) do not insure house = MAX[69,800, 0] = 69,800

(5) Select the alternative with the lowest of these maximum regrets, which is to insure the house.

WORKED EXAMPLE 10.7

Use the Savage criterion on the example of the fruit stall at a local gala described by the following gains matrix.

		Event		
		Weather good	Weather average	Weather poor
	Large quantity	<u>10</u>	4	−2
Alternatives	Medium quantity	7	<u>6</u>	2
	Small quantity	4	1	<u>4</u>

SOLUTION

(1) The best outcome for each event is underlined above (i.e. with good weather a large quantity, with average weather a medium quantity and with poor weather a small quantity).

(2) The regret for every other entry in the column is the difference between this underlined value and the actual entry. Thus if the weather is good and a medium quantity had been bought the regret would be $10 - 7 = 3$. If the weather was good and a small quantity had been bought the regret would be $10 - 4 = 6$, and so on.

(3) Form these regret figures into a regret matrix, replacing the original profit figures.

		Event		
		Weather good	Weather average	Weather poor
	Large quantity	0	2	6
Alternatives	Medium quantity	3	0	2
	Small quantity	6	5	0

(4) For each alternative find the highest regret:

   (a) large quantity   = MAX[0,2,6] = 6
   (b) medium quantity = MAX[3,0,2] = 3
   (c) small quantity   = MAX[6,5,0] = 6

(5) Select the alternative with the lowest of these maximum regrets. This is the medium quantity.

In summary

Situations of uncertainty have a number of possible events, but reliable probabilities can not be given to these. Decision criteria can be used to suggest the best alternative. A number of different criteria are available for different circumstances, including Laplace, Wald and Savage.

10.3.4 Maximum fee worth paying for perfect information

Sometimes it is possible to buy more information about a problem from a consultant or equivalent expert in the field. We would expect this additional information to allow better decisions. The question we should ask is how much better the decisions are and how much we should be prepared to pay for the extra information.

Suppose, for example, a company is about to launch a new product, the success of which depends on the economic climate in the area of launch. The product can be made in three styles (deluxe, standard and basic) and the company must decide which style to adopt. A gains matrix, with entries in thousands of pounds of profit a year, is as follows.

	Economy stagnant	Economy medium	Economy buoyant
Launch deluxe version	10	15	30
Launch standard version	5	20	10
Launch basic version	15	10	−5

If there is no further information we could use decision criteria to suggest the best alternative. It might be possible to hire an economic forecaster to give detailed information on the state of the economy in the launch area. The company could then make a more informed decision and would expect subsequent profits to be raised.

Assuming the information given by the economic forecaster is correct (in other words he supplies perfect information) the company would know in advance which event will occur. Then it would select the alternative which gives the maximum profit for this event. If the economic forecaster said the economy would be stagnant the company would launch the cheap product and make a profit of £15,000 a year. If the forecaster said the economy would be medium the company would launch the standard product with a profit of £20,000 a year. If the forecaster said the economy would be buoyant the company would launch the deluxe version with a profit of £30,000 a year. From these profits the company would have to subtract the forecasters fee, F. The company has effectively added a fourth alternative of 'Pay a fee of F for perfect information' which can be added to the gains matrix.

	Economy stagnant	Economy medium	Economy buoyant
Launch deluxe version	10	15	30
Launch standard version	5	20	10
Launch basic version	15	10	−5
Pay fee of F for info.	$15 - F$	$20 - F$	$30 - F$

The revised problem could now be tackled in the usual way, but with the solution phrased in terms of F.

Using the Laplace criterion, average values for alternatives are:

(a) deluxe version $(10 + 15 + 30)/3$ $= 18.3$
(b) standard version $(5 + 20 + 10)/3$ $= 11.7$
(c) cheap version $(15 + 10 - 5)/3$ $= 6.7$
(d) pay fee of F $(15 - F + 20 - F + 30 - F)/3 = 21.7 - F$

The largest of these is either 18.3 or $21.7 - F$. In particular, it will be worth paying a fee when:

$$21.7 - F \geq 18.3$$
$$F \leq 3.4$$

The maximum fee worth paying for perfect information is £3400 with the recommended action being to pay for information if the fee is less than £3400 and otherwise launch the deluxe product.

Other decision criteria might make different suggestions. Wald would calculate the worst outcomes as:

(a) deluxe version   MIN[10,15,30] $= 10$
(b) standard version MIN[5,20,10] $= 5$
(c) basic version   MIN[15,10,−5] $= -5$
(d) pay fee of F MIN[$15 - F, 20 - F, 30 - F$] $= 15 - F$

The best of these is either 10 or $15 - F$. The Wald criterion would suggest paying the fee provided:

$$15 - F \geq 10$$
$$F \leq 5$$

The maximum fee worth paying for perfect information is £5000 and the recommended action is to get the information if the fee is less than £5000 and otherwise launch the deluxe version.

Finally, we can consider the Savage criterion which would form the regret matrix as follows.

	Economy stagnant	Economy medium	Economy buoyant
Launch deluxe version	5	5	0
Launch standard version	10	0	20
Launch basic version	0	10	35
Pay fee of F for info.	F	F	F

The highest regret for each alternative is:

(a) deluxe version   MAX[5,5,0]   = 5
(b) standard version MAX[10,0,20] = 20
(c) basic version   MAX[0,10,35] = 35
(d) pay fee of F MAX[F,F,F]   = F

The lowest of these is either 5 or F and the suggested action would be to pay for information if the fee is less than £5000 and otherwise launch the deluxe version.

WORKED EXAMPLE 10.8

Calculate the cost of perfect information for the following gains matrix.

		Event 1	2	3
	a	142	150	119
Alternative	b	124	161	135
	c	102	147	150

SOLUTION

Adding a fourth alternative (d) of paying a fee of F for perfect information gives the revised gains matrix:

		Event 1	2	3
	a	142	150	119
Alternative	b	124	161	135
	c	102	147	150
	d	$142 - F$	$161 - F$	$150 - F$

Laplace criterion would suggest the alternative with the highest of:

(a) 411/3   = 137
(b) 420/3   = 140
(c) 399/3   = 133
(d) 453/3 $- F = 151 - F$

Alternative (d) is chosen if $151 - F \geq 140$, i.e. $F \leq 11$. Otherwise alternative (b) is chosen.

Wald criterion would suggest the alternative with highest of:

(a) 119
(b) 124
(c) 102
(d) $142 - F$

Alternative (d) is chosen if $142 - F \geq 124$, i.e. $F \leq 18$. Otherwise alternative (b) is chosen.

Savage criterion would form the regret matrix:

		Event 1	2	3
	a	0	11	31
Alternative	b	18	0	15
	c	40	14	0
	d	F	F	F

Savage would suggest the alternative with the lowest of:

(a) 31
(b) 18
(c) 40
(d) F

Alternative (d) is chosen if $F \leq 18$. Otherwise alternative (b) is chosen.

10.3.5 Selecting the criterion to use

Often different criteria will recommend the same alternative, but there are times when this does not happen. In such cases the most relevant criterion should be used. If, for example, the decision maker is working as a consultant and will be held responsible to others for the quality of his decisions there may be a case for using the Savage criterion. If the decision is made for a small company which can not afford to risk high losses, then Wald may be best. If there is really nothing to choose between the different events Laplace may be useful.

Although it is difficult to go beyond these general guidelines one other factor should be noted. Both Wald and Savage criteria effectively recommend their decision based on one outcome (the worst for Wald and the one which leads to the highest regret for Savage). This means the choice might be dominated by a few atypical results. The Laplace criterion is the only one which uses all values to make its recommendation.

It could be that none of the criteria we have looked at is suitable. Those described are only illustrative and there is a range of others which could be used. An ambitious organization might aim for the highest profit and use a criterion which selects the alternative which gives the highest return (a 'maximax profit' criterion). Alternatively it may try to balance the best and worst outcomes for each event and use a criterion based on selecting the best value for:

$$\alpha * \text{best outcome} + (1 - \alpha) * \text{worst outcome}$$

Different criteria will often suggest the same alternative, this perhaps reduces the importance of selecting the 'right' one for a particular application. Certainly it is often felt that the main strength of decision criteria is not their ability to recommend good alternatives but their use in formalizing the structure of a problem and allowing sensible discussion based on a clear picture of consequences.

SELF ASSESSMENT QUESTIONS

10.4 What is meant by decision making under uncertainty?

10.5 List three useful decision criteria.

10.6 How many of these criteria take into account all outcomes associated with a particular alternative?

10.7 Are the listed criteria the only ones available? If not suggest others which might be useful.

10.8 What is meant by 'the maximum fee worth paying for perfect information'?

10.4 DECISION MAKING UNDER RISK

In the last section we considered decision making under uncertainty, where a number of events could occur but there was no indication of the relative likelihood of each. The main characteristic of decision making under risk is that there are again a number of events which might occur, but now reliable probabilities can be given to each of them. As every event should be included, these probabilities should add to one. A simple example of decision making under risk would be to gamble on the outcome of spinning a coin. The events are the coin coming down heads or tails and reliable probabilities can be put to these (0.5 in each case).

10.4.1 Expected values

The method of solution for such problems is to calculate the expected value for each alternative and select the alternative with the best expected value. This involves two stages:

(1) Calculate the expected value for each alternative. (Expected value is defined as sum of probability times value of the outcome.)

(2) Select the alternative with the best expected value (i.e. highest value for gains and lowest value for costs).

The expected value for an alternative is the average gain (or cost) which would be expected if the decision were repeated a large number of times. It is not the value which would be returned *every* time but the average value for a large number of repetitions.

WORKED EXAMPLE 10.9

What is the best alternative for the following gains matrix?

		Events			
		1 $P = 0.1$	2 $P = 0.2$	3 $P = 0.6$	4 $P = 0.1$
	A	10	7	5	9
Alternatives	B	3	20	2	10
	C	3	4	11	1
	D	8	4	2	16

SOLUTION

Calculating the expected value for each alternative as the sum of the probability times the value of the outcome gives:

A $0.1 * 10 + 0.2 * 7 + 0.6 * 5 + 0.1 * 9 = 6.3$
B $0.1 * 3 + 0.2 * 20 + 0.6 * 2 + 0.1 * 10 = 6.5$
C $0.1 * 3 + 0.2 * 4 + 0.6 * 11 + 0.1 * 1 = 7.8$
D $0.1 * 8 + 0.2 * 4 + 0.6 * 2 + 0.1 * 16 = 4.4$

As these are gains the best alternative is C with an expected value of 7.8. If this decision is made the average return in the long run would be 7.8: if the decision is made only once the gain could be any of the four values 3, 4, 11 or 1.

WORKED EXAMPLE 10.10

A transport firms bids for a long term contract to move newspapers from printing works to wholesalers. It can submit one of three tenders: a low one based on an assumption of increased newspaper sales and hence reduced unit transport costs, a medium one which would give a satisfactory return if newspaper sales stayed the same, or a high one which assumes that newspaper sales will decline and unit transport costs will increase. The probabilities of newspaper sales and profits (in thousands of pounds) for the transport firm are shown in the following table. Based on this matrix, which tender should it submit?

| | Newspaper sales | | |
	decrease $P = 0.4$	stay same $P = 0.3$	increase $P = 0.3$
Low tender	10	15	16
Medium tender	5	20	10
High tender	18	10	−5

SOLUTION

Calculating the expected value for each alternative:

- low tender $\quad 0.4 * 10 + 0.3 * 15 + 0.3 * 16 = 13.3$
- medium tender $0.4 * \quad 5 + 0.3 * 20 + 0.3 * 10 = 11.0$
- high tender $\quad 0.4 * 18 + 0.3 * 10 - 0.3 * \quad 5 = \quad 8.7$

As these are profits the best alternative is the one with highest expected value, which is the low tender.

With decisions under uncertainty we were able to calculate a value of perfect information by adding an extra alternative 'pay a fee F for perfect information'. A similar approach could be adopted for decision making under risk. Suppose, for example, that a specialist market research agency was able to conduct a test which would say, with certainty, whether the sales of newspapers in the above example would increase, stay the same or decrease. We would expect this additional information to assist in decision making and lead to a higher return.

If we know in advance which event will occur, we will make the decision which gives the highest return. If, in the example above, a market research group suggested newspaper sales would decrease the transport company would put in a high tender and make a profit of

£18,000. If the research group said sales would stay the same the company would submit a medium tender for profits of £20,000, and if the group said sales would increase the company would put in a low tender for profits of £16,000. From each of these the company would have to subtract the fee, F. Adding the extra alternative 'pay a fee of F for perfect information' gives the revised gains matrix:

| | Newspaper sales | | |
	decrease $P = 0.4$	stay same $P = 0.3$	increase $P = 0.3$
Low tender	10	15	16
Medium tender	5	20	10
High tender	18	10	−5
Pay fee F for info.	$18 - F$	$20 - F$	$16 - F$

Then calculating the expected values as before:

(a)   low tender   = 13.3

(b)   medium tender   = 11.0

(c)   high tender   = 8.7

(d)   pay fee F for info = $0.4 * (18 - F) + 0.3 * (20 - F)$
$$+ 0.3 * (16 - F)$$
$$= 18.0 - F$$

The highest of these is either 13.3 or $18.0 - F$ and the fee should be paid if:

$$18 - F \geq 13.3$$
$$F \leq 4.7$$

The suggested decision is to pay for information if the fee is less than £4700 and otherwise submit a low tender.

In summary
Expected values can be used to suggest the best alternative in situations of risk. An expected value for perfect information may be calculated.

10.4.2 Using Bayes' theorem to update probabilities

In Chapter 8 we discussed how Bayes' theorem could be used to update conditional probabilities.

$$\text{Bayes' theorem } P(a/b) = \frac{P(b/a) * P(a)}{P(b)}$$

where: $P(a/b)$ = probability of a happening given that b has already happened (wanted probability)

$P(b/a)$ = probability of b given that a has already happened (known)

$P(a), P(b)$ = probabilities of a and b respectively (known).

If you cannot remember the details of Bayes' theorem it would be worthwhile rereading the relevant section in Chapter 8.

Bayes' theorem can be used for updating conditional probabilities of events, as illustrated by the following worked examples.

WORKED EXAMPLE 10.11

The crowd for a sports event might be small (with a probability of 0.4) or large. To help organization of the event the advance sales of tickets can be analysed a week before the event takes place. These can be classified as high, average or low, with the probability of advance sales conditional on crowd size given by the following table.

		Advance sales		
		High	Average	Low
Crowd size	Large	0.7	0.3	0.0
	Small	0.2	0.2	0.6

The organizers must choose one of two plans in running the event and the table below gives the net profit in thousands of pounds for each combination of plan and crowd size.

		Plan 1	Plan 2
Crowd size	Large	10	14
	Small	9	5

If the organizers used the information on advance sales what strategy would maximize their expected profits?

SOLUTION

We can use the abbreviations:

(a) *CL* and *CS* for crowd size large and crowd size small;
(b) *ASH*, *ASA* and *ASL* for advance sales high, average and small.

We will start by assuming the organizers do not use the information on advance sales, in which case the best they can do is to use the probabilities of large and small crowds (0.6 and 0.4 respectively) to calculate expected values for the two plans.

Plan 1 $0.6 * 10 + 0.4 * 9 = 9.6$

Plan 2 $0.6 * 14 + 0.4 * 5 = 10.4$ . . . better plan

The organizers would use plan 2 with an expected value of £10,400.

Now, let us assume the organizers do use the information on advance ticket sales. We are given conditional probabilities of the form $P(ASH/CL)$, $P(ASH/CS)$, etc. and we would really like them the other way around, $P(CL/ASH)$, $P(CS/ASH)$, etc. We use Bayes' theorem to get these, with the calculations shown in the following table.

	ASH	ASA	ASL		ASH	ASA	ASL
CL	0.7	0.3	0.0	0.6	0.42	0.18	0.00
CS	0.2	0.2	0.6	0.4	0.08	0.08	0.24
					0.50	0.26	0.24
			CL		0.84	0.69	0.00
			CS		0.16	0.31	1.00

The probability of advance sales being high is 0.5. If this happens the probability of a large crowd is 0.84 and of a small crowd is 0.16. Then, if the organizers choose plan 1 the expected value is $0.84 * 10 + 0.16 * 9 = 9.84$; if the organizers choose plan 2 their expected value is $0.84 * 14 + 0.16 * 5 = 12.56$. This shows that if advance sales are high they should choose plan 2.

This reasoning can be extended to the other alternatives:

ASH: Plan 1 $0.84 * 10 + 0.16 * 9 = 9.84$

Plan 2 $0.84 * 14 + 0.16 * 5 = 12.56$ . . .

ASA: Plan 1 $0.69 * 10 + 0.31 * 9 = 9.69$

Plan 2 $0.69 * 14 + 0.31 * 5 = 11.21$ . . .

ASL: Plan 1 $0.00 * 10 + 1.00 * 9 = 9.00 \ldots$
        Plan 2 $0.00 * 14 + 1.00 * 5 = 5.00$

The overall strategy which maximizes the organizers' profit is:

- if the advance sales are high or medium select plan 2;
- if they are low select plan 1.

We can go a little further with this analysis, as we know the probability of high, average and low advance sales are respectively 0.5, 0.26 and 0.24. Thus, we can calculate the overall expected value of following the recommended strategy as:

$$0.5 * 12.56 + 0.26 * 11.21 + 0.24 * 9 = 11.35$$

This can be compared with the expected profit of £10,400 when the advance sales information is not used, and using the additional information raises expected profits by $11,350 - 10,400 = £950$, or over 9%.

Finally, we could calculate a value of perfect information on advance ticket sales. If we knew with certainty that crowd size would be large we would use plan 2 with an expected profit of £14,000, and if we knew that crowd size would be small we would use plan 1 with a profit of £9000. The probability of large and small crowd is 0.6 and 0.4 respectively so the profit with perfect information would be $0.6 * 14 + 0.4 * 9 = 12$.

To summarize these results, the expected value:

(a) with perfect information   = £12,000
(b) using advance sales information   = £11,350
(c) not using advance sales information = £10,400

WORKED EXAMPLE 10.12

An oil company drills an exploration well in deep water off the Irish coast. The company is uncertain of the amount of recoverable oil it will find, but experience suggests it could be classified as minor (with a probability of 0.3), significant (with probability 0.5) or major. It now has to decide how to develop the find and has a choice of either moving quickly to minimize the cost of long term debt, or moving slowly to ensure continued income generation. The profits for every combination of size of find and development speed are given in the following table, where entries are in millions of pounds.

	Size of find		
	Minor	Significant	Major
Develop quickly	100	130	180
Develop slowly	80	150	210

Some further geological tests can be done to give a more accurate picture of the size of the find, but these will cost £2.5 million and are not entirely accurate. The tests give results classified as A, B and C with conditional probabilities of results given size of find shown in the following table.

| | | Test result | | |
		A	B	C
Find size	Minor	0.3	0.4	0.3
	Significant	0.5	0.0	0.5
	Major	0.25	0.25	0.5

The oil company wants to maximize its profits. Should it do the geological tests? What would be the value of perfect information?

SOLUTION

Defining the abbreviations:

(a) MIN, SIG and MAJ for minor, significant and major finds;
(b) QUICK and SLOW for the quick and slow development.

Without using the further geological test, the expected values with both speeds of development are:

QUICK $0.3 * 100 + 0.5 * 130 + 0.2 * 180 = 131$
SLOW $0.3 * 80 + 0.5 * 150 + 0.2 * 210 = 141 \ldots$

The company should develop the find slowly with an expected value of £141 million.

From the geological test the company will want information in the form $P(MIN/A)$ etc., but it is actually presented in the form $P(A/MIN)$, so Bayes' theorem should be used.

	A	B	C		A	B	C
MIN	0.3	0.4	0.3	0.3	0.09	0.12	0.09
SIG	0.5	0.0	0.5	0.5	0.25	0.00	0.25
MAJ	0.25	0.25	0.5	0.2	0.05	0.05	0.10
					0.39	0.17	0.44
			MIN		0.23	0.71	0.20
			SIG		0.64	0.00	0.57
			MAJ		0.13	0.29	0.23

Now the best development speed can be found for each test result.

A: QUICK $0.23 * 100 + 0.64 * 130 + 0.13 * 180 = 129.6$

SLOW $0.23 * 80 + 0.64 * 150 + 0.13 * 210 = 141.7 \ldots$

B: QUICK $0.71 * 100 + 0.00 * 130 + 0.29 * 180 = 123.2 \ldots$

SLOW $0.71 * 80 + 0.00 * 150 + 0.29 * 210 = 117.7$

C: QUICK $0.20 * 100 + 0.57 * 130 + 0.23 * 180 = 135.5$

SLOW $0.20 * 80 + 0.57 * 150 + 0.23 * 210 = 149.8 \ldots$

The best policy would be to develop slowly if test results were A or C and quickly if the test results were B. This policy would have an expected value of:

$$0.39 * 141.7 + 0.17 * 123.2 + 0.44 * 149.8 = 142.12$$

Profit without doing the tests is £141 million while doing the test raises it to £142.12 million minus the cost of £2.5 million. In these circumstances it is not worth doing the tests, and would not be worth doing them unless their cost was less than £1.12 million.

The value of perfect information is:

$$0.3 * 100 + 0.5 * 150 + 0.2 * 210 = 147.$$

10.4.3 Utilities

Expected values are easy to use but they have drawbacks. In particular, it may be argued that they do not always reflect real preferences, as illustrated by the following example. Consider an investment represented by the payoff matrix below, which has a 90% chance of yielding a loss.

		Events	
		Gain $P = 0.1$	Lose $P = 0.9$
Alternatives	Invest	£500,000	−£50,000
	Do not invest	£0	£0

The expected values are:

- invest $\quad 0.1 * 500{,}000 - 0.9 * 50{,}000 = £5000$
- do not invest $0.1 * 0 + 0.9 * 0 \qquad = £0$

Expected values would suggest investing even though there is a 90% chance of losing. Expected values represent the average value in the

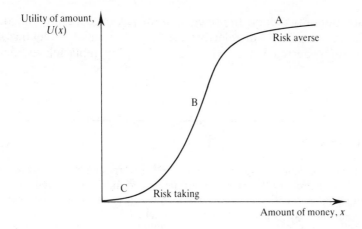

Figure 10.2 A typical utility curve relating amounts of money to their value.

long run when the decision is repeated a large number of times. If the decision is made only once they may give misleading advice. For this reason 'utilities' have been developed which reflect more accurately the real value of money.

The use of expected values assumes a linear relationship between the amount of money and its value. Then £100 has a value a hundred times as great as £1, and £1,000,000 has a value ten thousand times as much as £100. In practice this strict linear relationship must be doubted and utilities have been suggested to show a more realistic relationship. One graph of a typical utility function is shown in Figure 10.2. Unfortunately, each individual and organization has a different appreciation of the value of money and therefore will work on a different utility function. Moreover these curves tend to vary over time.

The generalized utility function in Figure 10.2 has three distinct regions. At the top, near point A, the utility is rising slowly with the amount of money. A decision maker in this region would not put a high value on a gain of money, but would certainly not like to lose money and move nearer to point B where the utility falls rapidly. Gaining an amount of money is not very attractive but losing it is very unattractive. This leads to a conservative decision maker who does not like to take risks.

Region B on the graph has the utility of money almost linear, which is the assumption of expected values. At point C losing an amount of money will not appreciably affect the utility, but gaining money and moving nearer to B would have a high value. A decision maker here will be keen to make a gain and not unduly mind a loss, which is characteristic of a 'risk taker'.

The main problem with utilities is the difficulty of defining a reasonable utility function. This is so difficult that relatively little practical use is made of utility theory. In principle, however, once a utility function is established the process of selecting the best alternative is identical to calculation of expected value, with expected utility replacing expected value.

WORKED EXAMPLE 10.13

Suppose, for convenience, someone's utility curve is a reasonable approximation to $\sqrt{x}$. In other words, in the range we are interested in, the perceived value of an amount of money x is $\sqrt{x}$. They have to make a decision described by the following gains matrix. Which is their best alternative?

		Events		
		A $P = 0.7$	B $P = 0.2$	C $P = 0.1$
Alternatives	1	14	24	12
	2	6	40	90
	3	1	70	30
	4	12	12	6

SOLUTION

For interest we will start by calculating the expected value of each alternative:

1. $0.7 * 14 + 0.2 * 24 + 0.1 * 12 = 15.8$
2. $0.7 * 6 + 0.2 * 40 + 0.1 * 90 = 21.2 \ldots$
3. $0.7 * 1 + 0.2 * 70 + 0.1 * 30 = 17.7$
4. $0.7 * 12 + 0.2 * 12 + 0.1 * 6 = 11.4$

Using expected values the best alternative is number 2.

Now if we repeat the calculations but replacing the amount of money by its utility (in this case by its square root) we get:

1. $0.7 * \sqrt{14} + 0.2 * \sqrt{24} + 0.1 * \sqrt{12} = 3.95. \ldots$
2. $0.7 * \sqrt{6} + 0.2 * \sqrt{40} + 0.1 * \sqrt{90} = 3.93$
3. $0.7 * \sqrt{1} + 0.2 * \sqrt{70} + 0.1 * \sqrt{30} = 2.92$
4. $0.7 * \sqrt{12} + 0.2 * \sqrt{12} + 0.1 * \sqrt{6} = 3.36$

Although the difference is small, the best alternative has shifted to 1. This is because the value put on various amounts of money has changed, and in particular the relative attractiveness of the gain of 90 in alternative 2 has declined.

In summary
Utilities are designed to reflect the value of different amounts of money. Expected utilities can be used to help decisions in situations of risk, provided a realistic utility function can be defined.

SELF ASSESSMENT QUESTIONS

10.9 What is meant by 'decision making under risk'?

10.10 What is the 'expected value' of a course of action?

10.11 Could a 'subjective probability' be assigned to events under risk?

10.12 When could Bayes' theorem be used to calculate expected values?

10.13 Why might expected utilities be a better measure than expected values?

10.14 How, in respect to their utility function, do risk averse and risk taking decision makers differ?

10.5 SEQUENTIAL DECISIONS AND DECISION TREES

The implicit assumption so far in this chapter is that once a decision has been made there is no follow-up or further action. There are many situations where one decision leads to a series of other decisions. If, for example, we decide to buy a car the initial decision might be to choose a new or second-hand one. If a new car is chosen, this opens the choice of British, Japanese, French, German, Italian or others. If the choice here is a British car the choice is Rover, Jaguar, Ford, Rolls Royce, Vauxhall and so on. Then if a Rover is chosen a range of other decisions have to be made. At each stage in the decision process the selection of one alternative opens up a series of other choices (or sometimes events). These can best be represented by a 'decision tree', where the alternatives (or events) are represented by the branches of a horizontal tree, as illustrated in Figure 10.3.

Although decision trees are most useful for tackling complex, sequential decisions they can be used for simple ones. Consider an example where a company approaches a bank manager for a loan to finance an expansion plan. The bank manager has to decide whether or not to grant the loan. If the bank manager grants the loan the company expansion may be successful or it may not. If the bank manager does not grant the loan, the company may continue banking as before or it may move its account to another bank.

This problem can be represented by the decision tree shown in Figure 10.4. This decision tree shows the sequence of alternatives and

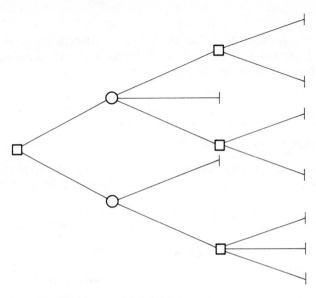

Figure 10.3   General form of a decision tree.

events. There is a notional time scale going from left to right with early decisions or events on the left followed by later ones towards the right. There is only one decision in this example followed by events over which the bank manager has no control, so the sequence is:

- the manager makes a decision
- one of several possible events happens.

In the decision tree the alternatives and events have been represented by the branches, so each branch represents a different path (decision or event) which may be followed through the tree. There are also three distinct types of nodes.

|	–	terminal node. These are at the right hand side and show the ends of all sequences of decisions and events.
O	–	random node. These represent points at which things happen, so that all branches leaving random nodes are events with known probabilities.
☐	–	decision node. These represent points at which decisions are made, so that all branches leaving a decision node are alternatives, the best of which should be selected.

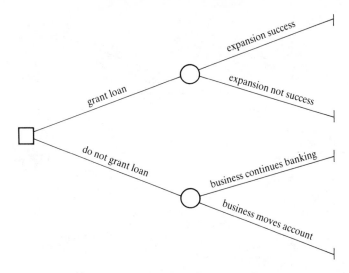

Figure 10.4 Example of a decision tree.

This is the basic structure of the tree, but probabilities and values still have to be added. Suppose the bank currently values its business with the company at £2000 a year. If the manager grants the loan and the expansion succeeds the value to the bank of increased business and interest charges is £3000 a year. If the expansion does not succeed the bank will still have business valued at £1000 a year (reduced because of reduced volume and allowance for writing off bad debt). There is a probability of 0.7 that the expansion plan will prove successful. If the manager does not grant the loan there is a probability of 0.6 that the company will transfer its account to another bank.

These figures can be added to the tree as shown in Figure 10.5.

The probabilities are now entered on the appropriate event branches (ensuring all events are included and the sum of the probabilities from each random node equals one). Values have been put on terminal nodes, representing the total cost of moving through the tree and ending at the terminal node. In this case these values are the annual business expected by the bank. If a longer term view is needed these figures could be multiplied by an appropriate number of years.

The next stage of the analysis moves from right to left through the tree and assigns a value to each node in turn. This is done by determining the best decision at each decision node and the expected value at each random node.

At each decision node the alternative branches leaving are connected to later nodes. The values on these are compared, the best branch is selected and the node value is transferred

At each random node the value is the expected value of the

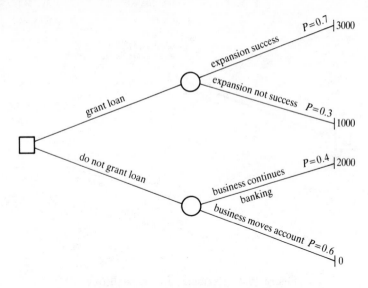

Figure 10.5 Decision tree with added probabilities and terminal values.

leaving event branches (i.e. the sum, for all branches, of the probability of leaving by a branch times the value of the node at the end of the branch).

Using this procedure on the tree in Figure 10.5 gives the results shown in Figure 10.6.

The calculations are as follows:

At random node A calculate expected value:

$$0.7 * 3000 + 0.3 * 1000 = 2400$$

At random node B calculate expected value:

$$0.4 * 2000 + 0.6 * 0 = 800$$

At decision node C select the best alternative:

$$MAX[2400, 800] = 2400$$

The best policy is to grant the loan and this will have an expected value of £2400.

In summary

To analyse sequential decisions using a decision tree:

- determine the alternatives, events and their probabilities, outcomes, etc.;

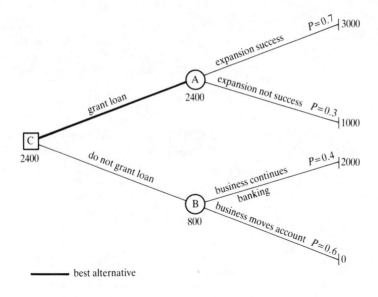

Figure 10.6 Analysis of decision tree.

- draw a tree (moving from left to right) showing the sequences of events and alternatives, and setting the values at terminal nodes;
- analyse the tree (moving from right to left) selecting the best alternative at decision nodes and calculating the expected value at random nodes.

We can now apply these principles to larger decision trees, including those which use Bayes' theorem to update conditional probabilities.

WORKED EXAMPLE 10.14

A workshop is about to install a new machine for stamping and pressing parts for domestic appliances. Three suppliers have made bids to supply the machine. The first supplier offers the Basicor machine which automatically produces parts of acceptable, but not outstanding, quality. The output from the machine is variable (depending on material supplied and a variety of settings) but could be 1000 a week (with probability 0.1), 2000 a week (with probability 0.7) or 3000 a week. The notional profit for this machine is £4 a unit made. The second supplier offers a Superstamp machine which makes higher quality parts. The output from this can be 700 a week (with probability 0.4) or 1000 a week, with a notional profit of £10 a unit. The third supplier offers the Switchover machine which can be set to

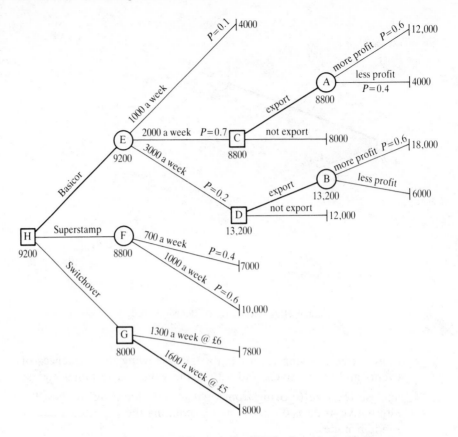

Figure 10.7 Decision tree for Worked example 10.14.

either produce 1300 high quality parts a week at a profit of £6 a unit, or 1600 medium quality parts a week with a profit of £5 a unit.

If the machine produces 2000 or more units a week, it is possible to export all production as a single bulk order. Then there is a 60% chance of selling for 50% more profit, and a 40% chance of selling for 50% less profit.

What should be done to maximize expected profits?

SOLUTION

The tree for this decision is shown in Figure 10.7. The terminal node values are weekly profit found by multiplying the number produced by the profit per unit. If 1000 are produced on the Basicor machine the value is £4000 and so on. If the output from Basicor is exported profit may be increased by 50% (i.e. to £6 a unit) or reduced by 50% (i.e. to £2 a unit).

Calculations at each node are as follows:

A. expected value at random node

$$= 0.6 * 12{,}000 + 0.4 * 4000 = 8800$$

B. expected value at random node
    $= 0.6 * 18,000 + 0.4 * 6000 = 13,200$

C. best alternative at decision node
    $= MAX[8800, 8000] = 8800$

D. best alternative at decision node
    $= MAX[13,200, 12,000] = 13,200$

E. expected value at random node
    $= 0.1 * 4000 + 0.7 * 8800 + 0.2 * 13,200 = 9200$

F. expected value at random node
    $= 0.4 * 7000 + 0.6 * 10,000 = 8800$

G. best alternative at decision node
    $= MAX[7800, 8000] = 8000$

H. best alternative at decision node
    $= MAX[9200, 8800, 8000] = 9200$

The overall best policy is to buy the Basicor machine and if it produces more than 2000 units, export all production. The expected profit from this policy is £9200 a week.

WORKED EXAMPLE 10.15

A new reservoir, designed to provide a nearby city with drinking water, has been built by damming a river. A farmer lower down the river valley now finds the water supply to his cattle has dried up. He is faced with the options of either connecting to the local mains water supply at a cost of £22,000 or drilling a new well. The cost of the well is not known with certainty but could be £16,000 (with a probability of 0.3), £22,000 (with a probability of 0.3) or £28,000, depending on the underground rock structure and depth of water.

A local water survey company can be hired to do on-site tests. For a cost of £300 they will give either a favourable or an unfavourable report on the chances of easily finding water. The reliability of this report (phrased in terms of the probability of a favourable report given the drilling cost will be low, etc.) is given in the following table.

	Drilling well costs		
	£16,000	£22,000	£28,000
Favourable report	0.8	0.6	0.2
Unfavourable report	0.2	0.4	0.8

Draw a decision tree of the farmer's problem and identify his best course of action and expected cost.

SOLUTION

We know the conditional probabilities one way around, but need them the other way around for the decision tree. These are calculated from Bayes' theorem, as shown opposite. These probabilities and the other values can be added to the farmer's decision tree as shown in Figure 10.8.

Completing the analysis shows the farmer's best option is to use the survey and follow its advice, with an expected cost of £21,340.

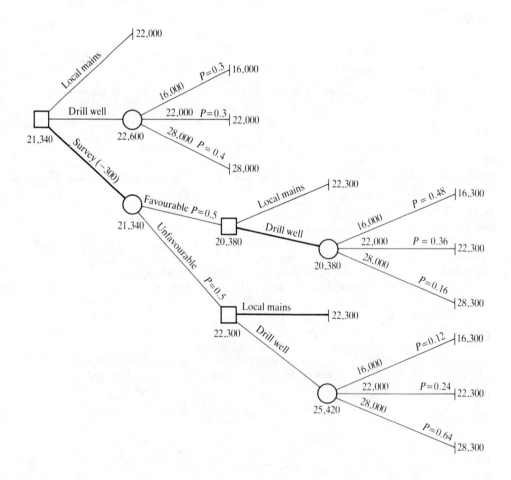

Figure 10.8 Decision tree for Worked example 10.15.

	FAV	UNFAV		FAV	UNFAV
16,000	0.8	0.2	0.3	0.24	0.06
22,000	0.6	0.4	0.3	0.18	0.12
28,000	0.2	0.8	0.4	0.08	0.32
				0.50	0.50
			16,000	0.48	0.12
			22,000	0.36	0.24
			28,000	0.16	0.64

SELF ASSESSMENT QUESTIONS

10.15 Why should sequential decisions be considered differently from a series of separate decisions?

10.16 List the three types of node in a decision tree.

10.17 How is the node value calculated at:

(a) a terminal node
(b) a decision node
(c) a random node?

10.18 How is the best policy determined from a decision tree?

CONCLUSIONS

This chapter has described some aspects of decision analysis. Everybody makes a continuous stream of decisions and usually these are tackled on the basis of previous experience, intuition and subjectivity. Sometimes a more important decision needs a certain amount of attention.

The first difficulty of decision making is the complexity of situations in which decisions have to be made. Maps, payoff matrices and decision trees are useful in showing the structure of problems and interactions which occur.

There are some standard features of all decision situations, including a decision maker who wants to achieve some objective, a set of alternatives, a set of events, and consequences for each combination of events and alternatives.

We described decision making in a number of situations. With decision making under certainty there is only one event and the solution procedure is to list the consequences and select the one with the best value.

Decision making under uncertainty has a number of possible events, but there is no way of saying which are more likely. Then decision criteria may be used. Decision making under risk allows probabilities to be assigned to events and expected values or expected utilities may be used.

Finally we looked at sequential decisions which could be represented by decision trees.

PROBLEMS

10.1 A pub on the seafront at Blackpool notices that its profits are declining. The landlord has a number of alternatives for increasing his profits (attracting more customers, increasing prices, getting customers to spend more, etc.) but each of these has follow on effects. Draw a map illustrating interactions for this situation.

10.2 Select the best alternatives in the situation of certainty described by the following gains matrix.

		Event
	a	100
	b	950
	c	−250
Alternatives	d	0
	e	950
	f	500

10.3 Use the Laplace, Wald and Savage decision criteria to select alternatives in the following matrices.

(a) cost matrix

		Events				
		1	2	3	4	5
	a	100	70	115	95	60
	b	95	120	120	90	150
Alternatives	c	180	130	60	160	120
	d	80	75	50	100	95
	e	60	140	100	170	160

(b) gains matrix

		Events			
		1	2	3	4
Alternatives	a	1	6	3	7
	b	2	5	1	4
	c	8	1	4	2
	d	5	2	7	8

10.4 What is the highest fee worth paying for perfect information in the payoff matrices of problem 10.3?

10.5 (a) What is the best alternative in the following situation of risk described by the following gains matrix?

		Events		
		1	2	3
		$P = 0.4$	$P = 0.3$	$P = 0.3$
Alternatives	a	100	90	120
	b	80	102	110

(b) Would this decision change if a utility function $U(x) = \sqrt{x}$ were used?

10.6 A company can launch one of three versions of a new product, X, Y or Z. The profit depends on market reaction and there is a 30% chance that this will be good, a 40% chance it will be medium and a 30% chance it will be poor.

(a) Which version should the company launch if profits are given in the following table?

		Market reaction		
		Good	Medium	Poor
Version	X	100	110	80
	Y	70	90	120
	Z	130	100	70

(b)   A market survey can be done to give more information on market reaction. Experience suggests these surveys give results A, B or C with probabilities $P(A/\text{Good})$, etc. shown in the following table.

		Result		
		A	B	C
Market reaction	Good	0.2	0.2	0.6
	Medium	0.2	0.5	0.3
	Poor	0.4	0.3	0.3

How much should the company be prepared to pay for this information?
    What is the value of perfect information?

10.7   A road haulage contractor owns a lorry with a one year old engine. He has to decide now, and again in one year's time, whether or not to replace the engine. If he decides to replace it it will cost £500. If he does not replace it there is an increased chance it will break down during the year and the cost of replacing an engine then is £800. If an engine is replaced during the year the replacement engine is assumed to be one year old at the time when the next decision is taken. The probability of breakdown of an engine during a year is as follows:

	Age of engine in years		
	0	1	2
Probability of breakdown	0.0	0.2	0.7

Draw a decision tree for this problem and find the decisions which minimize cost over the next two years.

10.8   An organization is considering launching an entirely new service. If the market reaction to this service is good (which has a probability of 0.2) the organization will make £3000 a week; if market reaction is medium (with probability 0.5) it will make £1000 a week, but if reaction is poor (with probability 0.3) it will lose £1500 a week. The organization could run a survey to test market reaction with results A, B or C. Experience suggests the reliability of such surveys is described by the following matrix of $P(A/\text{good})$, etc. How much should the organization be prepared to pay for this survey?

		Result		
		A	B	C
Market reaction	Good	0.7	0.2	0.1
	Medium	0.2	0.6	0.2
	Poor	0.1	0.4	0.5

CASE STUDY – JOHN SPARROW'S PETROL ADDITIVE

Two years ago John Sparrow was working as a postgraduate student of chemistry when he developed an additive for petrol which could marginally increase the fuel consumption of cars. He published a report of this in a technical journal and a fuller account was given in his PhD thesis.

Since John left university he has been working for a small plastics company, but this is now closing down and he will soon be unemployed. His most straightforward option would be to find a new job. Although he enjoyed working for the plastics company, John feels this may be the time to start a business of his own. One possibility for this would be the commercial development of his petrol additive.

John was not sure if there would be any interest in his additive, so he began by approaching an established company and seeing if they would be willing to manufacture and market it. His first talks were with the new developments section of Bonded Chemicals who owned the plastics company John worked for. Bonded Chemicals had read John's technical reports on the additive (this persuaded them to employ him in the first place) and were confident in his abilities. A quick response showed they would be interested in making a conditional offer for the additive. This would be based on a cash payment of £50,000 to John and further royalties based on the success of the product. In effect Bonded Chemicals would manufacture and market the additive and if they considered it a commercial success would give royalties of 2% of profit to John, but if they considered it a failure they would give him no royalties at all. Unfortunately, there is no means of saying, in advance, if the additive will be a commercial success or not. The experiences of other people offered similar contracts suggest there is a 50% chance of the company considering the product successful and royalty payments then average £25,000 a year. If the additive proves successful in the first year the company often (on 60% of occasions) offers a cash payment of £60,000 to the developers instead of paying any further royalties.

Another option open to John would be to set up his own company and start making and marketing the additive himself. Unfortunately, he is still young and has no business experience or proven skills. He has consulted the local Development Agency Small Business Encouragement Division who were able to offer a limited amount of advice. They were encouraging in some respects, but said that only 20% of small businesses could be judged a success over the first three years of operation. 40% of others ceased trading and the remaining 40% continued to operate but were only just covering costs. They also recommended a marketing firm which could be hired to prepare a market evaluation to see if the additive is likely to sell. This marketing firm specializes in assessing the potential demand for new products and for a fee of £15,000 will run a series of interviews, surveys and trials. At the end of these they make one of three reports: either the product has potential for good sales, or it does not have potential for good sales, or it is too new and not enough information is available to judge its likely sales.

John went home and analysed the information he had been given and did some calculations. Firstly, it seemed unrealistic to plan beyond three years, so he decided only to consider his income and costs over this period. Then, if his company is a success he could expect to take a salary and profits of £30,000 a year. If the company just covers costs he could take a salary of £15,000 a year. If the company closes down he could expect to have a net loss over three years of £10,000. Secondly, he looked at the reliability of the marketing firm and found that they said a new product had potential for good sales 30% of times, it did not have potential for good sales 45% of times, and the could not say 25% of times. Their reliability could also be described by the following table of conditional probabilities. This shows the probability that the marketing company said that a product had potential for good sales given that it eventually sold well and the new company was successful, etc.

	Company successful	Company covered costs	Company ceased trading
Potential for good sales	0.7	0.2	0.3
No potential for good sales	0.2	0.4	0.4
Not enough information	0.1	0.4	0.3

After receiving results from the marketing firm, John could still decide to simply find another job, or go into business on his own, or sell the additive to Bonded Chemicals. However, Bonded Chemicals would certainly have heard about the survey and if they were now being offered the product would infer that the survey was not optimistic. Hence, they would exactly halve all payments made in their offer without the survey. Because they were a large company with considerable experience in the area, the probabilities that Bonded Chemicals could make a success of the product are not affected by the marketing firm's report which is based on a small company environment.

There is one final course that John could take. If he starts his own company and finds it is a success, he could consider expansion or selling out to a larger company. He talked about these options to his bank manager who said that if he expands and the business really takes off there is no reason why his pay and profits should not reach £40,000 a year, but the probability of this is only about 0.3. It is more likely that an expansion so soon will not cover costs and leave John with a total income of £25,000 a year. On the other hand if John has a successful business he thinks it likely that a buyer could be found to pay John a total of about £100,000 over three years.

John must decide what to do fairly quickly. At the moment he is rather confused by the details of his problem. The only decision he has made so far is that he should aim to maximize his own expected income over the next three years.

SOLUTIONS TO SELF ASSESSMENT QUESTIONS

10.1 Decisions often must be made in complex situations and it is difficult to envisage all courses of action, or the effects that one course of action may have on wider issues. The purpose of these representations is to give structure to the situation and clearly show alternatives and consequences.

10.2 The five characteristics are:

- a decision maker;
- a number of alternatives, one of which must be selected;
- a number of events, one of which will happen;
- a set of measurable outcomes associated with each combination of alternative and event;
- an objective of selecting the best alternative.

10.3 With decisions under certainty there is only one event. The method of solution is to list the outcomes and select the alternative

which leads to the best. In practice this is not as easy as it sounds.

10.4 One of several events may occur, but there is no way of telling which events are more likely. In particular probabilities can not be given to events. 'Uncertainty' is not the same as 'ignorance' where events, outcomes and even alternatives are unknown.

10.5 The three criteria described here are due to:

Laplace – select alternative with best average outcome
Wald – select alternative with best value for worst outcome
Savage – select alternative with lowest value for highest regret.

10.6 Only the Laplace criterion.

10.7 No. There are a large number of criteria which could be devised to fit a particular

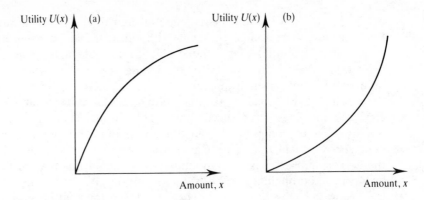

Figure 10.9 Utility curves for different approaches to risk: (a) utility curve for a risk averse decision maker; (b) utility curve for a risk taking decision maker.

situation. Ones mentioned are maximax profit and $\alpha *$ best outcome $+ (1 - \alpha) *$ worst outcome.

10.8 Perfect information implies that we know in advance which event will occur. If we know this we will select the alternative which gives the best returns. Having perfect information will give higher benefits than not having it and the difference between the two is the maximum fee worth paying for perfect information.

10.9 There are several events which may occur and probabilities can be given to each of these. As all events should be included the sum of the probabilities equals one.

10.10 The expected value is the sum of the probabilities multiplied by the values of the outcomes.

$$\text{Expected value} = \Sigma \, P * V$$

10.11 Yes. But care should be taken in how the results are interpreted and how reliable they are. Often there is little benefit in guessing a subjective probability.

10.12 Bayes' theorem is used for updating conditional probabilities in situations of risk.

10.13 Expected values assume the value of money rises linearly with the amount. In practice this may not be true and the perceived value of money is described by the utility function.

10.14 Two utility curves are shown in Figure 10.9. The first of these shows a risk averse utility function where the decision maker is relatively content with their present position. A gain of money will have little additional value while a loss would considerably reduce their utility. The second curve shows a risk taking decision maker, where a loss of money will have little effect, but a gain could have a substantial rise in utility.

10.15 A decision tree enables the whole of a situation to be examined rather than looking at separate parts. As the separate parts are all related, earlier decisions and events affect later ones. This can be represented most easily on a decision tree. Arguments based on utilities could also be used, as the utility of later decisions may depend on results from earlier decisions.

10.16 Decision node, random node, terminal node.

10.17 (a) The value of a terminal node is the total cost or benefit of reaching that node.
  (b) The value of a decision node is the best value of nodes reached by leaving alternative branches.
  (c) The value of a random node is the

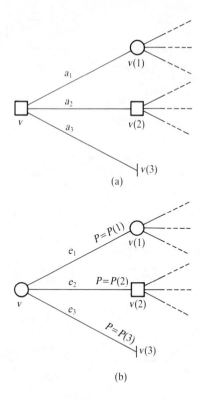

Figure 10.10 Calculation of node values: (a) at decision node V is the best of $V(1)$, $V(2)$, $V(3)$; (b) at random node
$$V = p(1) * V(1) + p(2) * V(2) + p(3) * V(3).$$

expected value of the leaving branches (that is, the sum, for all branches, of the probability times the value of the node at which the branch ends) (see Figure 10.10).

10.18 At each decision node the best alternative is selected. The value given at the lefthand, originating node is the overall expected value of following the best policy.

REFERENCES FOR FURTHER READING

Brown R.V., Kahr A.S. and Peterson C. (1974). *Decision Analysis for the Manager* New York: Holt, Rinehart and Winston

Buchanan J.T. (1982). *Discrete and Dynamic Decision Analysis* Chichester: John Wiley

Bunn D.W. (1984). *Applied Decision Analysis* New York: McGraw-Hill

Holloway C.A. (1979). *Decision Making Under Uncertainty* New Jersey: Prentice Hall

Lindley D.V. (1971). *Making Decisions* London: John Wiley

Moore P.G., Thomas H., Bunn D.W. and Hampton J. (1976). *Case Studies in Decision Analysis* Harmondsworth: Penguin Books

Newman J.W. (1971). *Management Applications of Decision Theory* New York: Harper & Row

Rivett P. (1980). *Model Building for Decision Analysis* Chichester: John Wiley

Chapter 11

Queues and simulation

SYNOPSIS

This chapter introduces the ideas of queueing theory. We are all familiar with queues when we wait to pay for groceries in a supermarket, go to a bank, catch a bus or any number of other activities. Not all queues, however, have people waiting for a service. Programs queue to be processed in computer systems, faulty machines queue to be repaired, airplanes queue to land and so on. There are many applications where analysis of queues could be beneficial. The objective of these analyses usually includes some balance between a high quality service with a large number of servers (which is expensive but keeps queues short) and a low quality service with few servers (which is cheap, but causes long queues and can lead to lost custom).

Unfortunately, analytical solutions to queueing problems are complex and are generally limited to simple situations. In this chapter analytical approaches are illustrated by single server and multi server queues where both arrivals and service times are random.

A more robust method of tackling complex queueing problems is simulation. This imitates the operations of a system so that results can be collected for a typical period without actually observing the system. If we want to find the average length of a queue it can be calculated (which may be difficult), or it may be measured from observation (which may be time consuming and unpopular), or the operation may be simulated over a typical period.

Simulation is widely used and can tackle many problems which are too complex to consider by other means. These complex models involve large amounts of arithmetic, so computers will almost inevitably be used in practice. Flow charts are used to describe the logic of complex situations.

OBJECTIVES

After reading this chapter and doing the numerical exercises you should be able to:

- appreciate the scope of queueing problems;
- describe a range of queueing problems and their objectives;
- calculate the characteristics of queues at a single server where both arrival and service times are random;
- calculate the characteristics of queues where a single line is formed for a number of parallel servers (with random arrival and service times);
- appreciate the complexity of real queueing problems and the role of computers;
- describe the characteristic approach of simulation;
- do manual simulations of simple queueing systems;
- use random numbers to draw samples from populations with various characteristics;
- draw simulation flow charts to describe the logic of a process;
- appreciate the use of computers in simulation.

11.1 INTRODUCTION TO QUEUEING THEORY

Queuing theory is concerned with situations where customers want a particular service but must wait to be served. This situation is familiar to us all and happens, for example, when:

- buying a ticket for a train
- getting money from a bank
- at the check-out of a supermarket
- waiting for traffic lights to change

and in many other circumstances.

We are all familiar with queues of people, but many queues do not involve people at all:

- a queue of jobs waiting to be processed on a computer;
- items waiting to move along an assembly line;
- telephone calls waiting for equipment to become free;

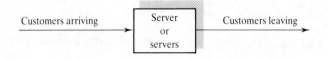

Figure 11.1 A general queueing system.

- faulty equipment waiting for maintenance engineers;
- ships waiting for a berth;

and so on.

All queues have characteristics in common and can be described by the general situation shown in Figure 11.1. By convention a 'customer' is anyone or anything wanting a service and a 'server' is the person or thing providing that service.

Queues are caused when a customer wants a particular service, but arrives to find the server is busy so they can not be served immediately. Other customers may already be waiting for service. The new arrival could see the queue and decide not to use the service, but more usually they decide to wait and line up in the queue. This queue can take many forms:

- customers may form a single queue or they may form separate queues for each server;
- they may arrive singly or in batches (for example, when a train arrives);
- arrivals may be at random or spread out by an appointment system;
- they may be served individually or in batches (at, for example, a bus stop);
- servers may be in parallel (where each does the same job) or in series (where each provides part of the service and then passes the customer on to the next stage);
- service time may be constant or variable;
- customers may be served in order of arrival or some other order (hospitals may admit patients in order of urgency etc.).

It is unpleasant for people to wait and if queues of any type form there are delays with associated costs. The service provided by the server is, therefore, in part determined by the time customers have to wait. The length of the queue depends on:

- the rate at which customers arrive to be served;
- the time taken for a server to deal with a customer;
- the number of servers available.

If there are a lot of servers the queues will be short, but providing the service may be expensive; if there are few servers the cost of providing the service will be less but potential customers might see the length of the queues and go elsewhere. A balance is needed which seems reasonable to all parties. This will differ according to circumstances. When visiting a doctor's surgery it is common to wait a long time. This is because doctor's time is considered expensive while patients' time is cheap: to ensure the doctor does not wait for patients to arrive they are given appointments close together and are expected to wait. Conversely, in petrol stations the cost of servers (petrol pumps) is low and customers will generally drive to a competitor if there is a queue. Then a large number of servers is provided and, although the utilization of each server is low, customers have a short time in any queue.

There are a wide variety of queueing problems and the detailed analysis of many of these is very difficult. Here we will illustrate the results of some analyses starting with the fundamental analysis of queueing theory, where a queue forms in front of a single server.

In summary
Queues arise in many situations, not all of which involve people. It is generally undesirable for customers to wait in queues and a balance is needed between large numbers of servers and reasonable costs.

SELF ASSESSMENT QUESTIONS

11.1 What are the main characteristics of a queue?

11.2 It is undesirable to make customers wait in a queue, so ideally enough servers should be provided to eliminate queues. Is this statement:

(a) true
(b) false
(c) partly true?

11.2 SINGLE SERVER QUEUES

The fundamental result of queueing theory refers to a single server dealing with a queue of customers with both random arrivals of customers and random service times. To be more specific this model assumes:

- a single server
- random arrivals
- random service time
- first come first served service discipline
- the system has reached its steady state
- there is no limit to the number of customers allowed in the queue
- there is no limit on the number of customers who use the service
- all arrivals wait to be served

11.2.1 Random arrivals

In Chapter 8 we said that random occurrences could be described by a Poisson distribution where the probability of r events is calculated from:

$$P(r) = \frac{e^{-\mu} * \mu^r}{r!}$$

where: r = number of events

μ = mean number of events

e = exponential constant (2.71828. . .)

Consider the random arrival of customers. If the average number of customers arriving per unit time is Φ the probability of r arrivals in the unit time is:

$$P(r) = \frac{e^{-\Phi} * \Phi^r}{r!}$$

11.2.2. Random service time

Arrivals are described by a discrete distribution but service time can take any value and must be described by a continuous distribution (see Figure 11.2). Experience suggests that the negative exponential distribution is useful for this (see Figure 11.3). We are not interested in the details of this distribution, but need only note that it is similar to the Poisson distribution and is described by the function:

$$f(t) = \mu * e^{-\mu * t}$$

where μ = mean service rate

= the average number of customers served per unit of time.

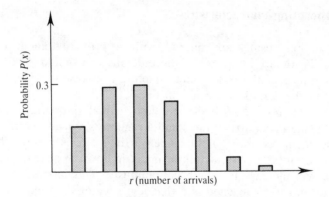

Figure 11.2 Random arrivals follow a Poisson distribution.

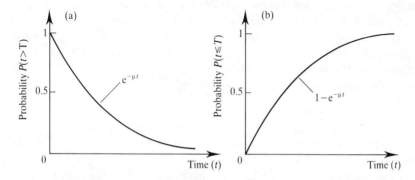

Figure 11.3 Random service times follow a negative exponential distribution: (a) probability service not completed within time T; (b) probability service completed within time T.

The distribution has the useful property (given without proof) that the probability of service time not exceeding some specified value, T, is given by:

$$P(t \le T) = 1 - e^{-\mu * T}$$

Conversely the probability that service is not completed by time T is:

$$P(t > T) = 1 - P(t \le T)$$
$$= e^{-\mu * T}$$

Random arrivals   Queue   Single server   Leaves system

(Poisson distribution)

(Negative exponential distribution of time)

513

11.2.3 Operating characteristics

[In this section results are quoted with a brief statement of their derivation. If you are interested in more details you should look them up in the references at the end of this chapter. Conversely if you are only interested in the results you can skip the details here.]

We have now described a random arrival rate of customers in terms of Φ (the mean arrival rate) and a random service time in terms of μ (the mean service rate). If the mean arrival rate is greater than the mean service rate, the system will never settle down to a steady state but the queue will increase in length continuously. This analysis assumes a steady state has been reached and that μ is greater than Φ.

The average proportion of time the system is busy is Φ/μ. Here 'busy' is defined as having at least one customer either being served or in the queue. This is also the average number of customers being served at any time. If, for example, the mean service rate is four an hour and the mean arrival rate is two an hour, we have $\Phi/\mu = 2/4 = 0.5$. This means the system will be busy half the time or there is an average of half a customer in the system.

The probability that there is no customer in the system is:

$$P_0 = 1 - \Phi/\mu$$

This is the probability that a new customer can be served without any wait.

Similarly, the probability that there are n customers in the system is given by:

$$P_n = P_0 * (\Phi/\mu)^n$$

This result (which may not be intuitively obvious but can be accepted as generally true) allows us to calculate some other characteristics of the queue. To start with, the average number of customers in the system is given by:

$$L = \sum_{n=0}^{\infty} n * P_n = \frac{\Phi}{\mu - \Phi}$$

The average number of customers in the queue is equal to the average number in the system minus the average number being served:

$$L_q = L - \frac{\Phi}{\mu} = \frac{\Phi}{\mu - \Phi} - \frac{\Phi}{\mu} = \frac{\Phi^2}{\mu * (\mu - \Phi)}$$

If L is the average number of customers in the system and Φ is the mean arrival rate, the average time any arriving customer has to spend in the system is given by:

$$W = \frac{L}{\Phi} = \frac{1}{\mu - \Phi}$$

The average time spent in the queue is the average time in the system minus the average service time:

$$W_q = W - 1/\mu$$

$$= \frac{\Phi}{\mu * (\mu - \Phi)}$$

In summary

The main operating characteristics of a queue are:

- probability the system is empty, P_0
- probability there are n customers in the system, P_n
- average number of customers in the system, L
- average number of customers in the queue, L_q
- average time spent in the system, W
- average time spent in the queue, W_q.

With:

$$
\begin{aligned}
P_0 &= 1 - \Phi/\mu \\
P_n &= P_0 * (\Phi/\mu)^n \\
L &= \frac{\Phi}{\mu - \Phi} \\
L_q &= \frac{\Phi^2}{\mu * (\mu - \Phi)} \\
W &= \frac{1}{\mu - \Phi} \\
W_q &= \frac{\Phi}{\mu * (\mu - \Phi)}
\end{aligned}
$$

These equations can now be used to make various calculations about a queueing system.

WORKED EXAMPLE 11.1

People arrive randomly at a bank teller at an average rate of 30 an hour. What are the average numbers of customers in the queue if the teller takes an average of 0.5 minutes to serve each customer? What happens if average service time changes to 1.0, 1.5 or 2.0 minutes? What are the average times in the queue for each service time?

SOLUTION

The average arrival rate is $\Phi = 30$. If the teller takes an average of 0.5 minutes to serve each customer, this is equivalent to a service rate of 120 an hour. Then the average number of customers in the queue (excluding anyone being served) is L_q.

$$L_q = \frac{\Phi^2}{\mu * (\mu - \Phi)} = \frac{30^2}{120 * (120 - 30)} = 0.083$$

The average time in the queue is W_q.

$$W_q = \frac{\Phi}{\mu * (\mu - \Phi)} = \frac{30}{120 * (120 - 30)} = 0.003 \text{ hrs}$$

Similarly substituting $\mu = 60$ and 40 (corresponding to average service times of one minute and 1.5 minutes respectively) gives:

$\mu = 60$: $L_q = 0.5$ $W_q = 0.017$ hrs
$\mu = 40$: $L_q = 2.25$ $W_q = 0.075$ hrs

If the average service time is raised to 2 minutes, the service rate is $\mu = 30$. This does not satisfy the condition that $\mu > \Phi$ and the system will not settle down to a steady state.

To find the average number of people in the system rather than the queue:

$$L = L_q + \Phi/\mu$$

Similarly the average time in the system is:

$$W = W_q + 1/\mu$$

Then:

$\mu = 120$: $L = 0.083 + 30/120 = 0.333$
$\qquad\quad W = 0.003 + 1/120 = 0.011$ hrs $= 0.66$ mins

$\mu = 60$: $L = 0.5 \quad + 30/60 \quad = 1.0$
$\qquad\quad W = 0.017 + 1/60 \quad = 0.034$ hrs $= 2.04$ mins

$\mu = 40$: $L = 2.25 \quad + 30/40 \quad = 3.0$
$\qquad\quad W = 0.075 + 1/40 \quad = 0.1$ hrs $\quad = 6.0$ mins

WORKED EXAMPLE 11.2

Customers arrive randomly at a railway information desk at a mean rate of 20 an hour. The single server manning the desk takes an average of two minutes with each customer. Calculate the characteristics of the queueing system.

SOLUTION

The mean arrival rate, Φ, is 20 an hour and the mean service rate, μ, is 30 an hour.

Probability that there is no one in the system is:

$$P_0 = 1 - \Phi/\mu = 1 - 20/30 = 0.33$$

Conversely there is a probability of 0.67 that a customer has to wait to be served.

Probability of n customers in the system is:

$$P_n = P_0 * (\Phi/\mu)^n = 0.33 * (0.67)^n$$

That is:

$$P_1 = 0.22, \ P_2 = 0.15, \ P_3 = 0.10, \ P_4 = 0.07, \text{ etc.}$$

The average number of customers in the system is:

$$L = \Phi/(\mu - \Phi) = 20/(30 - 20) = 2$$

The average number of customers in the queue is:

$$L_q = \frac{\Phi^2}{\mu * (\mu - \Phi)} = \frac{20^2}{30 * 10} = 1.33$$

The average time a customer spends in the system is:

$$W = 1/(\mu - \Phi) = 1/(30 - 20) = 0.1 \text{ hrs} = 6 \text{ minutes}$$

The expected time a customer spends in the queue is:

$$W_q = \frac{\Phi}{\mu * (\mu - \Phi)} = \frac{20}{30 * 10} = 0.0667 \text{ hrs} = 4 \text{ minutes}$$

SELF ASSESSMENT QUESTIONS

11.3 Define the variables Φ and μ in a queueing system.

11.4 What happens in a queue if $\Phi \geq \mu$?

11.5 What are the assumptions of the single server queue model?

11.6 Describe the operating characteristics of a single server queue.

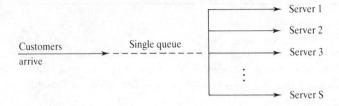

Figure 11.4 A single queue multi server queueing system.

11.3 MULTI SERVER QUEUES

If mean arrival rate is greater than mean service rate, or if queue lengths are unacceptably long, the service offered can be improved by increasing the number of servers. An extension to the single server analysis would look at the characteristics of queues with multiple servers. In particular we will consider the case where a single queue of customers is served by S servers. Here customers arrive and join a single queue; whenever a server becomes free the next customer in line is served. See Figure 11.4.

We can start by making similar assumptions to those for the single server model.

- S identical servers
- random arrivals
- random service time
- first come first served service discipline
- the system has reached its steady state
- there is no limit to the number of customers allowed in the queue
- there is no limit on the number of customers who use the service
- all customers wait to be served

If we now take μ to be the service rate for each of the servers, we can drop the requirement that μ is greater than Φ and replace it by $S * \mu > \Phi$. In other words the total service rate is greater than the total arrival rate. Unfortunately, the arithmetic now becomes a little more complex and rather than explaining the derivation we will simply state the results which are equivalent to those found for the single server queue.

The probability that all S servers are idle and there is no-one in the system is:

$$P_0 = \cfrac{1}{\sum_{n=0}^{S-1} \cfrac{(\Phi/\mu)^n}{n!} + \cfrac{(\Phi/\mu)^S * \mu}{(S-1)! * (S * \mu - \Phi)}}$$

The probability of n customers in the system is:

$$P_n = \frac{(\Phi/\mu)^n}{S! * S^{n-S}} * P_0 \qquad \text{for } n > S$$

$$P_n = \frac{(\Phi/\mu)^n}{n!} * P_0 \qquad \text{for } 0 \le n \le S$$

The average number of customers waiting for service is:

$$L_q = \frac{(\Phi/\mu)^S * \Phi * \mu}{(S-1)! * (S * \mu - \Phi)^2} * P_0$$

Average number of customers in the system is:

$$L = L_q + \Phi/\mu$$

Average time a customer waits in the queue is:

$$W_q = L_q/\Phi$$

Average time a customer spends in the system is:

$$W = W_q + 1/\mu$$

These equations look rather messy, but their use can be demonstrated by the following worked example.

WORKED EXAMPLE 11.3

A fast service, car exhaust replacement centre has customers arriving randomly at a rate of 25 an hour. It has three service bays each of which can handle up to 10 customers an hour. Find the characteristics of the queues.

SOLUTION

The mean arrival rate is $\Phi = 25$ while the mean service rate for each channel is $\mu = 10$. The number of servers, S, is 3.

Then the probability that all three service bays are idle and there is no one in the system is:

$$P_0 = \cfrac{1}{\displaystyle\sum_{n=0}^{S-1} \frac{(\Phi/\mu)^n}{n!} + \frac{(\Phi/\mu)^S * \mu}{(S-1)! * (S * \mu - \Phi)}}$$

$$P_0 = \cfrac{1}{\displaystyle\sum_{n=0}^{3-1} \frac{(25/10)^n}{n!} + \frac{(25/10)^3 * 10}{(3-1)! * (3 * 10 - 25)}}$$

Now $\displaystyle\sum_{n=0}^{2} \frac{(25/10)^n}{n!} = 1 + (25/10) + \frac{(25/10)^2}{2}$

$$= 1 + 2.5 + 3.125$$

$$= 6.625$$

So $\quad P_0 = \dfrac{1}{6.625 + 7.813 * 2} = 0.045$

The probability of n customers in the system is:

$$P_n = \frac{(\Phi/\mu)^n * P_0}{S! * S^{n-S}} \qquad \text{for } n > 3$$

$$P_n = \frac{(\Phi/\mu)^n * P_0}{n!} \qquad \text{for } 0 \leq n \leq 3$$

Thus $\quad P_1 = \quad 25/10 \quad * 0.045 = 0.113$

$$P_2 = \frac{(25/10)^2}{2} * 0.045 = 0.141$$

$$P_3 = \frac{(25/10)^3}{6} * 0.045 = 0.117$$

$$P_4 = \frac{(25/10)^4}{6 * 3} * 0.045 = 0.098$$

$$P_5 = \frac{(25/10)^5}{6 * 9} * 0.045 = 0.081$$

$$P_6 = \frac{(25/10)^6}{6 * 27} * 0.045 = 0.068$$

and so on for increasing values of n (the probability of more than six in the system is about 0.337).

The average number of customers waiting for service is:

$$L_q = \frac{(\Phi/\mu)^S * \Phi * \mu}{(S-1)! * (S * \mu - \Phi)^2} * P_0$$

$$L_q = \frac{(25/10)^3 * 25 * 10}{(3-1)! * (3 * 10 - 25)^2} * 0.045$$

$$= 3.51$$

Average number of customers in the system is:

$L = L_q + \Phi/\mu$

$\quad = 3.51 + 25/10$

$\quad = 6.01$

Average time a customer waits in the queue is:

$W_q = L_q/\Phi$

$\quad = 3.51/25$

$\quad = 0.14$ hours or 8.4 minutes

Average time a customer spends in the system is:

$W = W_q + 1/\mu$

$\quad = 0.14 + 1/10$

$\quad = 0.24$ hours or 14.4 minutes

The calculation for P_0, which is the basis for several of the other figures, can be quite tedious. It is clearly much more difficult to solve problems with multi servers than with a single server. There are two ways to avoid such calculations:

- use a computer to do the arithmetic
- use some other method of solution.

We will illustrate the way in which computers can help with the arithmetic in Section 11.4. The second approach is useful as it allows us to introduce a completely new solution procedure called simulation. This is described later in the chapter.

In summary
Models can be built for queueing systems with many servers but the arithmetic for these can be very tedious. Alternative ways of dealing with this are to use computers or to use a different type of solution procedure.

SELF ASSESSMENT QUESTIONS

11.7 Why might a queueing system have multiple servers?

11.8 Why is the condition $\mu > \Phi$ not used for multi server systems?

(a)
```
                         Input Data of The Problem Server


                                  M/M/1

        Customer arrival rate (lambda)      =    40.000

                          Distribution      :    Poisson

                    Number of servers       =    1

            Service rate per server         =    60.000

                          Distribution      :    Poisson

                    Mean service time        =    0.017  hour

                  Standard deviation         =    0.017  hour

                        Queue limit          =    Infinity

            Customer population              =    Infinity
```

(b)
```
                          Final Solution for Server
                                  M/M/1
        With lambda = 40 customers per hour    and μ = 60 customers per hour

                         Utilization factor (p) =    .6666667
           Average number of customers in the system (L) =    2
           Average number of customers in the queue (Lq) =    1.333333
              Average time a customer in the system (W) =    .05
              Average time a customer in the queue (Wq) =    3.333333E-02
           The probability that all servers are idle (Po)=    .3333333
           The probability an arriving customer waits(Pw)=    .6666667


     P(1) =0.22222   P(2) =0.14815   P(3) =0.09877   P(4) =0.06584   P(5) =0.
     P(6) =0.02926   P(7) =0.01951   P(8) =0.01301   P(9) =0.00867   P(10) =0


                      10
                      Σ   P(i) =0.655106
                      i=1
```

Figure 11.5 Illustrating a typical computer package for queueing theory:
(a) data input; (b) operating characteristics output.

11.4 COMPUTER SOLUTIONS TO QUEUEING PROBLEMS

In practice queueing problems can be very complicated, with different
distributions for arrivals and service times, arrivals rates which vary over
time, interconnected queues, varying availability of servers, and so on.
The models of such systems are often very complicated and difficult to
solve. Fortunately it is fairly easy to develop computer software for some
queueing models and there are a number of packages available. These
allow the descriptions of queues to be specified and the operating
characteristics are calculated automatically. Figure 11.5 illustrates the
input and results from a typical package working with a single server
queue.

(a)
```
              Input Data of The Problem Four Server


                          M/M/4
Customer arrival rate (lambda)      =    60.000
                   Distribution     :    Poisson
          Number of servers         =    4
    Service rate per server         =    20.000
                   Distribution     :    Poisson
          Mean service time         =    0.050   hour
        Standard deviation          =    0.050   hour
                   Queue limit      =    Infinity
        Customer population         =    Infinity
```

(b)
```
                   Final Solution for Four Server

                          M/M/4
  With lambda = 60 customers per hour   and μ = 20 customers per hour

                      Utilization factor (p) =   .75
    Average number of customers in the system (L) =   4.528302
    Average number of customers in the queue (Lq) =   1.528302
       Average time a customer in the system (W) =   7.547171E-02
       Average time a customer in the queue (Wq) =   .0254717
  The probability that all servers are idle (Po)=   3.773585E-02
  The probability an arriving customer waits(Pw)=   .509434

  P(1) =0.11321  P(2) =0.16981  P(3) =0.16981  P(4) =0.12736  P(5) =0.09552
  P(6) =0.07164  P(7) =0.05373  P(8) =0.04030  P(9) =0.03022  P(10) =0.02267

                        10
                        Σ  P(i) =0.894263
                       i=1
```

Figure 11.6 Illustrating a computer package for a multi-server system: (a) data input; (b) operating characteristics output.

The heading 'M/M/1' is a description of the queueing system using a notation devised by Kendall. The two letters show that arrivals and service times are both random (using M for Markovian or random) and there is one server. Figure 11.6 shows a typical output for a multi server system with random arrivals and service time, but four servers (hence the system is described as M/M/4).

Many packages find the operating characteristics for a system and then calculate some financial figures. Typically the costs of providing a server, performing the service, forceing customers to wait and losing custom can be entered and used to calculate total operating costs.

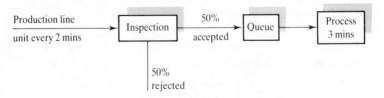

Figure 11.7 A simple system for simulation.

11.5 SIMULATION MODELS

The term 'simulate' is used quite widely (simulate anger, simulated leather, etc.). Here we are going to use it in the same general sense, but specifically referring to the imitation of real situations by quantitative models. We have already described a number of quantitative models, so we might ask what makes simulation models different from these. The essential characteristic of simulation is that it is dynamic and duplicates the continuous operation of a system. An ordinary model of an inventory system looks at the system, collects data for some point and draws conclusions: simulation follows the operations of the system and sees exactly what happens over time. A simple analogy has an ordinary model providing a snapshot of the system at some fixed point, while a simulation model takes a movie of the system.

We will demonstrate this approach with the following illustration (see Figure 11.7). Units move along a production line at a rate of one every two minutes. At some point there is an inspection, which takes virtually no time. At this inspection 50% of units are rejected and the remaining 50% continue along the line to the next process. This process takes three minutes per unit.

We might be interested in answering a number of questions about this system:

- how much space should be left for the queue of units between the inspection and the next process;
- how long will each unit stay in the system;
- what is the utilization of the processor;
- are there any bottlenecks;
- and so on.

The system is essentially a single server queue where all data (including the distribution of arrival times) is known, so a queueing theory model could be used. Unfortunately, as we have already said, queueing theory models soon get complicated and difficult to solve. We would really benefit from finding another approach to such problems. One practical alternative would be to stand and watch the actual system operating over a typical period and see what happens. We could follow a few units through the system and, perhaps, record the information, as in Table 11.1.

Table 11.1

Unit no.	Arrival time	Accept or reject	Time joins queue	No. in queue	Time process starts	Time in queue	Time process finish	Time in system
1	0	A	0	0	0	0	3	3
2	2	A	2	0	3	1	6	4
3	4	A	4	0	6	2	9	5
4	6	R	–	–	–	–	–	–
5	8	R	–	–	–	–	–	–
6	10	A	10	0	10	0	13	3

Here the first unit arrived for inspection at some time which was arbitrarily set to 0. The unit was accepted and moved straight to processing which took three minutes. The total time the unit was in the system (consisting of inspection, queue and processing) was three minutes.

The second unit arrived at time 2 from the arbitrary start time, was accepted and joined the queue (the fifth column shows the number already in the queue when the next customer joins it). Processing could only start on unit 2 when unit 1 was finished at time 3. This processing then took three minutes and unit 2 left the system at time 6.

We could stand and watch the operation for as long as necessary to get a reliable view of its working. The figures collected could then be analysed to give the information needed. Unfortunately, using this approach has a number of disadvantages:

- it is time consuming to stand and watch the process;
- it might take a large number of observations to get reliable figures;
- only one method of operating the production line was observed: comparisons of different methods would each need to be implemented and the observations repeated;
- watching a system is unpopular with people working on it (as well as those doing the observation);
- observing a system might change its characteristics (to return to normal when the observer has left).

These disadvantages could be eliminated using simulation. In essence this imitates the actual process using a simulation model. In the illustration above, for example, we know all its characteristics so a simulation would be aimed at duplicating the sheet of observations without actually standing and watching the process.

There is one element of uncertainty in the system and that is whether a unit is going to be accepted or rejected. We need some method of randomly assigning these decisions to a unit, giving a 50% chance of acceptance and a 50% chance of rejection. An obvious way of doing this would be to spin a coin. If it comes down heads the unit is rejected and if it comes down tails it is accepted (or vice versa). A more formal way of doing the same thing would be to use random numbers. These are strings of digits in random order and might look like:

5284778016941356756454793017714943179046582

Half of these digits are even and half are odd so we could assign rejection and acceptance based on this. When the first unit arrives we could look at the first random digit. If this is even (including 0) the unit would be accepted and if it is odd the unit would be rejected (or vice versa). This is repeated for subsequent units, taking each random digit in turn, and we could develop typical results for the process which might be obtained during some period of inspection. (The idea of using random numbers for sampling has already been mentioned in Chapter 9.)

These decisions can be used to construct a table of 'observations' like that shown above. We would then have simulated the system and got results for a typical period without actually observing its operation.

Table 11.2 can be used to develop simulated data. We can start by giving each unit arriving a unique identifying number (in column 1). Then we know that one unit arrives for inspection every two minutes, so column 2 can be completed. For column 3 we scan the sequence of random digits above. The first is odd so the first unit is rejected. The second, third and fourth digits are even, so the second, third and fourth units are accepted. The fifth digit is odd so the fifth unit is rejected, and so on. This allows column 3 to be completed.

Units which are rejected leave the system, while those which are accepted join the queue at their arrival time (assuming the inspection takes no time). This completes column 4. Column 5 shows the number already in the queue, while column 6 shows the time at which processing starts. If there is already a unit being processed, a queue is formed until the processor becomes free (shown in column 7): if there is no unit being processed work can start immediately (at the time shown in column 4).

Processing finishes three minutes after it starts (shown in column 8) and the time spent in the queue (column 7) is the difference between arrival time and time processing starts. Column 9 shows the total time in the system which is the difference between arrival time and time processing is finished.

Table 11.2 Simulated results for ten units arriving.

1	2	3	4	5	6	7	8	9
Unit no.	Arrival time	Accept or reject	Time joins queue	No. in queue	Time process starts	Time in queue	Time process finish	Time in system
1	0	R	–	–	–	–	–	0
2	2	A	2	0	2	0	5	3
3	4	A	4	0	5	1	8	4
4	6	A	6	0	8	2	11	5
5	8	R	–	–	–	–	–	0
6	10	R	–	–	–	–	–	0
7	12	A	12	0	12	0	15	3
8	14	A	14	0	15	1	18	4
9	16	R	–	–	–	–	–	0
10	18	A	18	0	18	0	21	3

The general rules for calculating each column in Table 11.2 are:

(1) number increases by one for each unit entering;

(2) arrival time increases by two for each unit entering;

(3) a unit is accepted if the corresponding random number is even and rejected if it is odd;

(4) accepted units join the queue straight away (i.e. at arrival time) while rejected ones leave the system;

(5) the number already in the queue is one more than it was for the last arrival, minus the number which have left since the last arrival;

(6) processing starts at the arrival time if the equipment is already free, or when the equipment next becomes free (the previous entry in column 8);

(7) the time in the queue is the difference between the arrival time in the queue and the time processing starts (column 6 − column 4);

(8) processing finishes 3 minutes after it starts (column 6 + 3);

(9) the time in the system is the difference between the arrival time and the finish of the processing (column 8 − column 2).

The simulation has been run for ten units arriving and the figures obtained can be used to give a number of results. To start with we can note that there was at most one unit in the queue for the processor. Also we could find:

- number accepted = 6 (in the long run this would be 50% of units);

- number rejected = 4 (again 50% in the long run);
- maximum time in queue = 2 minutes;
- average time in queue = 4/6 = 40 seconds;
- maximum time in system = 5 minutes;
- average time in system = 22/6 = 3.67 minutes;
- average time in system including rejects = 22/10 = 2.2 mins;
- processor was busy for 18 minutes;
- utilization of processor = 18/21 = 86%.

It is important to ask how reliable these figures are. The simulation certainly demonstrates the working of the system through a typical period of 10 units, but this is a very small number of observations. The current results are not likely to be very accurate, so the next step would be to extend this simulation for a much larger number of observations. When information has been collected about several hundred arrivals we would be fairly confident that the results are reliable. As the process includes a random element we can never be positive that the results are accurate, but large numbers of repetitions should give a reasonable picture. Unfortunately, to repeat the simulation over a large number of observations involves a lot of simple, repetitive arithmetic. This is the kind of process which is ideally suited to computers so most real simulations are done on computers.

WORKED EXAMPLE 11.4

One customer has an appointment at a reception desk (A) every eight minutes. After answering some standard questions, which takes two minutes, they are passed on to one of two areas (B or C). 50% of customers are passed to B for five minutes each and 50% are passed to C for ten minutes each. Finally all customers go to area D when they fill in forms for six minutes before leaving. Simulate this system for ten arrivals and find the utilization of each area.

SOLUTION

The system is shown in the following diagram.

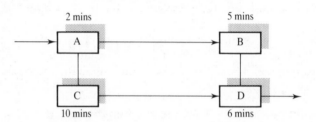

We are only interested in the times spent in each area so we can do the analysis using Table 11.3.

Table 11.3

1	2	3	4	5	6	7	8	9	10
Arrival no.	Start A	Leave A	Random no.	Start B	Leave B	Start C	Leave C	Start D	Leave D
1	0	2	6	–	–	2	12	12	18
2	8	10	4	–	–	12	22	22	28
3	16	18	5	18	23	–	–	28	34
4	24	26	4	–	–	26	36	36	42
5	32	34	7	34	39	–	–	42	48
6	40	42	9	42	47	–	–	48	54
7	48	50	3	50	55	–	–	55	61
8	56	58	0	–	–	58	68	68	74
9	64	66	1	66	71	–	–	74	80
10	72	74	7	74	79	–	–	80	86

Column 1 is the unit number arriving, while column 2 shows an arrival every eight minutes starting from a notional time of zero. Column 3 adds two minutes for processing at A before each customer is ready to move to B or C. The random numbers in column 4 are from the sequence given previously, starting at an arbitrary point about half way along. Units corresponding to odd random digits are sent to area B while those corresponding to even digits are sent to area C. After leaving A a customer can start immediately in areas B or C (if empty) or must wait until the next time their area will become empty (shown in columns 5 and 7). Columns 6 and 8 show the finishing times in areas B and C, found by adding five and ten minutes respectively to the starting times. Column 9 shows the starting time in area D which is either the finishing time in B or C (if D is empty) or the next time D will be empty (if it is busy). Column 10 shows the finish time in area D by adding 6 to the start time.

The utilization of each area can be found from the proportion of time between, say, minutes 20 and 80 when they were busy. These calculations give:

A: $14/60 = 23\%$ B: $28/60 = 47\%$
C: $22/60 = 37\%$ D: $48/60 = 80\%$

These figures are approximations and many more results would be needed before reliable figures are found (25%, 31%, 63% and 75% respectively).

In summary

Simulation provides a way of dynamically modelling problems. The purpose of simulation is to reproduce a typical set of results from operations without actually running the operation. It produces realistic, but artificial results. A major benefit of simulation is that it allows solutions to be found for complex problems.

11.9 What is meant when simulation is described as a 'dynamic' representation?

11.10 Simulation can be used to model complex situations. Is this statement:

(a) true
(b) false
(c) partly true?

11.6 RANDOM SAMPLING IN SIMULATION

The last section illustrated the general approach of simulation using an inspection on a production line. This was a straightforward example which had only one variable which could take two values (acceptance or rejection) with probabilities of 0.5. When more complex problems are tackled we will need more sophisticated ways of giving values to variables. How would a probability of acceptance of 0.6 be dealt with? Most simulation is based on Monte Carlo methods which use random sampling from distributions to assign values to variables. In this section we will look at some aspects of random sampling.

Almost all sampling is based on random numbers (a table of random numbers is given in Appendix E). If, as suggested above, we need a probability of acceptance of 0.6, one way of achieving this would be to use random digits 0 to 5 to represent acceptance and 6 to 9 to represent rejection. Then the string:

528477801694135675645479301771149431790465825

would represent accept, accept, reject, accept, reject and so on.

This approach could be extended to allow sampling from more complex patterns. If 50% of units are accepted, 15% sent for reworking, 20% for reinspection and 15% rejected we might use the following approach.

(a) split the stream of random digits into pairs:

52 84 77 80 16 94 13 56 75 64 54 79 30 17 71 etc.

(b) then let

00 to 49 (i.e. 50% of pairs) represent acceptance

50 to 64 (i.e. 15% of pairs) represent reworking

65 to 84 (i.e. 20% of pairs) represent reinspection

and   85 to 99 (i.e. 15% of pairs) represent rejection.

The stream of random digits would then represent rework, reinspect, reinspect, reinspect, accept and so on. In the long term the proportion of outcomes will be as required, but in the short term there will obviously be random variations. Here three out of the first four will need reinspecting and while there is an temptation to 'adjust' such figures this should not be done. Simulation is based on the principle that a large number of repetitions is needed to show typical figures and these will include fairly unlikely occurrences from time to time.

Such sampling could be extended to more complex forms, including sampling from probability distributions. If the process we are simulating has a Poisson distribution with mean 1.0 the probability of one event is 0.3679. To represent this we could split the stream of random digits into groups of four:

5284 7780 1694 1356 7564 5479 3017 7149 4317 9046 etc.

Then

0000 to 3678 represent 1 event   (probability = 0.3679)

3679 to 7358 represent 2 events   (probability = 0.3679)

7359 to 9196 represent 3 events   (probability = 0.1839)

9197 to 9809 represent 4 events   (probability = 0.0613)

9810 to 9962 represent 5 events   (probability = 0.0153)

9963 to 9993 represent 6 events   (probability = 0.0031)

9994 to 9998 represent 7 events   (probability = 0.0005)

9999   represents 8 events (probability = 0.0001)

Then our random number string would give 2, 3, 1, 1, 3 events and so on.

Sampling from continuous distributions is usually a little more complicated, but there is a straightforward way of sampling from a Normal distribution. For this we need to:

- split the stream of random digits into pairs;
- add twelve of these and subtract 600;
- put a decimal point in front of the result to give a random value selected from a Normal distribution with mean 0 and standard deviation 1;
- translate this to a random value from a Normal distribution with mean μ and standard deviation σ by multiplying the result by σ and add μ.

Using the stream:

52 84 77 80 16 94 13 56 75 64 54 79 30 17 71

Adding the first 12 pairs of numbers gives 744 and subtracting 600 leaves 144. Then 0.144 is a random value from a Normal distribution with mean 0 and standard deviation 1. To find a random value from a Normal distribution with mean 20 and standard deviation 5 calculate:

$$(5 * 0.144) + 20 = 20.72$$

WORKED EXAMPLE 11.5

Use the following stream of random digits to take random samples from:

(a) a Binomial distribution for samples of size six and probability of success equal to 0.25;
(b) a Poisson distribution with mean 1.5;
(c) a Normal distribution with mean 50 and standard deviation 10.

Random digits: 729946601590256421416749445530498

SOLUTION

(a) Binomial tables in Appendix B show the probability of r successes with $n = 6$ and $p = 0.25$ as:

$P(0) = 0.1780 \quad P(1) = 0.3560 \quad P(2) = 0.2966 \quad P(3) = 0.1318$

$P(4) = 0.0330 \quad P(5) = 0.0044 \quad P(6) = 0.0002$

A sampling plan would divide random digits into groups of 4 with:

0000 to 1779 representing 0 successes

1780 to 5339 representing 1 success

5340 to 8305 representing 2 successes

8306 to 9623 representing 3 successes

9624 to 9953 representing 4 successes

9954 to 9997 representing 5 successes

9998 to 9999 representing 6 successes

The string of random digits would give:

Random numbers: 7299 4660 1590 2564 2141 6749 4453 0498

Sample value: 2   1   0   1   1   2   1   0

(b) Poisson tables in Appendix C show the probability of r successes with mean = 1.5 as:

$P(0) \quad = 0.2231 \quad P(1) = 0.3347 \quad P(2) = 0.2510 \quad P(3) = 0.1255$

$P(4) \quad = 0.0471 \quad P(5) = 0.0141 \quad P(6) = 0.0035 \quad P(7) = 0.0008$

$P(>8) = 0.0002$

A sampling plan would divide random digits into groups of 4 with:

0000 to 2230 representing 0 events

2231 to 5577 representing 1 event

5578 to 8087 representing 2 events

8088 to 9342 representing 3 events

9343 to 9813 representing 4 events

9814 to 9954 representing 5 events

9955 to 9989 representing 6 events

9990 to 9997 representing 7 events

9998 to 9999 representing 8 events

The random string of digits would give:

Random numbers: 7299 4660 1590 2564 2141 6749 4453 0498

Sample value: 2   1   0   1   1   2   1   0

(c) To take samples from a Normal distribution requires twelve pairs of random digits. Then, following the procedure described above:

- sum of 72 99 46 60 15 90 25 64 21 41 67 49 = 649
- subtract 600 and put in decimal point gives 0.049
- multiply by 10 (σ) and add 50 (μ) gives 50.49.

WORKED EXAMPLE 11.6

The stock of an item is checked at the beginning of each month and an order is placed so that:

$$\text{order size} = 100 - \text{initial stock}$$

The order is equally likely to arrive at the end of the month in which it is placed or one month later. Demand follows the pattern:

Monthly demand	10	20	30	40	50	60	70
Probability	0.1	0.15	0.25	0.25	0.15	0.05	0.05

Assuming there are 40 units in stock at the beginning of the first month, simulate the system for 10 months and say what values can be calculated from the results.

SOLUTION

The variables are delivery time and demand. Samples for these can be found using the following schemes.

Delivery time:

even random number means delivery in current month

odd random number means delivery in next month

Demand:

demand	10	20	30	40	50	60	70
probability	0.1	0.15	0.25	0.25	0.15	0.05	0.05
random number	00–09	10–24	25–49	50–74	75–89	90–94	95–99

Two streams of random digits were found from tables:

delivery time: 2 5 9 1 0 7 3 8 7 6

demand: 83 50 56 49 37 15 84 52 66 41

Following the system through 10 months gives the results in Table 11.4. In this the stock at the end of a month is found from the initial stock plus arrivals minus demand.

Table 11.4

Month	1	2	3	4	5	6	7	8	9	10
Initial stock	40	50	10	20	80	150	130	80	60	60
Order	60	50	90	80	20	0	0	20	40	40
Arrival RN	2	5	9	1	0	7	3	8	7	6
Arrival month	1	3	4	5	5	7	8	8	9	10
Demand RN	83	50	56	49	37	15	84	52	66	41
Demand size	50	40	40	30	30	20	50	40	40	30
Arrival	60	0	50	90	100	0	0	20	40	40
Closing stock	50	10	20	80	150	130	80	60	60	70
Shortages	0	0	0	0	0	0	0	0	0	0

In month 1 the initial stock is 40, so 60 are ordered. The arrival random number determines that this will arrive in the same month. The demand random number determines a demand of 50 in the month so the closing stock is:

$$\text{closing stock} = \text{initial stock} + \text{arrivals} - \text{demand}$$
$$= 40 + 60 - 50$$
$$= 50$$

There are no shortages and the closing stock is transferred to the opening stock for month 2. These calculations are repeated for the following ten months.

The conclusions from this very limited simulation are not at all reliable. If, however, the simulation is continued for longer, reliable figures could be found for measures such as distribution of opening and closing stock levels (including mean, maximum and minimum), distribution of orders (mean, minimum and maximum), mean demand, shortages and mean lead time. Adding costs to the model would allow a range of other calculations.

WORKED EXAMPLE 11.7

A company is extending its production facilities and wants to know how profitable this will be. Estimates for fixed and variable costs are £60,000 a year and £20 a unit. Production is increased by 5000 units a year and selling price is £35. Unfortunately, the figures are subject to variability and it is felt that normal distributions would be a better description of the values, with standard deviations of £8000 for fixed costs, £3 for variable costs, 500 for production and £5 for selling price. Use simulation to find the distribution of profits.

SOLUTION

The simple solution to this would avoid any variability and say:

Profit = (selling price − variable cost) * number produced − fixed costs

= (35 − 20) * 5000 − 60,000

= £15,000 a year.

This would give a point estimate but give no indication of variability.

The approach using simulation would be to calculate random values from the distributions for each factor and then calculate a profit.

Selling price:

Random numbers 49 57 11 03 65 34 52 13 77 34 86 49

Sum = 530

This leads to a random value from a Normal distribution with mean 0 and standard deviation 1 of −0.070.

Multiplying this by 5 (the standard deviation) and adding 35 (the mean) gives a random value for the selling price of £34.65.

Repeating this calculation for the other three variables, using similar streams of random numbers, gives the following results.

Variable cost:

Random numbers 27 63 25 09 87 91 37 30 77 36 20 43

Sum = 545 to give a decimal of 0.055

Sample value = −0.055 * 3 + 20 = 19.835

Production:

Random numbers 52 28 92 42 09 91 53 93 27 86 60 71

Sum = 704 to give a decimal of 0.104

Sample value = 0.104 * 500 + 5000 = 5052

Fixed cost:

Random numbers 14 49 36 55 19 25 14 16 42 96 64 27

Sum = 457 to give a decimal of −0.143

Sample value = −0.143 * 8000 + 60,000 = 58,856

Substituting these values gives a profit of:

profit = (34.65 − 19.835) * 5052 − 58,856

= £15,989

Repeating this a large number of times would give not only a mean value for expected profits, but also its distribution.

11.11   Why are random numbers used in simulation?

11.12   Random numbers can only be used to give sample values from certain distributions.

Is this statement

(a)   true
(b)   false
(c)   partly true?

11.7   SIMULATION FLOW CHARTS

The examples we have looked at so far are relatively simple and the logic can be followed from tables of simulated values. In more complex problems this would not be possible. Simulation is most useful for complex situations which can not be tackled by any other means. As the models get more complex the benefits of using computers become more obvious and we will assume that almost all real problems are run on computers. This means we need to describe problems clearly so that models can be built and transferred to a computer. For this description we will use simulation flow charts.

The first illustration of simulation was an inspection on a production line.

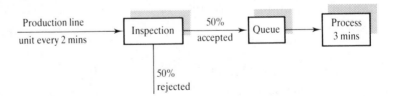

We have already described the logic of the system in the set of instructions needed to calculate each column in a set of simulated data. Another way of viewing this system would be to start a clock and take a series of views of the system at one minute intervals. At time 0 the first unit arrives at the inspector and is rejected. At time 1 nothing happens. At time 2 unit 2 arrives for inspection, is passed and moves on to processing. At time 3 nothing happens. At time 4 unit 3 arrives for inspection and joins the queue of the processor. At time 5 unit 2 finishes processing and leaves the system while unit 3 moves on to processing. The logic behind this approach can be described by the flow diagram in Figure 11.8.

This approach is known as 'next time' simulation where the clock is moved forward one unit (minute in this example) and any changes in the

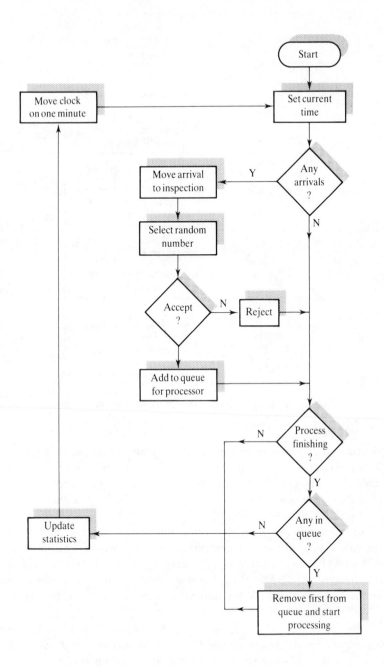

Figure 11.8 Flow chart for production line inspection example.

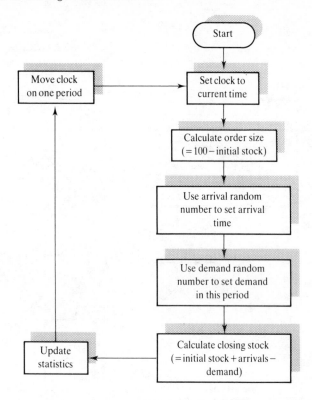

Figure 11.9 Flow chart for Worked example 11.6.

period are noted. Some time can be saved using 'next event' simulation where the clock is moved forward to the next time when something happens. In our example nothing happened in times 1 and 3, so next event simulation would ignore these and move directly to the next time when something actually happens.

Flow diagrams can be built for complex systems and here we will demonstrate a start for one application. Consider worked example 11.6, where the level of inventory was calculated each month. The steps in this simulation were relatively straightforward and could be calculated from the table of observations. We could also describe the logic by the 'next time' flow chart in Figure 11.9.

This initial flow chart could easily be extended to allow for more circumstances. Figure 11.10 shows the same basic chart, but adjusted to allow for a different ordering policy, shortages and costs.

By repeatedly adding more and more parts of the system to the flow chart a complicated model could be developed. This flow chart could then be programmed using an ordinary computer language such as Pascal, FORTRAN or BASIC or using a special purpose simulation language.

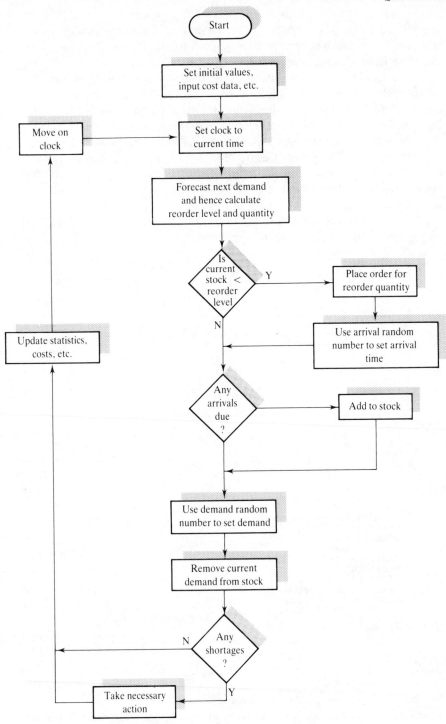

Figure 11.10 Extended flow chart for inventory.

Specialized languages make the development of simulation models quick and easy by including features like random number generation, random sampling from a range of distributions, scheduling routines to keep track of all events occurring in simulated time, diagnostics to check the logic of the model, automatic statistical analysis of results and flexible output report writers. Widely used simulation languages include GPSS (General Purpose Simulation System) developed by IBM in the early 1960s, Simula and Simscript which were developed about the same time by the Norwegian Computing Centre and the Rand Corporation. Other languages which may be met are Slam (simulation language for alternative modelling) and ECSL (extended control and simulation language).

Typical results from a simulation program for the model described in Figure 11.10 are shown in Figure 11.11.

(a)

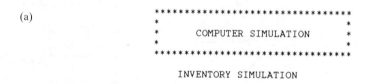

```
**********************************
*                                *
*      COMPUTER SIMULATION       *
*                                *
**********************************
           INVENTORY SIMULATION


PROBLEM:   inventory


HERE IS WHAT YOU ENTERED:

        ORDER QUANTITY AND REORDER POINT          AUTOMATIC
        QUANTITY ORDERED                          210
        REORDER POINT                             900
        SYSTEM PARAMETERS                         USER DEFINED
        CARRYING COST                             1
        ORDERING COST                             75
        STOCKOUT COST                             50
        DEMAND DISTRIBUTION                       UNIFORM
        LOWEST DEMAND VALUE                       100
        HIGHEST DEMAND VALUE                      500
        LEAD TIME                                 VARIABLE
        NUMBER OF PERIODS                         10
        RANDOM NUMBER SEQUENCE                    RANDOM
```

Figure 11.11   (a) Typical input for an inventory simulation; (b) output from the simulation run.

(b)   SYSTEM INFORMATION:

BEGINNING INVENTORY = 1500 UNITS

AVERAGE USE PER PERIOD = 300 UNITS

SIMULATION RESULTS

WEEK	BEGINNING INVENTORY	WEEKLY DEMAND	ENDING INVENTORY	UNITS SHORT
1	1,500	331	1,169	
2	1,169	372	797	

ORDER PLACED FOR 210 UNITS

3	797	229	568	

ORDER PLACED FOR 210 UNITS

4	568	205	363	

ORDER PLACED FOR 210 UNITS

5	363	397	0	34

ORDER PLACED FOR 210 UNITS

6	0	227	0	227

ORDER PLACED FOR 210 UNITS

7	0	215	0	215

ORDER £ 1 RECEIVED AT END OF PERIOD 7 210 UNITS

8	210	326	0	116

ORDER PLACED FOR 210 UNITS

ORDER £ 2 RECEIVED AT END OF PERIOD 8 210 UNITS

9	210	329	0	119

ORDER PLACED FOR 210 UNITS

ORDER £ 3 RECEIVED AT END OF PERIOD 9 210 UNITS

10	210	336	0	126

ORDER PLACED FOR 210 UNITS

ORDER £ 4 RECEIVED AT END OF PERIOD 10 210 UNITS

SIMULATION SUMMARY:

NUMBER OF PERIODS =	10	(weeks)		
AVERAGE INVENTORY =	396.2	(units)	CARRYING COST = $	76.19
ORDERS =	8		ORDERING COST =	600.00
STOCKOUTS =	837.0	(units)	STOCKOUT COST =	41,850.00
AVERAGE DEMAND =	296.7	(units)	TOTAL COST = $	42,526.19
AVERAGE LEAD TIME =	5	(weeks)		

END OF OUTPUT

Figure 11.11 (cont.)

The early simulation languages made writing programs much easier, but they worked as batch jobs. This meant that response time would generally be slow and rerunning the program for small adjustments to the model or data could be time consuming. Interactive models were developed which speeded up this response. Unfortunately the model and results were still essentially represented by tables of results of the type shown earlier. A more useful development came with 'visual interactive simulation' where these tables were replaced by symbols and graphics. Such packages are now widely available and they allow simulation to be a simple, as well as powerful, tool for management.

In summary

We can use the following steps in solving a problem by simulation:

- initial observation of the system, identification of major elements, measurement of parameters;
- detailed description of the system, probably in terms of a logic flow diagram;
- more detailed observation of the system to find distributions for variables and any details needed for the model;
- develop a program for the simulation and run this enough times to get reliable results;
- analyse the results of the simulation and test these for accuracy and reliability;
- make any adjustments necessary to the model and rerun it if necessary;
- draw conclusions and present them.

SELF ASSESSMENT QUESTIONS

11.13 Why are flow charts used to represent simulation models?

11.14 There is only one correct flow chart for a given situation. Is this statement:

(a)   true
(b)   false
(c)   partly true?

CONCLUSIONS

Queues occur widely in a number of circumstances. This chapter described some aspects of queueing theory which analyses the operations of queues. It started by discussing the general characteristics of queues and the need to balance the quality of service offered with its cost.

A model was developed for a single server queue where both arrivals and service times were random. Operating characteristics were developed, including measures for average queue lengths and times.

Unfortunately, analytical solutions to queueing problems are complex and are generally limited to simple situations. In this chapter these approaches were illustrated by single server and multi server queues where both arrivals and service times are randomly distributed.

A more robust method of tackling complex queueing problems is simulation. The general approach of simulation is to imitate typical operations of a system by duplicating them rather than direct observation. Simulation is widely used and can tackle many problems which are too complex to consider by other means. A means of describing the logic of simulation models is to use a flow chart.

Simulations can be complex and involve large amounts of computation, so computers will almost inevitably be used in practice. Visual interactive simulation allows models to be developed efficiently.

PROBLEMS

11.1   Describe the operating characteristics of a single server queue where arrivals are random at an average rate of 100 an hour and service time is random at an average rate of 120 an hour.

11.2   Describe the operating characteristics of a queueing system with one queue and five servers if arrivals are random at an average rate of 100 an hour and service time is randomly distributed with a mean of two minutes.

11.3   Confirm the results shown in Figures 11.5 and 11.6.

11.4   A self employed plumber offers a 24-hour emergency service to deal with burst pipes. For most of the year calls arrive randomly at a rate of six a day. The time he takes to travel to a call and do the repair is randomly distributed with a mean of 90 minutes. Forecasts for February suggest weather will be cold and last time this happened emergency calls came in at a rate of 18 a day. Because of repeat business, the plumber is anxious not to lose a customer and wants average waiting time to be no longer in February than during a normal month. How many assistants should he employ to achieve this?

11.5 Use random digits to take samples from:

(a) a Binomial distribution for samples of size eight and probability of success equal to 0.3

(b) a Poisson distribution with mean 2.0

(c) a Normal distribution with mean 1500 and standard deviation 125.

11.6 Customers arrive randomly at server A at a mean rate of 12 an hour. Service time is normally distributed with mean four minutes and standard deviation 1.25 minutes. After finishing with server A the customers are interviewed (which takes three minutes) and then 60% are passed to server B, 30% leave the system and 10% are returned to server A. Service time at server B is normally distributed with mean seven minutes and standard deviation two minutes. After finishing with server B customers are again interviewed (which takes three minutes) and then 85% leave the system, 10% are returned to server B and 5% are returned to server A. Simulate this system and develop a table of typical observations.

11.7 Draw a flow chart for the system described in problem 11.6.

CASE STUDY – CITY ASSISTANCE

Jim Peters left university with a law degree and joined an international oil company. There he met David Bryant who had recently finished training to be a chartered accountant. Two years ago they became involved in a charity fair where they ran a 'business advice stall'. Anyone with a small business problem could pay £1 and get some instant advice. This stall proved remarkably successful and at the end of the fair they had talked briefly to over 300 people.

A month after the fair a local businessman's club offered a small payment if the pair would give four evening sessions of the same kind. Club members could ask any question related to the running of their business, provided an answer could be given in about ten minutes. Large numbers turned up for these sessions, most of whom were self-employed or were employed by small companies which lacked expertise in some areas. The questions often concerned basic information about taxes, contracts, finances, liabilities and so on.

These evening engagements were repeated several times. They became so successful, and requests for follow up advice so time consuming, that Jim Peters and David Bryant decided to leave their company and found 'City Assistance'. For the past six months this has operated from a shop near the commercial centre of the city. The clientele has widened a little, but is still mainly businessmen with a small problem who ask for advice on a very informal basis. Typically the owner of a small company might receive a letter about Value Added Tax and will drop in to ask what the letter means and what is the best way to reply. A manager might have a letter from a dissatisfied customer and could drop into City Assistance for a few words of cheap, friendly and reliable advice.

The shop has an initial queue at a receptionist. This queue must be short or potential customers are discouraged and will go elsewhere for advice. The receptionist talks to the customer for a few minutes, decides who can best answer their question and passes them either to Jim Peters for legal questions, David Bryant for financial questions or both of them together for more complicated problems. A third consultant was hired to answer general management questions and he always works alone.

Ordinarily the office is quiet, but there are periods when business is brisk and fairly long queues form. Many people leave when there is an obvious queue, but others stay and wait their turn.

City Assistance are keen to make the business a success. Although they feel optimistic about the future they have little data about the company, except a feeling that business will increase about 30% in the next six months and a further 50% in the following year. To cope with this they are thinking of making changes to the structure of the shop. Their current idea is to reduce the size of reception areas and free space for other employees to increase overall capacity.

To get some feeling for the numbers involved everyone in the company was asked to keep a log of their activities during one typical week. Although there is no way of knowing how applicable these figures will be in the future they can form the basis of some reasoned ideas. The company wants a robust operation which can adjust to changing circumstances. In particular, if the business grows new employees should be fitted to provide the best service possible.

Summary of data collected during trial week

General

The shop is open from 8.30 in the morning to 4.30 in the afternoon. No appointments are accepted, and if follow-up meetings are needed these must be outside normal working hours. The emphasis is on providing a quick, efficient service for people who can walk in off the street.

The shop consists of a reception area with a single queue at the receptionist. There is plenty of space here, but easy chairs are only provided for four people. Leading from the reception area are four waiting lounges for finance, law, joint finance and law and general questions. Each of these provides free coffee and snacks and can comfortably seat 20 people. An office leads from each lounge.

Receptionist

Arrivals come randomly at a mean rate of 22 an hour. The time spent with each customer is randomly distributed with mean of three minutes. None of the customers who came in stayed if there were more than three already in the queue, and only half of those who came in stayed when the queue was three long. 40% of those who stayed were directed to the finance lounge, 20% to the law lounge, 10% to the joint finance and law lounge and 30% to the general lounge.

Finance office

The time spent with a customer is randomly distributed with a mean of 10 minutes. 10% of customers pose problems which are broader than finance alone and a joint meeting with law is arranged. These happen when the current customer leaves the law office. Although there is enough space for 20 customers to queue, 60% of those who are passed to the lounge leave if there are already four people queueing, and no one stays if there are already five in the queue.

Law office

The time spent with a customer is randomly distributed with a mean of 15 minutes. 20% of customers arriving are referred to joint meetings with finance. These happen when the current customer leaves the finance office. 40% of customers passed into the law lounge leave if there are already three people waiting, while no one stays if there are already four people in the queue.

Joint finance and law meetings

If either the finance or law office arrange these visits the duration is randomly distributed with a mean of 15 minutes. If meetings are arranged directly by the receptionist the duration is randomly distributed with a mean of 20 minutes. The priority of these customers is a little vague, but the aim is that they should not be kept waiting for more than 20 minutes. If either office becomes free they start talking to the customer and the meeting starts in earnest next time the other office is free. There is only a 10% chance that customers for joint meetings will wait if there are two other customers in the queue, and no chance of them waiting if there are three customers in the queue.

General office

The duration of these meetings is randomly distributed with a mean of 20 minutes. 10% of customers are redirected to the law office and 15% to the finance office. Only 10% of customers wait if there are already three customers in the queue, and none wait if there are four in the queue.

Suggested questions

- What factors might affect the volume of custom to City Assistance?
- Are there any reasons for dramatic changes in custom?

- Does the present organization seem reasonable?
- Are there any bottlenecks in the system?
- What changes might be made to the layout of the shop?
- What are the utilizations of each consultant?
- Are present staff levels satisfactory?
- How might future staff levels be set to meet expected demands?
- How much custom is being lost because of queues?
- Is it possible to estimate cost for the operation?

SOLUTIONS TO SELF ASSESSMENT QUESTIONS

11.1 Customers wanting a service and a server who is busy at some times, forcing the customer to wait.

11.2 (c) partly true. It is usually undesirable to make customers wait, but a balance is needed between large numbers of servers and high costs.

11.3 Φ is the average arrival rate and μ is the average service rate.

11.4 Customers arrive faster than they are served and the queue continues to grow.

11.5 Assumptions include: a single server, random arrivals, random service time, first come first served service discipline, the system has reached its steady state, there is no limit to the number of customers allowed in the queue, there is no limit on the number of customers who use the service and all customers wait until they are served.

11.6 The main operating characteristics of a queue are:

- probability the system is empty, P_0
- probability there are n customers in the system, P_n
- average number of customers in the system, L
- average number of customers in the queue, L_q
- average time spent in the system, W
- average time spent in the queue, W_q

11.7 Because the queue length would be too long with a single server. If the queue length is too long the only other alternative would be to reduce service time, but this could reduce customer service.

11.8 μ is the service rate for each server, so the system can be in equilibrium if $S * \mu > \Phi$.

11.9 Ordinary quantitative analyses describe a problem at some point of time and build a model accordingly. Simulation models follow the operation of a process over time.

11.10 (a) true. Simulation can be used to model very complex situations which could not be tackled by any other means. Complex systems of queues are one example of these.

11.11 To give typical (i.e. random) values to variables. Many other methods could be used for assigning random values, but random numbers are reliable, convenient, easy and cheap.

11.12 (b) false. Random numbers can be used to assign random values from any distribution.

11.13 To allow the logic of complex models to be followed. They also allow easy translation for computer use.

11.14 (b) false. There could be a number of different flow charts which describe the same situation, with different levels of detail, assumptions and so on.

REFERENCES FOR FURTHER READING

Banks J. and Carson J.S. (1984). *Discrete-Event Simulation* New Jersey: Prentice-Hall

Cooper R.B. (1972). *Introduction to Queueing Theory* New York: Macmillan

Cox D.R. and Smith W.L. (1971). *Queues* London: Methuen

Gordon G. (1978). *System Simulation* New Jersey: Prentice-Hall

Gross D. and Harris C.M. (1974). *Fundamentals of Queueing Theory* New York: John Wiley

Law A.M. and Kelton W.D. (1982). *Simulation Modelling and Analysis* New York: McGraw Hill

Lee A.M. (1966). *Applied Queueing Theory* London: Macmillan

Newell G.F. (1971). *Applications of Queueing Theory* London: Chapman & Hall

Payne J.A. (1982). *Introduction to Simulation: programming techniques and methods of analysis* New York: McGraw-Hill

Shannon R.E. (1975). *Systems Simulation* New Jersey: Prentice-Hall

Solomon S.L. (1983). *Simulation of Waiting-Line Systems* New Jersey: Prentice-Hall

Watson H.J. (1981). *Computer Simulation in Business* New York: John Wiley

White J.A., Schmidt J.W. and Bennett G.K. (1975). *Analysis of Queueing Systems* New York: Academic Press

Chapter 12

Review

12.1 AIMS

This is the last chapter of this book and it has several aims. Firstly, it gives a very brief review of earlier chapters and describes the links between them. Secondly, it mentions some points on implementation, and thirdly, it suggests some current developments which show future directions for management science.

12.2 A BRIEF REVIEW OF CHAPTERS

This book tries to give a balanced view of management science. It concentrates on quantitative models, but steers clear of mathematical complexity. The purpose of this is to introduce a range of ideas which has proved useful to management and is in common use.

These ideas are developed in a logical sequence. In particular, the book falls into two parts. The first seven chapters are limited to deterministic models. Many people find statistical ideas difficult to understand, so these are introduced in Chapters 8 to 11.

Chapters 1 to 7 – deterministic
Chapters 8 to 11 – probabilistic

Chapter 1 introduces the ideas of management science by defining the term and summarizing its aims. It is suggested that the methods of science can be used to tackle a variety of problems met by management. The emphasis of the book is on the use of quantitative models. The development of such models and their implementations can be viewed as a management science project for which a methodology is described.

Such methodologies give guidelines but are only an approximation to the steps actually taken. Cynics have exaggerated the differences to suggest stages in a project along the lines of:

(1) search for a project we can understand
(2) total confusion with the details
(3) wild enthusiasm
(4) disillusionment
(5) denial of responsibility
(6) reward of those not connected with the project.

Although this is meant as a comic parody, there are familiarities with badly planned and executed studies. Perhaps we should look on it as a list of things to avoid.

Chapter 2 expands the use of quantitative models by illustrating a number of areas where they are useful. It starts with a break even analysis. This is directly related to measures of capacity and utilization, which in turn are related to financial figures such as discounted cash flows. The chapter ends with a look at some replacement and scoring models.

The next five chapters examine specific areas in more detail. Chapter 3 looks at models for controlling stocks. The characteristics of inventories are described, followed by calculations for optimal order sizes in different circumstances. A second approach uses materials requirement planning which can be extended to just-in-time systems. One useful tip for practical stock control is to visit the warehouse and look for untidiness or dirt. These are symptoms of poor organization and show immediately where improvements can be made.

Efficient stock control depends on reliable forecasts of future demand. Various methods of forecasting are described in Chapter 4, including judgemental, projective and causal. Although forecasts are of central importance to almost all decisions, they are notoriously unreliable. This is partly due to the reliance on historic data which may not be valid in the future. An analogy can be drawn between basing decisions for the future on historic data, and driving a car by looking in the rear view mirror.

Many self-contained studies can be described as projects, and network analysis can help with their organization. This technique is described in Chapter 5. Assigning scarce resources to projects is an example of constrained optimization which can be tackled by linear programming. Chapter 6 describes the characteristics of linear programmes and solution methods. The chapter assumes that computers will be used for real problems and discusses the output from standard packages. Chapter 7 continues the theme of scheduling by describing a number of sequencing, scheduling and routing problems. These form a set of problems which occur very commonly, but are notoriously difficult to solve. Even apparently simple problems, like finding the minimum distance which can be travelled by a set of delivery vehicles, have not yet been solved.

The ideas discussed so far have been deterministic, with variables having finite values. The rest of the book considers stochastic models where probabilities are assigned to values. Chapter 8 lays the foundation for this by discussing some statistical ideas, including data description, probabilities and probability distributions.

Chapter 9 is similar in tone to Chapter 2, using a number of models to illustrate a general approach. The chapter extends some models mentioned previously and then discusses sampling and hypothesis testing.

Chapter 10 looks at decision analysis. This is concerned with the way in which decisions can be made in complex circumstances, particularly in situations of certainty, uncertainty and risk. One of the difficulties with any decision making is that decision makers do not necessarily act in a 'rational' way. One illustration of this is the 'voter's paradox', based on an apparently irrational preference for candidates from three different political parties. In this a person may prefer candidate A to B, candidate B to C, and yet still prefer candidate C to A.

Chapter 11 looks at queueing theory models. Unfortunately, these are very complicated and it is easier to use a different method of solution. The characteristic approach of Monte Carlo simulation is described.

We have described a number of different problem areas, and perhaps this is an appropriate time to mention some points about implementation.

12.3 IMPLEMENTATION OF MANAGEMENT SCIENCE

This book has aimed at showing how the rational analyses of science can be used for a variety of management problems. We have deliberately avoided a long discussion about the meaning of 'science' and have simply assumed that it allows a logical analysis of problems and suggests rational solutions.

It may be argued that people do not act rationally, as illustrated by the voter's paradox mentioned above. There are many circumstances where problems of this type could arise. What happens if the logical solution is for a decision maker to resign and make way for his more able replacement? Would the owners of a company like to maximize its profits if it meant them working 112 hours a week all year round? Is it better to spend government money on nuclear arms or health service? What would a politician's reaction be if they were told the good of their constituents would be served best by a member of the opposing party? Such questions begin to illustrate some of the problems in making real decisions. Situations are complex, constraints are varied and objectives are unclear.

Nonetheless there are considerable benefits to be gained by overcoming such problems and implementing rational policies. No organization deliberately set out to act irrationally, so the use of management science may depend on successful marketing within an organization. Perhaps this starts by creating a successful 'image' of management science as a means of improving the efficiency and effectiveness of operations.

Throughout this book we have examined ways in which numerical models can tackle management problems. In particular, we have concentrated on applications rather than theory: formal mathematical proofs have been avoided and models are described by examples rather than theoretical argument. Nonetheless, some people have the idea that management science is inevitably highly mathematical. This can make implementing solutions more difficult. Nobody likes working with things they do not understand, and a well known maxim says: 'I would rather live with a problem I understand than a solution I don't'.

We can disprove the theory that management science always uses complex mathematics by a couple of trivial examples.

WORKED EXAMPLE 12.1

A family of three is having steak for dinner. The steaks will be grilled for an average of 10 minutes on each side. Unfortunately, their grill pan is only big enough to grill two steaks at once. This means that cooking takes a total of 40 minutes, and two members of the family can start their steaks 20 minutes before the third member's is cooked. How might this arrangement be improved?

SOLUTION

There are three steaks each with two sides, so we can label the steaks A, B and C and the sides 1 and 2. The family obviously adopts the usual practice of:

- cooking the first sides of two steaks
- turning these over and cooking the second sides
- eating these while the first side of the third steak is cooking
- turning the third steak and cooking its second side.

This can be described by the time-table:

time 0 to 10 minutes cook $A1$ and $B1$

time 10 to 20 minutes cook $A2$ and $B2$

time 20 to 30 minutes cook $C1$

time 30 to 40 minutes cook $C2$

A simple model would suggest there are three steaks or six sides. Two sides can be grilled at once, so there are $6/2 = 3$ cooking sessions of 10 minutes each. This can be achieved with the time-table:

time 0 to 10 minutes cook $A1$ and $B1$

time 10 to 20 minutes cook $A2$ and $C1$

time 20 to 30 minutes cook $B2$ and $C2$

This arrangement has the advantages of taking a total of 30 minutes cooking and having one family member starting to eat only ten minutes before the other two.

WORKED EXAMPLE 12.2

A tennis tournament has all entrants playing in the first round. Those that win in the first round move on to the second round where they play again, and so on. Players are progressively eliminated until there are four in the semi-finals, two in the finals and one who becomes the overall winner. This year 369 people applied to take part in the tournament. This gives 184 matches in the first round, with one player given a 'bye' to the second round. Then there are 92 games in the second round with one 'bye', and so on. How many games have to be organized in total?

SOLUTION

To answer this we do not have to add 184 to 92 and so on, but can concentrate on the structure of the tournament. 369 players take part, each of these loses once, except the player who becomes overall winner. Then 368 players lose: each game has one loser, so there must be 368 games in total.

Often a problem can be tackled without any calculation at all. One famous study concerned people working in a tall office block who complained about the time they waited for lifts. Some simple data collection showed that average waiting time was only a minute or two, but this was enough for people to become bored. Efforts could be made to speed-up the lifts, but this ignored the underlying problem which was not that the lifts were slow, but that people became bored waiting for them. The solution was to fit mirrors and other distractions in the waiting area. This was cheap and reduced the complaints substantially.

We have implicitly described two possible difficulties in implementing management science. The first is a belief that its is overly mathematical, and the second arises because managers who do not understand the methods will avoid using the results. Several other difficulties may exist and typically these centre around:

- resistance to change,
- shortage of time to perform analyses,
- lack of data needed for analyses,
- simplifications and assumptions necessary in models.

Listing these problem areas is not meant to imply that management science is inevitably difficult to implement. Organizations are successfully implementing results from management science studies all the time. In an increasingly competitive environment organizations see management science as a means of gaining a lead over competitors, or even surviving. The difficulties are listed to show the kind of problem which may be faced and the areas where caution is needed. Everybody in an organization should be concerned with its efficient operation, and if a management scientist presents a solution to a problem in the right way it should be enthusiastically received. If it is not, there may be faults in either the analyses or their presentation.

A more detailed survey by Watson and Marett ranks the following ten problem areas:

- difficulties of selling management science techniques to management;
- top and middle management do not have the educational background to appreciate management science;
- there is not enough reliable data;
- there is not enough time to analyse a problem properly;
- those who use the results do not understand where they come from;
- it is hard to define problems exactly;
- less complicated methods may be used to give acceptable results;
- there are not enough people to do the necessary analyses;
- management scientists may have a poor reputation as problem solvers;
- people feel threatened by management scientists and their methods.

Again, we should emphasize that these difficulties are listed to show areas where special attention is needed rather than reasons why management science may be difficult to implement. With proper planning and communications management science can have a profound effect on the efficiency and effectiveness of an organization.

12.4 THE FUTURE OF MANAGEMENT SCIENCE

Management science has been studied, under different names, for many years. It had a surge of popularity in the 1940s with the development of Operational Research, but has become much more widely used since the 1960s. This is partly due to the development of better models, but is primarily due to the almost universal availability of computers. Originally, computers were thought of as calculating machines which allowed more complex mathematical models to be solved in a usefully short time. Soon they were being used to store virtually limitless amounts of information and could provide reliable data for quantitative models. At this stage the combination of data availability and arithmetic processing meant that management science could make a real contribution to the running of organizations.

As computer power increased it was possible to integrate the flows of data in an organization into a consolidated management information system. The purpose of these was to collect and analyse data so that it was available to management to enable them to make informed decisions. Part of this process could include the use of management science models.

More recently, management information systems have developed into decision support systems, where managers become integral parts of a system which works interactively to arrive at decisions. A core element of such systems is an interactive facility where managers ask 'what would be the effect of making this decision?' and management science models feed back the results. These approaches are expanding in many areas including expert systems and artificial intelligence.

These brief comments imply there are four directions in which management science is moving.

- Existing management science models and techniques are being used by a wider set of organizations. This is due in part to a wider awareness of the subject, and in part to the increased availability of computers.

- New techniques are being developed to tackle a wide range of new problems.

- Many existing models are considered 'theoretical' as they are too complex for use. Developments in computing are allowing these to be introduced for tackling real problems.

- As decision support systems develop, management science models have a more central part in the decision making of organizations.

These trends can be observed now, and will continue for the foreseeable future. This ensures management science will continue its growth in scope and impact.

CONCLUSION

This book gives an introduction to management science. We have concentrated on quantitative models, and in particular those models which are of practical importance. In this chapter we have made some comments about the implementation of results, and suggested that this must be done carefully. The end result will be an organization with improved efficiency, and one which can cope with an increasingly competitive environment.

Management science is already having a profound effect on the way in which organizations operate. We have suggested that the subject is growing and is likely to have an increasing impact in the future. Developments of various kinds show that management science has considerable potential and will allow future operations to be more effective and efficient. The consequent increase in prosperity and well-being should affect us all and improve our expected 'quality of life'. This seems an appropriately optimistic note on which to end.

REFERENCES FOR FURTHER READING

Alter S.L. (1980). *Decision Support Systems: current practices and continuing challenges* Reading: Addison-Wesley

Bennett J.L. (1983). *Building Decision Support Systems* Reading: Addison-Wesley

Gaither N. (1975). The adoption of operations research techniques by manufacturing organisations *Decision Sciences* **6**, 797–813

Gupta J.N.D. (1977). Management science implementations: experiences of a practicing O.R. manager *Interfaces* **7**, 84–90

Keen P.G.W. and Scott Morton M.S. (1978). *Decision Support Systems: an organizational perspective* Reading: Addison-Wesley

Kroeber D.W. and Watson H.J. (1984). *Computer-based Information Systems* New York: Macmillan

Schultz R.L. and Slevin D.P. (1975). *Implementing Operations Research/Management Science* New York: Elsevier

Watson H.J. and Marett P.G. (1979). A survey of management science implementation problems *Interfaces* **4**, 124–128

Wysocki R.K. (1979). OR/MS implementation research: a bibliography *Interfaces* **9**, 37–41

Appendix A

Basic quantitative methods

This book describes some methods of management science, emphasizing the development of quantitative models. It is not a book on mathematics and does not get bogged down in the details of proofs and analyses. Concepts are demonstrated through examples rather than rigorous derivation of results and a high level of mathematical ability is not required.

Nonetheless, some numerical skills are assumed. As students of management science come from a number of different backgrounds it would be wrong to assume they have a common body of mathematical knowledge. The aim of this appendix is to describe briefly some mathematical techniques which are used in the rest of the book. If you have difficulties with these, you might be advised to refer to a more detailed text, some of which are listed at the end of this Appendix.

NUMBERS, VARIABLES AND ARITHMETIC OPERATIONS

The main assumption in this book is that you are familiar with basic arithmetic operations and can do simple calculations accurately. As calculators and computers are widely available we will assume that arithmetic need not be done by hand.

It is also assumed that you have no problems with fractions, decimals and percentages. If a company made a net profit of £12 million last year and £3 million of this came from overseas, we could make the equivalent statements:

- fraction of profit from overseas = 3/12 = 1/4
- proportion of profit from overseas = 0.25
- percentage of profit from overseas = 25%

Such calculations can be extended to more complex arithmetic. The total income from selling an item, is calculated as the number of units sold multiplied by the price charged for each unit.

total income = number of units sold times price per unit.

This equation could be abbreviated to:

$$I = np$$

where:

I = total income

n = number of units sold

p = price per unit

If p keeps the same value during the period we are interested in, it is called a constant: if the values of I and n can change they are called variables. Equations and arithmetic expressions show the relationships between constants and variables.

There are several different ways of describing the calculation above. Computers are now widely used and this has an effect on the way equations are stated. In particular:

- longer, meaningful names are given to variables;
- arithmetic operators are always given explicitly;
- equations are often put on a single line;
- nested parentheses are used to clarify logic;
- upper case (capital) letters are used more frequently;
- Greek symbols and subscripts are avoided.

Using these conventions the equation above could equally be written as:

INCOME = NUMBER * PRICE

or   INC = NUMB * PRIC

or   I = N * P

The last of these is the compromise used in this book, where variables are generally given names of one or two upper case letters. Arithmetic operators for multiplication (*), division (/), addition (+) and subtraction (−) are always given explicitly and implicit multiplication is avoided. Then:

$$A(I + 10P) \text{ is written as } A * (I + 10 * P).$$

Sometimes the result is a bit longer than necessary, but the logic should be clearer. Any possible ambiguity is removed by parentheses or brackets. Then, the order for evaluating expressions is:

(1) things inside brackets
(2) raising to powers
(3) multiplication and division
(4) addition and subtraction.

Subscripts are largely avoided by using descriptors in parentheses. Then, the subscripted variable I_n is written as $I(n)$. (Note that lower case letters are used for descriptors.)

Some of these points are illustrated by the following alternative representations.

$y = ax + b$	becomes $Y = A * X + B$
$y = a_0 + a_1x_1 + a_2x_2$	becomes $Y = A(0) + A(1) * X(1) + A(2) * X(2)$
$r = \dfrac{p^2 q}{s}$	becomes $R = (P^2 * Q)/S$
$x_{n+1} = 0.1x_n + 0.9y_n$	becomes $X(n + 1) = 0.1 * X(n) + 0.9 * Y(n)$
$Z = \dfrac{3x^{a+b} + (p + q)^3}{7(x + 1)^{c-1}}$	becomes $Z = \dfrac{3 * X^{(A+B)} + (P + Q)^3}{7 * (X + 1)^{(C-1)}}$

OTHER NOTATION

We have described the conventions used for variables, arithmetic operators and expressions. A few other conventions are used in this book.

Usually numbers are represented as integers (which do not have decimal points) or real numbers (which do have decimal points). Thus 7 and 128 are integers while 10.2 and 147.803 are real numbers. There is no general rule for the number of decimal places which should be used for real numbers, but two points can be mentioned.

- Only use the number of decimal places which is useful. Avoid answers like £120.34782659 and quote the figure as £120.35, or even £120.

- Results from calculations are only as accurate as the data used. When multiplying a forecast average demand of 32.63 units by a forecast cost per unit of £17.19 we should not describe the projected total cost as £560.9097. A more reasonable answer would be £560.91 or even £561.

For clarity, long numbers (those over four digits) are divided into groups of three digits by commas (for example 1,247,822). For very large or very small numbers it is more convenient to represent them as a number between 0 and 10 multiplied by the appropriate number of tens. Thus:

1200 could be represented as $1.2 * 10^3$.

1,380,197.892 as about $1.38 * 10^6$

0.00000429 as $4.29 * 10^{-6}$

In this notation 10^3 means 10 multiplied by itself three times (i.e. 1000) and 10^6 means 10 multiplied by itself six times (i.e. 1,000,000). 10^{-1} means 1/10 and 10^{-6} means $1/10^6$.

A value followed by an exclamation mark, such as $B!$, is 'B factorial' which is equal to:

$$B! = B * (B - 1) * (B - 2) * (B - 3) \ldots \ldots * 4 * 3 * 2 * 1$$

Thus

$$4! = 4 * 3 * 2 * 1 = 24$$
$$8! = 8 * 7 * 6 * 5 * 4 * 3 * 2 * 1 = 40,320$$

By convention 0! is defined as 1.

A few standard functions are used in the book. These are commonly used calculations which can be easily abbreviated. The minimum of a set of numbers A, B, C, ... is described as:

MIN[A, B, C, . . .]

Then:

MIN[10, 15, 20, 25] is 10

MIN[1.54, 3.28, 19.42, 0.53, 2.19] is 0.53

Conversely the maximum of a set of numbers A, B, C,. . . . is written as:

MAX[A, B, C, . . .]

Then:

MAX[10, 15, 20, 25] is 25

MAX[1.54, 3.28, 19.42, 0.53, 2.19] is 19.42

Another standard function is the absolute value of a number. This simply ignores negative signs and takes the positive value.

ABS[1.4]   = 1.4

ABS[−1.4] = 1.4

ABS[−15] = 15

etc.

GRAPHS AND DIAGRAMS

Some people are able to follow numerical arguments by looking at the equations and expressions. Most, however, find it easier to draw some kind of diagram. Management science uses diagrams of many different types, but perhaps the most common are graphs. There are many kinds of graph, but the most widely used has rectangular axes with the vertical scale (Y) representing the dependent variable and the horizontal (X) the independent one (see Figure A1).

Using, for example, the equation $I = 10 * N$, N is the independent variable which can take any value and I is the dependent one whose value is fixed by N. This can be represented by the graph in Figure A2.

This is a specific example of a linear relationship:

$$Y = A * X + B$$

where:

A is the gradient or slope of the line and

B is the intercept or point where the line crosses the Y axis.

This is illustrated in Figure A3.

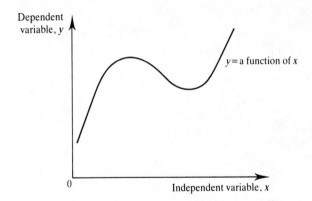

Figure A1 General graph of Y against X.

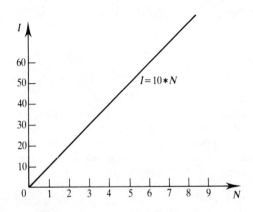

Figure A2 Graph of $I = 10 * N$.

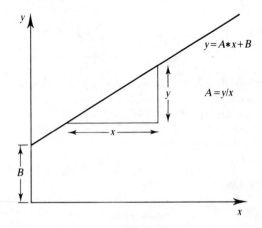

Figure A3 Graph of $Y = A * X + B$ (A = gradient y/x, B = intercept).

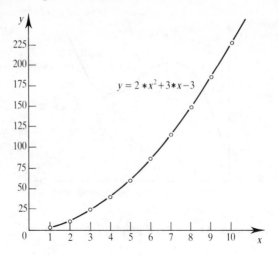

Figure A4   Graph of $Y = 2 * X^2 + 3 * X - 3$.

The easiest way to draw such graphs is to take a series of convenient values for the independent variable and substitute these into the equation to find corresponding values for the dependent variable. This gives a series of points for (X, Y) which can be plotted and a line drawn to join them. Straight line graphs need only two such points, but more complex functions need more.

To illustrate this approach we can draw the graph of $Y = 2 * X^2 + 3 * X - 3$. The shape of this graph is not obvious, but if we are interested in values of Y for X between 1 and 10 we could calculate the following coordinates by substitution. When $X = 1$, $Y = 2 * 1^2 + 3 * 1 - 3 = 2$, etc.

X	1	2	3	4	5	6	7	8	9	10
Y	2	11	24	41	62	87	116	149	186	227

When these points are plotted on rectangular axes and joined together the graph in Figure A4 is given.

Graphs of this type are called 'line graphs'. Other common forms of graph are scatter diagrams, histograms, horizontal bar charts and pie charts, examples of which are given in Figure A5.

SOLVING EQUATIONS

If an equation has only one variable whose value is to be found, the equation can be manipulated until the variable is on one side of the equals sign and everything else is on the other side. So:

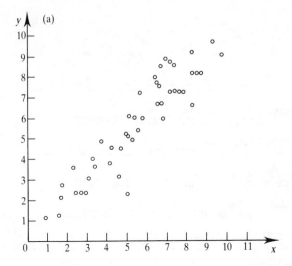

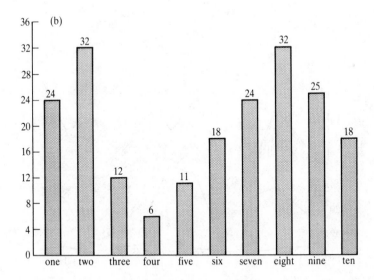

Figure A5 Graphical representation of data: (a) scatter diagram; (b) vertical bar chart or histogram; (c) horizontal bar charts; (d) superimposed line graphs; (e) pie chart.

(c)

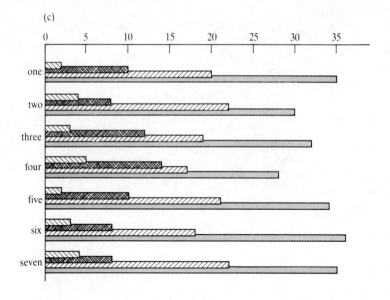

(d)

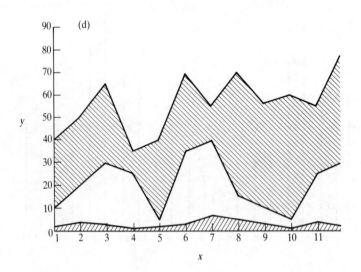

Figure A5 (cont.)

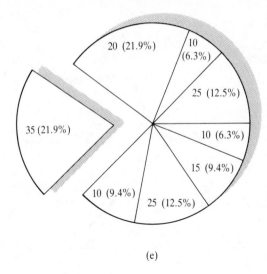

20 (21.9%)

10 (6.3%)

25 (12.5%)

35 (21.9%)

10 (6.3%)

15 (9.4%)

10 (9.4%)

25 (12.5%)

(e)

Figure A5 (cont.)

$$5 * X - 10 = X - 2$$

is solved by moving all the terms of X to the left hand side of the equals sign and all other terms to the right.

$$5 * X - X = 10 - 2$$

or $4 * X = 8$

or $X = 2$

In general, if we want to find values for n variables we must have n independent equations relating them. In the above illustration there was only one variable, X, so we could find this using one equation. A useful extension has two unknown variables and therefore needs two simultaneous equations to find a solution. Suppose we have the following equations and want to find values for X and Y:

$$3 * Y = 4 * X + 2 \tag{1}$$

$$Y = -X + 10 \tag{2}$$

One way of finding a solution would be to draw graphs of the lines and the solution is the point where the lines cross. In Figure A6 the solution can be read from the graph as about $X = 4$ and $Y = 6$.

It is difficult to draw graphs exactly and this approach would not be accurate if the graphs were complicated or the scales were small. More accurate results can be found by solving the equations algebraically. This involves multiplying one of the equations by a suitable number so that adding or subtracting the two equations eliminates one of the variables. Here we can multiply equation (2) by 3 to give the two equations:

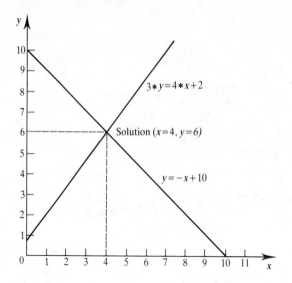

Figure A6 Solution of simultaneous equations $Y = -X + 10$ and $3 * Y = 4 * X + 2$.

$$3 * Y = 4 * X + 2 \qquad \text{(1) as before}$$
$$3 * Y = -3 * X + 30 \qquad \text{(2)}$$

Subtracting (2) from (1) gives:

$$0 = 7 * X - 28$$

or $\qquad X = 4$

Substituting this into one of the original equations, say (1) gives:

$$3 * Y = 4 * 4 + 2$$

or $\qquad Y = 6$

Equations containing variables raised to powers are more difficult to solve. We might also remember in passing that:

$$A^m * A^n = A^{(m+n)}$$

Because of the complexity, we will only use equations where a single variable is squared. These are quadratic equations with the general form:

$$a * X^2 + b * X + c = 0$$

There are two solutions to quadratic equations which are given by:

$$X = \frac{-b +/- \sqrt{(b^2 - 4 * a * c)}}{2 * a}$$

where:

+/− means 'plus or minus'

√ means the square root

The two values of X are given by:

$$X = \frac{-b + \sqrt{(b^2 - 4*a*c)}}{2*a} \text{ and } X = \frac{-b - \sqrt{(b^2 - 4*a*c)}}{2*a}$$

Taking, for example, the equation:

$$2*x^2 + 3*x - 2 = 0$$

the two solutions are found by substituting $a = 2$, $b = 3$ and $c = -2$.

$$X = \frac{-b + \sqrt{(b^2 - 4*a*c)}}{2*a} \text{ and } X = \frac{-b - \sqrt{(b^2 - 4*a*c)}}{2*a}$$

$$X = \frac{-3 + \sqrt{(3^2 + 4*2*2)}}{2*2} \text{ and } X = \frac{-3 - \sqrt{(3^2 + 4*2*2)}}{2*2}$$

In these equations $-4*2*(-2)$ has been simplified to $+4*2*2$.

$$X = \frac{-3 + \sqrt{25}}{4} \qquad \text{and } X = \frac{-3 - \sqrt{25}}{4}$$

$$X = 2/4 \qquad \text{and } X = -8/4$$

$$= 0.5 \qquad = -2$$

Checking these values by substitution in the original equation confirms:

$$2*0.5^2 + 3*0.5 - 2 = 0 \quad \text{and } 2*2^2 - 3*2 - 2 = 0$$

The same results could have been found approximately from a graph. Taking a range of values from $X = -5$ to $X = +4$ and substituting into the original equation gives:

X	−5	−4	−3	−2	−1	0	1	2	3	4
Y	33	18	7	0	−3	−2	3	12	25	42

The solutions are the points where the curve crosses the X axis.

MAXIMUM AND MINIMUM VALUE OF A FUNCTION

Sometimes functions have a distinct maximum or minimum. The graph of Figure A7, for example, has a minimum value of about −3 when $X = -1$. Maximum or minimum points can be identified approximately if graphs are drawn, but it is usually more convenient and accurate to do a calculation. Such calculations are described by differential calculus. We will only look at this very briefly, but if you find it too difficult you can simply skip the details in this part.

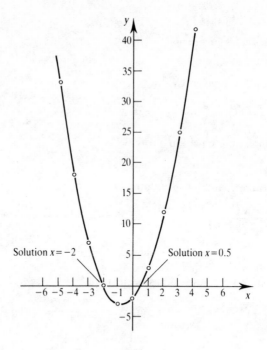

Figure A7 Solutions to a quadratic equation $2 * X^2 + 3 * X - 2 = 0$.

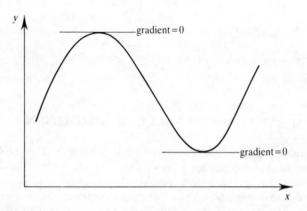

Figure A8 Maxima and minima occur when the gradient of a graph is zero.

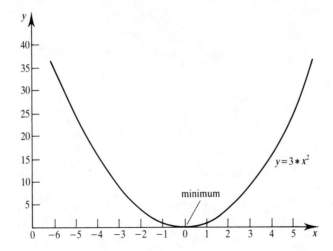

Figure A9 Showing the minimum of $Y = 3 * X^2$ when $X = 0$.

To find the maximum or minimum of a function we differentiate the function (differentiation gives the gradient at any point on the graph). Then the point where the gradient is zero identifies a maximum or minimum (see Figure A8).

Equations of the general form:

$$Y = A * X^n$$

can be differentiated to give the standard result $n * A * X^{(n-1)}$ and equating this to zero gives the point where the gradient is zero. To find whether this is a maximum or minimum we can either draw the graph or take the second differential $n * (n - 1) * A * X^{(n-2)}$. If this second differential is negative a maximum has been found and if it is positive a minimum has been found.

Consider the equation $Y = 3 * X^2$. This can be differentiated to give $3 * 2 * X = 6 * X$. Equating this to zero gives $X = 0$, so there is either a maximum or minimum of the function at the point where $X = 0$. The second differential of $6 * X$ is 6, which is positive and shows that a minimum has been found. This can be confirmed from the graph in Figure A9.

If a function has several terms, they can treated in the same way. Consider the function $Y = X^3 - 2 * X^2$. This can be differentiated to give $3 * X^2 - 4 * X$. Equating this to zero gives $3 * X^2 - 4 * X = 0$ which has two solutions of $X = 0$ and $X = 4/3$. Taking the second differential gives $6 * X - 4$. When $X = 0$ is substituted this has the value -4 which is negative and indicates a maximum value of the function. When $X = 4/3$ is substituted the second differential has the value 4, which is positive and indicates a minimum at this point (see Figure A10).

In summary

There are many ways of tackling management science. In this book we have chosen a quantitative approach, but have illustrated this by examples rather than

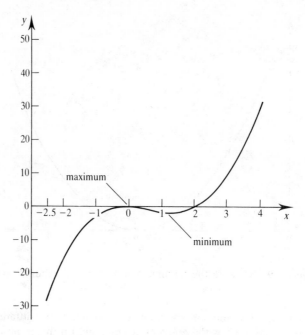

Figure A10   Graph of $Y = X^3 - 2 * X^2$ (with maximum at $X = 0$ and minimum at $X = 4/3$.

mathematical rigour. The level of mathematics required is not, therefore, excessive. If you have any problems in the text, some help may be found in this Appendix. If you want more details on any point it would be worthwhile looking at a textbook on mathematics, many of which are available. The following suggestions might be useful starting points.

REFERENCES FOR FURTHER READING

Battersby A. (1966). *Mathematics in Management* Harmondsworth: Penguin Books

de Lisle C. (1979). *The Martin Book of Management Calculations* Cambridge: Martin Books

Harper W.M. (1982). *Statistics* London: Macdonald & Evans

Johnson D. (1986). *Quantitative Business Analysis* London: Butterworth

Kemeny J.G., Snell J.L. and Thompson G.L. (1970). *Introduction to Finite Mathematics* New Jersey: Prentice-Hall

Morison A.M.C., Burden R. and Crabtree

M.G. (1971). *Understanding Modern Business Mathematics* London: Gee

Owen G. (1970). *Finite Mathematics* Philadelphia: W.B. Saunders

Scottish Mathematics Group (1969). *Modern Mathematics for Schools* (latest edition) Glasgow: Blackie/Chambers

Stafford L.W.T. (1979). *Business Mathematics* London: Macdonald & Evans

Stern M.E. (1963). *Mathematics for Management* New Jersey: Prentice-Hall

Ullman J.E. (1976). *Quantitative methods in Management* New York: McGraw-Hill (Schaum)

Appendix B

Probabilities for the Binomial distribution

n	r	.05	.10	.15	.20	.25	.30	.35	.40	.45	.50
1	0	.9500	.9000	.8500	.8000	.7500	.7000	.6500	.6000	.5500	.5000
	1	.0500	.1000	.1500	.2000	.2500	.3000	.3500	.4000	.4500	.5000
2	0	.9025	.8100	.7225	.6400	.5625	.4900	.4225	.3600	.3025	.2500
	1	.0950	.1800	.2550	.3200	.3750	.4200	.4550	.4800	.4950	.5000
	2	.0025	.0100	.0225	.0400	.0625	.0900	.1225	.1600	.2025	.2500
3	0	.8574	.7290	.6141	.5120	.4219	.3430	.2746	.2160	.1664	.1250
	1	.1354	.2430	.3251	.3840	.4219	.4410	.4436	.4320	.4084	.3750
	2	.0071	.0270	.0574	.0960	.1406	.1890	.2389	.2880	.3341	.3750
	3	.0001	.0010	.0034	.0080	.0156	.0270	.0429	.0640	.0911	.1250
4	0	.8145	.6561	.5220	.4096	.3164	.2401	.1785	.1296	.0915	.0625
	1	.1715	.2916	.3685	.4096	.4219	.4116	.3845	.3456	.2995	.2500
	2	.0135	.0486	.0975	.1536	.2109	.2646	.3105	.3456	.3675	.3750
	3	.0005	.0036	.0115	.0256	.0469	.0756	.1115	.1536	.2005	.2500
	4	.0000	.0001	.0005	.0016	.0039	.0081	.0150	.0256	.0410	.0625
5	0	.7738	.5905	.4437	.3277	.2373	.1681	.1160	.0778	.0503	.0312
	1	.2036	.3280	.3915	.4096	.3955	.3602	.3124	.2592	.2059	.1562
	2	.0214	.0729	.1382	.2048	.2637	.3087	.3364	.3456	.3369	.3125
	3	.0011	.0081	.0244	.0512	.0879	.1323	.1811	.2304	.2757	.3125
	4	.0000	.0004	.0022	.0064	.0146	.0284	.0488	.0768	.1128	.1562
	5	.0000	.0000	.0001	.0003	.0010	.0024	.0053	.0102	.0185	.0312
6	0	.7351	.5314	.3771	.2621	.1780	.1176	.0754	.0467	.0277	.0156
	1	.2321	.3543	.3993	.3932	.3560	.3025	.2437	.1866	.1359	.0938
	2	.0305	.0984	.1762	.2458	.2966	.3241	.3280	.3110	.2780	.2344
	3	.0021	.0146	.0415	.0819	.1318	.1852	.2355	.2765	.3032	.3125
	4	.0001	.0012	.0055	.0154	.0330	.0595	.0951	.1382	.1861	.2344
	5	.0000	.0001	.0004	.0015	.0044	.0102	.0205	.0369	.0609	.0938
	6	.0000	.0000	.0000	.0001	.0002	.0007	.0018	.0041	.0083	.0516
7	0	.6983	.4783	.3206	.2097	.1335	.0824	.0490	.0280	.0152	.0078
	1	.2573	.3720	.3960	.3670	.3115	.2471	.1848	.1306	.0872	.0547
	2	.0406	.1240	.2097	.2753	.3115	.3177	.2985	.2613	.2140	.1641
	3	.0036	.0230	.0617	.1147	.1730	.2269	.2679	.2903	.2918	.2734
	4	.0002	.0026	.0109	.0287	.0577	.0972	.1442	.1935	.2388	.2734
	5	.0009	.0002	.0012	.0043	.0115	.0250	.0466	.0774	.1172	.1641
	6	.0000	.0000	.0001	.0004	.0013	.0036	.0084	.0172	.0320	.0547
	7	.0000	.0000	.0000	.0000	.0001	.0002	.0006	.0016	.0037	.0078

Probabilities for the Binomial distribution (cont.)

n	r	.05	.10	.15	.20	.25	.30	.35	.40	.45	.50
8	0	.6634	.4305	.2725	.1678	.1001	.0576	.0319	.0168	.0084	.0039
	1	.2793	.3826	.3847	.3355	.2670	.1977	1373	.0896	.0548	.0312
	2	.0515	.1488	.2376	.2936	.3115	.2965	2587	.2090	.1569	.1094
	3	.0054	.0331	.0839	.1468	.2076	.2541	2786	.2787	.2568	.2188
	4	.0004	.0046	.0815	.0459	.0865	.1361	.1875	.2322	.2627	.2734
	5	.0000	.0004	.0026	.0092	.0231	.0467	.0808	.1239	.1719	.2188
	6	.0000	.0000	.0002	.0011	.0038	.0100	.0217	.0413	.0703	.1094
	7	.0000	.0000	.0000	.0001	.0004	.0012	.0033	.0079	.0164	.0312
	8	.0000	.0000	.0000	.0000	.0000	.0001	.0002	.0007	.0017	.0039
9	0	.6302	.3874	.2316	.1342	.0751	.0404	.0207	.0101	.0046	.0020
	1	.2985	.3874	.3679	.3020	.2253	.1556	.0605	.0339	.0176
	1	.2985	.3874	.3679	.3020	.2253	.1556		.0605	.0339	.0176
	2	.0629	.1722	.2597	.3020	.3003	.2668	.2162	.1612	.1110	.0703
	3	.0077	.0446	.1069	.1762	.2336	.2668	.2716	.2508	.2119	.1641
	4	.0006	.0074	.0283	.0661	.1168	.1715	.2194	.2508	.2600	.2461
	5	.0000	.0008	.0050	.0165	.0389	.0735	.1181	.1672	.2128	.2461
	6	.0000	.0001	.0006	.0028	.0087	.0210	.0424	.0743	.1160	.1641
	7	.0000	.0000	.0000	.0003	.0012	.0039	.0098	.0212	.0407	.0703
	8	.0000	.0000	.0000	.0000	.0001	.0004	.0013	.0035	.0083	.0716
	9	.0000	.0000	.0000	.0000	.0000	.0000	.0001	.0003	.0008	.0020
10	0	.5987	.3487	.1969	.1074	.0563	.0282	.0135	.0060	.0025	.0010
	1	.3151	.3874	.3474	.2684	.1877	.1211	.0725	.0403	.0207	.0098
	2	.0746	.1937	.2759	.3020	.2816	.2335	.1757	.1209	.0763	.0439
	3	.0105	.0574	.1298	.2013	.2503	.2668	.2522	.2150	.1665	.1172
	4	.0010	.0112	.0401	.0881	.1460	.2001	.2377	.2508	.2384	.2051
	5	.0001	.0015	.0085	.0264	.0584	.1029	.1536	.2007	.2340	.2461
	6	.0000	.0001	.0012	.0055	.0162	.0368	.0689	.1115	.1596	.2051
	7	.0000	.0000	.0001	.0008	.0031	.0090	.0212	.0425	.0746	.1172
	8	.0000	.0000	.0000	.0001	.0004	.0014	.0043	.0106	.0229	.0439
	9	.0000	.0000	.0000	.0000	.0000	.0001	.0005	.0016	.0042	.0098
	10	.0000	.0000	.0000	.0000	.0000	.0000	.0000	.0001	.0003	.0010
11	0	.5688	.3138	.1673	.0859	.0422	.0198	.0088	.0036	.0014	.0005
	1	.3293	.3835	.3248	.2362	.1549	.0932	.0518	.0266	.0125	.0054
	2	.0867	.2131	.2866	.2953	.2581	.1998	.1395	.0887	.0513	.0269
	3	.0137	.0710	.1517	.2215	.2581	.2568	.2254	.1774	.1259	.0806
	4	.0014	.0158	.0536	.1107	.1721	.2201	.2428	.2365	.2060	.1611
	5	.0001	.0025	.0132	.0388	.0803	.1321	.1830	.2207	.2360	.2256
	6	.0000	.0003	.0023	.0097	.0268	.0566	.0985	.1471	.1931	.2256
	7	.0000	.0000	.0003	.0017	.0064	.0173	.0379	.0701	.1128	.1611
	8	.0000	.0000	.0000	.0002	.0011	.0037	.0102	.0234	.0462	.0806
	9	.0000	.0000	.0000	.0000	.0001	.0005	.0018	.0052	.0126	.0269
	10	.0000	.0000	.0000	.0000	.0000	.0000	.0002	.0007	.0021	.0054
	11	.0000	.0000	.0000	.0000	.0000	.0000	.0000	.0000	.0002	.0005

Probabilities for the Binomial distribution (cont.)

n	r	.05	.10	.15	.20	.25	.30	.35	.40	.45	.50
12	0	.5404	.2824	.1422	.0687	.0317	.0138	.0057	.0022	.0008	.0002
	1	.3413	.3766	.3012	.2062	.1267	.0712	.0368	.0174	.0075	.0029
	2	.0988	.2301	.2924	.2835	.2323	.1678	.1088	.0639	.0339	.0161
	3	.0173	.0852	.1720	.2362	.2581	.2397	.1954	.1419	.0923	.0537
	4	.0021	.0213	.0683	.1329	.1936	.2311	.2367	.2128	.1700	.1208
	5	.0002	.0038	.0193	.0532	.1032	.1585	.2039	.2270	.2225	.1934
	6	.0000	.0005	.0040	.0155	.0401	.0792	.1281	.1766	.2124	2256
	7	.0000	.0000	.0006	.0033	.0115	.0291	.0591	.1009	.1489	.1934
	8	.0000	.0000	.0001	.0005	.0024	.0078	.0199	.0420	.0762	.1208
	9	.0000	.0000	.0000	.0001	.0004	0015	.0048	.0125	.0277	.0537
	10	.0000	.0000	.0000	.0000	.0000	.0002	.0008	.0025	.0068	.0161
	11	.0000	.0000	.0000	.0000	.0000	.0000	.0001	.0003	.0010	.0029
	12	.0000	.0000	.0000	.0000	.0000	.0000	.0000	.0000	.0001	.0002
13	0	.5133	.2542	.1209	.0550	.0238	.0097	.0037	.0013	.0004	.0001
	1	.3512	.3672	.2774	.1787	.1029	.0540	.0259	.0113	.0045	.0016
	2	.1109	.2448	.2937	.2680	.2059	.1388	.0836	.0453	.0220	.0095
	3	.0214	.0997	.1900	.2457	.2517	.2181	.1651	.1107	.0660	.0349
	4	.0028	.0277	.0838	.1535	.2097	.2337	.2222	.1845	.1350	.0873
	5	.0003	.0055	.0266	.0691	.1258	.1803	.2154	.2214	.1989	.1571
	6	.0000	.0008	.0063	.0230	.0559	.1030	.1546	.1968	.2169	.2095
	7	.0000	.0001	.0011	.0058	.0186	.0442	.0833	.1312	.1775	.2095
	8	.0000	.0000	.0001	.0011	.0047	.0142	.0336	.0656	.1089	.1571
	9	.0000	.0000	.0000	.0001	.0009	.0034	.0101	.0243	.0495	.0873
	10	.0000	.0000	.0000	.0000	.0001	.0006	.0022	.0065	.0162	.0349
	11	.0000	.0000	.0000	.0000	.0000	.0001	.0003	.0012	.0036	.0095
	12	.0000	.0000	.0000	.0000	.0000	.0000	.0000	.0001	.0005	.0016
	13	.0000	.0000	.0000	.0000	.0000	.0000	.0000	.0000	.0000	.0001
14	0	.4877	.2288	.1028	.0440	.0178	.0068	.0024	.0008	.0002	.0001
	1	.3593	.3559	.2539	.1539	.0832	.0407	.0181	.0073	.0027	.0009
	2	.1229	.2570	.2912	.2501	.1802	.1134	.0634	.0317	.0141	.0056
	3	.0259	.1142	.2056	.2501	.2402	.1943	.1366	.0845	.0462	.0222
	4	.0037	.0348	.0998	.1720	.2202	.2290	.2022	.1549	.1040	.0611
	5	.0004	.0078	.0352	.0860	.1468	.1963	.2178	.2066	.1701	.1222
	6	.0000	.0013	.0093	.0322	.0734	.1262	.1759	.2066	.2088	.1833
	7	.0000	.0002	.0019	.0092	.0280	.0618	.1082	.1574	.1952	.2095
	8	.0000	.0000	.0003	.0020	.0082	.0232	.0510	.0918	.1398	.1833
	9	.0000	.0000	.0000	.0003	.0018	.0066	.0183	.0408	.0762	.1222
	10	.0000	.0000	.0000	.0000	.0003	.0014	.0049	.0136	.0312	.0611
	11	.0000	.0000	.0000	.0000	.0000	.0002	.0010	.0033	.0093	.0222
	12	.0000	.0000	.0000	.0000	.0000	.0000	.0001	.0005	.0019	.0056
	13	.0000	.0000	.0000	.0000	.0000	.0000	.0000	.0001	.0002	.0009
	14	.0000	.0000	.0000	.0000	.0000	.0000	.0000	.0000	.0000	.0001

Probabilities for the Binomial distribution (cont.)

n	r	.05	.10	.15	.20	.25	.30	.35	.40	.45	.50
15	0	.4633	.2059	.0874	.0352	.0134	.0047	.0016	.0005	.0001	.0000
	1	.3658	.3432	.2312	.1319	.0668	.0305	.0126	.0047	.0016	.0005
	2	.1348	.2669	.2856	.2309	.1559	.0916	.0476	.0219	.0090	.0032
	3	.0307	.1285	.2184	.2501	.2252	.1700	.1110	.0634	.0318	.0139
	4	.0049	.0428	.1156	.1876	.2252	.2186	.1792	.1268	.0780	.0417
	5	.0006	.0105	.0449	.1032	.1651	.2061	.2123	.1859	.1404	.0916
	6	.0000	.0019	.0132	.0430	.0917	.1472	.1906	.2066	.1914	.1527
	7	.0000	.0003	.0030	.0138	.0393	.0811	.1319	.1771	.2013	.1964
	8	.0000	.0000	.0005	.0035	.0131	.0348	.0710	.1181	.1647	.1964
	9	.0000	.0000	.0001	.0007	.0034	.0116	.0298	.0612	.1048	.1527
	10	.0000	.0000	.0000	.0001	.0007	.0030	.0096	.0245	.0515	.0916
	11	.0000	.0000	.0000	.0000	.0001	.0006	.0024	.0074	.0191	.0417
	12	.0000	.0000	.0000	.0000	.0000	.0001	.0004	.0016	.0052	.0139
	13	.0000	.0000	.0000	.0000	.0000	.0000	.0001	.0003	.0010	.0032
	14	.0000	.0000	.0000	.0000	.0000	.0000	.0000	.0000	.0001	.0005
	15	.0000	.0000	.0000	.0000	.0000	.0000	.0000	.0000	.0000	.0000
16	0	.4401	.1853	.0743	.0281	.0100	.0033	.0010	.0003	.0001	.0000
	1	.3706	.3294	.2097	.1126	.0535	.0228	.0087	.0030	.0009	.0002
	2	.1463	.2745	.2775	.2111	.1336	.0732	.0353	.0150	.0056	.0018
	3	.0359	.1423	.2285	.2463	.2079	.1465	.0888	.0468	.0215	.0085
	4	.0061	.0514	.1311	.2001	.2252	.2040	.1553	.1014	.0572	.0278
	5	.0008	.0137	.0555	.1201	.1802	.2099	.2008	.1623	.1123	.0667
	6	.0001	.0028	.0180	.0550	.1101	.1649	.1982	.1983	.1684	.1222
	7	.0000	.0004	.0045	.0197	.0524	.1010	.1524	.1889	.1969	.1746
	8	.0000	.0001	.0009	.0055	.0197	.0487	.0923	.1417	.1812	.1964
	9	.0000	.0000	.0001	.0012	.0058	.0185	.0442	.0840	.1318	.1746
	10	.0000	.0000	.0000	.0002	.0014	.0056	.0167	.0392	.0755	.1222
	11	.0000	.0000	.0000	.0000	.0002	.0013	.0049	.0142	.0337	.0667
	12	.0000	.0000	.0000	.0000	.0000	.0002	.0011	.0040	.0115	.0278
	13	.0000	.0000	.0000	.0000	.0000	.0000	.0002	.0008	.0029	.0085
	14	.0000	.0000	.0000	.0000	.0000	.0000	.0000	.0001	.0005	.0018
	15	.0000	.0000	.0000	.0000	.0000	.0000	.0000	.0000	.0001	.0002
	16	.0000	.0000	.0000	.0000	.0000	.0000	.0000	.0000	.0000	.0000
17	0	.4181	.1668	.0631	.0225	.0075	.0023	.0007	.0002	.0000	.0000
	1	.3741	.3150	.1893	.0957	.0426	.0169	.0060	.0019	.0005	.0001
	2	.1575	.2800	.2673	.1914	.1136	.0581	.0260	.0102	.0035	.0010
	3	.0415	.1556	.2359	.2393	.1893	.1245	.0701	.0341	.0144	.0052
	4	.0076	.0605	.1457	.2093	.2209	.1868	.1320	.0796	.0411	.0182
	5	.0010	.0175	.0668	.1361	.1914	.2081	.1849	.1379	.0875	.0472
	6	.0001	.0039	.0236	.0680	.1276	.1784	.1991	.1839	.1432	.0944
	7	.0000	.0007	.0065	.0267	.0668	.1201	.1685	.1927	.1841	.1484
	8	.0000	.0001	.0014	.0084	.0279	.0644	.1134	.1606	.1883	.1855
	9	.0000	.0000	.0003	.0021	.0093	.0276	.0611	.1070	.1540	.1855
	10	.0000	.0000	.0000	.0004	.0025	.0095	.0263	.0571	.1008	.1484
	11	.0000	.0000	.0000	.0001	.0005	.0026	.0090	.0242	.0525	.0944
	12	.0000	.0000	.0000	.0000	.0001	.0006	.0024	.0021	.0215	.0472
	13	.0000	.0000	.0000	.0000	.0000	.0001	.0005	.0021	.0068	.0182
	14	.0000	.0000	.0000	.0000	.0000	.0000	.0001	.0004	.0016	.0052
	15	.0000	.0000	.0000	.0000	.0000	.0000	.0000	.0001	.0003	.0010
	16	.0000	.0000	.0000	.0000	.0000	.0000	.0000	.0000	.0000	.0001
	17	.0000	.0000	.0000	.0000	.0000	.0000	.0000	.0000	.0000	.0000

Appendix C

Probabilities for the Poisson distribution

					μ					
r	.005	.01	.02	.03	.04	.05	.06	.07	.08	.09
0	.9950	.9900	.9802	.9704	.9608	.9512	.9418	.9324	.9231	.9139
1	.0050	.0099	.0192	.0291	.0384	.0476	.0565	.0653	.0738	.0823
2	.0000	.0000	.0002	.0004	.0008	.0012	.0017	.0023	.0030	.0037
3	.0000	.0000	.0000	.0000	.0000	.0000	.0000	.0001	.0001	.0001

					μ					
r	0.1	0.2	0.3	0.4	0.5	0.6	0.7	0.8	0.9	1.0
0	.9048	.8187	.7408	.6703	.6065	.5488	.4966	.4493	.4066	.3679
1	.0905	.1637	.2222	.2681	.3033	.3293	.3476	.3595	.3659	.3679
2	.0045	.0164	.0333	.0536	.0758	.0988	.1217	.1438	.1647	.1839
3	.0002	.0011	.0033	.0072	.0126	.0198	.0284	.0383	.0494	.0613
4	.0000	.0001	.0002	.0007	.0016	.0030	.0050	.0077	.0111	.0153
5	.0000	.0000	.0000	.0001	.0002	.0004	.0007	.0012	.0020	.0031
6	.0000	.0000	.0000	.0000	.0000	.0000	.0001	.0002	.0003	.0005
7	.0000	.0000	.0000	.0000	.0000	.0000	.0000	.0000	.0000	.0001

					μ					
r	1.1	1.2	1.3	1.4	1.5	1.6	1.7	1.8	1.9	2.0
0	.3329	.3012	.2725	.2466	.2231	.2019	.1827	.1653	.1496	.1353
1	.3662	.3614	.3543	.3452	.3347	.3230	.3106	.2975	.2842	.2707
2	.2014	.2169	.2303	.2417	.2510	.2584	.2640	.2678	.2700	.2707
3	.0738	.0867	.0998	.1128	.1255	.1378	.1496	.1607	.1710	.1804
4	.0203	.0260	.0324	.0395	.0471	.0551	.0636	.0723	.0812	.0902
5	.0045	.0062	.0084	.0111	.0141	.0176	.0216	.0260	.0309	.0361
6	.0008	.0012	.0018	.0026	.0035	.0047	.0061	.0078	.0098	.0120
7	.0001	.0002	.0003	.0005	.0008	.0011	.0015	.0020	.0027	.0034
8	.0000	.0000	.0001	.0001	.0001	.0002	.0003	.0005	.0006	.0009
9	.0000	.0000	.0000	.0000	.0000	.0000	.0001	.0001	.0001	.0002

Probabilities for the Poisson distribution (cont.)

μ

r	2.1	2.2	2.3	2.4	2.5	2.6	2.7	2.8	2.9	3.0
0	.1225	.1108	.1003	.0907	.0821	.0743	.0672	.0608	.0550	.0498
1	.2572	.2438	.2306	.2177	.2052	.1931	.1815	.1703	.1596	.1494
2	.2700	.2681	.2652	.2613	.2565	.2510	.2450	.2384	.2314	.2240
3	.1890	.1966	.2033	.2090	.2138	.2176	.2205	.2225	.2237	.2240
4	.0992	.1082	.1169	.1254	.1336	.1414	.1488	.1557	.1622	.1680
5	.0417	.0476	.0538	.0602	.0668	.0735	.0804	.0872	.0940	.1008
6	.0146	.0174	.0206	.0241	.0278	.0319	.0362	.0407	.0455	.0504
7	.0044	.0055	.0068	.0083	.0099	.0118	.0139	.0163	.0188	.0216
8	.0011	.0015	.0019	.0025	.0031	.0038	.0047	.0057	.0068	.0081
9	.0003	.0004	.0005	.0007	.0009	.0011	.0014	.0018	.0022	.0027
10	.0001	.0001	.0001	.0002	.0002	.0003	.0004	.0005	.0006	.0008
11	.0000	.0000	.0000	.0000	.0000	.0001	.0001	.0001	.0002	.0002
12	.0000	.0000	.0000	.0000	.0000	.0000	.0000	.0000	.0000	.0001

μ

r	3.1	3.2	3.3	3.4	3.5	3.6	3.7	3.8	3.9	4.0
0	.0450	.0408	.0369	.0334	.0302	.0273	.0247	.0224	.0202	.0183
1	.1397	.1304	.1217	.1135	.1057	.0984	.0915	.0850	.0789	.0733
2	.2165	.2087	.2008	.1929	.1850	.1771	.1692	.1615	.1539	.1465
3	.2237	.2226	.2209	.2186	.2158	.2125	.2087	.2046	.2001	.1954
4	.1734	.1781	.1823	.1858	.1888	.1912	.1931	.1944	.1951	.1954
5	.1075	.1140	.1203	.1264	.1322	.1377	.1429	.1477	.1522	.1563
6	.0555	.0608	.0662	.0716	.0771	.0826	.0881	.0936	.0989	.1042
7	.0246	.0278	.0312	.0348	.0385	.0425	.0466	.0508	.0551	.0595
8	.0095	.0111	.0129	.0148	.0169	.0191	.0215	.0241	.0269	.0298
9	.0033	.0040	.0047	.0056	.0066	.0076	.0089	.0102	.0116	.0132
10	.0010	.0013	.0016	.0019	.0023	.0028	.0033	.0039	.0045	.0053
11	.0003	.0004	.0005	.0006	.0007	.0009	.0011	.0013	.0016	.0019
12	.0001	.0001	.0001	.0002	.0002	.0003	.0003	.0004	.0005	.0006
13	.0000	.0000	.0000	.0000	.0001	.0001	.0001	.0001	.0002	.0002
14	.0000	.0000	.0000	.0000	.0000	.0000	.0000	.0000	.0000	.0001

μ

r	4.1	4.2	4.3	4.4	4.5	4.6	4.7	4.8	4.9	5.0
0	.0166	.0150	.0136	.0123	.0111	.0101	.0091	.0082	.0074	.0067
1	.0679	.0630	.0583	.0540	.0500	.0462	.0427	.0395	.0365	.0337
2	.1393	.1323	.1254	.1188	.1125	.1063	.1005	.0948	.0894	.0842
3	.1904	.1852	.1798	.1743	.1687	.1631	.1574	.1517	.1460	.1404
4	.1951	.1944	.1933	.1917	.1898	.1875	.1849	.1820	.1789	.1755
5	.1600	.1633	.1662	.1687	.1708	.1725	.1738	.1747	.1753	.1755
6	.1093	.1143	.1191	.1237	.1281	.1323	.1362	.1398	.1432	.1462
7	.0640	.0686	.0732	.0778	.0824	.0869	.0914	.0959	.1002	.1044
8	.0328	.0360	.0393	.0428	.0463	.0500	.0537	.0575	.0614	.0653
9	.0150	.0168	.0188	.0209	.0232	.0255	.0280	.0307	.0334	.0363
10	.0061	.0071	.0081	.0092	.0104	.0118	.0132	.0147	.0164	.0181
11	.0023	.0027	.0032	.0037	.0043	.0049	.0056	.0064	.0073	.0082
12	.0008	.0009	.0011	.0014	.0016	.0019	.0022	.0026	.0030	.0034
13	.0002	.0003	.0004	.0005	.0006	.0007	.0008	.0009	.0011	.0013
14	.0001	.0001	.0001	.0001	.0002	.0002	.0003	.0003	.0004	.0005
15	.0000	.0000	.0000	.0000	.0001	.0001	.0001	.0001	.0001	.0002

Probabilities for the Poisson distribution (cont.)

μ

r	5.1	5.2	5.3	5.4	5.5	5.6	5.7	5.8	5.9	6.0
0	.0061	.0055	.0050	.0045	.0041	.0037	.0033	.0030	.0027	.0025
1	.0311	.0287	.0265	.0244	.0225	.0207	.0191	.0176	.0162	.0149
2	.0793	.0746	.0701	.0659	.0618	.0580	.0544	.0509	.0477	.0446
3	.1348	.1293	.1239	.1185	.1133	.1082	.1033	.0985	.0938	.0892
4	.1719	.1681	.1641	.1600	.1558	.1515	.1472	.1428	.1383	.1339
5	.1753	.1748	.1740	.1728	.1714	.1697	.1678	.1656	.1632	.1606
6	.1490	.1515	.1537	.1555	.1571	.1584	.1594	.1601	.1605	.1606
7	.1086	.1125	.1163	.1200	.1234	.1267	.1298	.1326	.1353	.1377
8	.0692	.0731	.0771	.0810	.0849	.0887	.0925	.0962	.0998	.1033
9	.0392	.0423	.0454	.0486	.0519	.0552	.0586	.0620	.0654	.0688
10	.0200	.0220	.0241	.0262	.0285	.0309	.0334	.0359	.0386	.0413
11	.0093	.0104	.0116	.0129	.0143	.0157	.0173	.0190	.0207	.0225
12	.0039	.0045	.0051	.0058	.0065	.0073	.0082	.0092	.0102	.0113
13	.0015	.0018	.0021	.0024	.0028	.0032	.0036	.0041	.0046	.0052
14	.0006	.0007	.0008	.0009	.0011	.0013	.0015	.0017	.0019	.0022
15	.0002	.0002	.0003	.0003	.0004	.0005	.0006	.0007	.0008	.0009
16	.0001	.0001	.0001	.0001	.0001	.0002	.0002	.0002	.0003	.0003
17	.0000	.0000	.0000	.0000	.0000	.0001	.0001	.0001	.0001	.0001

μ

r	6.1	6.2	6.3	6.4	6.5	6.6	6.7	6.8	6.9	7.0
0	.0022	.0020	.0018	.0017	.0015	.0014	.0012	.0011	.0010	.0009
1	.0137	.0126	.0116	.0106	.0098	.0090	.0082	.0076	.0070	.0064
2	.0417	.0390	.0364	.0340	.0318	.0296	.0276	.0258	.0240	.0223
3	.0848	.0806	.0765	.0726	.0688	.0652	.0617	.0584	.0552	.0521
4	.1294	.1249	.1205	.1162	.1118	.1076	.1034	.0992	.0952	.0912
5	.1579	.1549	.1519	.1487	.1454	.1420	.1385	.1349	.1314	.1277
6	.1605	.1601	.1595	.1586	.1575	.1562	.1546	.1529	.1511	.1490
7	.1399	.1418	.1435	.1450	.1462	.1472	.1480	.1486	.1489	.1490
8	.1066	.1099	.1130	.1160	.1188	.1215	.1240	.1263	.1284	.1304
9	.0723	.0757	.0791	.0825	.0858	.0891	.0923	.0954	.0985	.1014
10	.0441	.0469	.0498	.0528	.0558	.0588	.0618	.0649	.0679	.0710
11	.0245	.0265	.0285	.0307	.0330	.0353	.0377	.0401	.0426	.0452
12	.0124	.0137	.0150	.0164	.0179	.0194	.0210	.0227	.0245	.0264
13	.0058	.0065	.0073	.0081	.0089	.0098	.0108	.0119	.0130	.0142
14	.0025	.0029	.0033	.0037	.0041	.0046	.0052	.0058	.0064	.0071
15	.0010	.0012	.0014	.0016	.0018	.0020	.0023	.0026	.0029	.0033
16	.0004	.0005	.0005	.0006	.0007	.0008	.0010	.0011	.0013	.0014
17	.0001	.0002	.0002	.0002	.0003	.0003	.0004	.0004	.0005	.0006
18	.0000	.0001	.0001	.0001	.0001	.0001	.0001	.0002	.0002	.0002
19	.0000	.0000	.0000	.0000	.0000	.0000	.0000	.0001	.0001	.0001

Appendix D

Probabilities for the Normal distribution

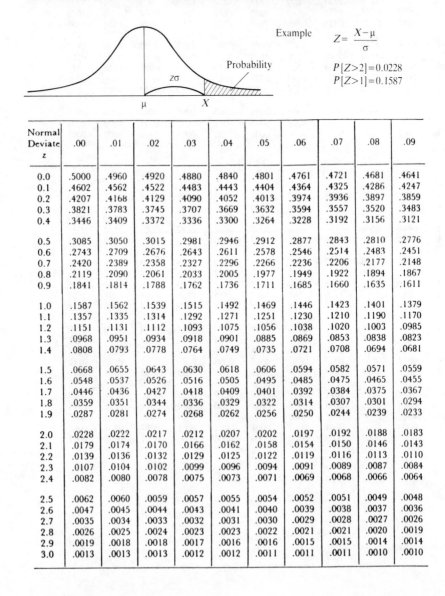

Example $Z = \dfrac{X-\mu}{\sigma}$

$P[Z>2]=0.0228$

$P[Z>1]=0.1587$

Normal Deviate z	.00	.01	.02	.03	.04	.05	.06	.07	.08	.09
0.0	.5000	.4960	.4920	.4880	.4840	.4801	.4761	.4721	.4681	.4641
0.1	.4602	.4562	.4522	.4483	.4443	.4404	.4364	.4325	.4286	.4247
0.2	.4207	.4168	.4129	.4090	.4052	.4013	.3974	.3936	.3897	.3859
0.3	.3821	.3783	.3745	.3707	.3669	.3632	.3594	.3557	.3520	.3483
0.4	.3446	.3409	.3372	.3336	.3300	.3264	.3228	.3192	.3156	.3121
0.5	.3085	.3050	.3015	.2981	.2946	.2912	.2877	.2843	.2810	.2776
0.6	.2743	.2709	.2676	.2643	.2611	.2578	.2546	.2514	.2483	.2451
0.7	.2420	.2389	.2358	.2327	.2296	.2266	.2236	.2206	.2177	.2148
0.8	.2119	.2090	.2061	.2033	.2005	.1977	.1949	.1922	.1894	.1867
0.9	.1841	.1814	.1788	.1762	.1736	.1711	.1685	.1660	.1635	.1611
1.0	.1587	.1562	.1539	.1515	.1492	.1469	.1446	.1423	.1401	.1379
1.1	.1357	.1335	.1314	.1292	.1271	.1251	.1230	.1210	.1190	.1170
1.2	.1151	.1131	.1112	.1093	.1075	.1056	.1038	.1020	.1003	.0985
1.3	.0968	.0951	.0934	.0918	.0901	.0885	.0869	.0853	.0838	.0823
1.4	.0808	.0793	.0778	.0764	.0749	.0735	.0721	.0708	.0694	.0681
1.5	.0668	.0655	.0643	.0630	.0618	.0606	.0594	.0582	.0571	.0559
1.6	.0548	.0537	.0526	.0516	.0505	.0495	.0485	.0475	.0465	.0455
1.7	.0446	.0436	.0427	.0418	.0409	.0401	.0392	.0384	.0375	.0367
1.8	.0359	.0351	.0344	.0336	.0329	.0322	.0314	.0307	.0301	.0294
1.9	.0287	.0281	.0274	.0268	.0262	.0256	.0250	.0244	.0239	.0233
2.0	.0228	.0222	.0217	.0212	.0207	.0202	.0197	.0192	.0188	.0183
2.1	.0179	.0174	.0170	.0166	.0162	.0158	.0154	.0150	.0146	.0143
2.2	.0139	.0136	.0132	.0129	.0125	.0122	.0119	.0116	.0113	.0110
2.3	.0107	.0104	.0102	.0099	.0096	.0094	.0091	.0089	.0087	.0084
2.4	.0082	.0080	.0078	.0075	.0073	.0071	.0069	.0068	.0066	.0064
2.5	.0062	.0060	.0059	.0057	.0055	.0054	.0052	.0051	.0049	.0048
2.6	.0047	.0045	.0044	.0043	.0041	.0040	.0039	.0038	.0037	.0036
2.7	.0035	.0034	.0033	.0032	.0031	.0030	.0029	.0028	.0027	.0026
2.8	.0026	.0025	.0024	.0023	.0023	.0022	.0021	.0021	.0020	.0019
2.9	.0019	.0018	.0018	.0017	.0016	.0016	.0015	.0015	.0014	.0014
3.0	.0013	.0013	.0013	.0012	.0012	.0011	.0011	.0011	.0010	.0010

Appendix E

Sample of random numbers

```
83635 18471 01664 97316 13751 22904 46465 55782 13047 64812
66791 25482 48893 34611 07709 24016 81064 00876 11197 35664
46879 05246 13006 17669 16587 25597 24106 67913 05438 97013
98520 97410 96305 57421 23489 67492 31647 85500 69477 55523
68227 06488 52064 30027 66988 20333 47881 20944 67822 01668
20034 17909 14246 28346 10972 38106 20079 99555 24768 25009
03504 71668 64982 34679 97643 18164 28640 27913 64820 57913
59731 12389 60071 04587 32881 66749 12400 64478 94613 00457
00456 67910 17219 89404 62840 37898 74613 01346 78994 00657
98015 67623 15678 01541 34613 26546 51255 25245 53345 42031
19994 64313 43100 32065 40324 60354 60106 14659 01346 43213
79844 57645 00247 61683 09830 98401 87410 01964 30687 46280
19601 68163 54387 46338 46324 57621 05151 23544 57987 98037
69771 02344 00168 98884 23467 90120 34970 35668 76137 90173
14865 05576 58425 97031 26459 73156 87109 01348 76218 40245
83116 77102 00886 01134 46905 58766 41003 28979 84341 28752
46103 25571 93826 40319 73150 46283 79134 67229 87766 35441
90087 51685 24641 35794 58525 81000 17991 77851 00356 48440
16624 00975 11300 24687 12665 78941 12265 02399 54613 87291
03154 67913 83739 19726 48505 64213 58467 91349 72344 31164
```

Index